THE NEW TURKEY AND

SIMON A. WALDMAN
EMRE CALISKAN

The New Turkey
and Its Discontents

HURST & COMPANY, LONDON

First published in the United Kingdom in 2016 by
C. Hurst & Co. (Publishers) Ltd.,
41 Great Russell Street, London, WC1B 3PL
© Simon A. Waldman and Emre Caliskan, 2016
All rights reserved.

The right of Simon A. Waldman and Emre Caliskan to be identified as the authors of this publication is asserted by them in accordance with the Copyright, Designs and Patents Act, 1988.

A Cataloguing-in-Publication data record for this book is available from the British Library.

ISBN: 9781849045667 *paperback original*

This book is printed using paper from registered sustainable and managed sources.

www.hurstpublishers.com

Printed by Bell and Bain Ltd, Glasgow.

CONTENTS

ACKNOWLEDGEMENTS

In writing this manuscript the authors owe many debts of gratitude. We would like to thank our publisher Michael Dwyer and his team at Hurst and Co. for all their hard work and effort. We benefited from the comments of the first and second readers of this manuscript, which we appreciate. We are also thankful for the support of Professor Rory Miller of the Georgetown University School of the Foreign Service in Qatar and Professor Michael Kerr of the Department of Middle Eastern Studies at King's College London.

While conducting research for this book, which involved several trips to Turkey, we received logistical support and advice from friends old and new. Thanks are due to Ceren Kenar, Aykan Erdemir, Nuray Mert, Kumru Baser, Firuzan Melike Sumertas, Irfan Askan, Gulcan Barut, Burak Kurkcu, Ezgi Cestepe, Ralph Hubbell III, Koray Serdar Tekin and Erkan and Pinar Kandemir. We are also grateful to our interviewees for taking the time out of their busy schedules to talk to us. A special thank you to Nesil Cazimoglu and Rivka Bihar.

We would like to thank our dear parents, Antony and Bonnie Waldman, and Giliman and Ismail Caliskan. It is to them that this book is lovingly dedicated.

LIST OF ABBREVIATIONS AND ORGANISATIONS

AKP	Adalet ve Kalkinma Partisi, Ak Parti, Justice and Development Party
ANAP	Anavatan Partisi, Motherland Party (centre-right)
AP	Adalet Partisi, Justice Party (centre-right)
BDP	Baris ve Demokrasi Partisi, Peace and Democracy Party (Kurdish)
CHP	Cumhuriyet Halk Partisi, Republican People's Party (secular Kemalist)
DEHAP	Demokratik Halk Partisi, Democratic People's Party (Kurdish)
DP	Demokrat Parti, Democrat Party (centre-right)
DSP	Demokratik Sol Partisi, Democratic Left Party
DYP	Dogru Yol Partisi, True Path Party (centre-right)
EC	European Commission
EU	European Union
FP	Fazilet Party, Virtue Party (Islamic)
HADEP	Halkin Demokrasi Partisi, People's Democracy Party (Kurdish)
HDP	Halklarin Demokratik Partisi, Peoples' Democratic Party (Kurdish)
HEP	Halkin Emek Partisi, People's Labour Party
Huda	Par Hur Dava Partisi, Free Cause Party (Kurdish-Islamic)
IMF	International Monetary Fund
IP	Workers' Party (Patriotic Party since 2015)

LIST OF ABBREVIATIONS AND ORGANISATIONS

ISIS	Islamic State in Iraq and Syria
KCK	Koma Civaken Kurdistan, Group of Communities in Kurdistan
KRG	Kurdistan Regional Government (Iraq)
MGK	Milli Guvenlik Kurulu, National Security Council
MHP	Milliyet Hareket Partisi, Nationalist Action Party (right-wing)
MIT	Milli Istihbarat Teskilati, National Intelligence Organisation
MNP	Milli Nizam Partisi, National Order Party (Islamic)
MSP	Milli Selamet Partisi, National Salvation Party (Islamic)
MUSIAD	Mustakil Sanayici ve Isadamlari Dernegi, Independent Industrialists' and Businessmen's Association
OECD	Organisation for Economic Co-operation and Development
OSCE	Organization for Security and Co-operation in Europe
PJAK	Partiya Jiyana Azad a Kurdistane, Party of Free Life of Kurdistan (Iranian)
PKK	Partiya Karkeren Kurdistan, Kurdistan Workers' Party
PUK	Patriotic Union of Kurdistan (Iraqi)
PYD	Partiya Yekitiya Demokrat, Democratic Union Party (Syrian Kurdish)
RP	Refah Partisi, Welfare Party (Islamic)
RTUK	Radyo ve Televizyon Ust Kurulu, Radio and Television Supreme Council
SHP	Sosyaldemokrat Halkci Parti, Social Democratic Populist Party
SP	Saadet Partisi, Felicity Party (Islamic)
TAK	Teyrebazen Azadiya Kurdistan, Kurdistan Freedom Falcons
TEMA	Turkiye Erozyonla Mucadele Agaclandirma ve Dogal Varliklari Koruma Vakfı, Turkish Foundation for Combatting Soil Erosion
TIB	Telekomunikasyon Iletisim Baskanligi, High Council for Telecommunications
TMSF	Tasarruf Mevduati Sigorta Fonu, Savings Deposit Insurance Fund of Turkey

LIST OF ABBREVIATIONS AND ORGANISATIONS

TSK   Turk Silahli Kuvvetleri, Turkish Armed Forces

TUSIAD   Turk Sanayicileri ve Isadamlari Dernegi, Turkish Industry and Business Association

TUSKON   Turkiye Isadamlari ve Sanayiciler Konfederasyonu, Confederation of Turkish Businessmen and Industrialists

TIMELINE OF KEY EVENTS

1960	first military coup, followed by new constitution
1971	second military coup
1978	founding of the PKK
1980	third military coup
1982	new constitution written under military tutelage
1984	PKK begins armed conflict against Turkish state
1997	"post-modern" coup leads to the ousting of Necmettin Erbakan's coalition government
1999	capture of PKK leader Abdullah Ocalan; first PKK ceasefire
2001	AKP is founded
2002–7	first AKP government
2004	PKK resumes armed struggle
2007–11	second AKP government
2007	Republic Protests; Abdullah Gul replaces Ahmet Necdet Sezer as president
2008	AKP closure trial
2009	Ahmet Davutoglu becomes foreign minister
2010	referendum and constitutional amendments
2011–15	third AKP government
2013	Gezi Park protests; corruption investigations; second PKK ceasefire and withdrawal to northern Iraq; Solution Process begins
2014	Prime Minister Erdogan elected president; Davutoglu becomes prime minister

TIMELINE OF KEY EVENTS

July 2015	PKK resumes armed struggle—end to Solution Process
Nov 2015–	fourth AKP government
July 2016	Binali Yildirim replaces Davutoglu as prime minister; failed military coup

LIST OF KEY FIGURES

Ahmet Davutoglu Turkish academic turned politician. Started his political career as chief advisor to Prime Minister Erdogan (2003–9). Became minister of foreign affairs in 2009 until he assumed the post of prime minister in 2014. A rift with President Erdogan led to his resignation in 2016, despite his having led the AKP to electoral victory the previous year. Davutoglu is considered the architect of Turkey's foreign policy under the AKP.

Suleyman Demirel A right-wing politician and prime minister on several occasions during the 1960s and 1970s and the early 1990s. He later became president from 1993 to 2000. His first premiership (1965–71) came to an end after the 1971 military intervention. Despite returning to the office more than once in subsequent years, he was ousted again after the 1980 coup, whose leaders banned him from office. A constitutional amendment in 1987 allowed him to return to politics and in 1991–3 he presided over a coalition government. He served as president from 1993, after Ozal's unexpected death, to 2000.

Bulent Ecevit Centre-left politician first elected to parliament in 1957. For much of his long political career he served as leader of the Kemalist CHP and of the Democratic Left Party in various ministerial roles. Most notably he was prime minister on several occasions (Jan-Nov 1974, June–July 1977, 1978–9, 1999–2002).

Necmettin Erbakan Islamist politician and leader of the Welfare Party, which saw success in the 1996 general elections. Erbakan subsequently became prime minister of a coalition government, but was forced to resign by the military's "post-modern coup" in 1997 for his Islamist policies. A year later the Welfare Party was shut down.

Recep Tayyip Erdogan Co-founder of the AKP in 2001. Rose to prominence as Mayor of Istanbul (1994–8). Served four months in prison (March–July 1999) for reciting a poem considered incitement to religious violence and hatred. Became prime minister a year after the AKP's 2002 election, serving three terms. In 2014 he became Turkey's first popularly elected president.

Abdullah Gul Co-founder of the AKP in 2001. After the first AKP electoral victory in 2002, he served as prime minister until 2003, when Erdogan's ban from office was lifted; he then became foreign minister. He served as president from 2007 until he retired from office in 2014.

Fetullah Gulen Turkish preacher in self-imposed exile in Pennsylvania. Once fellow travelers of the AKP, the Gulen Movement has been accused of infiltrating many institutions of state and conspiring against the AKP on a number of occasions, most notably the July 2016 coup attempt, in which military officers seemingly loyal to Gulen attempted to overthrow the government. Gulen and his organisation are considered terrorists by the Turkish government, which seeks Gulen's extradition.

Abdullah Ocalan Founder and leader of the Kurdistan Workers' Party (PKK). Led a violent armed separatist struggle against the Turkish state from 1984 until his capture in 1999. Convicted and sentenced to death, his life was spared after Turkey abolished the death penalty. Instead he remains incarcerated in seclusion on Imrali Island near Istanbul.

Turgut Ozal Founder and leader of the centre-right Motherland Party (ANAP), Ozal was prime minister in 1983–9, winning the first general election in Turkey since the 1980 military coup. In November 1989, he became the eighth president of the Republic, until his unexpected death in 1993. To this day, many in Turkey, not satisfied with the explanation of a heart attack, allege foul play.

Hilmi Ozkok Chief of the General Staff of the Turkish Armed Forces between 2002 and 2006, a period that coincided with the AKP's first term in government. Many within the ranks were deeply disappointed with Ozkok's performance in dealing with and standing up to the AKP.

Binali Yildirim Elected as an AKP deputy to the National Assembly in 2002, Yildirim served two terms as minister of transport, maritime and communications (2002–2013, 2014–15). Considered a staunch Erdogan loyalist, he was made prime minister after Davutoglu was ousted in 2016.

INTRODUCTION

The New Post-Military Turkey

Turkey has seen tumultuous changes in the past decade and a half. The Turkey of today bears little resemblance to the Turkey of yesteryear. From the ashes of recession and economic crisis, Turkey's GDP has grown significantly and it is now in the G20. It has a young and dynamic civil society. Education levels have improved. Turkey has grown more assertive in the field of foreign policy, and it has even made steps toward resolving the Kurdish problem despite recent developments that have reignited conflict between Ankara and the Kurds. The rise and popularity of the Justice and Development Party (AKP), despite its origins in political Islam, has shown the maturity of Turkish politics. Perhaps most significantly, the age of military tutelage is over.

The once powerful military, which was unafraid of interfering in civilian politics, is now confined to the barracks. Indeed, the demise of the military as a political force is perhaps the most important development since the founding of the Turkish Republic in 1923. Responsible for initiating three direct coups in 1960, 1971 and 1980 respectively and a "post-modern" coup in 1997, as well as an attempted coup by an Islamist faction within the military in 2016 (an anomaly which will be explained), the military's role as the guardians of the secular state has come to an end. However, this was a highly turbulent process with repercussions felt to this very day. This book explains how and why the military was ousted from the Turkish political landscape and examines the consequences.

1

THE NEW TURKEY AND ITS DISCONTENTS

It must be recalled that the Turkish armed forces' presence in civilian politics was, by its very nature, highly undemocratic. In any real democracy, decision making at the uppermost level should be by the elected government. The tragedy of Turkish politics today is that, despite the removal of the military from the political scene, Turkey's democracy remains deficient in many spheres. This book examines this disappointing reality from many angles affecting Turkey. It offers an analysis of contemporary Turkey since the dawn of the new millennium and the development of the "New" Turkey. In writing this book, the authors hope that the reader will receive an introduction to contemporary Turkey and insights into the problems it faces. It identifies and explains the nature and origins of Turkey's struggles by charting the decline of the military in political affairs and the rise of the AKP. It dissects the problems with Turkey's press and the lack of media freedom, and it evaluates Turkish foreign policy as well as the Kurdish question. It also examines the unstable nature of Turkey's democracy and its political system.

Turkey's politics and foreign affairs are highly turbulent. The government has become personalised and authoritarian. Military tutelage has given way to AKP patrimony. Perhaps this is an inevitable consequence of Turkey's post-military evolution: the AKP, whose founders were suppressed by the military and its networks, are fearful and want to destroy any semblance of its traces. They believe they are righting old wrongs.[1]

The decline of the military has opened many new opportunities not only for democracy and accountability, but also for solving Turkey's long-lived Kurdish question. The importance of Turkey's struggle with Kurdish separatists cannot be underestimated. On many levels it has shaped the Turkish military's mind-set. The very nature of Turkey's counterinsurgency against Kurdish guerrillas in the 1980s and '90s fused warfare with state-building. In addition to fighting militants, the military also destroyed villages, forcing migrations, while resettling others. As the south-east was under military rule, providing utilities and services such as sewage, running water, construction of schools and paving roads came under the purview of the armed forces.[2] It is therefore no wonder that the military maintained belief in its supremacy over the civilian government, and its role in the state as above that of civilians.

INTRODUCTION

Moreover, since the 1980s there have been virtually two states in Turkey; one that resembles any peacetime European state, albeit with its problems, and another that is governed by military law, curfews, violence and disappearances, where killing is common and account-ability and the rule of law virtually non-existent. For a period under the AKP, the south-east of Turkey was no longer under emergency rule, and as the military declined in its power and in political life, there was the emergence of a potential peace process to put an end to the decades-long war between Turk and Kurd that has claimed the lives of at least 40,000 souls. Alas, this was short-lived and, at the time of writ-ing, the south-east has once again descended into conflict.

This book assesses the Kurdish insurgency and the peace overtures made to the Kurds under the AKP. Unfortunately, the diagnosis is far from positive; however, the problem is not terminal. As yet there is no real peace process between Turkey and the Kurdistan Workers' Party (PKK). The gulf between the two sides remains large and significant. Sadly, despite the decline of the military, vestiges of its thinking still linger. The government continues to view the Kurdish issue as a ques-tion of cultural and democratic rights, while the Kurdish movement sees it as a national struggle.

Despite the shocking scale of the loss of human life and dislocation, the spotlight on Turkey has never been on its Kurdish problem. This is true of both domestic and international observers of Turkey. An impor-tant reason for this is the lack of an open press. The media has never been free in Turkey. Military tutelage would not allow journalists during the 1980s and 1990s to report on the Kurdish conflict. They were, however, able to discuss the ins and outs of Turkish politics with some degree of freedom. This was due more to the ruling coalition politics of the day than to a long-term commitment to freedom of expression.

Turkey's press is still not free. In addition to a climate of bullying by politicians against reporters critical of governmental policy, media owners' business links with other companies in different sectors have made the Turkish media virtually impotent. Owners rely on the gov-ernment for lucrative contracts and tenders and therefore lean heavily on journalists under their employ to toe the government line.

The media therefore does not serve as a check on the power of gov-ernment. Nor does it make it more accountable. What is more, the chinks in Turkey's democratic armour have been hammered and beaten over time, making it highly susceptible to attack in the form of autocratic tendencies. For example, there is no clear separation of powers between the executive, legislature and judiciary. The courts are open to government manipulation and influence over the appointment of judges, with the Ministry of Interior increasingly powerful. The government dominates parliament, a result of both the ruling party's popularity and the disparity between its number of seats and the number of votes it receives, as a result of its high electoral threshold of 10 per cent—another vestige of a constitution drafted by the military.

It is not new for Turkish politics to be dominated by a single charismatic leader. This has been the state of affairs since the founding of the republic in 1923 by the country's principal state-builder, the war hero Mustafa Kemal Ataturk, first president of Turkey. Reading Turkish political history is almost akin to reading biographies of its leading figures. In the 1940s there was Ataturk's trusted aide, Ismet Inonu. In the 1950s it was the ill-fated Adnan Menderes. During the 1960s and 1970s it was Suleyman Demirel and Bulent Ecevit; in the 1980s and 1990s, Turgut Ozal. Today, it is Recep Tayyip Erdogan.

One political figure after another tried to shape and mould Turkey into an image of its liking, and to influence the political and cultural direction of the state. However, this was always under the purview of the military, the self-styled guardians of the secular state, who would not hesitate to interfere in the political process. Sometimes this would be directly, as in 1960, 1971 and 1980. Other times it would be through the influence of the National Security Council, as in 1997, or through the secular Kemalist bureaucracy or individuals in prominent positions in civil society.

The exception to this was Prime Minister Erdogan, now President Erdogan, who led the AKP to three consecutive general election victories. He, too, had to face the very real threat of military intervention, either in a coup or through indirect means, such as a court case (a closure case) to shut down the party for violating secularism; the protest movement following the presidential crisis of 2007; or the attempted coup by a Gulenist faction in 2016. However, as the military's power declined, the AKP was rising. Erdogan and his party soon found themselves with free rein to navigate the treacherous terrain of

Turkish politics. Instead of consensus politics and pluralism, the Erdogan years—during his tenures as both prime minister and now president—have often been highly divisive and autocratic in style. Those chinks in the armour were now slowly cracking.

But the AKP was successful in governance. Not only did Turkey's economy develop, but more and more Turks were seeing the benefits of this growth through public spending on services and infrastructure. Meanwhile, Turkey's middle class also grew. The AKP's majoritarian style of politics was not to the liking of many younger, urbanised Turks who enjoyed the luxuries of the AKP's economic success. Many engaged in resistance, either through street demonstrations like the Gezi Park protests, or through their use of social and other online media. Indeed, a wave of social groups have made their voices heard in recent years, from LGBT activists to environmentalists. While Turkey's democracy has weakened, its civil society has grown stronger.

Indeed, what militates many Turks against the AKP is the issue of urban regeneration and large-scale public projects. They are concerned with the lack of transparency, the changing urban landscape and the ecological and environmental effects of such schemes. There is also the problem of corruption and accountability. Meanwhile, there are those who have benefited from such projects. The dwellers of what were once slums have seen urban renewal and development of their neighbourhoods and can now enjoy a middle-class lifestyle. The construction industry that drives the Turkish economy has seen successive years of growth.

In foreign policy, the decline of military tutelage has opened new directions for Turkey. No longer just an easterly extension of NATO, Turkey has sought to engage in the regions around it, especially the Middle East. There was some limited success. Turkey has certainly become more assertive and confident; no longer just an aspirant member of the European Union (EU), Turkey has sought to be a major power in its own right. Nevertheless, post-military Turkey was just a newcomer to the Middle East. It was caught unprepared for the Arab uprisings that began in 2011 and the subsequent Syrian Civil War. Soon it found itself virtually isolated in the region. It will take much planning and strategic thought to rebuild lost ties and undo the damage.

In short, the post-military Turkey is a new Turkey, with new challenges ahead.

THE NEW TURKEY AND ITS DISCONTENTS

Authoritarian Practices and the State

Given that some have described the AKP as authoritarian in nature, a question is raised: is Turkey a democracy without democrats? The answer, we think, is not so simple. We think that Erdogan considers himself a democrat and bases his legitimacy on electoral victories. What motivates his authoritarian style of governing, in his view, is the desire to strengthen the state and shake off the remnants of military tutelage and other subversive forces.

Indeed, the AKP has faced a rearguard attack. In order to appreciate how the military maintained its grip over Turkish politics, it is important to recognise that this often played out within the civil-legal institutions of state. Through committed secular Kemalists within the legal system and the bureaucracy, in addition to the extended powers of the National Security Council (MGK), the military was able to exert influence over civilian government. The closure case against the AKP in 2008 is a case in point. Despite being popularly elected in two consecutive polls, the AKP was nearly shut down on the dubious charge of being anti-secular.

It is in this context that the AKP has had to govern Turkey. The military's presence in political life, especially after the 1980 coup, was to the detriment of many groups within society, particularly Kurds, leftists and Islamists. In addition to battling such assaults from Turkey's military-Kemalist infrastructure, Erdogan is seeking to redress and correct what he and the AKP see as past injustices. This includes staffing the bureaucracy and the judiciary with AKP sympathisers and replacing secularists who are deemed to have been part of the military's grip on power. This, the party feels, is democratic—it is changing Turkey for the better, so that government institutions represent the will of the electorate.

Today, the AKP believes it faces another challenge, in the form of a "parallel state" or "parallel structure" within some institutions, which also needs correcting. This is especially the case after the failed July 2016 coup. In confronting this perceived challenge, the party is in the midst of another purge of the bureaucracy, this time against members or sympathisers of the Gulen movement, who are loyal to the self-exiled Islamic preacher Fetullah Gulen rather than to the government.

However, in attempting to right past wrongs, the AKP has alienated vast sections of the Turkish population, the 50 per cent or so who did not vote for Erdogan or the AKP. It has purged its critics from state institutions. The firebrand rhetoric of some of the AKP's leaders also has not helped. Another consequence has been the weakening of checks and balances against the ruling party. Power is increasingly centralised, democratic institutions weakened.

Weak State, not Deep State

In writing about Turkey, there are certain particularities that ought to be explained. One of them is the so-called "deep state". The term "deep state" has often been used to describe aspects of Turkish politics that may sound alien to Western observers. It is also a misappropriated term, one that the authors of this book use sparingly.

Simply put, in the context of Turkey, "deep state" means aspects of the military apparatus together with individuals or groups within civil society (journalists, civil servants, university rectors, and so on) who work together to form a network. For some, the term "deep state" has almost become a blanket term for any covert action by the state.[3] For the most part the "deep state" is an instrument of the military-Kemalist elite for maintaining the secularist nature of the state and fighting off challenges to Turkey. These include the threat from both Islamists and Kurdish separatists. However, the extent to which the "deep state" exerts its influence, and the interpretation of its scope, differs according to perspective.

For some, the real "deep state" was a clandestine network that derived from the military in its war against the PKK in south-eastern Turkey. In order to avoid accountability or civilian oversight, special squads were established in the 1990s to assassinate Kurdish leaders which often involved working with or sponsoring underground figures and movements. The origin of this "deep state" was the special warfare unit Gladios, a Cold War operation to defend against the Soviet Union in case of invasion and geared towards intelligence gathering. "Gangs" were organised, taking the form of a cell-like structure to fight the Soviets. However, they went on to be involved in the left-right battles of the 1960s and 1970s and were then used to combat the Kurdish insurgency during the 1980s and 1990s. Those within the cell, answerable to the military, would outsource and recruit individuals to launch an operation, which would be conducted autonomously. Sometimes those recruited would come from organised crime or the police. Soon this created a culture of impunity, especially in the south-east of Turkey, with death squads sometimes operating in public.[4]

For others, the "deep state" is simply individual public officials going beyond legal parameters on behalf of the state. However, in the eyes of the public, it is a stronger and much more structured organisation than what it really is. According to Ilhan Cihaner, a former public prosecutor, the 1990s assassination campaign in south-eastern Turkey was staged by criminal groups. But there was little deep state logic behind this; rather, it was part of the illegal activities of the "actual" state.[5]

For some, though, the "deep state" goes beyond the confines of national security issues and extends into the far reaches of the civil service and civil society. It was through such associations that the military was able to extend its influence. In other words, the military increased and maintained its power by dominating governmental institutions, and was therefore able to use legal and civilian means to protect the secular state without having to interfere directly. During the 1980s and 1990s, the south-east of Turkey was almost in anarchy and without the rule of law. Rival death squads would even compete with each other. However, in many respects, the political class was very much aware of what was going on and the structures that were in place (though not necessarily the details). In fact, they operated within the law.[6]

As previously stated, the authors of this volume have an aversion to the term "deep state", for several important reasons. For one, the different interpretations of the term create confusion. We prefer to be clear about the subject matter at hand wherever possible. Second, the idea of the "deep state" risks the government avoiding responsibility. We feel that regardless of whether the civilian government or high-ranking officers had knowledge of a specific paramilitary death squad in south-east Turkey, it is they who should be held accountable for the actions of such groups. Pleading innocence through ignorance is unacceptable in a modern democracy. Organisations such as anti-Kurdish death squads were acting and serving in the interests of the state, using equipment that belonged to the Turkish state, and were answerable to individual state officials. It is therefore the state that should be accountable for such activities.

One of Turkey's foremost investigators of the "deep state" is Nedim Sener. He also dislikes the term and believes that the "deep state" is actually just the state. Nevertheless, he uses the term because it is in popular parlance. He points to the assassinations of Armenians during the 1980s in operations against the Armenian Secret Army for the Liberation of Armenia (ASALA). These he says were conducted by the Turkish intelligence agency, MIT, which was under the jurisdiction of the National Security Council. Similarly, those who had engaged in extra-judicial killings of Kurds in the 1980s and 1990s were often those with official ranks.[7] The activities of JITEM, the illegal counterterrorism unit under the Gendarmerie, operated in south-east Turkey throughout the 1990s. This would indicate that, in reality, what some perceive as a "deep state" simply represents actions of the state that are beyond the law.[8]

Another important reason why the authors of this volume dislike the term "deep state" is that it draws attention to a symptom, rather than the problem facing Turkey today—namely, the weakness of the Turkish state. For many observers of Turkey, this statement may be somewhat surprising. Turkey has often been considered a father state with patrimonial inclinations and a top-down style of politics and organisation. This is, of course, true. From its inception, it was the state that led reforms and the process of modernisation. It was the state that led the population in a given direction in many periods of its history. Yet, while this may be the case, there is still weakness in the Turkish state. Consider, for example, the nature of the "deep state". Surely the very idea that elements within the state can act with impunity and engage in illegal activities such as extra-judicial killings is indicative of a lack of transparency and rule of law. Similarly, Turkey's high levels of alleged corruption, which can go without prosecution, indictment or conviction, are also symptoms of weakness within the state. So too is the dysfunctional political-judicial relationship, whereby the judiciary is appointed by politicians, again eroding the rule of law.[9]

Another example of this weakness is the concept that "parallel" structures exist within the state. This is an allegation that has been made by Erdogan and other members of the ruling AKP. The logic behind this argument is that followers of the self-exiled Turkish cleric

Fetullah Gulen have infiltrated the civil service with the agenda of subverting the AKP and bringing an Islamic state to power in Turkey or, at best, of taking direction from an exiled preacher as opposed to the elected government. Nedim Sener argues that there is indeed a parallel state whereby Gulen supporters act in their own interests and are effective within the police force, police academy and intelligence services and aspire to control every governmental department.[10]

Let us not forget that this "parallel" state is also far from unique to the "New" Turkey. In prior years, much of the bureaucracy was filled either with highly nationalist supporters, or at least ardent Kemalists. Today, the bureaucracy is divided among different groups organised into structures such as Alevis, leftists, nationalists, right-wing Nationalist Action Party supporters and different groups of conservatives.[11] But again, the idea that members of the bureaucracy are aligned to an ideological outlook, rather than to elected officials, highlights the fragility within the Turkish state.

The Coup of Many Ironies

On 15–16 July 2016 there was an attempted coup by a Gulenist faction within the armed forces. The events which took place represent a series of ironies within Turkish politics. Followers of Turkey would certainly have raised an eyebrow when it was revealed that the attempted putsch was orchestrated by a Gulenist military faction. Since the founding of the modern republic, Turkey's armed forces have been staunchly secular and considered themselves the guardian of the secular state. It comes as no surprise that, since the rise of the AKP, there have been stirrings of unrest within the military ranks on the basis of the party's Islamic background, perceived to be challenging the country's secular order. As this book will explain, the military's concern soon translated into indirect, behind-the-scenes action, in the form of campaigns such as the Republican Protests of 2007, the E-Memorandum, also in 2007, and the real or imagined coup plots of Ergenekon and Balyoz. However, the irony was that when a direct attempt to overthrow the AKP government took place (2016), it was instigated by an Islamic faction within the ranks, not the secular nationalists traditionally associated with the military—and not at the peak of the military's power, but at a time when the military wields considerably less influence than it once did.

Furthermore, while analysts have found evidence that at least elements within the Gulen network were the architects of the failed putsch,[12] the movement was also believed to be behind the trials, indictments, prosecutions and imprisonment of dozens of military officers during the Ergenekon and Balyoz cases beginning in 2008 (overturned completely by 2016). These cases, as will be explained in Chapter 1, ushered in the decline of the military as a major player in political life—yet the armed forces were the Gulenists' chosen instrument to overthrow military rule.

It is also highly ironic that the target of the attempted coup, the rule of President Erdogan and the AKP government, had turned a blind eye to the rise of the Gulen movement within state institutions. Seen as allies of the AKP against the possibility of a military intervention, the Gulen movement and the AKP had a marriage of convenience until 2013. However, as it transpired, it was the Gulenist infiltration into state institutions, no less the military, which proved to be the paramount threat to Turkey's democracy and to Erdogan's AKP. In the weeks after the coup, Erdogan expressed regret about the close cooperation between the AKP and the Gulen movement until at least 2010.[13]

In the aftermath of the coup, many sentiments were expressed of solidarity with President Erdogan and the ruling AKP, who utilised the coup as a means of obtaining the public's support for its purge against the Gulen movement. However, Erdogan and the AKP government have still not been held accountable for allowing the Gulen movement to penetrate state institutions such as the military and judiciary. The regime has avoided a public outcry and there have been few calls for ministerial resignations. If the Gulen movement was indeed behind the putsch, then surely it would be a scandal that the AKP, seeing the Gulen movement as an ally, had allowed this dangerous and nefarious group to embed itself within state apparatus. The true victim of the attempted coup was not the government, but rather the Turkish public. Public officials owe them a detailed explanation, which has not yet been forthcoming. This book touches on the relationship between the Gulen movement and the AKP, and its consequences.

Black Turk vs White Turk?

In analysing Turkey, it is very easy to view the country's struggles as between secularists devoted to the legacy of the nation's founder Mustafa Kemal Ataturk and Islamists wishing to replace the secular state with a more traditional one, in which Islam has a place in Turkish identity. This political struggle, which has obvious cultural ramifications, has even been referred to as one between "White Turks" (members of the secular, bureaucratic-military elite from Rumelia, the European Ottoman territory) and "Black Turks" (the conservative, rural Anatolian population).

After many rounds of arguing this subject in the coffee shops and restaurants frequented by the authors of this volume, we have come to the conclusion that in modern Turkey, such a division is a relic of the past.[14] Perhaps, during the period from the founding of the republic to as late as the AKP's first electoral victory in 2002, such simplifications of Turkey's problems might have been valid, if still problematic. In reality, social mobility and cultural identity is quite fluid in Turkey.

Take, for example, the ranks of the military. Until recently, this institution was a vehicle for upward mobility and cultural change. A staunchly secular institution, many officers come from the lower classes, from rural areas or sometimes even from pious families. By rising through the ranks, the individual becomes part of the elite, as do his children, who rarely enter a career in the military themselves, but instead attend good high schools and universities, then become professionals such as doctors, lawyers, teachers and academics. Within a generation, one may go from religious to secular, black Turk to white Turk.

Arabesk music has seen the same sociocultural change. The genre rose to great prominence and popularity in Turkey during the 1960s and '70s. With an Arab rhythm sung in Turkish, the style was primarily associated with the sentiments of the marginalised, the conservative or the socioeconomically depressed who had moved away from rural communities in search of a better life in the city. From its inception, the genre was frowned upon by the traditional secular elite, who preferred Western music, a legacy of the pro-Western Kemalist reforms following the establishment of the new Turkish Republic. However, with Arabesk's rising popularity, the genre blossomed into the mainstream while continuing to express feelings of anguish, alienation and the frustration of conservative men in trying to preserve traditional values and honour, particularly in the face of industrial employment and liberal women of the modern world.[15]

The gradual acceptance of Arabesk music represents how the once marginalised has gained legitimacy in Turkey. The lines between the establishment and the periphery have become intermeshed and blurred. White Turks and Black Turks have, perhaps, given way to Grey Turks.

One more example before we rest our case: consider the rise of the Anatolian bourgeoisie, which pre-dated the AKP. The members of this new business industrial elite are not merely rural and religiously pious. If social class is defined by profession and wealth, their status is certainly on par with that of the traditional Istanbul elite. They may be religious sympathisers, but they have no desire to live under Sharia and are content with Turkey's secular constitution. What is there to divide such people from so-called "White Turks", apart from religious belief? They too share similar concerns about the economy. They also aspire for their children to be doctors, lawyers and entrepreneurs, and to attend the best schools and universities. Many "Black Turks" do not even live in rural Anatolia or nearby cities but rather in the main population centres of Turkey—Ankara, Istanbul or Izmir. Their neighbourhoods have undergone development and many have benefited financially.

It seems that the differences between the two groups are more imagined than real. And although politicians and commentators still use such terms to describe identity politics, there is a generation emerging in Turkey that is becoming alien to such divisions. We would like to a see a Turkey whose political parties are not divided by such cultural identities, but rather are representative of left, right and centre, with a good dose of liberalism to boot—healthy, normalised politics for the new Turkey. This book dissects the historical and present-day barriers to this "new" politics, and the forces of dissent fighting to overcome them.

1

THE GENERAL'S LAST SIGH

Introduction

> "The army's attitude cannot be defined within democracy. Those who trust the power of weapons cannot build a democracy."[1]

Recep Tayyip Erdogan, July 2013

The above comment by the then Prime Minister Erdogan was not a reference to Turkey's troubled past. He was referring to events in Egypt, where the country's military intervened to overthrow the elected president, Mohammed Morsi. Erdogan was perhaps the world's most vocal critic of the Egyptian "coup". It had particular resonance for Turkey, with its turbulent history of military interventions. In the summer of 2013, Turkey had been gripped by street protests. These demonstrated represented the biggest public challenge to the government since the Justice and Development Party (AKP) had come to power over a decade previously. Protesters chanted, "*Tayyip Istifa!*", "Tayyip resign!" However, unlike in Egypt, there were no calls for the military to intervene. The political challenge against Erdogan's authority did not emanate from and was not supported by Turkey's once powerful military. Its ability to orchestrate such challenges had seemingly become a thing of the past.

Under Erdogan and the AKP, the dominance of the military in Turkish politics was both gradually and systematically eroded. The army was unable to deal with the rise of the AKP, partly because of a reduction in its power ironically due to EU-centred reforms that the military itself had advocated. However, as we will see, the military was also in many respects the author of its own decline, a result of infighting and both internal and external plots and intrigue. By the AKP's second term, tensions arose within the military's lower officer ranks over what they perceived as challenges to the secular state. This created disarray within the ranks at the same time as spurious conspiracies to overthrow the government were revealed and prosecuted, leading to a purge of the military's officers. By the time the AKP entered its third term in office in 2011, the military was a spent force in Turkish politics. Even though this did not stop a coup attempt from taking place in July 2016, the Islamist faction responsible represented an anomaly, against the military's traditional position as the secular guardian of the Turkish state. The failed coup turned out to be the swansong of the era of military interference, triggering additional reforms to the military's structure that should keep it out of politics for the foreseeable future.

Eighty-Five Years of Turkish Military Tutelage

Before that, though, scholars agree that Turkey's military was powerful, with a long history of engaging in political affairs. There were two sources of the Turkish military's power: its Ottoman legacy and its Kemalist foundations.[2] The military saw itself as the guardian not only of the secular state but also of the founding ideology of its first president, Mustafa Kemal Ataturk. After the collapse of the Ottoman Empire following World War I, Ataturk won a war of independence and established the new Turkish Republic on staunchly secular lines. The military's association with Ataturk was a significant source of legitimacy. However, from 1960 onwards, the military had virtual authority over the definition of what constituted a national security threat. This allowed it to impose its will over civilian politics, especially as such threats were multi-faceted and included the Cold War, the Cyprus issue, Turkey's regional disputes, the role of Islam in society and Kurdish separatism. Such military interference in politics left both the political elite and civilian institutions weak.

The guardianship culture of the Turkish military emanates from the historical foundations of the Ottoman Empire, especially the eighteenth and nineteenth centuries. The Ottoman elites, recognising the superiority of the European armies, sought to reform and modernise.[3] The new Ottoman military and the bureaucracy became revolutionary. The core figures of the Young Ottoman and later the Young Turk movements emerged from the military academy and were unafraid of interfering in politics to preserve the Ottoman state. For example, in the Young Turk Revolution of 1908, the military forced the Ottoman sultan to limit his rule by reinstating the modernising 1876 constitution, the Empire's first, which the sultan had abolished two years after its introduction in 1878.[4]

After Turkey's independence in 1923 it was Ataturk himself who tried to prevent military interference in politics. No longer embattled, Ataturk forced any military officer wishing to seek public office first to resign from the Turkish Armed Forces (TSK). This reduced the number of retired military personnel entering politics after Ataturk established his political party, the Republican People's Party (CHP).[5] Even during Turkey's transition to democracy after free and fair elections in 1950, the armed forces did not involve themselves in politics. This was despite the electoral victory of the opposition, the Democrat Party (DP) led by Adnan Menderes, who became prime minister.[6]

It was not until 1960 that Turkey saw the return of the military to the political process. Until then, despite the turbulence of Turkish politics, the TSK stayed out of the political fray and was for the most part directed by civilian ministers.[7] However, by 1960 the populist policies of Menderes were becoming increasingly authoritarian, and he had begun appealing to Islam for popular support. There was growing unrest, and the military decided to intervene, toppling Menderes and his government. This was the modern Turkish Republic's first military coup. Interestingly, the key drivers within the armed forces were a group of junior officers frustrated not only by what they considered to be incompetency among the political class, but also by the armed forces' lack of sophisticated equipment and low status in society compared with Turkey's NATO allies.[8] This group of young officers persuaded senior commanders to overthrow the elected government.[9] The military was now a major political player.

Menderes was put on trial, found guilty and sent to the gallows. The military then supervised the drafting of a new constitutional framework that increased the military's autonomy, political power and standing. The most significant development was the establishment of the National Security Council (MGK). This new body set up a direct communication channel between the chief of the general staff and cabinet ministers. In other words, the Council was the means by which the armed forces voiced its very strong opinions, especially on national security, to the elected civilian government.[10] This political involvement was reinforced by the 1961 Turkish Armed Forces (TSK) Internal Service Law No. 211. Article 35 nebulously stated that "the duty of the Turkish Armed Forces is to protect and preserve the Turkish homeland and the Turkish Republic as defined in the constitution".[11]

Following further interventions by the military, the National Security Council would soon enjoy additional, previously inconceivable powers. The TSK launched another coup in 1971, as the political parties in parliament seemed incapable of overcoming deadlock and the country was convulsed by economic crisis and political urban violence.[12] The 1973 constitutional amendments expanded the Council's mandate, allowing it to make recommendations to government especially in matters such as Islam, ethnic secessionism and the perceived threat from communist agitators.[13]

By 1980, left- and right-wing extremists battling in the streets had left the country reeling. On 12 September 1980 the military staged a third coup. The National Security Council's powers were expanded once again in the new 1982 constitution, drafted under the supervision of the military. Now the cabinet was obliged to prioritise implementing official decisions of the Council, and a new system of state security courts was established. For example, one of the three jury members of the National Security Courts now had to be a military prosecutor. The National Security Council also oversaw other governmental organisations, such as the Higher Education Council and the media regulator RTUK. This allowed the military to extend its influence beyond national security. Furthermore, the general chiefs of staff now had weekly meetings with the president and prime minister, allowing them to make their opinions heard on a regular and direct basis. Close ties were also established within bureaucratic institutions such as the Ministry of Foreign Affairs through regular working groups and other contacts.[14]

The military did not hesitate to use its powers. In subsequent years, the generals used the National Security Council as a mechanism to determine the country's security policies, veto governmental decisions and force counterproductive cabinets out of power. The decisions of the council included changing the content of the school curriculum, overseeing television broadcasts as well as the ability to shut television stations down, denying penal immunity to parliamentary deputies, especially those of the Kurdish-oriented Democracy Party, interfering in local bureaucratic appointments in the south-east region and determining the content of the laws relating to terrorism.[15] Simply put, from 1980 until the rise of the AKP in the 2000s, the military was by far the most powerful political player in Turkey.

"Vampires Roaming the Land"

Meetings of Turkey's powerful National Security Council usually only lasted a few hours. However, on the cold winter afternoon of 28 February 1997, deliberations continued until midnight. When the Council finally adjourned, it released a simple and terse communiqué. It stated that it would not tolerate "steps away from the contemporary values of the Turkish Republic", adding that "destructive and separatist groups are seeking to weaken our democracy and legal system by blurring the distinction between the secular and the anti-secular".[16] This was no mere statement. In effect, this represented a behind-the-scenes, indirect military intervention in politics.

The Council's statement has been referred to as a "soft" or "postmodern" coup.[17] Following this communiqué the Council issued a range of measures to be implemented in a twenty-point programme, which, six months later, would ultimately lead to the resignation of Prime Minister Necmettin Erbakan of the Welfare Party, an Islamic party. The Council's demands included the tightening of controls over religious brotherhoods and orders, the restriction of religious *Imam Hatip* high schools, the shutting down of television and radio stations considered anti-secular and restrictions on "green capital", or businesses that were owned by pious entrepreneurs—often from Anatolia—believed to be anti-secular.[18] Effectively the military was forcing the prime minister to initiate a crackdown against his own grassroots voters.

Although Erbakan initially resisted, telling supporters that "in Turkey, governments are formed in parliament, not in the National

19

Security Council,"[19] his resolve would gradually erode. He scribbled his name on the military's programme, which became known as the 28 February process. The Turkish public was clearly polarised as many secular protesters rallied across the country, against the Islamic-led government and in response to details of government corruption leaked, presumably, by the military, the Kemalist establishment or both. Soon the government, reeling from months of attacks by the secularist elite, lost its absolute majority in parliament, forcing Erbakan to resign in June 1997 after just eleven months in office.[20]

The military's intentions were two-pronged. It was concerned not only by a creeping Islamification of Turkey, but also that Erbakan's Islamic-oriented policies would detrimentally affect Turkey's standing with its Western allies. The military was both alarmed and incensed by developments such as Erbakan's visits to Iran and Libya, where he accused Israel and the US of supporting terrorism and called for a common Islamic community with a joint currency. In the eyes of the military, such visits and rhetoric weakened Turkey's standing with Washington and its Western allies.[21] Meanwhile, ahead of the coup, rumours had been circulating on national television and in the printed press of an apparent pending Islamic takeover, led by what was previously an unheard-of secretive brotherhood, the Aczmendi.[22] The straw that broke the camel's back was in Sincan in Central Anatolia, the same province as the capital Ankara. On 30 January, the military sent in tanks to quash a pro-Sharia and anti-Israeli demonstration where the Iranian ambassador was the guest speaker. Television stations beamed footage of a former bodyguard of the Islamist mayor slapping a female journalist.[23]

The impact of the 1997 "post-modern" coup was not limited to Erbakan's premiership. In January 1998, not only was Erbakan banned from parliamentary politics for five years, but the constitutional court also shut down the Welfare Party, freezing its funds on the basis that it had acted against the secular principles of the Republic.[24] Following the ban, the Virtue Party, also Islamic, was established in its place. Despite taking 15 per cent of the national vote in the 1999 general elections, the Virtue Party was also then banned, on the dubious charge of festering anti-secular activities. The original indictment against the party even likened it to "vampires roaming the land".[25] But the banning of the Virtue Party led to the creation of two new Islamic-oriented parties.

Some members formed the Felicity Party (SP). However, others created the Justice and Development Party, the AKP.

On 14 August 2001, Recep Tayyip Erdogan, the popular former Istanbul mayor who had served time in prison for reciting a poem considered anti-secular, established the AKP together with several other rising political stars. The party founders were a group of reform-minded politicians associated first with the Welfare and later the Virtue Party. Just over one year after this new party had been established, the AKP would sweep to power in spectacular fashion, having won the November 2002 general election with an impressive 34.3 per cent of the vote. Turkey's high electoral threshold of 10 per cent meant that several other political parties, including those who had been part of the previous ruling coalition such as the Nationalist Action Party (MHP), the centre-right Motherland Party (ANAP) and the Democratic Left Party, were prevented from winning any parliamentary seats. This meant that the AKP gained 363 seats of the 550 available in the Grand National Assembly. Although a clear majority, this still fell slightly short of the crucial two thirds required to elect a new president in the first two rounds of voting, or to make constitutional amendments without holding a referendum. However, it did give the AKP a three-fifths majority—enough to bring a constitutional change to referendum.[26]

Still, the AKP was careful to strike a balance between the military's dominance and its own populist policies. Unlike previous Islamic-oriented parties, the AKP was strongly committed to joining the EU. Accepting the lessons of the 1997 coup, one leading member of the AKP commented on the need to accept the military's guardianship role. "If we are to be realistic," he stated, "we should not come up against and clash with the military".[27] Indeed, despite the AKP's Islamist origins, from its inception until the run-up to the 2002 elections, it actively branded itself as moderately conservative and would not dispute the secular nature of the state. Not only did this broaden its support base beyond that of the Welfare Party,[28] it also helped it to avoid an immediate clash with the military. Nevertheless, as a former minister for women and family affairs would recall, the impact of EU reforms would gradually reduce the power of the military and contribute to its decline.[29]

"Europe, we're coming!"

Following the 1999 Helsinki Summit, the EU officially recognised Turkey as a candidate for membership.[30] The accession process was one of the most important developments in the alteration and, ultimately, limitation of the Turkish military's role in politics. In order to meet the EU's criteria for entry, the Turkish government introduced a series of reform packages. This began in 2001 under the coalition, before the AKP was elected. Some of the reforms pertained directly to the military. For example, the constitution was amended to alter the make-up of the National Security Council. The number of civilians at Council meetings was increased. In the wake of the 1999 trial of the captured PKK leader, Abdullah Ocalan, military judges were replaced with civilian judges in the State Security Courts. Further, Turkey did away with capital punishment, which meant that Ocalan's death sentence was commuted to life imprisonment. And, on 30 July 2002, emergency rule was finally lifted in the mainly Kurdish south-east.

The following month, in addition to passing legislation to abolish capital punishment, parliament also eased some restrictions on use of the Kurdish language. Such reforms led the Turkish daily *Milliyet* to run the headline "Europe, we're coming!"[31] These reforms were only the beginning of a long process and a series of further reforms to be carried out by the Turkish government, which would intensify under the AKP. In order to gain EU entry, Turkey needed to fulfil the Copenhagen criteria, which require a candidate country to meet certain standards before becoming eligible to join the EU. These include issues pertaining to minority rights, the upholding of the rule of law, the guaranteeing of human rights, legislative alignment with the laws of the EU and a functioning market economy. On 12 December 2002, the European Council stated that the EU would open entry negotiations if Turkey fulfilled the Copenhagen criteria.[32] By the time the decision was officially made on 16 December 2004, in a deal hotly debated by the then twenty-five member states,[33] Turkey had already put in place forty-eight measures on human rights.[34]

But fundamental to Turkey's bid for EU accession was the restructuring of civil-military relations. The EU required Turkey's military structures to be subordinated to democratic, civilian control. It was such military reforms that led lawmakers in Ankara on 30 July 2003 to vote in favour of an EU harmonisation package, which adjusted the make-up of the powerful National Security Council. Now, instead of the Council's secretary-general being appointed by the chief of the general staff, they would be appointed by the prime minister and could even be a civilian.[35] This amendment was soon enacted. In 2004, a civilian became secretary-general of the Council for the first time. The new legislation also detailed how Council meetings should be organised, and reduced their frequency from monthly to bimonthly. Soon, the defence budget was also under increased civilian supervision and overseen by the Court of Auditors.

The National Security Council also lost some control over state institutions and bodies. For example, the military lost its seat on the board of the Inspection of Cinema, Video and Musical Works, RTUK, the Council of Higher Education and the Supreme Communication Board in 2004. Later, in 2006, the Military Criminal Code was amended to prevent military courts from trying civilians during peacetime, with the exception of cases where military personnel and civilians stood accused of committing a crime together. If this were not enough, there were additional reforms in 2009. This time, new laws permitted civilian courts to try military personnel if their accused crimes occurred during times of peace. In 2010 came the annulment of the EMASYA Protocol on Cooperation for Security and Public Order, which was a covert blueprint that enabled the armed forces to launch internal operations without requiring prior permission. Not only was it annulled, its abolition obtained the consent of the chief of the general staff. Also in 2010, a national referendum approved a constitutional amendment allowing military personnel to appeal the decisions of the Supreme Military Council if the military body expelled or dismissed them.[36]

On a gradual basis, then, EU reform packages greatly reduced the power of the military in civilian affairs. The EU agrees. For example, the 2002 European Commission regular report on Turkey's progress to accession criticised the prevalence of the National Security Council in Turkish politics.[37] In contrast, by 2004, the European Commission reported that the "powers and functioning of the National Security Council (NSC) have been substantially amended, bringing the framework of civil-military relations closer to [the] practice in EU Member States".[38] The Commission's 2005 report went even further, acknowledging that in October 2004 the Council convened for the first time under a civilian secretary-general. Although the minutes of Council meetings were not made public, press releases were issued and on 30 November 2004 a press briefing was organised for the first time at the Council headquarters, including a question and answer session. The Commission report even noted improvement in parliamentary control over military spending following the Law on Public Financial Management and Control (PFMC) becoming effective in January 2005, and that there had been an amendment, not yet adopted, to Article 160 of the constitution, preventing state property from being owned by the military.[39] Undoubtedly, the successful implementation of EU reforms meant that the power of the military had been severely curtailed.

Soldiers of (Mis)fortune

Why did the military acquiesce to the decline of its own powers through EU reform packages? It is important to recall that since the 1990s, the military had supported Turkey's ambitions to become a member-state. This goal was deemed consistent with Westernisation and modernisation, key pillars of Kemalist ideology.[40] Although the military was no doubt aware that joining the EU would challenge its own superiority in Turkish politics, this was buttressed by the political and economic stability that EU membership offered Turkey. Nor were the generals impervious to the attitudes of the public who, along with the Istanbul bourgeoisie, had long supported EU membership. The EU was also perceived as a mechanism to tame both Islamist activities and Kurdish separatism. Following the arrest of Ocalan, there was also a reduction in the intensity of fighting in the south-east; this eased many of the military's concerns, especially over the implications of the EU process for Kurdish rights and identity. According to Edip Baser, a retired four-star general and deputy chief of the general staff, active until 2005, the military accepted even aspects of the EU reform package pertaining to the legislative curtailment of military power.[41]

However, this did not mean that the military was unconcerned by the possible impact of EU reforms on national security issues. Nor was it united on this issue. While initially the military was generally supportive of the democratic initiatives associated with the EU, it was highly critical of the EU's stance on certain issues such as Cyprus, especially the Greek Cypriot entry into the EU representing the island as a whole.[42] Some elements within the ranks held conspiratorial notions about certain EU member states (and the US), believing that they wanted to weaken Turkey, preventing it from becoming a great power competitor by creating a Kurdish state in Turkey's east.[43] As will be discussed, some within the military were greatly concerned about its declining fortunes, especially when it was suspicious of the AKP, deeming it an Islamist party. This would lead to resentment within the military that came close to open rupture with the chief of the general staff.

But, despite discontent in some quarters, the military accepted EU reforms that curtailed its power at least on the surface. It is important to remember that the reforms occurred at a time when the chief of the general staff was under the progressive leadership of Hilmi Ozkok. Unlike his predecessors, Ozkok adopted a relatively low profile. This was quite unusual and sparked rumours that the TSK had decided to withdraw from politics.[44] Ozkok's outlook was that the armed forces needed a new vision, and that officers needed to broaden their horizons intellectually. Ozkok considered Kemalism a worldview that was open and receptive to change, rather than a rigid ideological outlook. It was even said that Ozkok questioned the judgement of past military interventions and instead favoured democratic solutions to political problems. Even his style and manner were different from generals of the past. He could be reserved, and kept himself to himself. He would not invite his fellow officers to his home for social visits and appeared somewhat aloof from other generals, giving an impression of arrogance.[45] It did not help that, unlike previous chiefs of staff, Ozkok rose through the ranks from his engagement with NATO rather than the counter-insurgency warfare in the south-east, where the majority of high-ranking officers gained their stripes.[46] As a result, there had been resistance to Ozkok as head of the armed forces.[47]

Ozkok went as far as to believe that Turkish society had matured, that the military therefore needed to have more faith in people's judgement, and that pious people had the capacity to pursue secular politics.[48] This outlook was married with a respect for constitutionalism.

For example, Ozkok justified the military's not openly supporting parliament's resolution in favour of the Iraq War by citing the constitution, which states that the military can only make suggestions to government, not to parliament.[49] At times, the military under Ozkok even deferred to the judgement of the civilian body politic. For example, the office of the chiefs of staff saw their plan to invite their Iranian counterparts to Turkey dropped, after Foreign Minister Abdullah Gul told Ozkok that the move could be misinterpreted by Washington. Ozkok heeded Gul's advice.[50]

It should be no surprise, therefore, that Ozkok was a staunch advocate of Turkey's EU process. He publicly expressed his support for EU membership several times, even in the wake of the UN's Annan Plan for the future of Cyprus (1999–2004, see below). However, not all within Turkey's military were as forward-thinking as Ozkok, and soon dissent would grow up around him.

Dissension within the Ranks

The role of the Turkish general chief of staff is closer to demi-god than head of the armed forces. A towering figure to be unchallenged by the ranks and influential in promotions of officers, the power of the general chief of staff was deliberately designed, after the 1960 coup, to prevent lower-ranking officers from seizing power.[51] However, this did not prevent significant discontent among officers over Ozkok's conduct in the face of the military's toughest challenge: the threat of the AKP and its perceived Islamist activities, at a time when the military's power was already in decline.

The first signs of military fracture manifested themselves when the government pledged support for UN Secretary-General Kofi Annan's plan on the unification of Greek and Turkish communities under a federal state in Cyprus. Allegedly, according to the diaries of Admiral Ozden Ornek, the Cyprus problem created serious anti-EU sentiment among some of the top-ranking Turkish generals, who held fast to the belief that the EU would provoke Kurdish separatism, "break-up the republic" and "require Turkey to grant concessions on Cyprus".[52] Soon these grumblings of discontent within the lower ranks manifested themselves within the military command. For example, in 2003 the

National Security Council secretary-general, General Tuncer Kilinc, openly expressed his concerns over some of the details of the EU reform packages. In response, the then vice-chairman of the AKP, Dengir Mir Mehmet Firat, responded that "the Secretary-General of the MGK [National Security Council] has no right to criticize those reform packages in his own right".[53]

Following Gul's move to the Foreign Ministry and replacement as prime minister by Erdogan in March 2003, Ozkok (probably under pressure from fellow generals) and President Ahmet Necdet Sezer boycotted an official cocktail party, in protest against the AKP.[54] Later, on 5 May 2003, the military issued a press statement on secularism, describing itself as "the greatest guarantee of the secular, democratic and social characteristics of the Turkish Republic".[55] Soon there were even rumours of a pending coup by younger officers, over fears that the AKP was appointing religious radicals to important positions in the bureaucracy.[56] Ozkok had to deny such rumours in a press conference, especially in response to reports that younger officers were "uneasy" about the new government.[57] Indeed, Ozkok was facing "unbearable pressure" from officers over his working relationship with Erdogan, leading him to voice objections to the EU reform package on CNN Turk.[58] Several years later, and partly by Ozkok's own admission, it was revealed that there had indeed been a coup threat. It appears that Ozkok's uncharacteristic assertiveness against the civilian government was a possible attempt to placate dissension within the lower ranks.

These lower-ranking officers were seething at what appeared to be the good personal relationship that had developed between Ozkok and Prime Minister Erdogan. Generals Buyukanit and Basbug were concerned that Ozkok did not understand the threat to secularism posed by the AKP.[59] Many within the armed forces were incensed that Ozkok refused to allow anyone to accompany him into meetings with the prime minister (as was previously the norm) or for minutes to be taken.[60] There were even whispers among the lower ranks that Ozkok was "too liberal" and this view, making its presence felt within the military hierarchy,[61] soon became a recurring theme. There was a hard-core group of about six to eight senior officers who, on top of their reservations about his EU and US policies, believed that Ozkok was too soft on the AKP. It was even speculated in some quarters that this group of high-ranking generals was conspiring to force Ozkok to resign.[62]

It was with this challenge in mind that Ozkok allowed the military to make anti-government statements, such as one issued in May 2004 against an educational reform package that would allow graduates of the religious *Imam Hatip* schools to compete with other high school graduates for university places.[63] Still, this was not enough. Suspicion against Ozkok became so rife that talk within the military was either of getting rid of Ozkok or of making him more assertive.[64] Worse still, there were at least two to three four-star generals who were advocating that the military should once again intervene in civilian politics, under the old pretext that the constitution tasked the military with protecting the secular state. This intervention would take the form of a memorandum, or even "something more within legitimate limits"—in other words, a coup to oust the AKP.[65]

When you live with a tiger, don't pull its tail[66]

In 2006 and 2007, Turkish politics entered a period of crisis that was partially spurred by the change of personnel within the military. Ozkok retired as chief of the general staff and was replaced by Yasar Buyukanit in August 2006. Gone was the military chief determined to reach a modus vivendi with the ruling AKP; in his place was a staunch secularist of the old-school variety. Meanwhile, the presidential term of the respected secularist Ahmet Necdet Sezer expired in May 2007. Although largely a ceremonial role, the office of the president is important in Turkey, as it carries the power to return legislation passed by the Grand National Assembly deemed unconstitutional (although the president is obliged to accept it if parliament resubmits it). Sezer's secular credentials acted as a check on the power of the AKP. It was he who, in 2004, vetoed the proposed legislation to reform the education system against which the military had protested. Indeed, the military's new top man would not be anywhere near as low-key as Ozkok. The military was firm in its opposition to Erdogan's possible election as president and in its position that the AKP was filling state institutions with party sympathisers.[67]

At this stage, the AKP was reluctant to pursue its attempt to get Erdogan to assume the presidency, as this would usher in a presidential crisis pitting secularists and their military supporters against the government. Buyukanit had no qualms about making his position clear. He stated that Turkey needed a president "loyal to the principles of the republic".[68] Justice Minister Cemil Cicek responded by declaring, "it is inconceivable in a democratic state that the general staff would use any phrase against the government on any matter".[69]

During this presidential crisis there appeared to be a wave of popular support, both in the press and on the street, in what has been termed the "Republic Protests." In April 2007, a series of rallies in Ankara, Istanbul, Izmir, Manisa and other cities attracted hundreds of thousands and in some cases millions of demonstrators calling for the secular principles of the Republic to be upheld.[70] No doubt this was satisfying for the restless military, although the AKP had rescinded Erdogan's nomination and instead proposed Foreign Minister Abdullah Gul for the presidency.[71] Still, the prospect of a president whom the armed forces considered an Islamist, with a headscarf-wearing wife, alarmed them.

According to Turkish constitutional procedure at that time (amended since), a presidential candidate, who is obliged to be over the age of forty and have a university education, must win a two-thirds majority of the full membership of parliament in order to assume office during the first round of voting. If no candidate achieves this, a second round of voting ensues. If two thirds are still not in favour, the threshold is reduced to an absolute majority during the third or fourth rounds.[72] Gul was unable to win two thirds in the first round of voting that took place on 27 April 2007, falling short by several votes. Meanwhile, the CHP and other opposition parties boycotted the vote. Regardless, the vote in itself was enough to unsettle the military. Dubbed the E-Memorandum by some commentators, a statement appeared on the Turkish general staff's website which read:

> The problem that emerged in the presidential election process is focused on arguments over secularism ... Those who are opposed to Great Leader Mustafa Kemal Ataturk's understanding "How happy is the one who says I am a Turk" are enemies of the Republic of Turkey ... the Turkish Armed Forces maintain their sound determination to carry out their duties stemming from laws to protect the unchangeable characteristics of the Republic of Turkey.[73]

While this was no doubt a representation of Buyukanit's own thinking, it is probable that it emerged under pressure from the lower military ranks, as the style and grammar of the message differed from those of Buyukanit's earlier statements. Meanwhile, US officials noted in internal cables from Ankara to Washington that junior officers had been agitating for action against the AKP for some time.[74] However, the military's interference backfired. It elicited warnings from the EU and the US to stay out of the fray.[75] The CHP, the main opposition party, was also worried by the prospect of Gul becoming president. In order to prevent a second round of voting, the party appealed to the Constitutional Court on 1 May, arguing that because the CHP had boycotted the vote, and the opening of parliament, there had not been a required two-thirds quorum, making the vote—and the entire parliamentary session—illegal.

Controversially, the Constitutional Court agreed, declaring the vote null and void.[76] This crisis would later lead the AKP to spearhead amendments to the electoral process of selecting the president, reducing the presidential term to a re-electable five years and changing the procedure to a direct vote into office by the public.[77] In the meantime, however, an attempt to repeat the first round of voting on 6 May did not take place, as opposition deputies continued their boycotts. This forced Erdogan's hand; he had no choice but to announce early general elections.

The August 2007 general elections increased the AKP's share of the popular vote to 46.6 per cent, but, as several opposition parties managed to pass the 10 per cent threshold (Kurdish BDP deputies managed to sidestep this by running candidates as independents), this translated to 341 seats, less than the previous AKP tally of 363. Ahead of the next round of presidential voting, scheduled for 20 August, Prime Minister Erdogan sparked controversy by stating that whoever said that Gul was not their president should renounce their citizenship. It took three rounds of voting for parliament to elect Abdullah Gul on 28 August 2007—as this was the third round, just a simple majority was required.[78]

Despite this apparent victory, the AKP faced another significant hurdle. Turkey's chief prosecutor, Abdurrahman Yalcinkaya, brought a case to the Constitutional Court, asking it to shut down the AKP and to ban as many as seventy-one of its members from politics for five years, including Gul and Erdogan, on the basis that the party was engaging in anti-secular activities against the constitution.[79] Days before the court filed this closure case, the new chief of the general staff, Ilker Basbug, who had taken over in August 2008, had a "secret" meeting with the Constitutional Court judge, suggesting that Basbug may have had prior knowledge of the case or even orchestrated its outcome.[80] Although the Constitutional Court rejected the ban, it did remove 50 per cent of the party's state funding and issue it with a warning against anti-secular activities.[81] Gul's election and the failure of the "E-Memorandum" highlighted the diminished power of the military, especially after the AKP had increased its majority in the 2007 general election.[82] If anything, this episode proved that the days of military coups were over.[83] Soon, elements of the military itself would be put on trial for alleged coup plots and participation in "deep state" networks.

The Trials of the Century

"Deep state" conspiracies are not new to Turkey. In November 1996 a car accident killed three of the four passengers on board. The four made very strange bedfellows and the revelations that followed were more akin to a John le Carré novel than a real-life occurrence. This became known as the Susurluk scandal. The four passengers included a senior police official, Huseyin Kocadag; Abdullah Catli, a former leader of the Grey Wolves (an ultra-nationalist paramilitary group), wanted murderer and drug trafficker; his girlfriend, Gonca Us, a former beauty queen turned hitwoman; and centre-right DYP party member and Kurdish warlord Seda Bucak, who was from a large, state-supported anti-PKK village guard force and who survived the crash.[84] To make matters worse, guns, silencers and false documents were also found in the crashed car.[85] What were these four individuals were doing together? Susurluk revealed that elements of the Turkish security apparatus had developed ties with organised criminals to carry out the assassination of political dissidents, as part of an officially sanctioned counterterrorism campaign. In return, certain members of the political elite were turning a blind eye to criminal activities including murder and drug trafficking.[86]

It was during the AKP's second term in government that an explosive development took place. The Ergenekon and later Balyoz (Sledgehammer) investigations, which ended in trial and conviction, shook Turkey's political foundations to the core. They also destroyed whatever political power the military had left. The size and depth of the conspiracy would be much larger than the Susurluk scandal, and this time would directly implicate the military. Although many consider the Ergenekon and Balyoz investigations to mark the end of the military's power, we've seen that in reality it had already declined as a result of the EU reforms and the failure to suppress the AKP through the courts and the "Republic Protests" of 2007. Just as importantly, most of the military's "deep state" structures had already been dismantled after the Susurluk incident—though marred by obstacles and inconsistencies, investigations and reports resulted in several convictions, as well as restructuring, resignations of some and promotions of others within the security services. If the military had still had any influence, the Ergenekon and Balyoz investigations would not even have taken place.[87] Still, it's true that these two cases were the final nails in the military's coffin.

It all started after police in Istanbul discovered TNT and twenty-seven hand grenades inside a house belonging to a *muhtar*, or village head, in the rundown district of Umraniye in Istanbul. After questioning the building's owners and residents, the police went on to arrest two retired army officers, Oktay Yildirim and Muzaffer Tekin. The case was soon handed over to a public prosecutor.[88] These initial arrests led to a wave of further detentions across Turkey, such as those of nationalist businessman Kuddusi Okkir and retired major Fikret Emek, whose house in Eskisehir was raided. A cache of weapons was discovered including semi-automatic rifles and C3 explosives.[89] By 23 January 2008 thirty-three people, including retired general Veli Kucuk, had been taken into custody.[90]

Soon the Turkish press was full of reports of another "deep state" scandal similar to the Susurluk incident—but this time it was more prolific, and directly involved the military as well as key personnel within civil society in what appeared to be a coup plot to overthrow the democratically elected civilian AKP government. Before long the name of this deep-state organisation was revealed to be "Ergenekon", a name taken from the mythical birthplace of the Turkish people, a valley where the embattled race took refuge before being led to the Anatolian plains by a grey she-wolf. It was reported that this Ergenekon was a "gang", but in reality it better resembled an ultranationalist network that had attempted to stoke chaos and fear within the Republic in order to precipitate a military coup against the AKP.[91] Allegedly, some of these acts of violence aiming to discredit the government had already taken place. They included the murders of the prominent Armenian writer and newspaper editor Hrant Dink in 2007, of Italian Catholic priest Andrea Santoro and of a senior judge. Further assassinations were purportedly being planned against Nobel literature laureate Orhan Pamuk and pro-government journalist Fehmi Koru, as well as the high-profile Kurdish politicians Leyla Zana, Osman Baydemir and Ahmet Turk.[92]

The AKP was not surprised. By 2007 its members were already aware of plans for a possible coup.[93] Certain generals had wanted to send the government a strong message in conducting military training scenarios, led by former army commander Cetin Dogan.[94] These were recorded by the National Intelligence Organisation (MIT), which suggests that both the prime minister and the chiefs of staff would have been aware of the scenarios.[95]

However, the Ergenekon network's membership appeared to extend beyond the active military and retired officers to include civilians. For example, Dogu Perincek, leader of the Workers' Party, was arrested, as was the aging editor of the secular *Cumhuriyet* newspaper, Ilhan Selcuk, and Kemal Alemdaroglu, former president of Istanbul University.[96] Amid rising concern about the military's involvement in the Ergenekon case, Chief of the General Staff Buyukanit denied any link to the organisation, stating:

> An effort is being made at every opportunity to link such incidents to the Armed Forces. The Turkish Armed Forces are not a criminal organization, esteemed journalists. Those people in the Turkish Armed Forces who commit mistakes are punished by courts. Hence, it is a vain effort to link such incidents to the Armed Forces; such an attempt will be in vain.[97]

Despite there being no further statements from the prosecutors following the arrests, the investigations continued to dominate the Turkish media. Some called them a blow to a "deep state" dating back beyond Susurluk to the Cold War period, when paramilitary gangs were used to subvert communist agitators.[98] On 26 January 2008, eight members of the Ergenekon network were formally charged.[99] However, as more individuals were arrested and charged, more layers of this apparent "deep state" conspiracy were unravelled. This led to

33

even more detentions, and the extent of the Ergenekon network appeared to snowball larger than ever imagined. By 30 March, the number of those detained had increased to forty-seven.[100] In fact, the investigation had reached so many different organs of the state that it began to give the impression that Ergenekon's tentacles were wrapped around the media, the judiciary, business and practically all aspects of Turkish life.[101] What was also troubling about the investigation was that it did not make links with or look into the real clandestine organs of the state engaged in illegal acts, such as extra-judicial killings against Kurdish separatists and others in the south-east.[102]

Not everyone in Turkey was convinced that allegations of the plot were genuine. Some claimed that the conspiracy was political, an attempt by the AKP, aligned with the Gulen movement (followers of self-exiled religious preacher Fetullah Gulen), to rid itself of not only the military but also its political opposition. For example, Mehmet Demirlek, a lawyer representing one of the accused, argued: "This is 100 per cent political. It has all been cooked up by the government and by the imperialist powers, the CIA, Mossad and the Jewish lobby and the European Union to eliminate Turkish nationalism. There is no such thing as Ergenekon".[103] Another lawyer of many of the accused believed that the Ergenekon and later Balyoz trials were, in their early stages, a genuine attempt to destroy the "deep state", but later became a purge against the opposition, especially secularists and Kemalists.[104] This relied on flimsy evidence, sometimes offering no concrete links between the crimes and the suspects. At times it appeared that digital files were used as evidence, despite being of suspect origin and probably tampered with.[105] It is also alleged that the main instigators of the investigation were elements of the Gulen movement (see Chapter 2) engaging in a political witch-hunt against their secular opponents.[106]

A US cable released by Wikileaks in 2010 indicated that although there may have been some substance to the case, the investigation was political.[107] Arrests continued to be made. On 1 July 2008, a further twenty-two people were detained in raids in Ankara, Istanbul, Antalya and Trabzon, including a prominent journalist and two retired military officers, one of whom had been a leader of the anti-AKP rallies organised the previous year.[108] Finally, by mid-July, a 2,455-page indictment was issued against the eighty-six alleged coup plotters under terrorism charges.[109] Although the military denied any involvement with the network[110] and the indictment had not yet been available to the public, the alleged leaders of the organisation were named as Sener Eruygur, the retired head of the Gendarmerie, and retired general Hursit Tolon, along with journalists, academics and members of the Workers' Party.[111]

The trial did not begin until 20 October 2008, and was delayed by several hours after the judge ruled that the courthouse was overcrowded. Outside, supporters of the defendants waved flags.[112] Even after the start of the trial the waves of arrests did not stop. On 8 January 2009, the military held crisis talks with Prime Minister Erdogan and President Gul after an additional thirty-seven arrests were made, including two serving officers and three retired officers.[113] Two weeks later five active army officers and seventeen police officers were among those arrested.[114] Over the course of January, more retired military officers were detained, as well as a former head of Turkey's higher education board, who was also reportedly implicated in the 1997 "post-modern" coup.[115]

Ozkok, the former military chief, stated that when he had become aware of coup plots in 2003 and 2004, he had blocked them and sidelined their leaders. Ozkok even expressed willingness to testify about these previous attempts.[116] Further arrests continued throughout the year and included not only more retired officers but also Professor Mehmet Haberal, the respected doctor and rector of Baskent University in Ankara.[117] A second mass trial opened in July 2009, this time of two retired four-star generals and fifty-four other defendants. In the indictment, one of the generals was accused of commenting, "We should have sorted this business out on 28 February [1997], damn it … There wasn't the EU then … Now everything is much more difficult".[118] Also according to the indictment, after Ozkok had blocked a coup in 2003, the conspirators had changed tactics and attempted to destabilise the country and spread fear of Islam to usher in military intervention. In May 2006, in an apparent false flag operation, a grenade attack had been ordered against a secular newspaper but blamed on Islamists. Two weeks later, a lawyer had been shot dead at the Council of State with the same finger pointed.[119] In a later court hearing, it was stated that the NATO headquarters in Turkey was also going to be targeted, with twelve leading figures including the prime minister earmarked for assassination.[120]

If that was not enough for the military, even more arrests were made in early 2010, which included four serving admirals. But this was a separate investigation from Ergenekon, into a 2003 military plan that represented a coup plot against the AKP. The Balyoz case came to light after the daily *Taraf* published details of 5,000 stolen army papers relating to the plan, but not before a mass campaign of destabilisation that included bombing of mosques and even a war with Greece.[121] Among those arrested were a former deputy chief of the general staff, Ergin Saygun, and soon over 200 people were detained for their connection with Balyoz.[122] Although denying the existence of the coup plot, the military fell short of denying that it had made plans to prepare for war situations,[123] implying that the conspiracy was being confused with normal "war games" scenarios. Although three of the suspected lead conspirators were released, an emergency meeting had to be set up between Gul, Erdogan and the military chief, and calm was urged.[124]

In reality, these latest allegations were implausible. The draft of the action plan was alleged to have come from the First Army, which was unable to make such detailed plans—it was outside its scope. Moreover, the existence of such plans does not mean they were going to be acted upon.[125] Leaked cables indicate that although the US believed that there was some "fire behind the smoke", the investigating judiciary and police were behaving in a "thuggish" way; the cables noted that Erdogan wanted to see the military out of politics and reined in.[126]

As the Ergenekon and Balyoz cases developed, in January 2012, none other than Ilker Basbug, the former head of the joint chiefs of staff, was arrested. He was the highest-ranking officer to be linked with the alleged plot by the Ergenekon investigation.[127] Basbug stormed out of court on 27 March 2012, calling the trial an injustice to the armed forces.[128] By September 2012, 330 military officers were jailed for their part in the Balyoz plot. While some supported the verdict as an end to the military's involvement in politics, others highlighted inconsistencies in the evidence. For example, a document purportedly from 2002 referred to the Turkey Youth Union, a group that had not been established until a year later, in 2003.[129] Several months later, in August 2013, the Ergenekon trial drew to a close. Basbug was found guilty and sentenced to life in prison, while 275 others—included military personnel, politicians and journalists—were also convicted.[130]

However, in a shocking turn of events, some of the convicted generals, including Basbug, were released following the overturning of his sentence by the Constitutional Court, which found technical errors in the case. This came after the disbanding of the special courts that had tried defendants in the Ergenekon and Balyoz cases.[131] Soon other suspects were also released, such as journalist Tuncay Ozkan, the alleged coup plot leader Sedat Peker, retired Colonel Levent Goktas, the professor Yalcın Kucuk and retired colonel Dursun Cicek.[132] Cicek's daughter, also his attorney, made his campaign public, emphasising and highlighting discrepancies in the evidence used to indict him.[133] The investigations themselves were always marred by questions of the political motivation behind the cases, with critics claiming that evidence had been tampered with and that the investigations had more to do with settling old scores than upholding the rule of law.[134] Indeed, the indictments were full of inaccuracies, untruths, illogic and rumour, and were not even coherent.[135] It appears that the main fault of both investigations was to confuse coup plans with the actual intention of carrying them out. The evidence of such an intention was tenuous at best.

The timing of the releases added more fuel to the fire, encouraging speculation that the coup plot allegations and prosecutions were manufactured by members of the Gulen movement who had infiltrated the ranks of the police and judiciary. Indeed, Gulenists were fellow travellers of the AKP. Following a sharp split between the two groups (see below and Chapter 2), a police investigation was launched. A series of tapes leaked towards the end of 2013 and early 2014—again believed to be the work of Gulenists—indicated large-scale corruption on the part of AKP ministers, which led to the resignations of some cabinet ministers. It was on the back of this scandal, and a large reshuffle within the police and judiciary, that some of the Ergenekon offenders were released, perhaps pending a new trial. By April 2016, the court of appeals annulled the convictions of the 275 alleged coup plotters.[136] As for the Balyoz defendants, in June 2014, the Constitutional Court ruled that their rights had been violated, ordering a retrial.[137] By the end of March 2015 they were formally acquitted. Especially important to the verdict was expert testimony that key pieces of evidence had in fact been fabricated.[138]

Despite this definitive dismissal of the investigations' legitimacy, the Ergenekon and Balyoz cases essentially smashed for good the already dwindling power of the military in Turkish politics. This was evidenced before the releases, when leading members of the army, navy and air force simultaneously retired en masse. The most notable of the July 2011 retirees was the incumbent chief of the general staff, Isik Kosaner.[139]

After Erdogan became president in 2014, he created a permanent ceremonial military entourage at the presidential palace, Ak Saray. Initially met with laughter and scorn on social media, this division dresses in costumes resembling Turkey's Ottoman forefathers and consists of over 478 soldiers, the "Conquest Unit", accompanied by an eighty-four-man Ottoman band.[140] In many respects, this unit serves as a symbol for the army's subservience to the new political elite and, more generally, the rebranding of the Turkish armed forces as a "national army". This term has been used by Erdogan and the AKP to recast the military as a body subservient to the government, working for the national good, rather than a political actor in its own right.

The Emergence of a "National Army"

Following the political pacification of the military, generally viewed as aided overwhelmingly by Gulenists within the police force and the prosecution, the AKP and President Erdogan have sought better relations with the "national army", for two main reasons. One was the result of a conflict between the government and the Gulen movement. The other was the reigniting of the conflict with the PKK. From 2013, the AKP has considered the Gulen movement an internal challenge to its rule. In order to fend off the threat, considered acute because Gulen followers held key positions in the bureaucracy, police and judiciary, the AKP now turned to the pacified military.[141] Yalcin Akdogan, a senior advisor to Erdogan known for speaking at the latter's behest, hinted common cause and went as far as to announce that those who had taken action against the military (the Gulen movement by implication) were also those orchestrating attacks (the high-level corruption investigations and leaked recordings in late 2013 and early 2014) against key AKP government officials and allies. In his column in pro-government newspaper *Star Gazetesi*, Akdogan stated: "Those who plotted against their country's national army, intelligence, bank and the civilian government which won the heart of the nation know very well that they are not working for the good of this country".[142]

With this stance, Erdogan was claiming that the risk to Turkey was not a struggle between the generally pro-secular military and the elected Islamic-oriented government, but a third party: the very same persecutors of both the military's power and now the AKP. He therefore sought reconciliation with the army, stating that "there are members of the judiciary who are seeking to smear innocent people",[143] in order to confront the Gulenists, his one-time bedfellows.

Of course, as we've seen, Erdogan was seeking to reaffirm ties with the armed forces just as the age of Turkish military tutelage seemed to be over—as even Chief of the General Staff Necdet Ozel noted.[144] Instead, Prime Minister Davutoglu was stating that the military "is a national army" and would "obey whatever the political will decrees".[145] Erdogan even sided with the army on key occasions. For example, he spoke in favour of the military, even congratulating it, when the leader of the far-right Nationalist Action Party, Devlet Bahceli, criticised former chief of the general staff Necdet Ozel over the February 2015 evacuation of Turkish troops guarding the tomb of Suleyman Shah, grandfather of the Ottoman Empire's founder, Osman I. The tomb is located around 30 kilometres from Turkey's border inside Syria and, though considered Turkish sovereign territory, was believed to be encircled by ISIS fighters emboldened by gains during the Syrian Civil War.[146]

The troop evacuation, and Erdogan's defence of it, was important for two reasons. First, it showed the reconciliation between the AKP and the military leadership. Second, it demonstrated the military's diminished political power in operational terms. The Suleyman Shah incident saw opposition parties accuse both the army and the government of losing Turkish land for the first time since the establishment of the Republic—with the added irony that observers speculated that Turkey may have had to collaborate with groups such as Syrian Kurds, and possibly even ISIS, to follow through with the evacuation.[147]

One soldier died during the operation (later ruled accidental).[148] There were also reports that Turkey left as many as nine of its broken tanks behind. Indeed, the entire operation raised eyebrows concerning the capabilities of the Turkish armed forces.[149] In addition to Bahceli's comments ("For the first time since 1922 Turkey withdrew its troops from Turkish soil"),[150] Kemal Kilicdaroglu, the main opposition leader and head of the CHP, described the operation as a "washout". Nevertheless, the AKP defended the conduct of the politically crippled armed forces.[151]

The AKP needed the military to combat not only the Gulenists, but also the resurgent PKK. Following the 7 June 2015 general elections, Turkey found itself on the brink of armed conflict, against a backdrop of Kurdish armed separatism, the rise of ISIS and the ongoing Syrian Civil War.

After an ISIS suicide bombing on Turkey's Syrian border, which claimed thirty-three lives and injured over 100 in July 2015, there were increased tensions between Turkey and the PKK. Two police officers were killed by Kurdish militants in retaliation for Turkey's alleged tacit support for ISIS militants and its failure to prevent the ISIS-orchestrated attacks.[152] In response, President Erdogan declared that it was no longer possible to engage in a peace process with Kurdish fighters.[153] This spelled a de facto end to the fragile cease-fire between Turkey and the PKK, brokered in 2013.

At the time of writing, the streets of south-east Turkey resemble the dark days of the 1990s, when the Turkish-Kurdish conflict was at its zenith. As discussed in detail in Chapter 6, there has been an alarming increase in armed operations, Turkish air strikes, PKK ambushes, police patrols, suicide bombings and funerals for soldiers, militants and civilians. There has even been a declaration of "Special Security Zones", a new name for the infamous State of Emergency Rule of the 1990s.[154] In the context of a broader reconciliation, Erdogan and the AKP have naturally looked to the military to combat the PKK threat—but the government was caught by surprise when an attempted coup emerged from a faction within the armed forces.

The "Hope and a Prayer" Putsch

15 July 2016 was the longest night of many Turks' lives. As evening turned to night, news emerged that a faction within the military, believed by many to be a Gulenist faction, was staging a coup. As events unfolded it was unclear whether the putschists had been successful. The military had captured the key points and strategic arteries of Turkish cities, especially in the nation's capital, Ankara, and largest city, Istanbul. Airports were seized by tanks, most notably Istanbul's Ataturk

Airport, and flights were grounded. Bridges were taken while military planes and helicopters hovered ahead. As the night unfolded into the early hours of 16 July, more spectacular, worrisome and dramatic events unfolded. For several hours, there was not a word from President Erdogan, who was vacationing in the south of the country. Meanwhile, the military had attempted to take over media outlets, particularly broadcast media, and even managed to take the state broadcaster TRT off air (as well as the privately owned CNN Turk). When it returned, TRT broadcasted the message of the "Peace at Home Council", the supposed military junta, declaring that it had taken over the government and reinstated the constitutional order.

However, within hours, the coup plotters lost control. By the time daylight broke in the early hours of 16 July, it was clear that the putschists were losing control and the tide was turning in the government's favour. The junta's attempted curfew was being defied by the public who, heeding a call from President Erdogan and other leading politicians who had managed to get messages broadcast, were actively resisting the soldiers, forcing them out or overrunning their positions. It was soon clear that the putschists' presence within urban areas was thin and undermanned. By this time, the main body of the military was soon attacking the putschist forces with support from popular protests and the police. Politicians from all the mainstream parties declared their support for the government and condemned the actions of the junta. It was all too clear that the putschist forces had been defeated.

Several questions loom over the circumstances surrounding the coup. Who were the putschists? Why did they launch their attempted coup, and was it well organised, botched or simply badly planned? Why were the intelligence services unable to predict it?

In assessing whether the coup was well or badly planned, it is worth consulting one of the most controversial books ever to be written by a political scientist. In *Coup d'État: A Practical Handbook*, Edward Luttwak details the means, tactics and circumstances by which a successful coup can take place. Since its first print run in 1968, the book has no doubt guided many a coup plotter. Luttwak details the requirements for launching a coup that one would typically expect. He notes that it must be carried out with speed, to effectively neutralise any opponents.[155] In this regard, the July 2016 putschists were successful, as they struck by surprise. Though the military was—unexpectedly—able to rapidly seize key choke points in Istanbul and Ankara, it was unable to neutralise all of its opponents. However, while leading generals of the military were captured and held, important political figures such as Prime Minister Binali Yildirim were untouched; President Erdogan was able to escape capture and arrest.

Another factor that Luttwak emphasises is the need to recruit key officers within the military, chosen for their ethnic identity, career prospects and political views, and, on an executional level, those who preside over the technical structure of the military.[156] The coup plotters were only partially successful in meeting these criteria. While they were able to recruit enough officers to direct a coup that targeted key locations throughout the country as well as aircraft and some ground forces, they only managed to win the support of a small number of officers; within hours, the putschists faced opposition from the majority of the armed forces, who remained loyal to the elected government. Soon, troops under the command of the junta were overwhelmed and lost air superiority, which was essential to their strategy.

Luttwak also explains the importance of neutralising political forces, achieved by seizing infrastructural facilities and/or counteracting the police force and security agencies,[157] as well as isolating the interior minister, the minister of defence, party leaders, the prime minister and any other central leaders (such as the president).[158] In this regard, the plotters failed miserably. Noting their inability to detain leading political figures, Dani Rodrik, Professor of International Political Economy at Harvard University's John F. Kennedy School of Government, went as far as to call the putschists "amateurish," a sentiment shared by the equally baffled Steven A. Cook of the Council of Foreign Relations, who noted that this failure allowed such leading politicians to voice their calls for mobilisation in the media.[159] During its early stages, the putschists' actions were resisted by both police and security agencies, which were far from immobilised. Politicians from all parties—notably the ruling AKP, including cabinet ministers, no less—were free in their movements and able to speak to the mass media to oppose the coup. These included all those listed by Luttwak as needing to be neutralised: the prime minister, defence minister, foreign minister, interior minister and, after some initial concern and a lucky escape, the president as well. It is no surprise that Luttwak identifies the flow of information from mass media as the most important weapon for establishing authority in a coup; seizing of communications channels that the government would otherwise use to retain control is therefore required.[160] In this respect, too, the putschists performed badly. Despite their initial control of TRT and CNN Turk, they failed to maintain authority over the mass media.

According to Luttwak, coup plotters must also plan for the taking of city entry-exit roads, traffic points, airports and other transportation facilities, primarily to block the movement of loyalist forces.[161] He considers it equally necessary to target and possess public buildings, whether of symbolic value or the actual seat of power, as visual representations of the coup and the new authority are a necessity.[162] He notes the importance of primary targets such as presidential palaces, central police stations and army headquarters.[163] The military junta saw some success here. It was able to take control of Istanbul's bridges, airports and central Taksim Square. It did the same with key roads and government buildings in Ankara. Unable to fully capture parliament, it chose to bomb it instead, most probably in a bid to scare the public so that they would not challenge the coup attempt.[164] However, the coup plotters were undermanned on the ground, unable to withstand opposition. In other words, maintaining these locations was a significant source of failure.

This brings us to another important factor in the coup's failure: the plotters' inability even to create the impression that they were going to succeed. If people had believed that the attempted coup was likely to hold, they would have been less likely to take the risk of opposing it.[165] Only around fifty soldiers took one of the Bosphorus bridges in Istanbul. Just dozens captured the airport and Turk Telecom. In other words, the taking of strategic locations was more show than substance, presumably because the plotters hoped that they would then be bolstered by an outpouring of public support. Instead, the opposite happened.[166] As Steven A. Cook argues, Turkish society had changed and developed since previous interventions such as 1980 and 1997, and military intervention had become an "affront to whom Turks believe themselves to be," especially after years under the AKP of politicians resisting the dictates of Kemalist conformity.[167]

This leads onto another crucial requirement identified by Luttwak. It takes place where dialogue has broken down between ruler and ruled, or if the relationship has fallen to distrust.[168] This is certainly true in the case of Turkey, where a large portion of society feels alienated from the ruling AKP and the authoritarian style of President Erdogan. However, a large portion of the electorate still supports the government, having voted the AKP into office and supported it for well over a decade. Luttwak argues that a coup is more likely to succeed where the fortunes of the general population, the rank-and-file military and the bureaucracy are not bound to a victory for either side.[169] This highlights one of the most important reasons why the coup failed. Over half of the Turkish public supports Erdogan and the AKP. For them, the ruling party represents their interests, challenging the Kemalist order that, since the beginning of the Republic, had alienated the conservative Anatolian classes and denied the validity of traditional and religious values.

Indeed, under the AKP, vestiges of Kemalist elitism within institutions of state, the public sector, business enterprises and public offices have been eroded to favour the AKP's large constituency. In other words, many in Turkey stood to lose if the July 2016 junta was successful, and therefore did not support it. Meanwhile, as we've already discussed, by the time the attempted coup took place, the age of military tutelage was over in Turkey. Furthermore, not only had the military lost its power over civilian bodies, but many other opponents of the AKP, whether secularists or Gulenists, had been expunged from most state institutions such as the police force, the media, education and the judiciary. Those who filled the vacant positions were large enough in number for these institutions to have a vested interest in Erdogan and the AKP maintaining power. Other political parties, such as the CHP and the Nationalist Action Party (and the pro-Kurdish, pro-democratic HDP, for whom supporting a coup would be anathema), were opponents of the seeming culprits behind the attempt, the Gulen movement. For these opposition parties, the choice was between putschists with Islamist sympathies or Erdogan and the AKP, which, despite showing Islamist tendencies, had been democratically elected and held popular legitimacy. Inevitably they chose to side with the latter. Opposition parties stood to gain very little from the coup and had politically and economically matured in a post-military era. Their allegiance was naturally to the democratic order.

As has already been noted, the coup attempt was in all likelihood organised by a Gulenist faction within the military. Members of the Gulen movement have denied involvement in the coup and argued that they are being used as a scapegoat or smokescreen by Erdogan and the AKP so that they may redesign the military, judiciary and state bureaucracy to their own benefit.[170] Fetullah Gulen himself, denying involvement in the coup, even publicly condemning it while emphasising a commitment to democracy, has accused the Turkish president of staging the coup himself so that he could purge state institutions of Gulenist sympathisers.[171] Though the government has certainly been able to use the coup attempt to consolidate its power, Erdogan even calling it a "gift from God",[172] confessions by alleged ringleaders, reports in the domestic and international media and by politicians, and analysis of all stripes point to Gulenists.[173] Whether this was with or without the knowledge of the Pennsylvania-based Gulen is still an open question; no publicly available evidence has linked him personally to the plot.

The coup plot was months in the making; however, it was expedited after the intelligence service caught wind of the plot at around 4pm on 14 July.[174] It seems likely that it was originally planned to take place before a meeting to discuss promotions in August, where it was believed that Gulenist officers would be dismissed.[175] It appears that the air force was the most committed segment of the military to the plot. In many cases ground forces refused to fire on protesters approaching their positions; however, the section of the air force loyal to the plotters seemingly did not hesitate (with the exception of choosing not to shoot down Erdogan's plane to Ataturk airport, presumably because they were unsure whether it was his or a civilian aircraft).[176] As well as elements of the air force, especially in the Akinci air base just outside of Ankara—Akin Ozturk, the air force's commander-general, has been indicted as a ringleader—much of the coup was also planned within the Gendarmerie General Command Headquarters in Ankara.[177] Nevertheless, it appears that the majority of officers, like the rank and file, were not part of the conspiracy.

It's true that military intelligence, working together with the National Intelligence Organisation, failed to identify and expel Gulenists from the ranks of the military—but that doesn't mean they didn't try. Different methods were employed by military intelligence to identify and limit Gulenists within the military's ranks, such as interviewing suspected members and blocking entrance into the professional armed forces by those who had attended Gulenist schools; however, these methods proved unsuccessful. Much disinformation was circulated, so much so that many people were falsely identified as Gulenists when they were not, and there was a general lack of credible evidence on the subject.[178] Such is the extent of the intelligence failure that politicians such as Erdogan did not hear of the plot until it was underway. This sent fear into the heart of the government and has been a major factor in the subsequent wide-scale purges and restructuring of the military and state institutions.

Consequences for the military

The consequences of the failed coup have been swift and severe, especially within the ranks of the military. Since the coup failed, thousands of military officers—representing over 40 per cent of the officer class—have been removed from their posts. Such a rupture within the higher echelons of the armed forces is bound to have a negative impact on both morale and operative effectiveness. This was especially the case after similar removals, purges and reshuffles took place following the Balyoz and Ergenekon cases. However, in the post-15 July period, the changes to the military have been systemic, filtering down to its inner workings, organisation and recruitment, and are bound to have a lasting impact in the further pacification of the military in political affairs. Already significant changes have taken place. In a decree issued while the country was under emergency law, additional cabinet ministers are now allowed to sit on the National Security Council. Erdogan has decreed that his government is now able to give direct orders to all branches of the military, with the Gendarmerie directly answerable to the interior minister and the rest of the armed forces to the prime minister and defence minister.[179] Further reforms to the armed services extend to the military academy structure, with military schools closed and replaced by a national defence university.[180]

Another important change has come in the form of future recruitment to the officer class of the armed forces. Prime Minister Yildirim has intimated that broader segments of society will be encouraged to enter the professional armed forces, paving the way for graduates of *Imam Hatip* (religious) schools. Currently prohibited from joining the officer ranks, the presence of *Imam Hatip* graduates higher up in the military would have significant repercussions for the identity of the armed services, challenging their traditional self-perceived role as staunchly secular bastions of the Turkish state.

The military's attempted coup was resisted by the general population. It is important to note that even though the scenes of citizens fighting and attacking military troops shocked many Turks, even the staunchest critics of the AKP and President Erdogan were opposed to the attempted coup, which was a serious source of disappointment. The Turkish public has lost confidence and trust in the military. The armed forces will inevitably feel a decline in their physical and psychological capacity,[181] and the military must work hard to regain the trust of the people.

Regardless, the power of the military has been vastly curtailed, even before the coup. The culls and restructuring that followed it means that the military is highly unlikely to ever regain its standing as a powerful political player. Across military bases, installations and academies inside Turkey's cities such as Istanbul, Izmir and Ankara, the authorities blocked off entry/exit roads with emergency vehicles. This move was devised to prevent any military action against the post-coup crackdown, but it was also a symbol of the civilian government's supremacy, supported by public opposition to military interference in political matters, regardless of the affiliation of the plotters. The failed coup was clearly the final curtain call for the era of military tutelage.

Conclusion

The decline of the military as a political force between 2002 and 2016 has been spectacular. Once the dominant force in Turkish politics, author of four political interventions, it is no longer able to exert that influence. During the AKP's first, second and even third terms in office—from 2002 to 2015—there was significant discord within the ranks, especially against the leadership of Hilmi Ozkok, whose moderate stance was distrusted by younger officers. This insubordination within the ranks until 2014 divided the armed forces at a critical juncture in their history. Elements of the military went rogue, with some officers conspiring against Ozkok, while others, it appears, were making plans for a military coup against the government.

On top of this internal disunity, the Ergenekon and Balyoz trials and the EU-instigated structural reforms to the National Security Council crippled the military's ability to challenge the AKP. If there were any "deep state" organs left at its disposal, they were a shadow of what they once were after their dismantling in the wake of the Susurluk scandal. The 2007 "Republic Protests" and attempts to ban the AKP through the courts only strengthened the party's popularity and undermined the legitimacy of the military. The Ergenekon and Balyoz trials shattered morale as high-level officers served time in prison.

In 2013, Abdullatif Sener, deputy prime minister in the first Erdogan government, claimed that there were no longer conditions for a military coup.[182] He was right to some extent. There was little likelihood of the mainstream military staging a coup. However, the perceived threat after 2014 was from Gulenist insiders within the armed forces. Gulenists, purged by the AKP from state institutions, had allegedly been infiltrating the officer class of the military. Under attack by the AKP, they seemingly attempted a coup in a last-ditch effort to overthrow their once fellow travellers. This backfired spectacularly, and led to another round of purges within the armed forces, ushering in a new cultural and political era—one in which the military would become a professional instrument of the ruling political cadres.

2

THE IRRESISTIBLE RISE OF THE AKP

Introduction

In 2001, Recep Tayyip Erdogan and his associates formed the Justice and Development Party (AKP) out of the ashes of the dissolved Welfare and Virtue Parties. The November 2002 general election was a turning point in Turkish politics. Not only did the AKP come to power, but it also scored a majority of seats in parliament. The party's clear majority (thanks to Turkey's high 10 per cent electoral threshold) was a rarity in Turkish politics. It went on to win the subsequent general elections of 2007, 2011 and 2015 (twice) as well as changing the political landscape in Turkey for decades to come. This electoral success was unprecedented. Only on one previous occasion had a political party won three consecutive elections, but this was the first time that a party had increased its percentage of the popular vote in succeeding elections. To put this in figures, in 2002 34.28 per cent of the Turkish population voted for the AKP. This increased to 46.58 per cent in 2007 and then a huge 49.9 per cent in 2011.[1] No party or party leader in the history of Turkish politics has been as electorally successful as the AKP and Erdogan, not even the country's founder, Mustafa Kemal Ataturk. In 2014, Erdogan— then prime minister—won Turkey's first presidential elections; the AKP managed to secure vote shares of over 40 and 49 per cent respectively during the June and November general elections of 2015.

The spectacular rise of the AKP coincided with the military's decline. This offered a unique opportunity for a new political party with Islamic origins to come to power and, just as importantly, stay there. Overall, the AKP has performed well on many levels. There have been significant improvements in public health, transportation, public services and the economy, and a new middle class has emerged.[2]

The AKP was the result of merging political and ideological forces following the 1980 military coup, including the religious-political Milli Gorus movement and, more generally, the opening of Islamic discourse in what was known as the Turkish-Islamic Synthesis, a post-coup compromise solution that paved the way for the acceptance of Turkish Islam in the political sphere. This chapter charts and accounts for the party's navigation through the complex waters of Turkish politics, from its origins in Milli Gorus to the difficulties and controversies of governance and continual electoral victory, despite obstacles including opposition from the military and a split with the Gulen movement.

From Snowball to Avalanche: Milli Gorus and the Turkish-Islamic Synthesis

The ideological underpinnings of the AKP can be traced back to the Milli Gorus movement. Founded by members of the Naksibendi religious order, the movement was—according to Altan Tan, author and former Milli Gorus politician—based on the ideas of the *ummet* (community of believers), Turkish nationalism, economic order and respect for the military. Indeed, there was a strong nationalist strain within the movement in addition to those of piety and tradition. Not only did it believe that Islam was the only precondition to be a Turk, but it also held that from the moment Turks embraced Islam, they had become the natural leaders of the Islamic world. From this foundation stemmed the belief that Turkey was the heir of the Ottoman Empire, with the ability to unite all Muslims under it.[3]

Milli Gorus was also an attempt to reconcile traditional Islam with modernism, and particularly to incorporate Western science and technology with a commitment to Islamic ideals.[4] The Welfare Party was one of a long line of parties to emerge from this ideological prism. Arguably, part of its appeal was that it was able to mobilise voters who considered themselves disadvantaged by the so-called "White Turk" privileged class. It was a protest movement for the underrepresented.[5] In other words, the Welfare Party represented the more Islamic, Anatolian population of Turkey, rather than the Republican urban elite.

Another feature of the Milli Gorus movement is a uniquely Turkish form of anti-Semitism that borrows from elements of traditional anti-Semitic conspiracies. It blames the demise of the Ottoman Islamic caliphate on the *Donmes* (followers of the "false" messiah Shabbtai Zvi during the seventeenth century), who, they claim, established the secular Republic of Turkey.[6] There are plenty of examples of such discourse, including publishing houses that produced Turkish translations of *Mein Kampf* and the proven forgery *The Protocols of the Elders of Zion*, which were bestsellers in Turkey. Such conspiracies reverberate at higher political levels. For example, according to Sevket Kazan, a former Welfare Party justice minister under Prime Minister Erbakan, the 1980 coup in Turkey was conducted because of the Turkish government's condemnation of Israel declaring Jerusalem its capital.[7] This is a claim with which serious scholars of Turkey would not agree.

The evolution of political parties out of the Milli Gorus movement reads as a list of banned organisations. The National Order Party, whose support came from the *esnaf* (small traders or artisans) and religiously conservative Anatolian population,[8] was established in 1970 and shut down the following year; the National Salvation Party, which became part of the respective ruling coalitions following the 1974 and 1975 elections, was shut down after the 1980 military coup. Its successor was the Welfare Party, which would also have a relatively short life, but would at least see power at the highest levels until it was banned.[9] The political fortunes of the Milli Gorus movement would have remained in the background of Turkish politics had it not been for the policies adopted by the most unlikely of champions of a Turkish Islamic worldview (although not that of the Milli Gorus): the military, the traditional vanguard of Turkish secularism. Some time must be devoted to this peculiar synthesis of worldviews if one is to understand the rise of the AKP.

Top-Down Islam: The Turkish-Islamic Synthesis

General Kenan Evren, chief of the general staff, was the principal leader behind the 1980 coup. It brought him to the presidency following the establishment of the third Turkish Republic. He was, strangely, a rather likely candidate for inadvertently opening space for Islam to grow as a political force. The son of an imam, Evren was, paradoxically, a devout Kemalist. More than that, he was a die-hard anti-communist. It was Evren who had staked his military career as the commander of the Turkish branch of Operation Gladio, which aimed to counter communist movements in Europe and carried out other anti-communist operations in the Turkish Republic. The September 1980 coup was spearheaded by Evren to reinstall order as urban violence, pitting right-wing nationalists against socialists in pitched battles, erupted on Turkish streets. In the three years that followed the coup, Turkey was ruled by the MGK, the National Security Council. Evren became Turkey's primary military and political figure, overseeing the execution of at least fifty civilians and the arrest of hundreds of thousands, not to mention the many that disappeared. The primary targets of this brutal crackdown were students and activists with Marxist sympathies—or for that matter, anyone with a view to the left of, say, Ronald Reagan.

While physical force was a potent weapon against the rise of communist agitation, Evren was aware of the old adage that an idea cannot itself be killed. Meanwhile, there was an acute need to expand the social base of government support during this turbulent political period. Evren believed that Islam could be open to change and modernity and even work within a secularist political hierarchy. This would especially be the case if it were kept away from political influences.[10] The military needed an alternative ideological foundation for state identity, one which would annul the appeal of historical materialism and unite the masses upon stronger foundations, unifying what it meant to be a Turk. That ideological underpinning became the basis for the Turkish-Islamic Synthesis.

The immediate intellectual origins of the Turkish-Islamic Synthesis were twofold. They partly lay in Turkey's political opposition to the CHP, Ataturk's party. They also lay in Islamic nationalist movements such as the Aydinlar Kulubu, or the Club of the Enlightened, established in 1962, and its successor, known as the Hearth of the Enlightened.

The Hearth of the Enlightened was established in 1970 by university professors, *hocas* (religious leaders) and businessmen alarmed by the spread of left-wing ideology in Turkey.[11] They saw a formula to counter left-wing ideas that not only had voter appeal, but would also be an ideological protective wall against the left, which they deemed responsible for the violence of the 1960s. They also believed that this new ideological foundation could be an alternative to Kemalism.[12] Ideologically, the Hearth of the Enlightened was opposed to humanism and the strict secularism of the Turkish state. It was also ill-disposed towards atheism, communism, and any non-Muslim group such as Christians or Jews, who were deemed responsible for the collapse of the Ottoman state. This did not stop the movement from looking outside Turkey for inspiration, though. In fact, it looked to Japan as a model for its ability to be both modern and Western while retaining its "national" identity.[13]

Perhaps in a different political climate the worldview and ideological foundations of the Hearth of the Enlightened would either have been persecuted or have drifted into a theoretical backwater with other countless strands of nationalist and religious thought. However, the Synthesis was exactly what both the Islamists and the military needed: control of public political expression through cultural and religious motifs.[14] Indeed, the military's reign of power in the post-1980 period, and its desperate need to counter left-wing movements with a credible alternative by creating a cohesive and unifying national identity, gave such an ideology state sanction and sponsorship. For example, Article 24 of the Turkish constitution, drafted under military supervision in 1982, states that "Religious and moral education and instruction in religion and ethics shall be conducted under state supervision and control. Instruction in religious culture and moral education shall be compulsory in the curricula of primary and secondary schools".[15] Mosques were also built to bolster the organisational power of religious associations.

The Synthesis was based on some of the ideas of Ibrahim Kafesoglu, leader and main ideologue of the Hearth of the Enlightened. It held that Islam was attractive to the Turks because of its similarities to the pre-Islamic Turkish society—its sense of justice, morality and family life, and belief in the immortal soul. The Turks, it further held, were the soldiers of Islam.[16] It was not a programme for religious education but rather a policy of using Islam to forge a cultural identity in harmony with Turkish national identity. This led some analysts to conclude that Turkey had transformed itself into a semi-secular state, on the grounds that state supervision of religious authority is far from true secularism.[17] The initiative was designed to strengthen the Turkish state-building process, based on the idea that it was better for Turks to be Muslims than communists—that is, of course, if they were the right kind of Muslims.[18]

But what the adoption of the Turkish-Islamic Synthesis truly produced was space for Islam to grow, even extending to movements outside the military. The state-controlled version of Islam taught in schools coincided with some of the thinking already prevalent within political parties such as the right-wing Nationalist Action Party. In addition to being pushed in primary and secondary schools, the Synthesis was also propagated through state media such as TRT (the state-owned broadcast channel), the Council of Higher Education and university principals and education ministries affiliated with the Hearth.[19] It was also carried out by the state's Directorate of Religious Affairs, and during the 1980s there was a significant rise in the number of religious schools, mosque constructions and the publication and circulation of state-approved Korans.[20]

Reworked textbooks would represent the Turkish soldier as a defender of Islam, but, paradoxically, military academies were careful not to recruit graduates from religious schools.[21] This took place under the auspices of Prime Minister Ozal, leader of the centre-right Motherland Party (ANAP), which won the 1983 elections with a staggering 45 per cent of the vote. Ozal's popularity would keep him as prime minister for another six years until he became president in 1989. The only thing that stopped his political career was a fatal and sudden heart attack in 1993. Under Ozal liberal economic policies combined with an increased emphasis on traditional ties of kinship as well as the presence of Sufi orders and mosque associations, with the encouragement of religious expression and state support for religious institutions. Ozal himself even made a pilgrimage to Mecca, the first Turkish prime minister to do so.[22] Although non-Muslim minorities such as Christians and Jews were exempt from classes on the Koran at school, Alevis, a Shia-oriented mystical sect that accounted for up 10 to 20 per cent of Turkey's population, were not, and this angered many of them.[23]

The military's attitude towards Islam in the post-1980 period was ambiguous: it opposed Islamic radicalism, but promoted some Islamic activities.[24] The Turkish-Islamic Synthesis, it should be acknowledged, was about neither religiosity nor political Islam. Rather, it was a cultural phenomenon that emphasised not piety but the centrality of Islam to Turkish identity and history. It owed more to the nationalised version of Islam prevalent during the 1950s, when Turkey was led by Adnan Menderes and the moderately right-wing Democrat Party (DP), which won the country's first free and fair elections in 1950. It was Menderes who called for greater freedom in religious practice and respect for Islam. The DP had the support of the Nurcu and Naksibendi Islamic groups, but the party also had secular politicians and it worked within the parameters of the secular state.[25]

During the 1950s, not only was nominal Islamic identity a source of social cohesion, but it was also a form of political discourse that, although opposed to the secularism of the country's Western elite, was still within the limits of mainstream politics.[26] Even the military had to tread carefully on some matters pertaining to Islam. After the 1960 coup, on the other hand, the military was confident enough to rebury in an unknown location the body of Said Nursi, a highly influential Kurdish Muslim scholar and theologian of the early twentieth century. Even then, however, the military ensured that the call to prayer remained in Arabic and that state television did not cease broadcasting Koranic recitations or prevent mosques from operating normally.[27]

If anything, the 1961 constitution was in many places liberal, and this enabled the centre-right Justice Party (AP) to win the senate elections of 1964.[28] However, the AP still forged links and connections with Islamic organisations in a form of patronage whereby it offered religious groups access to public resources and protection from hostile elements of the secular state, in exchange for votes.[29] Later Ozal's ANAP deepened and extended these ties. He was shrewd enough to handpick candidates for his neo-liberal party from a wide range of backgrounds while also forging alliances with religious groups. This all translated into votes, many of which came from religious sectors of the electorate. Particularly important for Ozal was his connections to the Naksibendis, who became an influential religious group.[30]

It was in this political context that the Welfare Party, established in 1983, emerged. Unlike Ozal's ANAP, the Welfare Party was the latest in a long line of parties affiliated with the Milli Gorus tradition. It initially focused on local mayoral politics during the 1980s. In 1991 it ventured into national politics, at first as part of an electoral alliance with the secular Nationalist Action Party and the conservative nationalist Nation Party (MP); it managed to achieve 16.9 per cent of the vote, or sixty-two parliamentary seats (nineteen of which belonged to its allies). In the 1995 elections, the Welfare Party capitalised on this success, this time running alone—the party gained over 21 per cent of the popular vote and claimed 158 seats in parliament,[31] making it the single largest party. Initially kept out of the power by a short-lived ANAP-DP coalition, the Welfare Party managed to enter government, following a censure motion that toppled the ANAP-DP administration. Necmettin Erbakan, leader of Welfare, replaced the DP leader as prime minister, making the Islamic party the senior partner in a new Welfare-DP coalition.[32]

The reasons for the Welfare Party's rise were many. No doubt, the party was effective in its organisational structure at grassroots level, thanks to dedicated and highly committed activists who invested in community politics. They sought solutions to everyday needs in the constituency.[33] This grassroots politics was not limited to the Anatolian countryside, but also extended to rural migrants to Turkey's expansive cities, who experienced the social alienation associated with cultural dislocation, stigmatisation and economic hardship following Turkey's vast inflation since the 1970s (see Chapter 5). Erbakan promised them a "Just Order". This was not simply an Islamic-inspired political slogan. Before the 1995 election the aptly named Welfare Party doubled as a social welfare organisation. It distributed coal, food, clothing and other supplies to the urban and rural poor. On election day, its activists made it a priority to visit potential voters and canvas support, while mobilising further support from a network of youth groups, labour unions and Islamic-oriented businesses including publishers, radio stations and television channels.[34] This was at a time when secular parties were losing support due to years of real or perceived corruption and declining confidence in their ability to govern.

However, Erbakan's premiership was short-lived, due to the military's "post-modern coup" of 1997. It was one thing for the military to sponsor a synthesis of Islam and nationalism and quite another to accept Islamic policies in government. In municipalities under Welfare control such as Konya, alcohol was banned, women's clothing regulated and new mosques erected.[35] A rupture occurred in Turkish politics along secular-Islamic lines. Business organisations, NGOs, academics and labour unions called for Erbakan to be ousted. At football matches fans chanted in unison that Turkey would not become another Iran. More people celebrated Republic Day, further popularising the already cult-like figure of Ataturk. Meanwhile, secularist fears were not helped by incidents such as Istanbul restaurants serving alcohol being forced to remove their outside tables.[36] There was even talk of plans to build a mosque in Istanbul's central Taksim Square. On top of this was Erbakan's foreign policy orientation—his friendly ties with Qadaffi's Libya and visits to Iran, coupled with grandiose ideas of an Islamic financial union. This was all too much for the military, which initiated the "post-modern coup" process that led to the Welfare Party's decline and Erbakan's removal. But it was too late: in sponsoring the Turkish-Islamic Synthesis, the military had let the proverbial cat out of the bag.

The Emergence of the AKP

Like the Welfare Party, the AKP's political ideology stems from the Milli Gorus movement, which was divided between moderate innovationists and hardliners. This division formally manifested itself in the establishment of a new party in 1997–8, the Virtue Party. During its 2000 party congress, the moderates challenged the hardliners by nominating their own candidate, Abdullah Gul, to run against Erbakan's appointed candidate.[37] The traditionalists' emphasis on Erbakan's charisma paid off, and the moderates lost out, but the latter won nearly half of the delegates' votes, marking a permanent split in the movement.[38]

Although the AKP was a later successor of, and represented a departure from, the Milli Gorus tradition, many of its main leaders were alumni of the Welfare and Virtue Parties and had become highly skilled in the art of popular politics. Despite the military taking action against Welfare, the reality was that the party was a comparatively well-oiled machine. It had developed a popular support base by establishing pious foundations and youth wings, organising social activities and scholarships for university students. It had a database of potential supporters and a women's movement, found favour among the urban poor and promised to fight corruption. What is more, it received funding from Islamist businesses.[39]

The AKP was dominated by the popularity and charisma of three of its co-founders. Abdullah Gul hailed from the industrial and conservative central Anatolian city of Kayseri. The son of an air force mechanic, Gul won a place to read economics at Istanbul University and continued his studies to PhD level. Active in student politics, he joined the Islamist-oriented National Turkish Students' Union and went on to represent Kayseri as a member of parliament on the Welfare Party's list following the 1991 and 1995 elections. After Welfare was outlawed, Gul, ever the political pragmatist, maintained his seat by joining the replacement Virtue Party. When that party was banned in turn, he co-founded the AKP. Bulent Arinc was born in the industrial city of Bursa and grew up in the city of Manisa, towards the Aegean coast. After graduating in law from Ankara University, Arinc became Welfare Party deputy for his native city after the 1995 elections. Like Gul, he too joined the Virtue Party after Welfare was shut down, and left Virtue to co-found the AKP.

However, it was the charismatic Recep Tayyip Erdogan who dominated and defined the AKP. Born in the rough Istanbul neighbourhood of Kasimpasa to parents originally from the Eastern Black Sea province of Rize, Erdogan epitomised a Turkish rags to riches story. A teenage lemon seller and graduate of an *Imam Hatip* school, the young Erdogan went on to study business administration at what is now Marmara University. A typical product of the Milli Gorus movement, but highly pragmatic,[40] Erdogan tried his hand, or rather his feet, at semi-professional football. Like Gul, he was also involved in student politics through the National Turkish Students' Union. Erdogan joined the youth wing of Erbakan's National Salvation Party, where he rose to the rank of chair. Following the party's ban after the 1980 coup, the incorrigible Erdogan joined its successor, the Welfare Party; by 1994, he had secured the position of mayor of Istanbul. Politically savvy, Erdogan styled himself as a man of the people and was quick to publicise every municipal improvement and development. Erdogan's style of political activity featured in many aspects of society, including clubs, pubs, and even brothels.[41] His popularity soared. Following the dissolution of the Welfare Party, Erdogan found himself imprisoned on the dubious charge of reciting a poem that apparently incited religious hatred (although the poem was featured in Turkish school textbooks), which obliged him to give up his mayoral position. Released in 1999, his incarceration meant that he was barred from serving political office for several years. Still, he co-founded the AKP and, in a 2003 by-election, won a seat in parliament after a constitutional amendment overturned his ban from political office.[42]

Erdogan subsequently claimed the post of prime minister, on the back of the AKP's historic 2002 election victory. His role is central to the success of the AKP. His firebrand rhetoric and charismatic style have often surpassed the party machinery itself, so much so that some votes have been billed as referenda on Erdogan himself, such as the referendum on constitutional changes in 2010.[43] The same was the case in the 2014 local elections, which came amidst allegations of corruption within the AKP and Erdogan's inner circle.[44] His popularity finally brought him to the presidency in August 2014, after winning the country's first ever direct presidential election in the first round.

The AKP as Social Conservatives

At the same time, the power behind the AKP was not simply the result of the party's leading troika. The AKP was not a continuation of the Milli Gorus political tradition, but vocally rejected it, instead looking to steer the party in a new direction focusing on themes such as "democracy, human rights, freedoms and Turkey's EU membership".[45] Rather than pro-Islamist, the AKP declared itself to be "conservative-democratic" with a commitment to the free market. AKP leaders disavowed their *Milli Gorus* past at every opportunity.[46] During the party's inaugural press conference, a minute's silence was observed in honour of Turkey's staunchly secular founder, Mustafa Kemal Ataturk. The conference hall prominently featured a large, draped portrait of him.[47] The AKP stated that it regarded Ataturk's principles and reforms as fundamental for raising up Turkish society and that it considered these principles integral to social peace.[48]

Though light on concrete policy proposals, the AKP's 2001 manifesto, the "Development and Democratisation Programme", promised to maintain the unity of the Republic as a secular democracy.

Approaching the question of Islam and secularism from a centre-right perspective, the AKP insisted that it was neither a religious party nor a party that would exploit religion for political ends. According to Erdogan, the AKP values religion as a social value.[49] The AKP programme also characterises secularism as a crucial aspect of democracy, protecting freedom of religion and social harmony.[50] When he paid a visit to Egypt in September 2011, Erdogan even called on the Muslim Brotherhood to adopt a secular constitution and to advance the ideals of a secular state.[51]

Erdogan claims that the AKP has become "the undisputable single force of the centre-right in Turkey".[52] The party has included former members of the socially conservative ANAP. Political scientist Ergun Ozbudun agrees, arguing that the AKP has managed to resurrect the ANAP coalition of support that brought together centre-right voters, moderate Islamists, moderate nationalists and elements of the centre-left.[53] Such politicians notably included Ertugrul Gunay, a social democrat who had once been secretary-general of the secular CHP (now Turkey's main opposition party). There were also young and ambitious political first-timers such as Mevlut Cavusoglu (who went on to become foreign minister), the US-educated Egemen Bagis and Northwestern University alumnus Ali Babacan, both of whom also later assumed ministerial positions.

Arguably, the AKP's seeming moderation was due to its politicians having learned historical lessons of Turkish politics, especially the fate of Islamic parties. Some scholars, such as Gamze Cavdar, have argued that while the Turkish state had set up the framework for political action, EU incentives and the democratisation process created a "structure" of constraint. The AKP was also very well aware that if it attempted to increase the influence of Islam it would be swiftly blocked and left to face the wrath of the military and the secular bureaucratic establishment.[54] It is telling that while many of its female members wore headscarves, none were part of the party's parliamentary list, avoiding the risk of controversy—the headscarf was at that time banned in parliament.[55] The emphasis away from Islamic values can also be explained simply by the influence of those AKP members who'd previously belonged to secular parties.[56]

AKP ideologues explained the party's self-description as "conservative-democratic" as a "formulation of synthesis that aims at creating a harmonious fusion between 'conservatism' and 'democracy.'"[57] This definition of the party's orientation was then used by the AKP government to highlight Turkey as a country that could reconcile Islam with democracy, serving as an example for other countries in the region.[58] The AKP also emphasised that Turkey was a bridge between East and West, facilitating cooperation and coexistence between Islam and the West.[59]

Erdogan's top advisor in political affairs, Yalcin Akdogan, offered a more detailed definition of the AKP's conservative democracy, identifying eight main points: 1) natural and evolutionary reform instead of revolutionary change; 2) focusing on the politics and culture of reconciliation; 3) accepting that political legitimacy is obtained from the sovereignty of the people, the constitution and universal principles; 4) rejecting authoritarian and totalitarian styles of government and (notably vaguely) limiting rule; 5) considering small but effective government optimal, and resisting imposing government preferences on citizens; 6) supporting a pluralist democracy; 7) rejection of social engineering; 8) balancing idealism with realism.[60] While this may sound good on paper, some aspects, especially points 4, 5 and 6, were lacking in practice (see Chapter 3).

In the run-up to the 2002 elections, the AKP engaged in "moderate" and "non-confrontational" rhetoric while capitalising on middle- and working-class voters as well as the urban poor, who were dissatisfied with the economic policies of the incumbent coalition government, especially after the 2001 economic meltdown.[61] Indeed, the alternative parties had shown themselves not only incapable of dealing with an economic disaster, but also incapable of forming stable coalitions at a time when effective leadership was vital.[62] In 2002 voters were deeply frustrated with government corruption. The AKP, or the AK Party as it is formally known, is a clever abbreviation of its Turkish name: *ak* means clean (or white) in Turkish, allowing the party to brand itself as the clean party. The party's support was also buttressed by maintaining its traditional political base.

Following its election victory, one Turkish newspaper ran the headline "*Anadolu Ihtilali*" (Anatolian Revolution), a reference to the alienated conservative Muslim majority of rural Anatolia, long estranged politically and culturally by the secular civil and military elites.[63] This apparent cultural divide in Turkey has been described as a conflict between the "Rumelian" secular elite (White Turks) and the Anatolian masses (Black Turks).[64] Erdogan himself once quipped, "In this country there is segregation of Black Turks and White Turks ... Your brother Tayyip is a Black Turk".[65] Erdogan appealed to the working-class voter by styling himself as a man of the people, citing his childhood in Kasimpasa and his humility. Indeed, it has been argued that the AKP is in part a protest force built on marginal factions of society who feel they have been excluded from representation or even the benefits of globalisation, Western cultural values having been promoted from the 1970s onwards at the expense of traditional culture.[66]

In its 2002 landslide, the AKP won votes from former supporters of Turkey's other centre-right political parties, the ANAP and the DP. It even won votes from the ultra-nationalist Nationalist Action Party and managed to secure over half of the voters of the Islamist Virtue Party. What was also unforeseen was that the AKP secured around 10 per cent of the vote that had previously gone to the Democratic Left Party.[67] However, despite appealing to a broad base, the main source of the AKP's support was still the religiously pious. By one calculation, 60 per cent of AKP voters prayed five times a day, and 90 per cent prayed at least once a day; 99 per cent kept the fast during the holy month of Ramadan while 81 per cent considered themselves as Muslims before Turks.[68] However, only 22 per cent called for Sharia.[69]

Secret Liaisons: The AKP and the Gulen Movement

Once in power, the AKP benefited from the support of the Gulen movement, a religious and social movement with branches across the world and led by the self-exiled preacher Fetullah Gulen. Often his supporters refer to him as "Hocaefendi", a term of respect for a teacher held in high esteem. Gulen is one of Turkey's most influential and controversial Islamic scholars. His network of followers is active in over 140 countries and worth billions of dollars.[70] The movement classifies itself as a community, *Hizmet* (The Service), positioning itself as the modern face of moderate, as opposed to fundamentalist, Islam. However, it has also been accused of having a secret agenda to infiltrate the state and to Islamise Turkey. The true nature of the Gulen movement is subject to controversy and highly differing opinions, but worth exploring.

Some consider the organisation to be secretive, even criminal, with a hidden hierarchy and a dormant Islamic agenda. Its members have been instructed to integrate themselves into institutions of the state.[71] Persecuted by secular authorities (Turkey designated the movement a terrorist organisation in 2015), Gulen advocates that followers should work within state institutions as a means of protection. Emphasis is placed on the educational sector, especially profit-making private schools with scholarships for poorer students, to allow students from Gulen schools to enter the bureaucracy.[72]

According to Ihsan Yilmaz, who taught at the Gulenist Fatih University before its closure in 2016, the movement is a faith-inspired civil society organisation that comprises a loose network. It resembles more of a franchise between the different organisations and groups and therefore has a loose hierarchical structure, in which Fetullah Gulen has "moral authority". Bulent Kenes, former editor-in-chief of the English-language daily *Today's Zaman*, which was associated with the Gulen movement and also shut down, was arrested in October 2015 for insulting President Erdogan.[73] According to him, the movement wants people to be more pious, but is against using state means to do so because this would only create superficial commitment to Islamic values. Nor, Kenes argues, does the movement aim for regime change, but instead has focused on education, with centres in over 140 countries. It also tries to engage in interfaith dialogue and present an image of Islam that advocates peaceful harmony.[74]

However, others beg to differ—they believe that the Gulen movement is centralised and answerable directly to Fetullah Gulen, whose aim is to establish an Islamic state in Turkey.[75] For those who subscribe to this interpretation, its members have infiltrated the civil service with this agenda in mind. Journalist Nedim Sener argues that Gulenists have established a "parallel state", in which they act in their own interests and are effective within the police force, police academy and intelligence services, and seek to control every department.[76]

The roots of the movement were in both the right-wing nationalism of the 1950s and 1960s and in the religious writings and teachings of Said Nursi, an influential Turkish (of Kurdish extraction) Islamic scholar.[77] Unlike other *Nurcu* movements (followers of Nursi), the Gulen movement was keen to fuse together Islamic and Turkish principles to create a type of "state-centric" Turkish Islamic nationalism dedicated to education and a free economic market.[78] According to Hakan Yavuz, Fetullah Gulen and his ideas are the main impetus behind the Islamic version of nationalism present in Turkish politics today.[79]

While there are ideological similarities between the Gulen movement and the Milli Gorus, they differed in their political set-up and approach.[80] Under Erbakan, the Milli Gorus movement adopted staunchly anti-EU and anti-NATO positions. However, the Gulen movement embraces Turkey's EU membership ambitions, is less militant over the headscarf issue and as a result has attracted comparatively greater support. Some of this support has come from members of the secular establishment, including politicians, who consider the movement a far more attractive and tolerable alternative to the radical Islamic politics they perceived as driving Erbakan's Welfare Party.[81] However, the two movements had a common cause. Both the Gulenists and the Milli Gorus were deeply angered by the military's intervention in 1997 and considered the armed forces to be a threat to the state. It was after this post-modern coup that Gulen fled to the US. By 1999, Gulen had been charged in absentia of heading a clandestine organisation that threatened the Turkish state.[82]

Gulen's followers started to establish schools and dormitories in Turkey and Europe from the late 1970s and in Central Asia during the post-Soviet era, with the intention of creating a new kind of individual, both pious and educated.[83] In an attempt to increase its influence in Turkey, the media became a particular focus of the Gulen movement. This started through Feza Media, which was established in 1986 after members of the movement purchased a small newspaper. Feza Media grew considerably. Until its closure in 2016 following the attempted coup, it ran two nationally broadcast television stations, an English-language satellite station based in New Jersey and a radio station, which also broadcasted nationally. This was in addition to several newspapers, Turkey's most widely sold news magazine, *Aksiyon*, and a wire and news distribution agency, Cihan Haber Ajansı, all of which were later shut down. However, Feza Media's flagship outlet was *Zaman Gazetesi*, Turkey's highest-circulation newspaper.[84] By early 2016, its affiliation with the Gulen movement would see the newspaper taken over by a team of administrators, after a court order.

In 1994 Gulen founded the Journalists' and Writers' Foundation, which came to be accepted as the institutional face of the movement in Turkey.[85] Then, in the late 1990s, the movement started organising workshops and seminars such as the Abant Workshops, which aimed to ease divisions within Turkish society, find consensus and prevent polarisation.[86] These workshops, which ran annually, usually involved around fifty or so intellectuals from a variety of different backgrounds, discussing a range of topics. It was also a means to expand the movement's outreach to both liberals and conservatives.[87]

Members of the Gulen movement have often had a stormy relationship with Islamic-oriented political parties.[88] Following the AKP's open rejection of Milli Gorus, the Gulen movement forged an alliance with the governing party.[89] Throughout its rule the AKP closely associated itself with and consulted members of the Gulen movement. The media outlets owed by Gulen's followers were utilised, as were the Abant meetings, to spread the government's message.[90] This partnership was despite leading AKP figures, including Erdogan, having come from the Milli Gorus tradition, or other Sufi schools and religious orders, different from that of the Gulenists. Indeed, several prominent cabinet members were even known to be sympathetic towards the Gulen movement and to have participated in activities such as workshops and conferences.[91]

During this time, the Gulen movement was essentially operating in coalition with the AKP. This was a significant development, as the Gulen movement had not associated itself with the AKP's forerunner, the Welfare Party.[92] The AKP and the Gulen movement had shared goals, such as further integration of Turkey into the international economic system, privatisation and increased foreign investment in Turkey.[93] The Gulen movement not only supported the AKP's policies in its newspapers and on its TV channels, but its supporters took advantage of the government's new economic policies.[94] Some businesses associated with the movement even enjoyed the fruits of state contracts and concessions, enabling them to grow and develop rapidly.[95] Meanwhile, Gulenists are believed to have entered the ranks of the state bureaucracy, especially the police and judiciary, in an attempt to influence the direction of the state. It is important to understand that, as with any organisation, some members of the Gulen movement have been highly committed, moderate followers, others only pragmatists. Many nominal followers within the bureaucracy simply wanted a career and to provide for their families.[96]

The partnership between the AKP and the Gulen movement allowed the two to dominate the political landscape in Turkey for over a decade. Not only was the media highly favourable to the ruling government, its position that Islam was compatible with democracy and neo-liberal economic policies in a socially conservative environment seemed to work.[97] Meanwhile, the two forces' combined power enabled them to replace the military's tutelage. As the power of the military and its secular allies within the bureaucracy waned, the void was filled with AKP and Gulen sympathisers. Gulenists within the judiciary, police and other such institutions allowed the AKP to increase its influence and support in Turkish politics.[98] However, as we will see, this marriage of convenience would soon splinter into an explosive and messy divorce.

The AKP and the rise of the Islamic Bourgeoisie

It was the support of the rising Islamic bourgeoisie that helped the AKP come to power in 2002 and solidify its hold over government. The 2002 electoral victory came in the wake of a highly turbulent economic crisis in Turkey, especially after successive economic meltdowns in 2000 and 2001. The need for Turkey to expand and find new markets became more urgent. The AKP managed to achieve this and saw periods of stability and economic growth as well as an expansion into new global markets. The Islamic bourgeoisie certainly benefited, as the positive economic environment was receptive to their needs. Soon their power would grow, and pious businesses remained a strong support base for the AKP.[99]

Turkey had already seen a transformation since the 1980s, with the emergence of new industrial centres in central Anatolian towns and cities. At the end of the Cold War, many small- to medium-sized companies based in central Anatolia took advantage of the new global system to find new markets for exporting their goods. Soon these businesses became large billion dollar enterprises,[100] and became known as the Anatolian Tigers, essentially the core of the conservative bourgeoisie. Their presence in the Turkish economy increased during periods when conservative parties were at the helm—ANAP, the Welfare Party and most recently the AKP.[101] As we know, the AKP had shed its Milli

Gorus trapping but still appealed to Milli Gorus voters, at the same time as building votes from traditionally conservative supporters. It was therefore without much surprise that the AKP received the backing of the pious industrial elite of Anatolia and took on the stripes of the Anatolian Tigers. However, it is important to note that despite this burgeoning pious economic class, it was nowhere near the size or scale (in economic terms) of the traditional secular business elite represented by the Turkish Industry and Business Association (TUSIAD).[102]

To counter the TUSIAD and to have a body acting in their interests, in 1990 the Islamic bourgeoisie established their own business association, the Independent Industrialists' and Businessmen's Association (MUSIAD).[103] This became an increasingly important group under the AKP, as did a similar association, the Confederation of Turkish Businessmen and Industrialists (TUSKON). Both became important players especially in terms of foreign trade. They were also closely aligned to the AKP,[104] though TUSKON's influence diminished after the AKP-Gulen rift, as the association was linked with the Gulenist movement.

Indeed, an important reason why the AKP prioritised the EU accession process was that it met the demands and expectations of the Islamic bourgeoisie, which was essentially an AKP grassroots support base. The Islamic bourgeoisie saw the EU as important to the Turkish economy and their trade interests, which had developed after the 1980 coup and the subsequent process of economic liberalisation, boosted by a customs union agreement with Europe in 1996. It was during this time that the Islamic bourgeoisie had forged close ties and business interests with the EU.[105] Representing a new middle class, these new pro-European conservatives, often members of MUSIAD, supported the AKP, which committed itself to European reforms and entry into the supranational organisation.[106] In fact, many members of the association even joined the AKP to assist in the organisation and setting up of local party offices. Several members of MUSIAD even went so far as to run for office during the 2002 elections. Twenty entered parliament.[107]

It's the Economy, Stupid!

Turkey's economy has been in better shape under the AKP than at any other time in Turkey's modern history. The party has reaped the political dividends in its electoral successes. A 2013 study, noting the strong correlation between the AKP's popularity and the growth of the Turkish economy, cited a 2008 poll which revealed that a whopping 85 per cent of respondents who had voted for the AKP in 2007 said that they did so because of the economic situation.[108] Since 2008, Turkey has been facing considerable strains on its economic performance, yet the AKP remains highly popular.

It is true that under the AKP, Turkish GDP has more than tripled, reaching almost US$800 billion in 2014, up from US$231 billion in 2002.[109] In addition, Turkey's inflation rate fell from 29.7 per cent in 2002 to 6.2 per cent in 2012.[110] The economy experienced what can only be described as a golden age between 2002 and 2007, with an average 7 per cent growth rate.[111] Thanks to this economic stability, by 2005 Turkey had removed six zeros from its national currency, with the establishment of the new lira. This was a sign of optimism in Turkey that the economy was on the right track.

The success of Turkey's economy during the early years of AKP rule stemmed from the EU's structural reforms, which Turkey started to implement after becoming a membership candidate in 1999. Although this did not prevent the financial crisis that took place in 2001, in its wake Turkey signed a stand-by agreement with the International

Figure 2.1: Annual growth of Turkish GDP, 2002–14

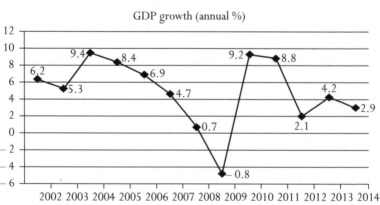

Source: World Development Indicators, World Bank.

Figure 2.2: Turkish GDP per capita in US dollars, 2002–14

GDP-per capita GDP ($) (annual)

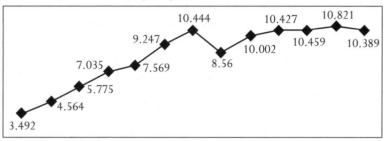

Source: Turkish Statistical Institute (TurkStat).

Monetary Fund (IMF). When the AKP came to power the following year, the party was prudent to pledge that it would continue to implement the incumbent coalition government's IMF-supported programme. Turkey's IMF stand-by agreements came to end in May 2008, by which time Turkey had borrowed US$45.8 billion from the IMF.[112]

However, from around 2007 onwards, Turkey saw a significant reduction in economic growth. After 2010 and 2011, when growth managed to reach higher levels, the slowdown resumed, averaging an increase rate of around 3 per cent. Meanwhile, the economy in 2016 is in a middle-income trap of around US$10,000 in GDP per capita. According to the IMF, without structural reforms, Turkey might not surmount this difficulty, and growth may continue to stagnate.[113]

The Turkish economy currently faces major challenges. One is its high current account deficit. In 2014 this was 6 per cent of GDP, the highest proportionately of all OECD member-states.[114] In no small part because of this, professional services firm PriceWaterhouseCoopers considers Turkey one of the most vulnerable economies within the emerging markets.[115] According to the IMF, the problem was caused by a lack of savings.[116] That being said, due to a sharp fall in the price of oil, in 2015 Turkey's deficit narrowed to a more healthy US$35 billion, which amounts to about 4.4 per cent of its GDP.[117] Political economist

Dani Rodrik has pointed out that, under the AKP, Turkey has chosen to borrow from the private sector rather than print money.[118] Although this has its benefits, it also means that at a period when Turkey was finding it difficult to attract sufficient foreign direct investment, Turkish banks ended up borrowing money overseas.[119]

The AKP also sought to bring down Turkey's current account deficit through a "golden loophole", which became a central theme in government corruption allegations in December 2013. Between March 2012 and July 2013, Turkey exported US$13 billion of gold to Iran, as international sanctions against Tehran prevented Iran from receiving payment in dollars or euros. In return, Turkey received natural gas and oil. For instance, in 2013, Turkey received 18 per cent of its natural gas and 55 per cent of its total gas from Iran.[120] According to economics professor Magfi Egilmez, the "gold for gas" loophole helped Iran to break the international sanctions regime and Turkey to accelerate the reduction of its current account deficit.[121]

A vexing problem for Turkey's economy is its high unemployment rate. In 2015, this rose to 10.3 per cent, the highest level since 2010.[122] While it is true that the Syrian Civil War and the influx of 2.7 million refugees has contributed to the increase, structural issues are also responsible for the high unemployment rate. Minimum wage is high. In 2011, for example, the ratio of the minimum cost of labour to the cost of the median worker was around 75 per cent, while the OECD average was 45 per cent. In other words, in terms of income inequality (the Gini coefficient), Turkey had the second worst record in the OECD.[123]

As Turkey's economy faced such difficulties, Erdogan started to blame the so-called "interest rate lobby". In addition to criticising this nebulous group, he also pointed the finger at some of his own officials, such as the director of the Turkish Central Bank, Erdem Basci, for apparently not increasing interest rate cuts,[124] and the minister dealing with the economy, Ali Babacan.

Despite the challenges, though, the market still considers the AKP the most business-friendly party in Turkey.[125] This perception also explains the party's success in the snap election of November 2015. It would appear that the public has not so much confidence in the AKP's ability to guide the economy steadily as the impression that it can still do a better job than any of the opposition parties. This in itself may be an unfair comparison. As Dr Bahadir Kaleagasi, the TUSIAD's international coordinator, notes, it is difficult to compare the AKP with previous governments, as the challenges of the international environment were different.[126] Still, Turkey's economic growth and development took place under the AKP's watch and it is therefore the AKP that reaps the electoral rewards.

Crisis of Legitimacy

Despite distancing themselves from the Milli Gorus tradition, upon assuming office, the "socially conservative" founders of the AKP were still distrusted by many secularists who sought to undermine the party's legitimacy.[127] The AKP found itself having to convince both the Turkish and Western publics that they did not have a "hidden agenda" to change the secular character of the state and transform it into an Islamic one. One of the policies that helped the AKP through this legitimacy crisis was its focus on EU membership accession and its strong prioritisation of starting entry negotiations. The party's commitment to the EU process, which enjoyed public support, helped it to create an image that it was progressive and reformist in both word and deed. During its first term in government the AKP passed constitutional amendments and EU harmonisation packages to synthesise Turkish law with EU law and standards.[128] This achieved several objectives. It helped the AKP to consolidate its power, while simultaneously reducing the role of the military, in the political arena.[129] The reform packages also benefited Turkey's democracy. For example, under a 2004 reform package, the government eased the legal obstacles to setting up NGOs. This paved the way for some groups, previously seen as marginal, to engage with political life. One such group was Turkey's LGBT organisation, KAOS GL.[130]

The AKP's first term in office (2002–7) was a relative success, built on not only EU-motivated democratic reform packages, but also effective management of the economy. This economic success extended beyond GDP income growth to the way wealth was divided among society, through the provision of public goods and services, improvement of public and private finance and overseeing growth in the economy until the global crisis of 2008–9, which it managed for the most part to overcome.[131] No doubt this goes a long way in explaining why the AKP managed to increase its vote share at the 2007 general elections to 46.6 per cent.

Perhaps a significant additional factor for the increase in popular support was the presidential debacle earlier in the year (see Chapter 1). A series of deadlocks and boycotts led to the blocking of the AKP's preferred candidate, Abdullah Gul. This was coupled with the "Republic Protests", in which hundreds of thousands of secular Turks rallied in Turkey's main cities to protest against the office of the president, a check on the power of the AKP, being held by a member of the ruling party, powerless to prevent the feared creeping Islamification of the country. The protests in themselves were legitimate in a democratic state; however, the "E-Memorandum", warning of the military's determination to protect the secular Republic,[132] was not, and appeared to backfire. Not only did the AKP win the general election of 2007, but within months Abdullah Gul was also president of the Republic.[133]

Following the elections, the AKP dominated the Turkish parliament, with 341 seats. By late 2007, the AKP began drafting an entirely new constitution, as it had promised during the electoral campaign. In January 2008, the Nationalist Action Party unexpectedly proposed a constitutional amendment that would lift the ban on headscarves in universities. The AKP's backing, which allowed the bill to pass, prompted Public Prosecutor Abdurrahman Yalcinkaya to apply to the Constitutional Court on 16 March, asking the court to shut down the AKP on the basis that it had become a "focus for anti-secular activities".[134] Though found to be violating secularism, the AKP managed to avoid dissolution: of the seven judges needed to rule that its offenses merited closure, only six voted in favour.[135]

In 2010, new rumours began circulating in the media that the public prosecutor might make another attempt to have the AKP shut down, this time in the Supreme Court.[136] This prompted the AKP to launch a package of constitutional amendments making such party closures more difficult. However, the same package was also aimed at changing the position of the Supreme Board of Judges and Prosecutors, which had previously been accused of blocking the AKP's policies. This package of twenty-seven amendments to the 1982 military-authored constitution was drafted as a bill. It managed to get a majority of support in the Grand National Assembly in April 2010, but fell short of the two thirds needed to change the constitution within parliament. However, it was passed by a three-fifths majority—enough for President Gul to sign the proposed amendments, but not enough to avoid presenting them to the public in a national referendum. On 12 September 2010, the Turkish electorate approved the constitutional changes with 58 per cent in favour. The AKP had managed to change the constitution, even when exposed to a popular vote.[137]

How to Lose Friends and Alienate People

Having won a third term in office in 2011, the AKP was at the height of its popularity. Having spent almost a decade in power, the party was turning into a divisive political force, believing that its unprecedented electoral success gave it a mandate to rush ahead with its policies without concern for the 50 per cent of the population that had not voted for it. Soon it was alienating many Turks. This was in stark contrast to the first and, to some extent, second terms. Soon the AKP's leaders were making statements or passing legislation that many Turks suspected of being motivated by Islam, or at least of invading their private lives. For example, speaking at the official inauguration of the Global Alcohol Policies Symposium held in Istanbul in April 2013, Prime Minister Erdogan declared that alcohol was the mother of all evil.[138] The following month, the Turkish parliament passed legislation that heavily regulated alcohol consumption, prohibiting its sale after 10pm, blurring alcohol products on TV shows, and restricting sales within 100 metres of mosques and schools.[139]

In September 2013, Erdogan commented that Turkish families should have four children, an increase on his earlier recommendation of three.[140] In November of the same year, Erdogan publically condemned co-ed dormitories, warning that the state should intervene.[141] This was reminiscent of the AKP's proposed legislation of 2004 banning adultery, which was quickly abandoned following an uproar at home and abroad.[142] Such instances of blatant interference in the private lives of citizens had contributed to the Gezi Park protests during the summer of 2013. These protests, which were initially against an urban regeneration project at one of Istanbul's last remaining green spaces, turned into an outpouring of opposition to the AKP's increasingly authoritarian measures, especially by middle-class urban secularists of various political affinities and ages who felt that they were being marginalised and ignored. This did not stop Erdogan or the AKP from making further statements. On 30 May 2016, President Erdogan declared that no Muslim family should consider birth control or family planning. On an earlier occasion, the president had declared that contraception was tantamount to treason.[143]

Although small, another social group increasingly estranged by the AKP were the liberals, who had initially backed the AKP, believing that the party represented a unique opportunity for reform and positive change. By the AKP's third term, it had lost this source of support. One study discovered that 13 per cent of the AKP's votes in 2002 were from voters who had previously supported the Democratic Left Party as well as 4 per cent who had previously supported the CHP.[144] While this indicates disillusionment with the traditional secular and liberal parties, it also signifies an attraction towards the AKP by liberal-minded Turks. Indeed, as Soner Cagaptay has argued, "[The] AKP attracted many moderate urban voters, who were appalled by the inefficient and corruption-ridden governments of the 1990s, as well as by the political instability and economic downturns that characterized this decade."[145] This liberal support was certainly due to the AKP's economic policies, but was also in approval of the AKP's democratic agenda and the EU reform packages.[146]

Turkey's liberals, according to journalist Mustafa Akyol, were then public intellectuals who were vehemently against the authoritarian nature of the secular Turkish state. They were fervently opposed to both military coups and secular issues such as prohibitions on headscarves at universities.[147] The Turkish liberals were not a particularly large source of support for the AKP, but they did offer the party intellectual power and credence. They were also important because their support helped Erdogan to claim that his party represented a centre-right position.[148] Although never ideological bedfellows, the European-looking AKP convinced its liberal supporters to ignore concerns about a hidden Islamist agenda and vote in Erdogan's favour.[149] However, it was a short-lived match, which erupted into open rifts following the Gezi

Park protests of 2013. But even before the protests, and despite openings in the Kurdish peace process which many liberals had advocated, they were increasingly targeted and isolated by Erdogan, removing them from pro-AKP media outlets in order to prevent any criticism of his government from reaching his core base of support.[150]

By 2010, the AKP had been overhauled with the purging of parliamentary party members seen to be too centrist or liberal. By the AKP's September 2012 congress, similar purges had taken place within the party's executive, although the press reported those purged as being sympathetic to Abdullah Gul.[151] Aziz Babuscu, the AKP's Istanbul branch head, even commented several months before the Gezi Park protests that although liberals had worked with the AKP for the past ten years, they would not be with them in the future.[152] However, even earlier, liberals were already concerned about the slowing down of the EU reform process after the AKP's 2007 re-election.[153] By the 2009 local elections, the AKP had seen a decrease in electoral support. An important factor was middle-class concern over the AKP's positioning of Turkey as a liberal European country following the party's increasing distance from Europe from 2005.[154] The brutal crackdown on the Gezi Park protesters, the government's harsh policies towards the Kurds—such as the mass arrests of members of the umbrella Kurdish movement Group of Communities in Kurdistan (KCK)—and Erdogan's increasing references to Sunni identity after the start of the Arab Spring all alienated liberals from the AKP.[155]

Another challenge facing Erdogan and the AKP was a wave of corruption allegations and arrests concerning bribery for construction projects, money laundering and circumventing sanctions against Iran. This led to the resignation of cabinet ministers whose sons were taken into custody.[156] A second wave of allegations even swirled around Erdogan's son, but neither the police nor the general prosecutor pressed charges.[157] Instead, details were leaked to the press, and a series of leaked tapes followed that also called into question government thinking on foreign policy, as well as telephone conversations between Erdogan and his family members concerning money. These corruption allegations, the most widespread in Turkey's history, have certainly been detrimental to the AKP. Also disconcerting was the extent of governmental association with big business and large conglomerates. After the corruption allegations emerged, this close connection immediately affected Turkey's economy, with inflation rising to 7 per cent, the currency losing value, and a reduction in foreign investment and exports.[158]

The AKP also had to worry about the source of the leaks and the investigations, believed by many to be coming from the Gulen movement. Before the constitutional changes of 2010, the AKP did not have concerns about a "parallel" state within the ranks of the judiciary.[159] Now Erdogan was condemning the Gulenists at virtually every opportunity while purging their ranks within government institutions. Apparently the government was shocked by the extent of this so-called "parallel state".[160]

What caused the rift between the AKP and the Gulen movement? There were several factors at play, including Turkish-Israeli relations and the Kurdish issue. The *Mavi Marmara* incident in 2010, for example, was not confined to foreign policy, but also had domestic repercussions. Nine Turks were left dead after Israeli commandos boarded a Turkish flotilla sent in an attempt to break the Israeli blockade of Gaza. Speaking from Pennsylvania, Gulen criticised the flotilla strategy as counterproductive,[161] angering Erdogan, who had made a point of criticising Israel over its policies in Gaza. Meanwhile, the Gulen movement disapproved of Erdogan's so-called Kurdish opening and the backroom talks between the PKK and the Turkish state. The Gulenists disagreed that the problem could be solved by negotiating with Abdullah Ocalan and the PKK.[162] It was rumoured that the Gulen movement was so disturbed by Erdogan's Kurdish policy that it instigated the leaking of taped discussions between PKK officials and the government delegation, including members of Turkey's secret service and Erdogan's then advisor, Hakan Fidan. It was in this context that, in November 2013, Erdogan announced that prep schools for university exams (*dershane*), many of which belonged to Gulenists, would be shut down.[163] One month later, Erdogan found the sons of three of his ministers implicated in the corruption investigations.

The corruption allegations of December 2013 and the rift with Gulen opened other wounds. Relations with the Gulen-linked business association TUSKON had soured. Meanwhile, despite still supporting the AKP, individuals such as Irfan Guvendi of MUSIAD were concerned about corruption and transparency, especially after the graft probes of December 2013.[164] Further, Guvendi had come to believe it was a myth that MUSIAD benefited significantly under the AKP, as contracts for large projects were awarded to big monopolies, not the medium-sized enterprises his organisation represented.[165] Guvendi's position represents significant concern among the AKP's grassroots supporters over the party's dealings with large businesses.

However, these corruption allegations, instead of hindering the AKP and Erdogan at elections, seemed to make little impact. During the local elections of March 2014, which came after bans of Twitter and YouTube and the Gezi Park crackdowns the previous summer, the AKP won over 42 per cent of the popular vote. In the presidential election of August 2014, Erdogan managed to secure 52 per cent of the vote, winning in the first round. The AKP also managed to win the November 2015 re-run of the June general elections, and maintain its hold in parliament. This in itself could not have been a surprise. In 2011, the AKP had won by a landslide despite WikiLeaks revelations that Ambassador Eric Edelman had reported "conflicts of interest or serious corruption in the party at the national, provincial and local level and among close family members of ministers" and that Erdogan himself had "eight accounts in Swiss banks; his explanations that his wealth comes from the wedding presents guests gave his son and that a Turkish businessman is paying the educational expenses of all four Erdogan children in the U.S. purely altruistically are lame".[166]

Bolstered by its electoral victories, the AKP continued its attack against the "parallel structure" of the Gulen movement. Backed into a corner, Gulenists within the military apparently staged a failed coup on 15 July 2016. If anything this only strengthened the AKP. With electoral victories under its belt, as well as outpourings of support for the government against the putschists, the AKP was able to administer Turkey under emergency rule and "cleanse" state institutions of Gulenist sympathisers. However, the AKP's visceral attacks on the Gulen movement before and after the July 2016 coup attempt raise concern over the government's judgement. If the movement was as nefarious as government politicians claim, why did the AKP use the Gulen movement to combat the military and secularists during its first two terms in office? The AKP's attitude towards the Gulen movement since the attempted coup brings to mind a bomb maker being maimed by his own explosives and then claiming to be the victim.

At the 2015 Polls

After his success at the 2014 presidential elections, Erdogan named his loyal ally Ahmet Davutoglu as the new prime minister and leader of the AKP. Arguably, Erdogan wanted a prime minister who was both loyal and weak, to enable him to push Turkey towards a presidential system while also being able to set priorities and governmental policies.[167]

Erdogan's presidential victory marked the start of a semi-presidential system whereby his office has gained increasing powers,[168] stretching its constitutional boundaries. For example, to mark the presidency's increasing importance, a new presidential compound was built, known as the Ak Saray (White Palace). The name itself is a play on the AK Party, the official name of the AKP. To rehouse the president's official residency was a controversial move, not least because of its soaring costs, to the tune of US$615 million.[169] It did not go unnoticed that a mosque was built on the estate of the president's new digs. In reality, the compound—with its 250 rooms standing on 150,000 square metres of grounds—is a symbol of prestige for the role of the presidency and its associated offices.

Erdogan has proceeded to raise the budget of the presidency and its number of directorates which went up from four to thirteen. He has set up a de facto shadow government to deal with issues such as internal security, foreign affairs, economic matters and even defence.[170] Rather than being a symbolic institution, Erdogan has used the office of the presidency to chair cabinet meetings on several occasions. According to the spirit, if not the letter, of the constitution, he is only supposed to chair such meetings when there is a special need. His predecessors resisted the urge as often as they could.[171] After 2014, it was all but clear that Erdogan was acting as the puppet master controlling the AKP government of the new Prime Minister Davutoglu.

The position of the president is supposed to be politically neutral. But ahead of the general elections in June and November 2015, Erdogan made his support for the AKP known in no uncertain terms as he went on overdrive with public appearances, attending official openings and giving public speeches. This was noted by the Organisation for Security and Cooperation in Europe (OSCE), which stated that:

> [the] President played an active role in the election campaign, even though under the Constitution he is obliged to be non-partisan and perform his duties without bias. The President attended an extraordinary number of public events, as head of state, along with local officials, however, these events were used as opportunities to campaign in favour of the ruling party and to criticize opposition figures.[172]

This observation was an understatement. For example, during the 7 June elections, in line with Erdogan's direction, Davutoglu put a new constitution and presidential system at the heart of his election campaign. The AKP's 100-article manifesto was called the "2023 New Turkey Contract", a reference to the Turkish Republic's centennial.[173] This New Turkey had already been used in the 2014 presidential elections, in effect also a referendum on Erdogan's ambitions for full executive powers. The AKP portrayed the 2015 elections as a choice between a "New Turkey" and a return to the old days of military tutelage, short-lived coalition governments and economic instability. During the election period, it hardly mattered whether Davutoglu was running, because the New Turkey and the future role of the president was emphasised more than Davutoglu's own leadership. Also during the campaign period, Erdogan actively asked for support for the constitutional change to a presidential system, and for the AKP's "New Turkey". Erdogan even asked people to vote for the ruling party, without directly mentioning it by name, to receive 400 deputies in parliament so that a shift to a presidential system could be instituted.[174]

Nevertheless, the outcome of the June 2015 general elections was not what Erdogan or the AKP had wanted. Instead of winning a majority in parliament, the party won 258 seats, having gained just under 41 per cent of the popular vote. This amounted to eighteen seats short of an outright majority, and far short of the two-thirds majority needed to change the constitution and transform the system without a referendum.[175] This pitched Turkey into uncertainty, as the AKP would need to form a coalition with the Kemalist CHP (131 seats), the far-right Nationalist Action Party (eighty seats) or the pro-Kurdish, left-wing HDP (eighty-one seats) in order to govern. The alternative was fresh elections.

The June 2015 result invites the question of whether the AKP or Erdogan was in fact losing support. Though Erdogan had won over 50 per cent of the vote in the previous year's presidential election, it is certainly the case that his hopes of establishing a new presidential system were dealt a sharp blow. Voters had made clear their reservations about sudden changes to the political system. Indeed, perhaps the fact that the personally popular Erdogan was not officially at the helm of the AKP was a reason for its sliding support. However, the election results point to another direction. The Kurdish-orientated HDP won conservative voters away from the AKP over discontent with the lagging Kurdish peace process. This put the HDP past the 10 per cent threshold to gain seats in parliament. AKP voters were also courted from the other side by the Nationalist Action Party, which increased its vote share by appealing to those disillusioned with the government's pursuit of a peace process in itself. In this context, the AKP's 40 per cent vote share was a significant achievement, bearing in mind that it was facing a corruption scandal, a fallout with the Gulen movement, liberal discontent after the suppression of the Gezi Park movement and Kurdish anger towards the AKP's inertia over the peace process, not to mention a foreign policy in tatters amidst extreme regional volatility. All of these subjects are discussed in the following chapters, but it is clear that despite being embattled, the AKP still appears to have considerable support and remains a force to be reckoned with.

Following the June elections, Turkey's political scene was dominated by potential coalition discussions. However, there was speculation in some quarters that Erdogan was actually pushing for fresh elections, rather than encouraging the AKP to find a coalition partner.[176] When the coalition talks collapsed, Erdogan refused to give a mandate to the leader of any other party represented in parliament, and called a snap election.[177] With political uncertainty on the horizon and increasing clashes between Turkish forces and the PKK, the AKP managed to achieve over 49 per cent of the vote in the re-run. Once again, the AKP could boast a considerable electoral success.

In the aftermath of the November 2015 election, the future of Turkey's political system and constitution was back at the top of the agenda. Erdogan believes that the current political system is "double-headed". To remedy this problem, he seeks to establish what he deems to be a uniquely Turkish presidential system.[178] However, what such a system would look like is not immediately clear. What is apparent is that Erdogan is not content with his current presidential powers. He also believes that his vision of a distinctly Turkish system would be more efficient. The AKP's election manifesto was vague and did not explain it.[179] The potential for controversy lies in the exact powers of the president. Would he be able to appoint members of the judiciary? Would he have legislative powers? Would he be able to order and pre-side over all cabinet meetings? Would he be able to make political appointments? Would he be able to veto laws passed in parliament? Would he be obliged to sever ties with existing political parties? How often would he run for office? Would he also act as a commander-in-chief, with the power to declare war and states of emergency?[180] These questions remained unanswered.

Conclusion

As the AKP and Erdogan continue to win elections, they do so at the expense of alienating those who do not vote for them. The 50 to 60 per cent of the population who did not vote for either the party or the president have grown tired and frustrated. Meanwhile, the scars of Gezi have not healed, and many secular or liberal Turks feel frustrated and angry. Little has been done to ease their concerns. Deputy Prime Minister Bulent Arinc's shocking comment in July 2014 that women should not laugh in public certainly did not help.[181] Turkey has become more polarised than ever under the AKP, while transparency and rule of law have suffered; a paradoxical twist from the party that elicited so much promise when it came to power in 2002.

Certainly a factor keeping the AKP in power is the lack of political alternatives. However, the AKP remains embattled. It faces a threat from the so-called "parallel state" of the Gulen movement, which has tried to delegitimise the AKP and whose members even appear to have attempted a military takeover in July 2016. Despite the post-coup spirit of national solidarity, there remains opposition to the AKP from secularists and Turkey's small group of liberals, as well as Kurds and even nationalists. The AKP may continue to win elections, but at what cost to Turkey's unity? This question is particularly pertinent as President Erdogan, with the backing of the AKP, seeks to change the country's political system and constitution, which may further alienate large segments of the population and sow further seeds of political division.

3

ERDOGAN'S WAY

TURKEY'S MAJORITARIANISM AND ITS DISCONTENTS

Introduction

In the early nineteenth century, having spent time in the newly independent United States of America, Alexis de Tocqueville penned one of political philosophy's most engaging and important works, *Democracy in America*.[1] Although impressed by the American system of governance, he warned about an important deficiency that has plagued the minds of even the most ardent democrats ever since: the "tyranny of the majority." In other words, the threat that those who had not voted for an elected official would become marginalised, isolated or even persecuted. Modern Turkey should pay heed to this warning, as should anyone citing Turkey as a model for other states to emulate. While no doubt a democracy, Turkey is a flawed one. It lacks significant democratic conditions both in its political culture and practices. Paradoxically, the style of Turkish democracy at times resembles aspects of authoritarian rule. This is due to a majoritarian system in which the political class, having won free and fair elections, see fit to make their mark on Turkey almost carte blanche. Once elected, prime ministers, often charismatic leaders, seek to dominate the political landscape. On the basis that general elections have unconditionally mandated their rule, Turkish politicians seek to suppress critics and dominate all aspects of the state, eroding systems of checks and balances and the separation of powers, in addition to dominating civil society discourse.

Which failures within Turkey's democratic system allow it to be dominated by majoritarian-style politics? How have Turkey's institutions of state, its electoral system, its separation of powers and the functions of each branch become dominated by political actors seeking to implant their respective cultural identity onto the nature of the Turkish state and stifle opposition? Historically the ambitions and abilities of politicians to dominate have been tempered by the presence of the military, the self-appointed guardian of Turkey's secular principles and the Kemalist definition of who and what is a Turk. Never a democratic institution, the military was the ultimate check on the power of the political class. The decline of its political power was once a promising development that could strengthen Turkey's democracy and political culture. But now, especially after the post-putsch purges of summer 2016, this possibility has been reduced to a mere flicker of hope and the government, while ruling the country under emergency law, has used the coup attempt as an excuse to purge the opposition from institutions of state and society, solidifying its dominance for years to come.

Nevertheless, there are traces of social movements in Turkey resisting the majoritarian system and the rule of the political class. As the Gezi Park protests showed, beyond political opponents of the government, social media and social movements are and have always been vibrant and dynamic forces in Turkish politics, refusing to be silenced.

Claims of Majoritarianism

In a widely circulated and influential *Foreign Affairs* article from 2012, public intellectual and political affairs commentator Fareed Zakaria discussed the rise of what he termed "illiberal democracies". Popular participation in politics, Zakaria noted, need not take place within a western liberal democratic model where protection of individual rights is a key aim of government and institutions of state. In fact, he said, illiberal democracies were on the rise.[2] Turkey's turbulent political history since its founding in 1923 lends credit to Zakaria's assertion that "Constitutional liberalism has led to democracy, but democracy does not seem to bring constitutional liberalism",[3] especially if we factor in military interventions, corruption, weak institutions, turbulent attempts at centralisation and a fragile system of checks and balances. Contemporary Turkish politics has highlighted the illiberal nature of the state. If anything, Turkey's very democratic structure and what is left of its liberal institutions serve as a facade for an increasingly authoritarian-minded government, which seeks to dominate all aspects of government and civil society.

On 8 June 2013, at the height of the Gezi Park protests, *The Economist* ran a controversial front-page article entitled "Turkey's Troubles: Democrat or Sultan", which depicted the face of Turkey's then Prime Minister Erdogan Photoshopped onto the body of a classical Ottoman sultan, sitting at leisure in full royal regalia. "For some observers," the article stated, "Turkey's upheaval provides new evidence that Islam and democracy cannot coexist. But Mr Erdogan's religiosity is beside the point. The real lesson of these events is about authoritarianism: Turkey will not put up with a middle-class democrat behaving like an Ottoman Sultan."[4]

The Economist was not alone in its analysis, which represented the views of many Turks. According to a poll commissioned by the daily *Today's Zaman* in June 2013, 49.9 per cent of Turks believed that the government was increasingly authoritarian and 54.5 per cent felt that the government was interfering more in their lives.[5] This view was also echoed by Turkey's celebrated Nobel laureate Orhan Pamuk, who stated that the plans to uproot Gezi Park without informing Istanbul's population represented "reckless politics", behind which were "the authoritative and oppressive tendencies of the government".[6] Indeed, beyond the planned demolition of the park, the increasing authoritarianism and state interventionism in Erdogan's Turkey was a prime reason for the large-scale protests during the summer of 2013.[7]

Even before the Gezi protests, accusations of increasing authoritarianism were levelled against Erdogan. After May Day protests were repressed with heavy-handed police tactics in 2013, the leader of the opposition, Kemal Kilicdaroglu of the CHP, commented that Erdogan was leading Turkey towards authoritarian rule. He had already commented that the then prime minister was a "post-modern dictator".[8] In what can only be described as a scathing critique of the AKP's Turkey, also written before the Gezi protests, British political commentator Mehdi Hasan slammed Erdogan for the restrictions on press freedom. He pointed to a "new climate of fear in Istanbul" among the press, concluding that "Turkey cannot be the model, the template, for post-revolutionary, Muslim-majority countries like Tunisia and Egypt until it first gets its own house in order".[9]

However, Turkey is still a democratic state. It is a republic with institutions that work within a democratic structure. There is a parliament, whose head is the prime minister; there is a presidency and a judiciary. Erdogan's party has been elected into office four times and the man himself has won not just elections, but landslides. The AKP's popularity is unprecedented. It won 50 per cent of the vote in November 2015. Addressing supporters in May 2013 during the Gezi crisis, Erdogan insisted that he was "not a king but a prime minister elected with a nation's votes ... I am your servant, not your master".[10]

As Turkish commentator Mustafa Akyol notes, when looking at Christian and Kurdish rights in modern Turkey, Erdogan deserves some praise for the reopening of churches and the easing of restrictions on the Kurdish language. Some limited progress has been made. On the other hand, the press has not been at all free. In other words, according to Akyol, Erdogan has advanced democracy in some areas while reducing it in others.[11] The picture is complicated. What Erdogan has come to represent is the charismatic leader not of a liberal democracy, but a majoritarian democracy, where voting allows the leading party to dictate the direction of the state, which in turn sees itself as a paternal guiding hand for its citizens.

Prior to the AKP's ascension to office, Turkey's political climate was subject to the presence of the military, whose dominance had been permanent since the 1980 coup. Not only did the military set the rules of civilian politics, the constitution was drafted and implemented under its auspices. Through bodies like the National Security Council, the military's presence served as a check on government power, but by no means a democratic one, and in a system controlled by the military itself, with a weak separation of powers. Though ostensibly a positive step toward democracy, the decline of the military also led to the erosion of checks and balances, paving the way for more majoritarian—and possibly more authoritarian—rule.

We've seen that the political history of the modern Turkish Republic has been marked by strains of authoritarianism and paternalism emanating from both the military and from civilian politicians. So how has life under the AKP been any different?

According to columnist Etyem Mahcupyan, who also served as advisor to Prime Minister Davutoglu, the driving force behind the AKP was a democratic one, seeking to transform Turkey from within and to overthrow the tutelage system; under such circumstances, he explains, the party felt obliged to try to win every election by over 50 per cent.[12] You could argue that the majoritarian nature of AKP rule is but the latest example of civilian government being dominated by a single party leader with a strong emphasis on top-down democracy. However, there are important differences. Under the AKP opportunities have presented themselves for Turkey to step away from its majoritarian legacy—namely, the decline of the military and the initiation of pro-EU democratic reforms. This led to a certain degree of hope, especially among liberals, democrats and the younger generation of Turks.

However, this short-lived opening was coupled with increasing concern about the growing lack of checks and balances in Turkey's political system, as well as the traditional secular elite's lack of confidence in the AKP, fearing a hidden Islamic agenda. This perpetual perception confronted the AKP with a crisis in its legitimacy despite its popular election and good governance of the economy. This uneasiness, the traditional fear of a military intervention and its popular mandate, pushed the AKP to attempt to steer Turkey in the direction for which it felt its electorate had voted, to right traditional wrongs and injustices. In order to achieve this vision, the AKP needed not only to tackle the makeup of the bureaucracy and judiciary, but also to enter the private sphere and attempt to introduce legislation that affected the private lives of many citizens. This was a radical departure from previous regimes and occurred at a time when checks were being eroded. According to columnist Ali Bayramoglu, a fundamental problem facing Turkish democracy is the division between conservatives and secularists, with the AKP representing Turkey's conservatives and protecting their interests.[13]

The party has gained significant political influence not only through electoral victories but also through informal means of suppressing checks on government power. Through the issuing of government contracts to media outlets, Erdogan's AKP has been able to intervene in the press (see Chapter 4). This is particularly serious as it accompanies a general lack of accountability. Even though the AKP's rise was partly due to the perceived corruption of the ruling secular parties, the AKP has only proved marginally better. Accountability of elected officials is difficult to obtain, as members of parliament enjoy immunity while in office. Despite some anti-corruption measures adopted by the AKP, Turkey ranked 61 out of 183 countries in Transparency International's 2011 Corruption Perceptions Index.

Worse still, Erdogan himself has been accused of being involved in cronyism and nepotism scandals, some of which were made public following the leaks of US cables.[14] Indeed, under his tenure, scandals such as the wiretapping of judges in 2009 have been revealed, with no public inquiries. Yet there have been few instances of public accountability or prosecutions. Then, of course, there are the corruption arrests and leaked tapes that emerged in 2013, all of which pointed to high levels of corruption and misconduct at the highest levels and inner circles of government.

According to Abdullatif Sener, deputy prime minister during the first AKP term, the government shapes the public and private economy by distributing loans, credits and contracts.[15] Even with parliamentary immunity, one would still expect a degree of transparency to be implanted within a party's structure. At minimum, this would gain some public confidence. For the most part, this has not been the case with the AKP. If anything, there has been a general reluctance to seek governmental accountability, especially during the party's third term in office (2011–15). For example, in 2012 the Court of Accounts did not send fiscal auditing reports to parliament before the 2013 budget. It was the first time that this had happened in Turkey's history. Nor did the Court submit the requisite External Auditing General Evaluation Report and General Evaluation Report on Performance. Even when they have been submitted, there has been criticism that Court of Accounts audit reports and annual reports by public institutions supply insufficient data in their descriptions—despite the hope that there would be an improvement following the passing of the 2010 Law on the Court of Accounts.[16]

Meanwhile, the AKP has made thirty amendments to the Law on Public Procurement since entering office, while the Parliamentary Planning and Budget Commission, most of whose members are from the AKP, "acts like a rubber stamp", preventing parliament from over-seeing spending or holding public institutions to account.[17] In Turkey's booming construction industry, corruption is an increasing problem, with two officials from the public housing administration charged with bribery and abuse of power—this in a body that has a monopoly on the redevelopment of private and public land, with a twenty-year budget of US$400 billion. To make matters worse, there is a public perception that under-regulated development is benefiting leading members of society, including AKP members and a company run by Erdogan's own son-in-law.[18]

Turkey's Majoritarian System: The Legislature and the Executive

After the era of military tutelage, Turkey's political structure was ripe for political dominance by a single political party and a single political figure. This has proved especially true during the AKP period, which has been marked by several important and historical developments. This includes the unprecedented electoral success of the AKP, the decline of the military as a political force and the 2010 constitutional amendments. These events, to which we will return, have resulted in the erosion of the checks and balances needed in any healthy democracy, in a political system that was already problematic and highly centralised.

On the surface, Turkey's political structure indicates that the necessary separation of powers between state institutions is present. There is a legislature, an executive and a judiciary. There is also a written constitution, although drafted under military supervision following the 1980 coup. Turkey's legislature is the Grand National Assembly of Turkey, which sits in Ankara, the capital since Turkey's War of Independence. Seats in the Assembly are allocated after general elections, which take place regularly—at least every four or five years, as in many other democracies. Turkey's electoral system is party list pro-portional representation (PR), brought in after the 1960 coup.[19] Meanwhile, the calculation of seat allocation employs the D'Hondt method, widely used in PR systems. The method calculates the highest average of votes to select parliamentary candidates, and has been criti-cised in countries where it is used for favouring larger parties.[20]

Turkey's parliament has 550 seats representing eighty-five provinces. The party with the majority of seats usually forms the government. The size of the voting districts, in terms of the number of representatives per district, has also been criticised for favouring the ruling party. This is particularly problematic in Turkey due to the unusually high electoral threshold: in order to gain any seats in the Assembly at all, a party must have gained at least 10 per cent of the popular vote. This is detrimental to smaller parties and works in favour of larger electoral blocs. Smaller parties, especially Kurdish parties, have been able to pass the threshold by fielding candidates as independents. This state of affairs has changed since the rise of the AKP. The 2002 elections were a watershed moment, as the AKP won just over one third of the popular vote and was only a few seats short of a two-thirds majority in the house, which would have allowed it to make constitutional amendments without public consultation.

The astonishing electoral success of the AKP in 2002, 2007 and 2011 was a significant break from the norm; in previous years multiple parties had been able to overcome the 10 per cent threshold. Just as importantly, Turkey's PR system was geared towards coalition govern-ments. With parties unable to form a majority, they relied on coalition partners to form a government. Although this was far from perfect and entailed significant democratic deficiencies, the coalitions would often lead to policy compromises reflecting a broader consensus. It worked almost as an internal check on the power of the leading party. The AKP's stunning electoral victories, however, overturned this. Although coalition government is by no means a pre-requisite for democratic legitimacy, its absence since 2002 has highlighted the systemic prob-lems in Turkey's political system that would soon allow for majoritar-ian, even authoritarian, rule achieved through the ballot box.

Turkey's legislative process is highly centralised. In theory, the law comprises ordinary law, amendments, by-laws and the constitution.[21] However, the constitution itself was a product of the 1980 military coup. Amendments are possible only if two thirds of parliament votes in their favour, as was the case in 2010.

Here, though, we should dwell on the most common form of legis-lation in Turkey: ordinary law. With an overwhelming majority in parliament, and only an absolute majority required, the present government has been able to pass new laws quickly, without broad public consultation and with little cross-party consensus or debate. Articles 87, 88 and 89 of the constitution outline the process: legislative bills for ordinary law or to abrogate existing laws are proposed by either the Council of Ministers or individual deputies, debated and adopted in parliament during its plenary session, then submitted to the president, obliged to ratify the legislation at the second pass.[22]

Very rarely does proposed legislation from opposition parties manage to enter serious political discussion. In fact, according to a report compiled by a joint EU-OECD initiative, Support for Improvement in Governance and Management, "Draft laws submitted by opposition deputies have scarcely any chance of becoming law"—little debate time is given to these bills, which are routinely voted down.[23] This means that new legislation is almost entirely in the hands of the Council of Ministers, headed by the prime minister, together constituting the executive branch. Even when a proposed law enters parliamentary committee level, where bills are scrutinised, there are tight deadlines (rarely met) for necessary amendments to be made. Only deputies who are members of parliamentary groups can be members of such committees,[24] and members of the Council of Ministers or the Assembly Bureau cannot serve on them. Membership of new committees is voted and approved in parliament.[25] This, of course, favours the ruling party—nearly every committee in Turkey today is dominated by the AKP. Between this and the fact that most laws are devised and implemented by the prime minister and his cabinet, the party enjoys almost complete control of the legislative process.

After a general election, the president asks the party with the most seats to form the government and the prime minister selects his cabinet members, who are then presented to the Assembly. They are subject to a vote of confidence by a simple majority. Thanks to the AKP's sizeable majority, the appointment of new ministers rarely faces opposition. Each member of the Council of Ministers heads a ministerial department and the prime minister acts as a head of the cabinet as well as supervising policy implementation.

While elections take place every four years, the prime minister also has the power to dissolve parliament and call new elections if supported by a majority of MPs. As head of both party and cabinet, the prime minister is by far the most powerful figure in Turkish politics. He or she possesses the power to appoint party officials and candidates for elections and therefore holds considerable influence over politicians' careers.[26] However, the primacy of the prime minister has been increasingly eroded since Erdogan became president in 2014. He has wielded much power among the party, the cabinet and the parliament, albeit by stretching the constitutional powers of his office as well as his personal influence over state and party institutions, built during his time as prime minister.

According to Abdullatif Sener, Erdogan when he was prime minister utilised his power to make decisions without consulting the rest of the parliamentary party. There was no real mechanism to question the authority of the party leader.[27] This changed when Erdogan was elected president. He was able to use his influence to reduce the power of his replacement, Ahmet Davutoglu. The events of May 2016 were a case in point. In what was dubbed by some as a "Palace Coup", Davutoglu resigned after clashing with Erdogan on a number of political issues, such as Davutoglu's commitment to greater transparency to prevent corruption, resuming talks with the PKK, the refugee deal with the EU and the pace of drafting a new constitution.[28] Davutoglu was replaced by Transport Minister Binali Yildirim, who is considered closer to Erdogan and believed to be more subservient to his will.[29]

The concentration of power in the hands of one man is particularly important in Turkey because the personality of leading political figures has always been of crucial importance. Erdogan is but the latest in a long line of prime ministers and presidents whose character has dominated the political landscape, including but not limited to Mustafa Kemal Ataturk, Ismet Inonu, Adnan Menderes, Bulent Ecevit, Turgut Ozal, Suleyman Demirel and Tansu Ciller. The importance of the "charismatic" leader in Turkish politics has been the subject of a study by political scientist Hakan Yavuz, who concluded that "personalities are always more important than party programs or institutions".[30] This is especially interesting because, despite Erdogan's dominance, Turkey is not a presidential system: the prime minister, head of the executive, is also not directly elected by the people. Ex-US ambassador Morton Abramowitz and international relations professor Henri Barkey have claimed in the *Wall Street Journal* that when Erdogan was prime minister he ruled his party with an iron fist, contemptuous of criticism. They added that, with the power he has accumulated and the praise he has received for his domestic and foreign policies, he seems to have developed a sense of invincibility.[31]

Not everyone agrees. Journalist Etyem Mahcupyan argues that Erdogan is not authoritarian, but paternalistic, and that though he feels offended when the Turkish public does not accept his views, he is nevertheless willing to change his own.[32] Still, noting inconsistencies between Erdogan's words and deeds, Istanbul-based analyst Gareth Jenkins has concluded "either that no one in his inner circle of trusted advisors has the courage to point them out—or that, if they do, Erdogan simply ignores them. But without anyone to restrain him, Turkey's future will remain highly vulnerable to Erdogan's personality".[33] But what is the personality of Recep Tayyip Erdogan?

One study has been conducted on this subject: Aylin S. Gorener and Meltem S. Ucal analysed Erdogan's personality in the context of its foreign policy implications. Assessing Erdogan's speeches in the English-speaking media, they concluded that Erdogan's scores on power as a personal motive can be considered close to the average for world leaders. Interestingly, his self-confidence score is slightly closer to the lower end of the spectrum. However, worryingly, Erdogan scored very highly on his belief that he could control events, and scored high on having a general dislike of others, but scored low on understanding conceptual complexity. This backs the contention of Yavuz, who asserts that "for Erdogan, party politics is about loyalty and obedience to the leader."[34]

Traditionally a largely ceremonial role in Turkey, the office of the president is still highly important, as the president's role is to ensure that new laws are in accordance with the constitution. This may serve as a check on the power of the government. Prior to 2007, Ahmet Necet Sezer, a respected secularist, was president. Sezer was not afraid to block AKP legislation. In June 2005, he refused to sign a new penal code, which would cut the penalty for anyone found guilty of teaching the Koran in unauthorised places.[35] But after the AKP's re-election in 2007 and the expiration of Sezer's term in office, the post fell to Abdullah Gul. The AKP was then able to pass legislation with fewer obstacles than during Sezer's term, with little incentive for consensus or consultation. Just before the Gezi Park protests of June 2013, the AKP made a controversial attempt to severely restrict the sale of alcohol, which was passed in parliament with little public consultation. Though the protests continued and ground Turkey to a halt, President Gul signed the bill into law.[36]

Majoritarianism and the dominance of individual politicians intensified after Erdogan's victory in the 2014 presidential elections, the first time that the president of the Republic had been directly elected by the people. Erdogan defeated his two competitors (Selahattin Demirtas of the Kurdish-oriented HDP and the joint CHP-Nationalist Action Party candidate Ekmeleddin Ihsanoglu) in the first round, with an impressive 51 per cent of the vote.[37]

Ihsanoglu was shocked by the attacks against him from Erdogan's campaign, which he accuses of making false claims against him, including that he did not know the Turkish national anthem and had not served in the military and that, if elected, he would prevent people from reading the Koran in Arabic.[38] Amidst legitimate claims that the Erdogan campaign was overwhelmingly supported by sympathetic media outlets giving him disproportionate coverage,[39] Erdogan's victory furthered the transformation of Turkey into a presidential system, giving him even more powers. However, for such changes to come into effect, the new president would need parliament to pass constitutional amendments, with the majorities discussed above.[40] Erdogan's hope lay with the AKP, the party that he had co-founded and led for over a decade.

According to the Turkish constitution, the president should not be affiliated with any political party: "If the President-elect is a member of a party, his/her relationship with his/her party shall be severed and his/her membership of the Grand National Assembly of Turkey shall cease".[41] But it was all too clear that Erdogan actively supported the AKP's campaigns in the June and November 2015 general elections. He called for the electorate to give him 400 deputies in parliament to make the necessary constitutional changes—presumably 400 AKP deputies.[42] This campaigning on behalf of the AKP utilised the resources of the office of the president and extended to going on rallies and making public appearances that were, in no uncertain terms, in support of the AKP.[43] Meanwhile, presidential powers have increased, with

Erdogan chairing cabinet meetings—a move widely seen as contrary to the spirit of the constitution—and seeing discretionary state funds allocated to the president.[44]

Adjusting the Judiciary: It's Complicated!

The separation of the judiciary from other powers is crucial to preventing political interference in the implementation of law. In Turkey, the judiciary consists of several levels: first instance courts, district courts and supreme courts. There is also a distinction between the civilian judiciary and military judiciary. Each is further divided into two groupings, the ordinary and the administrative judiciary.[45]

Essentially, this complex structure means that there are four distinct jurisdictional fields and, therefore, four supreme courts. In the civilian judiciary, these are the Court of Cassation (Supreme Court), the highest court in ordinary affairs, and the Council of State, the highest court in administrative affairs. These two civilian courts have their corresponding military counterparts: the Military Court of Cassation, the highest military court, although its mandate is criminal procedures, and the High Military Administrative Court, which gives the final verdict in administrative judicial affairs. It serves as both the Supreme Court and the court of first instance. As if this weren't complicated enough, it was deemed necessary to create yet another court, to resolve any disputes between the four: the Court of Jurisdictional Disputes. This brings the total number of supreme courts to five, or six if you count the Constitutional Court, which deals with issues pertaining to constitutional jurisdiction.[46]

During the first term of AKP rule (2002–7), the judiciary served as a check on the power of the government. However, this in itself was problematic. Staffed by secularists, the judiciary was often used by the military as a tool to limit the power of the elected government—and a means for the armed forces to maintain their political tutelage.[47] Towards the end of the AKP's first term, as the military's power to remove the government by direct means was starting to decline, it increasingly relied on the judiciary, particularly the Constitutional Court, to prevent the AKP from passing legislation that it felt threatened secularism.[48]

This was notably the case over the contentious issue of the ban on wearing a headscarf in public places. On 9 February 2006, the Second Chamber of the Council of State controversially upheld the Ankara Administration Court's ruling preventing a teacher from being promoted to headmistress because she chose to wear a headscarf—not inside school, but out of teaching hours. This made the Second Chamber a particular target of rage because many thought its judgment to be a very hard-line interpretation of the ban. AKP politicians, including Prime Minister Erdogan, let their frustration be known and condemned the decision, arguing that it was not within the court's remit to impose dress restrictions outside of a public servant's working life.[49] Tensions became so heated that on 17 May 2006, a gunman shot and killed a judge, wounding several others.[50] In a move that perhaps did little to curb tensions, Erdogan did not attend the funeral of the slain judge. Some of the heads of the high court made a joint statement after the funeral calling the killing a massacre and an attack "against the secular republic".[51] The chairwoman of the Council of State even went as far as to describe the attack as the result of careless rhetoric by government officials.[52] This incident highlights the extent to which the courts had become a political battleground in Turkey.

In the absence of a strong political opposition, the judiciary acted against Erdogan's government. The most striking example was the 2007 presidential vote in the Assembly. Concerned that respected secularist President Sezer would be followed by an AKP Islamist, hundreds of thousands rallied across the country in a series of "Republic Protests" in support of secularism, from April to May 2007.[53] Surprisingly, during the controversial Ergenekon trial (see Chapter 1), the "Republic Protests" were used as evidence of coup attempts.[54] The logic was that the protests were not an organic civilian movement, but organised by the military, which then later issued its "E-Memorandum".[55] One prominent organiser was the Ataturkist Thought Association, whose head at that time was the AKP critic Sener Eruygur, former general commander of the Gendarmerie (2002–4).

During this debacle, the Constitutional Court also annulled the initial parliamentary vote electing Abdullah Gul.[56] However, after Gul's election, the AKP was now rid of a checking and balancing institution, the presidency, and its representative, Ahmet Sezer. After assuming office, Gul gradually appointed new members to important institutions including the Constitutional Court. By the time his term as president drew to a close in late August 2014, he had been directly involved in the election and subsequent appointment of eleven of the Court's seventeen members.[57]

What explains such political interference in the judiciary? According to Sami Selcuk, the former first president of the Court of Cassation, in Turkey politicians are not concerned with the rule of law. Instead, they try to shape judicial structures for political purposes.[58] Politicians are even known to comment on judicial decisions. Ilhan Cihaner, CHP opposition deputy and former public prosecutor, believes that the problem lies not with the executive, but in the structure of the judiciary, especially as the judicial system is closely connected to politicians who have a greater say on promotion to high judicial office, through the Supreme Board of Judges and Prosecutors. He adds that the judiciary does not have its own judicial force. During investigations it has to work with the police, who are under the jurisdiction, if not the influence, of the Interior Ministry.[59]

On the other hand, from the AKP's perspective, it sought to restructure the judiciary because, unchanged, it would stand as an extension of military tutelage.[60] The party was angered and spurred into action by the ultimately failed attempt to close it in 2008. The 2010 constitutional amendments—approved by 58 per cent in a referendum—not only targeted the military, but overhauled the judicial system, allowing the AKP to strengthen its power. These constitutional changes, many of which were endorsed by the EU, gave the president and parliament greater authority over the selection and appointment of senior prosecutors and judges, and enlarged the Supreme Board of Judges and Prosecutors, extending government oversight. They also increased the size of the Constitutional Court.[61] The effect of this was to curtail the influence of secular judges in Turkey's high courts. Before these amendments, the Supreme Board was dominated by judges selected from the two civilian high courts, the Court of Cassation and the Council of State. Both of these institutions previously held very strong secular tendencies.[62] The constitutional amendments diluted this characteristic. They were designed to do so, and to erode the ability of the high courts to block governmental legislation.

For Osman Can, a former Constitutional Court reporter and the AKP's Central Executive Committee member, the 2010 amendments represented real progress, abolishing Kemalist hegemony in the judiciary and making it more pluralist, especially on the Supreme Board and in the Constitutional Court, though it was still not fully democratic—Can adds that high court judges should be appointed by parliament based on their electoral votes, to bring unrepresented groups such as the Kurds into the judiciary.[63] But in many respects, all the amendments really achieved was to replace Kemalist judges with conservative judges.[64] According to ex-public prosecutor Sami Selcuk, Supreme Board members should be selected mostly from the Court of Cassation and the Council of State. He feels that, at present, local judges are not independent, as the Supreme Board holds meetings with most local judges under the presidency of the Ministry of Justice. This is why local judges rarely vote differently from the Ministry of Justice or the Undersecretary of Justice. They want to be promoted to the Court of Cassation and the Council of State.[65]

There was also a restructuring of the military courts following the 2010 amendments. Crimes committed by members of the military against the constitutional order of the state were now to be tried in civilian rather than military courts. This was a game-changing development: now, if active or retired military officials were accused of plotting coups, it was the civilian courts that would charge and potentially prosecute them.[66] So the constitutional amendments drastically diluted the ability of both the military and the judiciary to challenge the AKP government.[67]

Following the amendments, new posts—especially within the Supreme Board—were filled mostly by Gulen-affiliated judges and prosecutors.[68] An AKP deputy party leader once said that while he was serving as justice minister, he knew of a judge who, before delivering a verdict, would first ask Fetullah Gulen for instruction.[69] By contrast, there are very few Alevis on the Supreme Board. According to Ilhan Cihaner, the former prosecutor, although numbering anywhere from 10 to 20 per cent of the national population, the Alevis, predominantly secularist and CHP-voting, numbered only two or three out of almost 100 members of the Supreme Board between 1990 and 2010. Today, he counted none. Similarly, there is no governor in all of Turkey's eighty-one provinces with an Alevi background.[70]

After the corruption arrests of 17 December 2013, Erdogan held the newly restructured judiciary responsible for the investigation, which he deemed an attempted "judicial coup" orchestrated by the Gulen movement to undermine him in the run-up to local and presidential elections.[71] In response, the AKP passed a bill that aimed to tighten the government's control over judicial institutions and appointments. The government wanted to alter the structure of the Supreme Board and create stronger links between it and the Ministry of Justice, which is part of the executive arm of the state. Human Rights Watch condemned this legislation, as did the Council of Europe's commissioner for human rights and the EU's commissioner for enlargement.[72] On 11 April 2014, the Constitutional Court partly overturned what was becoming a highly controversial bill, recognising that it threatened to turn the judiciary from independent to dominated by the executive.[73]

Those damn bureaucrats!

Though not one of the three branches of state, the bureaucracy is a fundamentally important aspect of governance. While elected officials dominate the legislature and put forward policy, it is the rank and file of the administration that sees it through. In Turkey particularly, the bureaucracy is the frontline in a political battle. Traditionally, Turkey's bureaucratic elite was dominated by middle- and upper-class secularists who hailed from the main cities. In recent years, the AKP is believed to have been altering this status quo, so that the administration of departments of state employs what they deem a more representative sample of the population. Allegations are rife that the government favours the hiring of new personnel who are more ideologically inclined towards the worldview of the AKP. This is problematic. It is legitimate to argue that, since a political party may stay in power for several terms, it should be permitted to appoint bureaucrats, on the basis of its popular mandate after an election. It would make sense to appoint people that the governing party can work with.[74] However, the reverse of this argument is that appointees should be based on merit, and be apolitical. This would lead to greater efficiency. A system based not on merit, but on political or ideological affiliation, is intrinsically undemocratic and allows a particular worldview to dominate and transcend the will of the electorate.

Several Turkish examples illustrate this point. In April 2007, the Education Ministry temporarily eased criteria for the appointment of school headteachers. During this short period, around 4,500 people across forty cities were appointed as either principals or deputy principals. Meanwhile, according to an Education Ministry report to parliament, 836 personnel from the government's Religious Affairs Directorate were transferred to Education. The impact was visible. During the month of Ramadan, the lunchroom no longer served food, indicating that the majority were pious, fasting during the holy month.[75]

Meanwhile, some analysts point to the AKP's Islamist origins as a factor in the dearth of women among the higher echelons of Turkey's bureaucracy, citing a joint report by the prime minister's Office of Personnel and IRIS, an Ankara-based women's rights group.[76] Political players consider the bureaucracy pivotal in controlling the state and influencing the central administration to maximise each player's own interest. This has most recently been played out in the struggle between the AKP and the Gulen movement, but has a legacy from the Kemalist period.[77] Meanwhile, former deputy prime minister Abdullatif Sener (2002–7) has stated his belief that most of the trade unions, associations and chambers became pro-AKP out of fear.[78] Such a climate is unhealthy in a democracy.

The Putsch and the Purge

Less than twenty-four hours after the failed military coup attempt of 15 July 2016, the government was already initiating a crackdown against the alleged perpetrators. The purge within the military included dozens of generals and admirals such as General Erdal Ozturk, commander of the Third Army; General Adem Huduti, commander of the Second Army; and Akin Ozturk, the former chief of air staff. All in all, by 17 July 6,000 within the military had been either dismissed or detained.[79] However, such action was not limited to the ranks of the armed forces. There were also 18,000 detained or dismissed from the ranks of the police and judiciary. In what appeared to be a witch-hunt against not just Gulenist sympathisers, but any perceived enemies of President Erdogan and the AKP, the arrests and sackings kept coming.

By 20 July, 35,000 public sector workers had been affected, including 15,000 education workers removed from their posts and 1,500 university deans "asked" to resign. Over 250 officials working at the prime minister's office were sacked, as well as 492 clerics at the Directorate for Religious Affairs.[80] But even this was just the beginning. On the same day, President Erdogan declared a three-month state of emergency, allowing the cabinet and the president to bypass parliament and decree laws, and to restrict rights and freedoms without being challenged by the Constitutional Court. As a result, Turkey temporarily suspended the European Convention on Human Rights.[81]

In the following weeks, the purges within Turkey's state institutions and societal organisations reached alarming levels. By 30 July, Turkey had cancelled the passports of 50,000 citizens in an attempt to prevent them from leaving the country.[82] 100 members of the medical profession were issued with arrest warrants (apparently for fast-tracking favourable medical reports for Gulenists entering the military). By August, 9,000 police officers had been fired, 21,000 private school teachers suspended from duty as well as over 10,000 soldiers, 2,700 members of the judiciary, 1,500 officials from the Ministry of Finance and 21,700 officials from the Ministry of Education, not to mention over 100 media outlets closed, with dozens of journalists arrested.[83]

By the end of the first week of August, a total of over 60,000 had been detained, investigated or suspended, and plans formed to shake up the country's intelligence agency.[84] At the time of writing, this number is set to continue rising. Also worryingly, just two days after the state of emergency was announced, it was decreed that the legal limit for detention would be increased from two days to thirty.[85] This has alarmed the international community and human rights organisations. Amnesty International claimed that it had credible evidence to suggest that detainees were being subjected to beatings and torture.[86] US and European officials have expressed their disquiet. US Secretary of State John Kerry called on Turkey to respect the rule of law in the aftermath of the coup. EU foreign policy chief Federica Mogherini echoed this concern.[87] After the state of emergency was declared, Mogherini called the measures against public sector workers "unacceptable".[88]

The attempted coup was condemned vocally by all parties represented in the Turkish parliament. In fact, there even appeared to be some semblance of mutual respect, with the AKP supporting and participating in a CHP rally against the attempted coup on 24 July at

Istanbul's central Taksim Square.[89] However, CHP leader Kemal Kilicdaroglu also warned that the purge risked becoming a witch-hunt against anyone critical of Erdogan or the government.[90]

Indeed, this appears to have happened already. By arresting such large numbers within state institutions extending to the spheres of education, the media, foreign affairs and the judiciary, opponents of the AKP, not just Gulenists, have been not just pacified, but all but crushed. The coup attempt has also paved the way for the president to receive extraordinary powers even before a new constitution has been enacted. For example, on 31 July 2016, it was announced that the Gendarmerie and Coastguard would be transferred to the Interior Ministry's remit, while the military would be brought under the direct jurisdiction of the Ministry of Defence.[91] It is no secret that Erdogan ultimately intends for the military to be brought under presidential jurisdiction, but since that would require a constitutional amendment, he was at this juncture unable to pursue it, lacking the necessary two-thirds majority in parliament to avoid a referendum. This announcement came just days after the police were given the right to carry heavy weapons.[92] The path was being laid for new constitutional changes even as Turkey was still reeling from the attempted coup. Erdogan himself stated just after the coup attempt was foiled that it was a "gift from God", promising to build a "new Turkey".[93]

The end result of the failed coup and ensuing crackdown has been that the government, and especially President Erdogan, have at once reached both unprecedented levels of popularity among the Turkish public, and unprecedented levels of power, further entrenching their hold on Turkish politics.

Gezi Park: Resisting Turkey's Majoritarianism

However significant the attempted coup may have been, there were already signs of significant opposition to the AKP government's majoritarian and authoritarian politics prior to its outbreak. During the early hours of Friday 31 May 2013, peaceful activists gathered to protest the demolition of a small park in central Istanbul. They were met with tear gas and police batons. Soon protests spread across Turkey's commercial capital to demonstrate against the heavy-handed tactics of the police, who only intensified their brutal crackdown. Protests spread through-out Istanbul and other Turkish cities. Soon the protests that would engulf Turkey during the summer of 2013 would become an outpour-ing of discontent against Erdogan and the AKP. Some commentators have argued that the protests were initially environmental in nature, and that the majority of participants were peaceful, young, apolitical and middle class, before being joined by some marginal violent groups.[94] But this is an oversimplification; Gezi Park attracted many diverse groups within Turkish society worthy of further examination. Indeed, the Gezi movement managed to unite people from a diverse range of backgrounds and lifestyles against the politics and rhetoric of the government, brought together by an environmental cause symbol-ising the people's demand for their voices to be heard.[95]

Around 41 to 49 per cent of the demonstrators had voted for the CHP, the main secular opposition party, in 2011.[96] However, as field-work has shown, many of these voters were reluctant CHP supporters, who voted as such due to a lack of alternatives. Meanwhile other par-ticipants in the protests did not identify themselves with the CHP, and voted for other parties. There were also many who did not identify with any mainstream party, were apolitical or had not voted at all.[97]

The make up of those present at Gezi was varied in other ways, too. The movement consisted of a multiplicity of social groups, from LGBT activists to football supporter associations known as *Carsi*. One of the *Carsi* with a significant presence was the Istanbul-based football team Besiktas. Their participation was in many respects organic, as the asso-ciation has no formal hierarchy; once one member joined the move-ment, others followed.[98] Indeed, the *Carsi* are an interesting phenom-enon. Although anarchist in nature, members of the association have been involved in political protests demonstrating against a wide range of causes, from nuclear power to the high cost of football tickets. A movement without an ideological political platform, its loose, autono-mous membership ranges from anarchists to Kemalists and even to AKP supporters.[99]

The *Carsi* were demonstrating together with environmentalists, LGBT campaigners, anti-capitalist Muslims, leftists and the apolitical. These different groups came together during the protests.[100] As many as 50 per cent had been involved in other protests.[101] Soon Gezi Park and neighbouring Taksim Square, where the protesters resided, not only became a place for political expression, but also an important shared space. Over the following days a library, a food court, a concert stage and even a prayer area were opened.[102] While environmental concerns were of course one of the main impetuses for the Gezi Park protests, they were not limited to Istanbul. Environmental activists in other Turkish cities were angered by how urban construction could transform their cities and lives without any consultation—this feeling of anger and marginalisation was then bolstered by images of police brutality.[103]

Umut Guner, general coordinator of Ankara-based LBGT organisation KAOS GL, says that while Turkey becomes more conservative under Erdogan's AKP, thanks to the EU accession process, other people speak up. In fact, they are obliged to make their voices heard. KAOS GL has over 2,000 members and over 20,000 followers on Twitter and Facebook. Their website, which has attracted 1.5 million unique visitors, is sometimes difficult to access. Gezi was an important moment for the LGBT movement, as it brought together many LGBT individuals from diverse backgrounds and political ideologies.[104]

The LGBT community faces serious difficulties in Turkey. In June 2014, the government took measures to separate gay prisoners, supposedly to protect them from harassment.[105] The then minister of women and family affairs, Aliye Kavaf, called homosexuality a "disease".[106] Gay and trans individuals in Turkey confront daily stigma, no recognition of rights to civil partnership and, at times, violence from the authorities.[107]

Protesting together with the LGBT campaigners was a perhaps unlikely group, the anti-capitalist Muslims. These pious individuals were prominent at Gezi and were particularly angry at the government because of its lack of commitment to tackling corruption, its involvement in capitalist enterprises, the repressive behaviour of the state, and its cooperation with international powers to oppress weaker states.[108]

During the Gezi protests a disproportionate number of Alevis were hurt or killed. Of the seven people killed, the majority were of Alevi origin. An offshoot of Shia Islam with aspects of Sufi mysticism, the Alevi faith is not recognised in Turkey. Brief talks in the context of the government's "Alevi opening" between 2008 and 2011 came to nothing. The community's main grievance is that its prayer houses, also known as Cem houses, do not have legal status as a place of worship. There is also concern over the increase of Sunni or anti-Alevi government rhetoric and symbolism, such as the perceived insult in the naming of Istanbul's third bridge after Selim I, who massacred many Alevis during the sixteenth century.[109]

Turkey's Kurdish south-east was relatively quiet during the Gezi Park protests, with no clashes between the military and the PKK; both sides were engaged in a tentative ceasefire and dialogue. Although the soon-to-be-established Peoples' Democratic Party (HDP) would try to ride the waves of the "spirit of Gezi", many Kurds were suspicious, asking where these protesters had been when Kurds were facing arbitrary arrests and police brutality.[110]

During the protests the police used tear gas and other chemicals, rumoured to be "agent orange" because of the colour, but in reality a less nefarious agent. The use of tear gas was so widespread that in Ankara, for example, whole squares could not be seen. Even if the police thought that these drastic measures were needed, they should have used these weapons sparingly and not directed them straight at people as sometimes they were. In terms of the chemicals used, the Ankara Association of Medicine has said that the Health Ministry should state what chemicals had been used and will be used in future cases.[111] The Istanbul Doctors Association declared that pepper gas was used as a weapon rather than a method of crowd dispersal.[112] Later, the police even arrested several doctors who had treated the injured, and a new law was passed making it illegal for doctors to administer emergency first aid without government authorisation or face a fine of up to nearly US$1 million and three years in prison.[113]

In the period since the Gezi protests, there has been a crackdown on the movement. Some of the activists, including minors, have had custodial sentences passed down for attending the demonstrations, while others face lengthy prison terms, including members of Taksim Solidarity, one of the main organising groups.[114] Parliament also passed stiff public legislation to allow the police to use firearms if it faced Molotov cocktails. Police would also be allowed to detain protesters for forty-eight hours and expand their searches, and Ankara-appointed governors were given the authority to order police investigations and detentions.[115] Meanwhile, Ankara has invested in further crowd control equipment, spending US$205 million on armoured water cannons in 2015, ten times more than in the previous year.[116]

There has been much comment on the nature of the Gezi Park movement. Some have contended that the protests were a reaction to secular worries about increased Islamic morality in Turkish life and public areas.[117] Others, noticing the youthful nature of the movement, have suggested that Turkey's young could represent new actors in Turkish political life.[118] However, this is not quite the case—Turkey's average age stands at around twenty, but only 22 per cent of those present were under this age. However, over one third of those present were students, and over half were university-educated.[119] Gezi represented a range of social forces disaffected with the rule of the AKP. Nine out of ten of those involved opposed the government's policies and believed that, at some stage in their lives, they had been treated unlawfully or had their human rights violated.[120]

What is clear about the Gezi protests is that the military, unlike during the 2007 "Republic Protests", was not involved in their organisation or development.[121] In other words, Gezi represented an organic, bottom-up social movement that represented the discontent of a great many citizens with the nature of AKP rule.

Twitter Tactics: A New Generation Against Majoritarian Politics?

In 1976, Saul Bellow, that year's winner of the Nobel Prize in Literature, criticised the media for producing news that fomented "crisis chatter". He argued that this filled the population with "anxious phantoms".[122] By crisis chatter, Bellow was referring to the everyday conversation of ordinary people. Conversations on nearly every subject, from race, sex and politics to the economy, were not transmissions of real knowledge or insight. Rather, Bellow said, they were reflections of reactions born out of crisis or turmoil within society. Bellow blamed the media as the guilty purveyor of such crisis chatter, transmitting and making news out of it, while informing readers, listeners and viewers not of the truth, but of illusions and shades of the real story.

Bellow's observation was not only insightful regarding the traditional media of the late twentieth century; it was also prescient, considering the state of the new media and the use of present-day social networks. This is especially the case in societies like Turkey where the traditional media is constrained by government censorship or self-censorship. With the dissemination of news limited to 140 characters, it is doubtful that any meaningful analysis or commentary is truly possible. Instead, readers and users are faced with sound bites on which they reflect, spread and comment. Virtual crisis chatter ensues over mere fragments of news pieces, emanating from cyberspace, citizen journalism or the traditional and new media. In other words, social networks become a breeding ground for crisis chatter because they are outlets for citizens of a society in turmoil to let off steam. Indeed, there is the risk that political issues reduced to a slogan will polarise society, as they appeal to emotional rhetoric.[123]

However, Bellow's insights are only partially true in the Turkish case. Turkey in the twenty-first century has seen several trends emerge to create a new political generation which is young, dynamic and Internet savvy. Thanks to the economic policies of the AKP, the majority of Turks today are middle class (around 59 per cent), according to a survey by market research company Ipsos KMG, using an OECD definition of those with a purchasing power of between US$10 and US$100 a day.[124] Turks are also young, with 24.5 per cent of Turkey's 76 million population aged zero to fourteen[125] and 17 per cent aged fifteen to twenty-four.[126] Meanwhile, over 72 per cent of the population live in urban areas.[127]

Despite this, as of 2014, Turkey ranks thirty-eighth in the Web Index Global Ranking, which measures Internet access, freedom and openness as well as its content and ability to empower.[128] This mediocre ranking is despite the fact that 69.5 per cent of Turkish households now have Internet access,[129] and Turkey has one of the world's largest numbers of social media users. It hovers between fourth and seventh for the most Facebook users in the world. It is Twitter's eighth largest market globally.[130] In one month alone in 2014, it was reported that 26 and 17 per cent of the entire country used Facebook and Twitter respectively, and 69 per cent of social media users are between the ages of nineteen and twenty-nine.[131] The Turkish nation spends an average of 10.2 hours a month on social networking websites, against a global average of 5.7 hours per visitor.[132]

Turkey's demographics indicate that over 40 per cent of the population is too young to remember a time of overt military interference in politics, such as the 1997 post-modern coup. This 40 per cent spent their formative years under the AKP, which witnessed a vast improvement in the economy, and they are from homes with a disposable income. They have also grown up in an information age, with access or close proximity in early adolescence to the Internet, including online social media. And, coming from an urban middle-class background, many young Turks expect rights and freedom of expression like their peers in the Western world. This has created a new generation with the ability to use information technology as a means for social change and even action, as well as a news source and a means of mass communication with their peers. This does not necessarily mean that Turkey's Twitter generation is political. But, as the Gezi Park protests indicated, when the freedoms that they take for granted are under threat, they can become a social force for mobilisation, either through street demonstration or simply by circumventing Internet bans with the use of proxies and Virtual Private Networks (VPNs), which for many is second nature.

Social media in Turkey has been utilised for communication by politicians, activists and ordinary citizens alike. With such high user rates, public figures have realised the utility of broadcasting messages on social networks. Virtually every political figure in Turkey uses forums such as Twitter to feed information into the public realm. However, the use of modern communications by the political elite is not in itself a new development. What is significant is that Twitter is not fully controlled by the state and exists beyond the scope of its full influence, although it may fudge boundaries in its acceptable usage to certain degrees.

Linked to the high usage of social media is the lack of trust in the traditional mainstream media. During the initial stages of the Gezi movement, it was widely acknowledged that some of Turkey's major print and broadcast news outlets did not air the mass demonstrations. Some of the initial hashtags on Twitter reflected this frustration, such as #BugünTelevizyonlariKapat (Turn off your television today).[133] According to *Turkiye* columnist Ceren Kenar, Twitter picks up stories that have been ignored by the mainstream media. It can even offer a form of accountability in the absence of free traditional media.[134]

The lack of state regulation on the use of social media in Turkey is an important factor in its usage for the purpose of social and political organisation. With Twitter uptake in Turkey hovering at around 12 million users,[135] the possibility that such social networks offer for political mobilisation and activism is tremendous. Indeed, activist groups ranging from LGBT organisations to environmental groups have utilised such channels to broadcast their messages, mobilise people power and monitor and report state attempts to prevent their activities. During the Gezi protests, it was through social media that protesters shared news updates, links to YouTube videos, photographs on Flickr and information about how to survive during the police crackdowns. Messages were tweeted and retweeted where offers to help were posted from hotels and cafes with food, shelter and water.[136]

Through Twitter, it was easy for the Gezi movement to spread information, share locations and keep organisations politically intact.[137] Live-stream also became a factor, with links to live images of Turkish streets shared on Twitter and Facebook. Over a three-week period during the Gezi protests, Livestream had 2.9 million Turkish viewers, an almost three-fold jump.[138]

As two NYU PhD candidates, Pablo Barberá and Megan Metzger, recorded, within one day there were at least 2 million tweets with hashtags related to Gezi, and 3,000 every minute during the first days of the protests. What is striking was that these social media posts were delivered from the ground, with 90 per cent of the tweets on the protests coming from within Turkey itself. This is a very high volume, especially when compared with other protests movements in the region; only 30 per cent of tweets about Tahrir Square during the protest period actually came from Egypt.[139] The strength of social media in action was palpable in the case of Erdem Gunduz. After Gezi Park and Taksim Square had been cleared of protesters, Gunduz staged his own special form of resistance, which made him known as the "standing man". Gunduz stood still at the central Istanbul square while facing the Ataturk Cultural Center, also threatened with demolition. After it was realised what he was doing, tweets started to circulate, and soon the "standing man" was joined by hundreds of other protesters.[140]

Another example of Turkish activists using technology is the Video Documentation Collection. This project was set up in 2000 to work as a news agency without interruption or selected editing, and filmed protests over the Kurdish issue and other social problems such as honour killings and conscientious objection to military conscription. In addition to its own filming of the Gezi Park protests, the group invited others who had taken snapshots or video footage on mobile devices to submit their material to be archived. The agency now has over 600 hours of raw video footage, a real visual archive. It believes that, contrary to the title of Gil Scott-Heron's famous song, "the revolution *should* be televised".[141]

Many Gezi protesters used social networks not only for internal communication but to direct medical attention to wounded demonstrators and to share locations of makeshift medical centres. According to Dr Ozden Sener, who was one of many medical professionals treating the wounded, social media "was like magic", because the injured could seek treatment without risking arrest by going to a state hospital.[142]

As we've discussed, the Arab Spring makes it clear that protesters using social media is a phenomenon far from unique to Turkey. However, the statistics cited earlier indicate the particular prevalence of social media on the ground during Turkish protests. Why are rates of usage during demonstrations so high? One reason is the uniquely Turkish form of social media known as *Sozluk*. Literally translated as "information (dictionary)", the *Eksi Sozluk* (Bitter Dictionary) was established in 1999 as a digital knowledge archive and resource built by its users. This was an important development for the Turkish online community. Not only could users develop accounts and contribute or create entries, but also it was a means of circumventing prohibition of free speech. By the time Facebook and Twitter were created in 2004 and 2006 respectively, Turks had already had vast experience in utilising such platforms, encouraged by increasing mistrust of the traditional media.[143]

Beat 'Em at their Own Game: Twitter and the AKP

The success of these social media tactics provoked a two-pronged response on the part of the authorities. On the one hand, the government tried to crack down on Twitter users. At the height of the protests, for example, then Prime Minister Erdogan commented that "social media is the worst menace to society".[144] The police took note, and two days later arrests were made in the large coastal city of Izmir, where twenty-five social media users were taken into custody because of the content of their tweets.[145] Later in June, the Turkish government requested that Twitter set up a representative office in Turkey in order for the state to maintain a tighter grip on its usage.[146]

On the other hand, astute parties also use social media—and this includes the ruling AKP. In the words of Ertugrul Kurkcu, former co-chairman and current honorary president of the pro-Kurdish HDP, "everyone has understood, if you don't know how to use them [social networks] you must find someone who does!"[147] The AKP and its rivals have been quick to recognise this and to harness online social networks such as Facebook and Twitter for mobilisation and communication. And indeed, youth does not necessarily mean that Turkey's Twitter generation is in opposition to the AKP government or Erdogan's policies. Those in support often take to social media to voice their solidarity with the government.

Although believing that the events of 2013 were manipulated by dissenting media, the AKP is very aware that the Gezi protests, the number of imprisoned journalists, and the corruption investigation have damaged the party's image.[148] Supporters are therefore turning to social media to defend its reputation. Perhaps no political party in Turkey yet uses social media to maximum effect. Still, they are all using it, with rising frequency.[149]

Some members of the government used Twitter to communicate directly with the protesters. One minister even took to the social media platform to explain the government's actions, and activists were able to question and challenge these assertions live in cyberspace. Such occurrences represent something of a paradox, because while some members of the government consider social networks a social menace, the government also uses the very same networks to counter its critics. Journalist Emre Kizilkaya even discovered that after the Gezi Park protests it became common for scores or even hundreds of commentators to attack scholars or journalists posting criticism of the government online. These pro-government users would mobilise, make offensive hashtags and encourage others to slur the critic. Meanwhile, it has been reported that the AKP has a 6,000-strong online volunteer team,[150] which has been particularly active in the run-up to elections, specifically the local elections of March 2014.[151] This force was created to

111

counter the government's online critics and to proactively set the agenda on social media through online groups such as "Wake Up Attack", associated with AKP's youth division.[152] Overall, those critical of the government on the Internet face pro-government trollers on the one hand, and state prosecution of posts considered "insulting" to the president on the other. Those arrested, prosecuted or sentenced have ranged from students and journalists to a former beauty queen.[153] Tweeting is not without its dangers.

Erdogan himself has a Twitter account, with a very impressive 9.3 million followers. The AKP mayor of Ankara, Melih Gokcek, also has a very respectable number of followers at around 3.5 million, and has himself written a staggering number of tweets—over 62,000. During the Gezi Park protests, Istanbul governor Huseyin Avni Mutlu, in a savvy move, gave out his personal telephone number on Twitter, offering to sit down with some of the demonstrators.[154] Indeed, to a limited extent, Twitter and other social media platforms have become a means not only for ordinary citizens and the political elite to broadcast messages to their own side, but for the two parties to communicate with one another. Politicians are aware of the popularity of social media and are increasingly developing social media strategies.[155]

Political use of social media has not been limited to a platform for politicians to engage with voters. The case of Deniz Baykal, former leader of Turkey's principal opposition party, raises a startling point. Baykal was forced to resign as leader of the CHP after a video was released and circulated on YouTube that purportedly showed him having an extra-marital affair. Baykal denied any wrongdoing and countered that he was a victim of a government-led smear campaign, allegations vehemently denied by Erdogan. However, in late March 2014, there was yet another leak of footage on YouTube, this time featuring none other than Erdogan himself, apparently ordering the Baykal recording to be transmitted. Now it was Erdogan's turn to claim victimhood. He stated that this recording was a deceiving montage and that he was actually calling for the Baykal video "to be withdrawn from the Internet". Unsurprisingly, YouTube was again banned for a couple of months following the release of the Erdogan video on the site.

Since Erdogan became president in 2014, more journalists, activists and, in some cases, even children have been tried or arrested on the grounds of insulting him. By August 2015, the number of those in court for insulting Erdogan reached an unprecedented 700. If one were to include cases against the press, the number reaches as high as 1000.[156]

Some examples are necessary to illustrate the severity of such cases for the defendant. Journalist Mehmet Baransu was sentenced to ten months in prison for insulting Erdogan on Twitter.[157] Bulent Kenes, former editor-in-chief of English-language Turkish daily *Today's Zaman*, was given a twenty-one-month suspended sentence for the same reason.[158] In December 2014, a sixteen-year-old student was arrested for insulting the president and spent two days in custody. He allegedly said, "we don't see Erdogan, the chief of corruption, bribery and theft, as this country's president but rather as thief Tayyip of the illegal palace."[159] Another student was sentenced at the age of twenty-three to fourteen months for calling Erdogan a dictator during the Gezi Park protests. He was put behind bars in March 2015. Following his request to take his exams at school, he was released sixteen days later.[160]

Social Media and the Attempted Coup

Some commentators have been quick to point out the apparent irony that, in order to defend against the allegedly Gulenist coup attempt of 15 July, President Erdogan and members of the ruling AKP took to social media, despite their suspicions of the phenomenon, used by political opponents to mobilise against them.[161] But this is an incorrect reading of the nature of Erdogan and his supporters' anti-coup activities. In reality, social media was barely a determining factor. Rather, it was the traditional television media and radio that played the most important role in defending against the coup, along with traditional means of mass mobilisation, most especially Turkey's network of mosques.

We have seen in Chapter 1 that, despite the putschists' attempts to cut off media outlets, Prime Minister Binali Yildirim and other cabinet members, past and present, were able to speak on television and radio channels such as the privately owned, government-friendly CNN Turk and NTV. They made pleas for citizens to resist the coup which, they stressed, was being orchestrated by a faction of the military acting against the chain of command. Erdogan was finally able to speak to the media, after a couple of hours of silence, in a live interview via FaceTime, which is not a social media outlet but an online telecommunications channel. Erdogan's presence was effective because it was broadcast live and repeatedly in the mainstream broadcast media. The president's message for the Turkish people to defy the junta's curfew and go out into the streets was heard loud and clear, especially after he had landed in Istanbul's Ataturk Airport, where he spoke again to the press and his supporters, this time directly. In other words, the traditional media played the leading role in galvanising opposition to the coup. Social media simply reflected the messages already being aired by the traditional media and therefore only played a supplementary role.

President Erdogan was once imprisoned for publicly reciting a poem written by the Turkish nationalist ideologue Ziya Gokalp, which read: "The minarets are our bayonets, the domes our helmets, the mosques our barracks and the faithful our soldiers." This brings us back to one of the main vehicles for mass gatherings of people on the streets to resist the coup, and another traditional source of mobilisation: the mosque.[162] During the events of 15–16 July and for weeks after, in addition to the five daily calls to prayer, messages were aired across Turkey's 85,000 thousand mosques rallying people to defend democracy against the coup plotters, either directly addressing worshippers or reciting the obligatory daily Sala prayer over and over.[163] For weeks after, messages against the coup and sporadic reading of the Sala prayer continued in mosques across the country, even after the attempted coup had been defeated. Later gatherings were facilitated by official circles, with municipalities offering free public transport and putting on entertainment and activities in the cities' public squares.

Many of those on the streets on 15–16 July were ordinary people, outraged by the military faction seeking to ouster their democratically elected government. But others were semi-organised groups, including some youth movements, loyal to either the AKP or the far-right Nationalist Action Party, who saw the attempted coup as their calling to defend their government. Some members of these groups were even armed. Some belonged to groups associated with political parties, such as the Heart of Ottoman, which had become a source of mobilisation for young supporters of the government during the Gezi Park protests.[164] It is worth recalling that during the Gezi period, Erdogan stated that for every 100,000 protesters against him, he would bring out 1 million in his support.[165] Taking action into their own hands, militant protesters attacked soldiers, often rank and file members unaware that their orders were not from the chain of command; they were beaten, lynched and, in one case, decapitated by an angry mob.[166] By utilising loyal media networks, the country's mosque networks and mobilising popular protest, the AKP and President Erdogan have managed to cement their hold over Turkish political life and marginalise their political opponents. The resistance to the 15 July coup attempt is not only the latest example of such action, but also a demonstration that the government can mobilise its support network on the ground to shore up its majoritarian political ambitions.

Internal Challenges?

With the increasing authoritarianism in Turkish politics, it is often wondered whether there is any credible challenge to Erdogan's power. Past election results would indicate not, unless that challenge comes from within the AKP, and it would seem that Erdogan's grip over the party is strong. However, there are some stirrings of discontent.

One of Erdogan's closest confidants is the head of the Turkish intelligence agency, Hakan Fidan. He resigned from his position to run as an AKP candidate in the 7 June 2015 elections. Fidan's resignation led to speculation that he might even become prime minister after the elections.[167] If true, this represented behind-the-scenes dissent within the AKP and Erdogan's inner circle. It is believed that Erdogan was not enamoured with Fidan's foray into politics. He even publicly stressed how vital the intelligence agency was to Turkey and that Fidan should not have resigned.[168] Following Erdogan's criticism, Fidan withdrew his candidacy and returned to his former position.

Hakan Fidan represents the younger generation of the AKP; he is close to Erdogan and a trusted ally.[169] Under Fidan, the National Intelligence Organisation became essential in the AKP's battle against the Gulen movement. National Intelligence was also involved in operations in Syria and was part of the secret talks with Ocalan and the PKK.[170]

According to *The Economist*'s then Turkey correspondent, Amberin Zaman, the dispute over Hakan Fidan's political career revealed rivalries within the AKP. According to her sources, Davutoglu did not like being Erdogan's puppet, and Davutoglu and Fidan have different approaches and ideas from Erdogan on issues such as the Kurdish problem and the Syrian conflict.[171] It is also an open secret that if Fidan had been elected to parliament, he would have been appointed foreign minister in Davutoglu's new cabinet.[172] M.K. Kaya believes that if he had managed to ascend to foreign minister, Fidan would have supported Davutoglu's position, tipping the balance of any conflict between the president and the prime minister in the latter's favour.[173] Regardless of the real reason, the Fidan incident has highlighted tensions within the upper echelons of the AKP.

However, this was not the first time there had been dissension. Old guards of the party such as former deputy prime ministers Ali Babacan and Bulent Arinc have come at odds with Erdogan. During the Gezi Park protest, Arinc, who was deputy prime minister at the time, expressed a position that appeared contrary to the party line: "government respects the right to non-violent protest and free speech, but that it must also protect its citizens against violence".[174]

Another sign of rivalry within the AKP became visible during the presidential elections of 2014. After his victory, Erdogan blocked Abdullah Gul from becoming head of the AKP. He set the date of AKP's general congress, which was to choose a new leader, for just one day before Gul's term had finished, preventing Gul from running himself.[175] According to the memoirs of Gul's chief press advisor, Ahmet Sever, Erdogan also tried to obstruct Gul's political career on two other occasions. The first was in 2007, when Gul wanted to run for president. The second was when Erdogan passed legislation through a parliamentary commission restricting the maximum presidential term in office to a single term, while Gul held that office.[176] In fact, Sever's book, *12 Years with Abdullah Gül*, gives more details about the deep discord between Erdogan and Gul. According to the book, which Gul approved before publication, Gul did not agree with the AKP's foreign policy on Syria and Egypt. In addition, Gul's opinion differed from Erdogan's over the Gezi protests. Gul's son brought ten friends to the presidential office who complained to his father of disproportionate police violence. In fact, the book's release date was very significant, hitting stores just as Erdogan was under pressure at home and abroad over his autocratic style, and Gul was being considered as a possible alternative.[177]

Nevertheless, opposing Erdogan is a risky business, as Davutoglu discovered when he found himself obliged to resign despite having led his party to election victory just six months prior. In a show of Erdogan's strength, Davutoglu's successor, Binali Yildirim, was the sole AKP candidate to replace him and was voted in by all 1,405 party delegates. Yildirim has thus far fulfilled expectations of taking his cue from the president.[178]

Regardless, despite challenges from both within and outside his party, Erdogan remains the most influential politician to lead Turkey since Mustafa Kemal Ataturk. His authoritarian style has not been detrimental to his popularity among his core support base. Meanwhile, after the July 2016 coup attempt, it is unlikely that there will soon be any challenges to Erdogan's rule, which, if anything, has been enjoying increased support.

Conclusion

Turkey's majoritarian politics is not a new phenomenon. It dates back to the earliest years of the Republic. It is also a representation of Turkey's turbulent political system, which can be and has been manipulated by key political players. The sometimes anti-democratic methods employed by the AKP have been put into place to address the imbalances of times past, when the judiciary and bureaucracy were dominated by secular republican elites under military tutelage. However, these overhauls have eroded Turkey's fragile system of checks and balances, and the deficiencies in Turkey's democratic system have been manipulated to give Erdogan and the AKP almost total control.

A system that was once dominated by the military now appears to be dominated by the AKP, led officially until August 2014 and since then unofficially by a charismatic leader with very strong paternalistic or authoritarian instincts, who has not only survived a violent challenge to his rule, but has thrived in its aftermath. This strength is supplemented by firebrand rhetoric that attempts to impose the will of the AKP's elected majority on the rest of Turkish society rather than seek consensus.[179] Nevertheless, there remain opponents to this authoritarian sway. There is a range of civil society movements and actors, young, digitally literate and often middle class, opposing and resisting Turkey's majoritarian system and the measures upholding it. But they are finding that the government they face is also becoming hi-tech savvy, utilising new media as well as traditional networks of mobilisation to extend its majoritarian outreach.

4

BREAKING THE NEWS

Introduction

The broadcasting of documentaries on television as large-scale demonstrations erupted in 2013, rather than coverage of the protests, has become a comedic symbol of the lack of press freedom in Turkey. However, press censorship is no laughing matter. These protests were the most important and vocal challenge to the rule of the AKP since it came to power in 2002. Yet, despite having the ability to report it, the vast majority of Turkish news outlets failed to cover a story that would have been seized upon by journalists in most democratic societies. It was only after public outrage that the media, which had been ignoring the protests' spread to many population centres across the country, started to feature them in news articles and broadcasts. Why did so many elements of the Turkish media fail to run the Gezi Park story as it broke?

The short answer is that the press in Turkey has never been fully free, open and fair. This chapter will explain the severe and systemic restrictions in place during the period of military tutelage. However, despite the armed forces being removed from political life, press censorship has intensified, not lessened, during the AKP years. Under the military, the press was severely curtailed, even compromised. While the erosion of the military's power is good for democracy, it is highly unfortunate that, instead of allowing the media to flourish, the government has manipulated it, co-opted it or attacked it fervently. The lack of a free and fair press in Turkey represents a significant democratic deficit. Not only does it prevent government accountability, but it also highlights severe restrictions on freedom of expression. The fear and self-censorship of the media diminishes the internal debate on Turkish politics and the direction of the country.

The Dynamics of the Turkish Media Landscape since 1980

The press in Turkey has faced restrictions and red lines ever since the birth of the Turkish Republic. However, this was particularly the case after the 1980 military coup and the 1982 military-drafted constitution, which superseded the constitution of 1961, also written after a coup. While it should be acknowledged that the 1961 constitution did actually extend press freedoms and guarantee civil liberties,[1] it still fell short of installing a fully independent and free media.

Under the post-1980 constitution (still in force), strict limitations were imposed. Particular articles were put in place which, supplemented by common law, prohibited the freedom of the press. For example, while Article 26 stated that "everyone has the right to express and disseminate his/her thoughts and opinions by speech, in writing, or in pictures or through other media", it went on to provide that "Regulatory provisions concerning the use of means to disseminate information and thoughts shall not be deemed as the restriction of freedom of expression and dissemination of thoughts as long as the transmission of information and thoughts is not prevented." However, the above passage was repealed in October 2001, and a later amendment brought the constitution in line with Article 10 of the European Convention on Human Rights (ECHR), which states: "The exercise of these freedoms may be restricted for the purposes of national security, public order, public safety".[2]

Other articles of the constitution are also ambiguous, overlapping with aspects of Article 10 of the ECHR. The constitution states that "The press is free, and shall not be censored" and that "The State shall take the necessary measures to ensure freedom of the press and information," but it also allows for the banning, with judicial notification, of reporting on events if they threaten the internal or external security of the state. Periodicals may also be suspended if they carry "material which contravenes the indivisible integrity of the State with its territory and nation, the fundamental principles of the Republic, national security and public morals".[3] These articles, despite seeming common characteristics with the ECHR, have enabled the press to be regulated and restricted, in conjunction with common law. For example, in November 1983, a press law was approved enshrining lengthy custodial sentences for journalists or editors who had published stories considered to have endangered public security or public morality. It also allowed for the temporary closure of the publication that printed the article.[4] This press law further permitted public prosecutors to halt the distribution of an outlet without a court order if it were deemed to be an "offence against the state", a somewhat vaguely defined phrase.[5]

If this were not enough, there were the added restrictions of the Turkish Penal Code. Some of the articles used during the 1980s to restrict the press (Articles 132 and 137) pertained to the publication of secret documents. Articles 161 and 162 were equally troublesome, as they related to publications that risked causing anxiety during times of war. Articles 192 and 268 were concerned with publications that could violate someone's wealth, honour, prestige or reputation and with the prevention of insulting a person in print. Article 426 restricted the publishing of pornography.[6] The broadness of these terms was fundamentally detrimental to press freedom.

Statutory law, too, played a part in hampering the openness of the press, including the Law on Crimes Against Ataturk, the Extraordinary Situation Law, the Law on the Introduction and Application of the Turkish Alphabet, the Law of Treason, the Law of Printing Presses, the Turkish Radio and Television Law[7] and, from 2005, the infamous Penal Code 301. This troubling piece of legislation allows for a person to be imprisoned for six months to three years if he or she "publicly denigrates Turkishness, the Republic or the Grand National Assembly of Turkey".[8] This raised international concern after the law was used to prosecute critically acclaimed authors of international standing such as Orhan Pamuk and Elif Shafak. It was also used against journalists; among these was Hrant Dink, editor of the Armenian-language weekly *Agos*, before his assassination in 2007.[9] Despite amendments to Article 301 in 2008, it remains vague and troublesome.[10]

The First Estate

There is more to press censorship than articles of law. It also concerns the nature of the relationship between the press and government, as well as the quality of news stories. Under Turgut Ozal, who was prime minister and later president during the post-coup neo-liberal period of the 1980s and early 1990s, there was increased sensationalism in Turkish journalism. Perhaps a sign of the times everywhere in the Western world, what seemed to be prioritised was profit, circulation and readership, as opposed to journalistic standards and factual accuracy.[11] This was particularly problematic in Turkey as, under Ozal's influence, not only were large corporations involved in the media, but also this state of affairs appeared to be encouraged by political patronage and support.[12] Ahmet Ozal, Turgut's son, became joint owner of the Uzan Group of STAR TV, Turkey's first private television channel, and by the 1990s, more privately owned channels were part of a portfolio of enterprises owned by large conglomerates.[13]

One consequence of this situation was a deepened relationship between media groups and politicians. During the 1995 elections, for example, a circulation war was waged between Turkey's main media groups through their flagship newspapers, *Hurriyet* and *Sabah*; each supported one of the main centre-right parties, the ANAP and the DYP respectively. The logic behind this was that if the two papers each picked a different political horse, the media group as a whole would have backed a winner. The only trouble was that neither party won in 1995—instead it was Necmettin Erbakan's Welfare Party.[14] Throughout the 1990s Turkey suffered political crisis after crisis, with six governments falling in nine years, making the support of the media highly desirable for political parties needing their influence every time the tables turned.[15]

The idiosyncratic relationship between the media and politics during the 1990s was highlighted by the common feature of leading columnists writing about their conversations with ministers and prime ministers over the phone or even at breakfast meetings.[16] In 1997 a columnist was even accused of blackmailing a minister to resign over allegations of corruption.[17] As Heper and Demirel cleverly put it, journalists had become the Second Estate in Turkish politics, after the politicians themselves.[18] Many observers went further and labelled the media Turkey's "First Estate".[19]

At times when they felt their interests could be jeopardised by the ruling party, media owners became vocal government critics.[20] This even contributed to the toppling of a government, during the 1997 post-modern coup ousting the Welfare Party's Erbakan as prime minister.[21] In this case, some media owners embraced the military's opposition to the Islamist prime minister, in order to maintain their political influence. Columnist Can Ataklı has explained that during this period newspapers even went as far as wording their headlines to suit the wishes of generals who were in effect setting the agenda and dictating the language of news stories.[22]

Politicians also attempted to heavily influence and steer media content by using the allure of state contracts in return for positive coverage. In the late 1990s, construction tycoon Korkmaz Yigit had bought two television stations and two national newspapers. He had also managed to gain a tender for the privatisation of the state-owned Trade Bank. However, soon Yigit found himself under arrest, after recordings were discovered of him discussing ways of eliminating other bidders for the Trade Bank tender with an infamous mafia figure. Yigit disclosed that he had actually been encouraged by Erbakan's successor, Prime Minister Mesut Yilmaz of the centre-right ANAP, and another minister to make his bid for the bank in exchange for favourable coverage. The revelation of this scandal contributed to the collapse of Yilmaz's coalition in 1999.[23] And, as we will see, this incident was not so dissimilar to later deals between the AKP and media owners.

Journalistic Quality and Censorship

Of course, media politicisation has a significant impact on the quality of Turkish journalism. To this day it is for the most part lacking, compared with that of many Western countries. Since the 1990s, it has been dominated not by reporters who transmit the news, but rather commentaries penned by self-interested journalists who like to "wear expensive watches and fancy suits like films stars". This is a long way from the real work of a journalist, who is supposed to speak truth to power.[24]

With several notable exceptions, journalistic standards in Turkey remain low. News reports often lack corroborative evidence. Instead, rumour and hearsay are prevalent, and become confused with verifiable facts and details that begin vaguely, "it has been announced" or "it has been claimed".[25] Just as importantly, it remains the case that politics has an influence on the content of stories and the work of journalists, because media owners consider political ties or commercial success more important than journalistic independence.[26] There is also no consensus on journalistic standards. Self-regulation and weak unions contribute to the low quality of reports, while financial remuneration is low.[27]

This sorry state of affairs is compounded by good old-fashioned censorship or, just as troublesome, self-censorship. Both have eliminated the press's ability to serve as a watchdog over government and other elected officials. This culture of self-censorship and even fear of reporting certain issues is pervasive in Turkish media. Journalists have been very aware of red lines in reporting the Kurdish question and obliged to turn a blind eye to human rights violations, especially during the 1990s when the conflict was at its height, or else risk facing the wrath of the armed forces.[28]

As Chapter 6 points out, an abundance of human rights violations were perpetrated by both sides, but especially by members of the military. There were many cases of murder, torture, depopulation and extra-judicial killing documented by different human rights groups. Although details of some of these crimes were reported outside of Turkey despite attempts to stifle them, some of the horrors of the Kurdish conflict did not reach news watchers and readers within the country, especially if they involved human rights abuses by the state, the military or its clandestine organs. Simply put, the Kurdish issue remained a taboo subject for journalists, especially reporters and commentators in the Turkish media. This was a subject regulated by the state, with lines drawn that journalists dared not cross for fear of imprisonment and other reprisals.

In fact, Human Rights Watch documented many instances of Kurdish journalists being killed, imprisoned and tortured by the Turkish state. Meanwhile, authorities banned or confiscated left-wing or pro-Kurdish journals including, but not limited to, *Ozgur Gundem*, *2000'e Dogru*, *Yeni Ulke*, and *Mucadele*. In the first six months of 1992 alone, Human Rights Watch reported, thirty-one journalists had been beaten with clubs, sticks or truncheons in twelve separate incidents. Some journalists had been tried and sentenced for their reporting under anti-terror laws that included nebulous terms such as "criticising" or "insulting" the president, public officers, Ataturk or the military, or for printing "anti-military propaganda", "praising an action proscribed as a crime" or publishing or distributing "separatist propaganda."[29] In other cases journalists were barred from reporting; in 1992, the town of Sirnak saw all but 2–3,000 of the town's 35,000 inhabitants abandoned due to fighting. In 1992 alone, thirteen journalists were believed to have been assassinated by special death squads.[30] A veteran journalist in the south-east region told the authors that he recalled a member of JITEM, the illegal counterterrorism unit of the Gendarmerie, putting a gun to his head and warning him to stop his story about an accused drug dealer affiliated with counterterror activities.[31]

The Media as a Government-Sponsored Organ under the AKP

A politically compromised media may not be a new phenomenon in Turkey, but this would reach new heights under the AKP. During the party's first term in government (2002–7), then Prime Minister Erdogan enjoyed unprecedented support from the media. This was much to do with the AKP's apparent acceptance of the secular state as well as its pro-EU stance and positive economic policies. Indeed, outlets such as the daily *Hurriyet*, owned by the Dogan Group, embraced the AKP as an antidote to Islamist politics and the declining Turkish centre.[32] As a result, in the early days of AKP rule, the Dogan Group, which has been compared with Rupert Murdoch's News Corp in terms of its power, became a significant beneficiary of AKP projects for privatisation.[33]

Soon, in a similar fashion to the 1990s, certain media organisations became central to the ruling party's strategy of advancing policy, as the government rewarded sympathetic media owners with other business interests, soft loans from state banks and lucrative state contracts. It was almost at the point where the television and newspaper coverage of some outlets was coming close to AKP propaganda.[34] This situation was different from the 1990s. Then, there were various competing political powers, making it possible to criticise the government.[35] But even today as in the '90s, the media was not a particularly profitable business, and needed to be buttressed with state contracts and loans for other business sectors in which media moguls also had ownership. This incentivisation, together with the AKP's monopolisation of political power, gave the AKP a level of influence over the media that its political predecessors could only dream of.[36]

During the first AKP term, several media companies became insolvent, were placed under the control of the Savings Deposit Insurance Fund (TMSF) and then changed ownership through public tenders.[37] Of particular note, the media outlets owned by the Ciner and Uzan groups were taken over by the TMSF and then sold to media owners more sympathetic to the AKP government. The Dogan Group, at that time on friendly terms with the AKP, was the main beneficiary. In September 2005 it took over Uzan's Star TV, making the Dogan Group Turkey's dominant media organisation. Then, in December 2007, Ciner's *Sabah*-ATV group was acquired by Calik Holding, whose media branch was led by none other than Erdogan's son-in-law. This was despite the fact that initially Calik was unable to fund the deal. No bother, two state-owned banks provided the necessary funding.[38]

These types of deals were not limited to the Calik and Dogan groups. Other media owners sympathetic to the AKP, such as Akın Ipek, Ethem Sancak and Fettah Tamince, also obtained newspapers and television stations through AKP patronage. Sancak was able to buy Uzan's *Star* newspaper from the TMSF and establish the Kanal 24 television channel.[39] Sancak did not even hide his affiliation with the government. He later stated that he was on a mission to serve the AKP and Prime Minister Erdogan.[40] When he faced financial difficulties with his new media acquisitions, it was Fettah Tamince, also closely associated with Erdogan and his then ally Fetullah Gulen, who fronted the cash.[41] It was a similar story with Akın Ipek, who owned the daily *Bugun*. He later was able to purchase television channel KanalTurk. After the purchase, it was no longer a staunchly Kemalist and anti-AKP outlet.[42]

On the other hand, disloyalty to the AKP was met with wrath and there was literally a very high price to pay if media owners fell out of favour with the government. They faced heavy-handed financial sanctions, including crippling tax fines. The Dogan Group is a particular case in point. Although close with the AKP during its first term, during the party's second term (2007–11) this would change dramatically. In April 2008, the Ministry of Finance took the unprecedented step of conducting a large-scale tax inspection of companies under the Dogan portfolio. This resulted in a penalty for Dogan that was worth around US$490 million. This was just the beginning. In 2009, another fine was issued, this time worth US$2.5 billion. To put the scale of this sum into perspective, its total was the equivalent of over four fifths of the market value of the whole Dogan Group.[43] The onslaught against the group did not stop there. Custodial sentences were given to the publisher Aydin Dogan and *Hurriyet*'s editor-in-chief Ertugrul Ozkok, as well as several other executives.[44] According to former deputy prime minister Abdullatif Sener, Erdogan personally ordered politically motivated tax inspections against the party's opponents.[45]

These fines against the Dogan Group do not merely reflect a problem over free speech, but also the complex and dangerous nexus between corporate interest, the media and the government. The conflict between the AKP and the Dogan Group emerged because Erdogan had refused to grant the group permission to build a refinery for petrol in the town of Ceyhan, located at an important intersection between pipelines.[46] Instead Erdogan apparently handed the contract to the Calik Group, headed by one of his associates.[47]

Also, in 2005, the Dogan Group had bought the Hilton Hotel during the AKP's privatisation period. The group's plans to build plots of residential compounds on the site were refused by local authorities dominated by the AKP. The Dogan Group retaliated through its newspapers, focusing on a story about a German corruption court case involving a Turkish-German charity that allegedly had contacts with members of the AKP. Erdogan accused the Dogan Group of using its papers to smear his government and even called for a boycott of the Dogan Group's media outlets.[48] The Dogan Group also had to face other economic pressures, including permits and licenses being delayed or withheld, and the AKP calling on businesses not to advertise in the group's media outlets.[49]

The AKP's interference in the media continued after the party's third electoral victory, in 2011. Outlets once again changed hands through the TMSF, in favour of pro-government owners. The Cukurova Group's television channel, Sky360, and its *Aksam* newspaper were both considered for ownership by the Kolin-Limak-Cengiz consortium, which later won the tenders for Istanbul's controversial third airport and third bridge.[50] In the end, the consortium decided not to go ahead with the purchase, and the two outlets were instead sold to Ethem Sancak for US$62 million.[51] The interesting circumstances surrounding the consortium's withdrawal were finally revealed after the December 2013 corruption investigation, when several recordings were leaked over the Internet indicating that Binali Yildirim, then minister of transport, and Bilal Erdogan, the son of the prime minister, had counselled the consortium to drop Sky360 and *Aksam* in favour of *Sabah*-ATV outlets.[52]

While the media sector in Turkey is hardly profitable in itself, it is an attractive investment, because pro-government coverage offers the possibility of being rewarded with contracts and tenders in other sectors. For instance, despite the fact that *Sabah* newspaper's finances were in quite a bad state in December 2013, with a deficit of US$73 million in 2012 and US$37 million in 2013,[53] the *Sabah*-ATV group was bought in December 2013 by the Kalyon Group, a major player in the construction industry and a partner of the Cengiz-Limak-Kolin consortium on the third bridge and airport projects.[54] Again, following the corruption investigation, it was alleged that Kalyon had formed a syndicate with the consortium to purchase *Sabah*-ATV.[55] Despite this backroom dealing, the press found itself unable to report on the matter; the courts soon imposed a black-out on covering the corruption investigation. In fact, Turkey's High Council for Telecommunications (TIB) went so far as to demand the deletion of a call for an inquiry from the personal webpage of opposition MP Umut Oran, who submitted the request for an inquiry to parliament, citing codes of conduct for purchasing media groups.[56]

There is one example even more disturbing than these dubious media transactions and business links. Cukurova Group's last remaining outlet was Show TV. On 24 May 2013, it was sold to Turgay Ciner, in the absence of a public tender.[57] The fact that the Ciner Group was the beneficiary of this deal was no great shock. After some of its media outlets were confiscated by the TMSF in 2007, the group established new ones that completely avoided criticism of the AKP. The Ciner Group had also, in 2012, become the proud owner of Kasımpasa Sports Club (Erdogan's home team; he is a keen supporter) and, for good measure, had appointed a friend of the prime minister, Mehmet Fatih Sarac, to the board of both the media group and the football team.[58] A leaked tape that surfaced after the December 2013 corruption investigation revealed that Erdogan had intervened directly in broadcasts by the Ciner Group-owned Haberturk TV and had ordered Sarac to cease airing a speech by Nationalist Action Party leader Devlet Bahceli criticising the government. Erdogan later confirmed that it was indeed his voice on the tape. In another recording, Erdogan tells Sarac to remove a news ticker that quoted Bahceli on the Gezi Park protests of June 2013.[59]

Another tape leaked after the 17 December corruption scandal was alleged to be a recording of Erdogan telephoning his son, Bilal, to instruct him to hide US$1 billion in cash in anticipation of a police search. The entire series of leaked tapes, believed by many to be a Gulenist move against the government following their rift, broke Turkish YouTube viewer records, reaching around two million listeners within a day.[60] This incident showed just how polarised the Turkish media had become. The pro-Gulen media, the Dogan Group (by now out of favour) and some smaller opposition outlets, were highly critical towards the government. However, pro-AKP outlets such as *Sabah*, Star TV, *Yeni Safak* and *ATV* were critical of the Gulen movement and portrayed Erdogan as a victim. The Ciner Group tried to stay out of it, not wanting a dispute with either Gulen or Erdogan, but a later leaked recording purported to reveal that Ciner personally told Fetullah Gulen that his "newspaper will never publish a story which would compromise you ... I shall never allow a piece which might embarrass His Eminence."[61]

In a reversal of the 1990s, under the AKP the media even had a hand in reducing the power of the military. During the Ergenekon and Balyoz investigations, media outlets associated with the AKP and the Gulen movement (which had not yet fallen out at that time) were central in shaping the way these alleged coup plots were reported.[62] The investigations themselves were triggered by stories featured in the pro-AKP and anti-military daily *Taraf*.[63]

What is particularly disconcerting is that, in an electoral democracy, even the state media has become an organ of government, rather than an impartial outlet representative of all Turkish viewpoints. The national public broadcaster, TRT, would toe the government line and dedicate many hours to speeches by AKP officials, ten times more than the airtime given other political parties. This was particularly the case in the presidential elections of August 2014. In the run-up to the vote, a report compiled at the request of an opposition figure by Turkey's regulator RTUK found that between 4 and 6 July, TRT devoted 533 minutes to Erdogan, but just three minutes and forty-five seconds to opposition candidates Ihsanoglu and Demirtas respectively.[64] This so angered Demirtas of the pro-Kurdish HDP that he used his airtime to criticise not his electoral rivals, but TRT itself, quipping, "I am excited and happy to address you on the screens of a precious institution like TRT, which as you all see is very objective and impartial and takes an equal approach to all presidential candidates".[65]

Similarly, RTUK reported that during the last month before the June 2015 elections, the AKP was given 54.4 hours of airtime on TRT. Erdogan was broadcast speaking for forty-five hours, while the CHP was given a mere fourteen. The Nationalist Action Party and the HDP got 14 hours and 7.5 hours respectively.[66] But it should be noted that even RTUK's impartiality has long been a source of concern for the EU; in its 2013 progress report,[67] the European Commission reminded RTUK that nine of its members were elected by parliament—though parliament is, of course, dominated by the AKP. Meanwhile, a 31 July report by the Organization for Security and Co-operation in Europe (OSCE) highlighted its concern about manipulation of the media on the presidential campaign trail.[68]

Overall, the AKP's dominance in the media has been to the detriment of universal journalistic standards. Award-winning journalist Nedim Sener, for example, takes a dim view of his profession and bemoans the results of a recent survey, which found that only 19 per cent of the Turkish public trust the media, while trust of the government was as high as 33.5 per cent, even after the 2013 corruption allegations.[69]

The Fear Factor

Despite the press restrictions, a period of general democratisation characterised the AKP's first and to some extent second terms. The impetus behind this was both entry into the EU and reducing the power and influence of the military. The AKP built on the precedence of democratisation packages launched in 2001 and introduced a wave of further measures to bring Turkey in line with European standards. This and the military's decline in political affairs initially had a positive effect on the freedom of the press as some issues that had been taboo, including the Kurdish question and the Armenian massacres of World War I, were more openly discussed.

Some subjects remained gagged by enduring legislation. Nevertheless, although there were significant issues concerning the relationship between the AKP and media owners, overall during the party's first term, the government was for the most part compliant with the media, perhaps in an attempt to prove its secular and democratic credentials to the intelligentsia, military and judiciary.[70] However, as we have seen, this was short-lived. The promise of openness eroded during the AKP's second term in office and especially in its third.

Media restrictions of past years came back into force, with reporters being arrested and imprisoned for the content of their stories. Soon Turkey became one of the world's leading prisons for journalists, with numbers comparable with China—somewhat embarrassingly, for a country with EU aspirations that claims democratic values. Several journalists found themselves imprisoned because of investigative articles or books written about the inner workings and aspirations of the then government-aligned Gulen Movement. Other journalists, particularly those of Kurdish origin, found themselves in trouble with the authorities on flimsy charges that either they themselves or their outlets were affiliated to the PKK or other designated terrorist groups.

Politicians within the government, and especially the prime minister and president, would openly criticise and condemn media reporters and pundits if they criticised policy decisions, Erdogan's conduct or the party's activities. Reporters or commentators would find themselves denounced in the prime minister's addresses or even directly telephoned by the prime minister or his staffers. Editors had a similar experience. This was not limited to the naming and shaming of media personnel. Erdogan and other AKP politicians would directly lean on media bosses to fire reporters or commentators deemed to be critical.

Journalists became a target of the Ergenekon investigation, with many arrested, especially those of secular orientation. By 2012, over 100 journalists had been arrested over allegations that they were part of a "deep state" conspiracy.[71] By August 2013, over twenty journalists had received sentences for their alleged involvement in the Ergenekon coup plot. Some were prominent and well known, but this did not stop them from receiving lengthy sentences.[72] Unfazed, the minister for EU affairs, Egemen Bagis, argued on the BBC's *Hardtalk* that no Turkish journalist had been imprisoned for practising his profession. Those journalists in jail, he insisted, had been convicted of wildly implausible crimes such as murder, bank robbery or sexual assault.[73]

In 2011, a Turkish court ordered the arrest of two prominent journalists, Nedim Sener and Ahmet Sik, under the spurious charge of being part of the Ergenekon organisation.[74] Sener had released a book entitled *The Dink Murder and Intelligence Lies*, which argued that officers connected with the Ergenekon network had also been involved in the murder of Armenian journalist and newspaper editor Hrant Dink. Sik, another investigative journalist, had written *The Imam's Army*, an inquiry into the activities of Fetullah Gulen and his followers, then in a close alliance with the AKP. Even before the book was published, a draft had been confiscated and banned (later defied by a publisher who printed it under a different name).[75] Eventually these journalists were released the following year pending trial. These developments did not seem to bother Prime Minister Erdogan. Amid growing concerns over freedom of the press in Turkey he, like Bagis, said that none of the journalists were arrested because of their work.[76] However, the European Court of Human Rights begged to differ. In July 2014, the ECHR ruled that the rights of Sener and Sik had been violated, that their lengthy detentions without reasonable cause had led to censorship in Turkey, and that Turkish courts unjustly created a connection between books criticising the government and a terrorist organisation. As a result Turkey was ordered to pay the journalists compensation.[77] Following the ruling, Sener aptly commented that "journalism is not terrorism and books are not bombs," a play on the words of Erdogan himself, who had likened Sener's book to a bomb in a 2011 interview.[78]

In a taste of things to come, after the 2010 constitutional changes, Erdogan himself convened a meeting of different media representatives to tell them of his own set of principles under which the media should operate.[79] Erdogan stayed true to his word. He criticised columnist and TV host Nuray Mert for her criticism of the government's policy towards the Kurds. Erdogan publically called her "despicable", using a play on words to change her surname, meaning brave and honest, to "Namert", which implies treason. Soon not only was she forced to leave her position at NTV, but she also received a barrage of threatening abuse and insults from the public, as well as having her phone tapped. Not long after, she was told by her bosses at the daily *Milliyet* that she should "take a break".[80]

Mert's experience is just one of several. Ece Temelkuran, a highly regarded and read journalist and columnist, was fired from her position at *Haberturk* in 2012 for her criticism of the government's handling of the Uludere massacre, in which thirty-four Kurdish smugglers were killed in an aerial raid. This came several months after Erdogan had convened media owners for a meeting where he stated that terrorism stories should be treated with more "sensitivity" and responsibility.[81] Meanwhile, Hasan Cemal of the *Milliyet*, "stepped down" over his story on secret contacts between government emissaries and imprisoned PKK leader Abdullah Ocalan. Erdogan had reportedly commented, "If this is journalism, down with it!"[82] It is not only journalists writing in the critical press who face censorship. Those who write for the pro-AKP outlets are also under pressure and engage in auto-censorship, knowing the editorial boundaries that they should not cross.[83] According to former deputy prime minister Abdullatif Sener, while he was a member of the government he recalled Erdogan personally ordering some reporters to be fired because of their stories.[84]

When the US ambassador to Turkey, Frank Ricciardone, broached the subject of detained journalists in 2011, especially in relation to the Ergenekon case, Erdogan simply dismissed him as a "a rookie ambassador."[85] If that were not enough, in another tirade against the press just ahead of the August 2014 presidential elections, Erdogan mixed the extra ingredient of misogyny into his outburst against *Economist* and *Taraf* reporter Amberin Zaman. He called her a "shameless woman", a "shameless militant disguised under the name of a journalist"[86] and, for good measure, added that she should "know your place".[87] Her only crime was to ask the opposition leader in an interview an interesting question about whether Muslim societies were capable of challenging authority.

Meanwhile, Erdogan has used litigation as a means to suppress freedom of expression in the media. For example, in 2005 he sued the publisher of the satirical magazine Penguin for depicting him as a series of animals in a cartoon. The following year, he sued left-wing publication *Gunluk Evrensel* and its columnist Yucel Sarpdere for defamation over an article twisting the lyrics of a popular AKP song to criticise the prime minister's anti-corruption policies. Erbil Tusalp of the left-leaning *Birgun* was also sued because she wrote an article that accused the AKP of being increasingly authoritarian. Veteran journalist Ahmet Altan, editor-in-chief of the daily *Taraf*, was sued twice (the first case in 2011 was dropped, but another was brought in 2012) for calling Erdogan a bully and then later "arrogant, uninformed, and uninterested".[88] The campaign of intimidation was so effective that it was not journalists who publicised some of the leaked tapes alleging corruption at the highest levels, but rather politicians, who had parliamentary immunity. Clearly, the ability of journalists to break the news has been hampered.[89] There has also been an effect on the integrity of their profession and the propensity to self-censor. Not only their profession is at stake, but also their livelihoods.[90]

Another side to media censorship in Turkey is its link with the Kurdish problem. Just as the Turkish media faced restrictions in its ability to report on the state's conflict with the PKK during the 1980s and 1990s, under the AKP an acute means of press restriction has developed of linking Kurdish journalists to outlawed Kurdish organisations such as the PKK and the KCK. By August 2012, around 70 per cent of journalists jailed in Turkey were Kurdish, charged with aiding terrorists because their stories covered the views or activities of these organisations. Among the journalists who have faced such charges are reporters and editors from the Kurdish daily *Azadiya Welat*, including its editor Ozan Kilinc, and the Dicle News Agency and its reporter Hamdiye Ciftci. According to findings by the non-profit Committee to Protect Journalists, through vague definitions in anti-terror legislation, the Turkish government was conflating journalists reporting the attitudes of outlawed groups such as the PKK with assisting such organisations.[91]

The crisis of the Turkish media became increasingly apparent during the Gezi Park protest of 2013. Not only did many media outlets fail to cover the waves of unrest that gripped Istanbul and other major population centres across the country, but to add insult to injury they instead aired Erdogan speeches, or wildlife documentaries. This shocked many Turks as the full scale of government media control was realised. Soon protesters spread their demonstrations to the headquarters of media outlets in protest of their initial lack of coverage.

Despite this, what is also disconcerting is the government onslaught against the media in the aftermath of the protests, especially for those outlets and journalists that did cover the demonstrations or were critical of the government. According to the Turkish Union of Journalists, fifty-nine colleagues were either dismissed or forced to leave in the wake of the protests. The opposition CHP put the number at seventy-seven. However, it could even be higher, as NTV-owned history magazine *NTV Tarih* was shut down entirely. The government, on the other hand, has said that there is no proof that these losses were related to the Gezi Park coverage.[92]

Turkish government or presidential attacks on journalists have also extended to the international media. *The New York Times* published a highly critical editorial on attacks against the press, specifically Erdogan's launching an investigation against the *Hurriyet* newspaper for its headline "The world is shocked! Death sentence for president who received 52 per cent of the vote", on the grounds that the Turkish daily was making a veiled attack against him (the headline and story were actually about events in Egypt). Erdogan responded by labelling the *New York Times* journalists "paid charlatans" and telling the newspaper's staff, like Amberin Zaman, to "know your place".[93] *The Guardian* also felt Erdogan's wrath after he (incorrectly) accused the newspaper of writing that "poor Muslims who are not entirely Westernised cannot be allowed to rule their countries on their own".[94] Not only was this inaccurate, but *The Guardian's* request for an apology[95] went unheeded.

Turkey's broad anti-terrorism laws have created an increasingly difficult environment not only for Turkish journalists, but also for international reporters. In January 2015, a Dutch journalist, Frederike Geerdink, was detained in Diyarbakir on charges of spreading PKK propaganda. She was eventually released after a strong response from the Dutch foreign minister, who was visiting Turkey at the time.[96] In August 2015, while covering fights between ISIS and the PKK, two British reporters and a translator from *Vice News* were arrested on the charges of "working on behalf of a terrorist organisation".[97]

In the aftermath of the government's fallout with the Gulen movement, affiliated outlets were targeted for closure or seizure. In

December 2014, Turkish police detained twenty-three people including journalists, producers, screenwriters and directors after a raid on opposition media outlets with close ties to the movement. Four people, including Samanyolu Broadcasting Group general manager Hidayet Karaca, were arrested on charges of forming and leading an armed terrorist organisation.[98] In March 2016, Turkey's highest-circulation newspaper, *Zaman*, was seized after a court order ruled that it should be under the administration of a panel appointed by the court. After the authorities had dispersed protesters, the following day, the newspaper toed the government line.[99]

Gulen-affiliated outlets have not been the only target. Two *Cumhuriyet* columnists, Ceyda Karan and Hikmet Cetinkaya, face up to four and a half years in prison for their republication of a cover image of the Prophet Muhammad from *Charlie Hebdo*.[100] Erdogan also openly threatened the editor-in-chief of *Cumhuriyet* newspaper, Can Dundar, for publishing a report that Turkey had sent arms to rebels in Syria, warning that he would "pay a heavy price". Erdogan kept his word; soon Dundar and his Ankara bureau chief Erdem Gul were arrested and incarcerated.[101]

Switching off the Internet

As a result of Turkey's lack of free press, many get their news from the Internet, notably from social media. After years of press restrictions, this was particularly the case in 2013, during and after the Gezi Park protests, and after the corruption investigation: the leaked tapes found their way onto the Internet, but not into the mainstream media. However, particularly under the AKP, social media, like traditional media, has been subject to severe restrictions, even when it has not been directly political.

In February 2014, President Abdullah Gul approved a new bill tightening restrictions on Internet usage. The original bill as passed by the National Assembly would have allowed the TIB, the High Council for Telecommunications, to block Internet material within four hours without needing a court order in the first instance. The law also required Internet providers to store data on web users for a two-year period and make it available to the authorities if requested.[102] It was drawn up following the aforementioned corruption scandal that shook the AKP. Gul's approval of the new Internet law was subject to amendments requiring a court order to access Internet traffic data, and, if access was blocked to online material on privacy grounds, a court order to uphold the block within twenty-four hours.[103]

After the bill was passed and signed into law by Gul, he—perhaps ironically—announced it on his Twitter account.[104] Police in Istanbul fired water cannon and tear gas at hundreds protesting the bill in Istanbul.[105] Gul's signing was a particular blow, as it had been hoped that the president would resist the new legislation. Disappointed social media users took to "unfollowing" him on Twitter.[106] According to a report by Reporters Without Borders, this new legislation, particularly in its pre-amendment form, would force Internet service providers to become "instruments of censorship and surveillance", as they would face losing their licenses if they did not join and install the surveillance tools demanded by the authorities and surrender data on demand.[107]

However, this has just been the latest development in Turkey, where Internet freedom has always been restricted. Freedom House's "Freedom on the Net 2013 Report" listed Turkey as only partly free, with a rating of 49 out of 100 (three points better than the previous year). The report noted social media and apps being blocked, bloggers and social media users being arrested and political and social content also being blocked. The report noted that almost 30,000 websites had been blocked and highlighted the case of Fazil Say, the Turkish pianist and composer who was given a ten-month suspended sentence for insulting religious values on the basis of a Tweet.[108]

The legislation approved by Gul was itself an amendment to Law No. 5651, which had come into effect in July 2007 and is widely referred to as the Internet Law. This law built on the two laws regulating Turkish media, the Press Law of June 2004 (5187) and the Law on the Establishment of Radio and Television Enterprises and Their Broadcasts, which cover print media and TV and radio broadcasts respectively.[109] For several years Turkey's Internet had been a "largely free medium", but this began to change in 2005 with a series of laws culminating in the 2007 Internet Law.[110] Section 8 of this legislation allowed a court to block any website where there was "sufficient suspicion" that a crime had occurred. The government's main concern was the availability of defamatory material, particularly in videos, against Ataturk.[111]

Since the passing of the Internet Law, thousands of websites have been blocked, including popular sites such as YouTube, DailyMotion, Google Sites, Farmville and Geocities, through either court orders or administrative blocking orders via the TIB.[112] According to Freedom House, in many instances these shutdowns represented "blunt efforts to halt circulation of specific content that is deemed undesirable or illegal by the government".[113] This was in stark contrast with the period between 2000 and 2007, when only a few blocking orders were made through the courts to prevent access to certain websites. After 2007 the hugely increased number of blocked websites included sites reporting events in south-east Turkey and Turkey's online LGBT community, as well as social network sites such as MySpace. By March 2014, over 40,000 websites had been banned in Turkey.[114]

The Internet Law drew wide criticism. The EU's progress report on Turkey for the year 2010 was blunt, stating that "Law No. 5651 on the Internet limits freedom of expression and restricts citizens' right to access information" and that it appeared not to be in line with international standards.[115] In 2010, Reporters without Borders added Turkey to the "list of countries under surveillance" in terms of Internet freedoms. In the following years, the EU's progress reports stated that Turkey's Internet law needed to be revised.[116] To a certain extent even Turkey's ruling echelons were aware of the absurdity of the Internet Law, which led to some of the world's most popular websites being blocked to Turkish users, although many found proxy servers or VPNs to bypass the restrictions. In June 2010, President Abdullah Gul himself used his Twitter account to announce that he did not endorse blocks on YouTube and Google.[117]

On 18 December 2012, the European Court of Human Rights ruled that it was a violation of the right to freedom of expression to block access to an entire online platform. Ahmet Yildirim, a Turkish national who maintains a website hosted by webpage creation tool Google Sites, had brought the case after his website, which he used to publish his views, opinions and academic work on a range of subjects, was blocked for insulting Ataturk. So was all of Google Sites.[118]

This did not stop the AKP government from simply ignoring the court's decision; it continued to enforce the ban under the 2007 Internet Law until new Internet legislation was introduced in 2014.

Turkey did lift its ban on YouTube in October 2010, but only after the videos that were considered insulting to Ataturk had been removed. Although YouTube has stated that it was not involved in deleting the offending videos, it was later discovered that a third party had managed to remove them by making a copyright complaint.[119] It was only the removal of these videos, not any commitment to freedom of expression, that induced the government to lift the ban.

Despite this relative easing of Internet restrictions, the ruling government once again clashed with the online community after the Gezi Park protests of summer 2013. It should be recalled that this was when Erdogan called Twitter a social menace. If Erdogan thought online media was a problem during the protests, this soon became the least of his worries. Following the corruption scandal in December, leaked audio footage surfaced indicating corruption and embezzlement within Erdogan's inner circle. Much of the audio was widely circulated in Turkey through social media outlets and video and streaming websites. It was in the context of dealing with this scandal, ahead of local elections, that the AKP passed the new Internet legislation of February 2014, enabling authorities to get webpages blocked within hours, and without a court order. The embattled prime minister then felt confident enough to threaten to ban such outlets, though President Gul ruled this out.[120]

Regardless, with such legislation now in place, the prime minister was ready to use it. During a campaign speech in Bursa, Erdogan not only threatened to ban Twitter, but added that he did not care about the international response and declared that "everyone will see how powerful the Republic of Turkey is". Dismissing Twitter as "Twitter, mwitter", he added, "We will wipe out all of these no matter what the rest of the world has to say about it".[121] Hours later, Twitter was blocked.[122] This move backfired as Turks, in the most widespread act of civil disobedience in modern Turkish politics, simply circumvented the ban, with levels of 17,000 Tweets. Twitter users also mocked the prime minister, while others of his own party, such as President Gul and Deputy Prime Minister Bulent Arinc, continued to tweet, even deeming the shutdown "unacceptable".[123] Later, after the leaking of further tapes—this time of top-level Turkish officials including ministers proposing contentious tactical military action in Syria—YouTube was temporarily banned. Again, users turned to VPNs for continued access.

The international condemnation of both bans was swift and forth-right. Amnesty International called it a "draconian measure" that limited freedom of expression and "shows the lengths the government is prepared to go to prevent anti-government criticism".[124] In a scathing condemnation, the US State Department called it "twenty-first-century book burning".[125] Stefan Fuele, European Union Enlargement Commissioner, commented that the Twitter ban cast doubt on Turkey's commitment to European values. Similar sentiments were expressed by Germany, and the British Foreign Office added that social media was vital for modern democracy.[126]

Although the move was initially justified as being the result of court orders, there is no specific court order that could have legitimately allowed for a blanket national shutdown of Twitter. The new Internet laws, as the European Court of Human Rights had ruled, do not allow the blocking of an entire social media platform. Quite tellingly, the TIB imposed the ban mere hours after Erdogan had announced his intention to "root out Twitter". Yaman Akdeniz, a professor of law at Istanbul's Bilgi University, commented that the TIB had acted on an assumption of authority and that the resulting shutdown was illegitimate.[127] In acknowledgement of the government's lack of judicial mandate for the Twitter ban, an Ankara court issued an injunction against the ban on 26 March 2014. However, the block remained in force in the run-up to Turkey's 30 March 2014 local elections and was only lifted that April after a constitutional court ruling.[128]

Even with Twitter and other social media outlets once again freely available in Turkey, there have been sporadic bans. For example, in April 2015 Twitter and Facebook were temporarily blocked after photographs were circulated of far-left militants holding hostage a prosecutor, later killed as security forces raided the Istanbul office where he was being held. Only after the images were removed was the ban lifted.[129] Following the 10 October 2015 terrorist attack in Ankara, which left over ninety-seven people dead, Twitter and Facebook were once again temporarily banned, on the prime minister's orders, to prevent images of the bombings creating "a feeling of panic".[130] This practice of placing temporary blocks on social media was repeated in the wake of subsequent terrorist outrages.

Whether through the traditional media or online social media, the Turkish government seeks to dominate the political discourse disseminated, and is prepared to violate democratic principles in order to achieve hegemony in the public forum. So far, it is winning that battle.

Conclusion

Media freedom constitutes a vital pillar in any real democracy. Not only is having an independent and open media an important element of freedom of expression, but it may also be a fundamental check on power that complements a system of checks and balances needed for any healthy democracy to flourish in practical terms. The restrictions that the Turkish press has suffered since 1980 and especially after the second and third AKP terms (2007–15) have directly impacted on the capacity for freedom of thought to proliferate in Turkey. Despite the hope and promise of the AKP, emerging at a period when military tutelage was in decline, Turkey's media is embattled. Political figures feel fit to directly intimidate journalists and pressure media bosses who dare to criticise them. Meanwhile, the government has the media firmly in its grip. It exploits a system that connects the wider business interests of media owners to the fortunes of the AKP, which prevents the media from criticising the government. Essentially, the corporatisation of the media has all but eroded the independent press.

This deplorable state of affairs was highlighted during the Gezi protests, when many media outlets failed to air this historic moment in Turkish politics. To make matters worse, even the alternative outlet, social media, has been subject to attack. However, unless Erdogan and the AKP wish to borrow the model of communist China and face the domestic and international repercussions, this is highly unlikely to be successful. As things stand, any future bans or blocks on social media will just be circumvented by an Internet-savvy population looking for alternative news sources and platforms to share their thoughts and ideas.

5

URBAN PLANNING, DEVELOPMENT
AND THE POLITICS OF THE *GECEKONDU*

Introduction

The protests over the planned destruction of Istanbul's Gezi Park and its replacement with an Ottoman-style barracks and shopping mall highlight the problem of urban regeneration in modern Turkey. Visitors to cities such as Istanbul and Ankara will no doubt see shiny new buildings, both office and residential, as well as cranes and building works. Turkey's construction industry is booming, an important driver of the economy. Meanwhile, "mega projects" such as a third airport in Istanbul and the widely ambitious artificial shipping canal project, Kanal Istanbul, are in their initial stages. Quite simply, Turkey's urban landscape and environment are being transformed, altering the lives of millions. However, there are multiple concerns surrounding Turkey's construction boom. The AKP's infatuation with building luxury homes, malls and large-scale projects has many opponents, unhappy that a large number of projects are approved with little to no public consultation. Others are concerned about the effects on the environment. There is also the question of corruption, and of the frequency of legal amendments to the law in order for projects to go ahead.

We will see in this chapter that the politics of urban development is not limited to ownership of public spaces and environmental concerns, but also encompasses a political patrimonial relationship between the AKP, big businesses and the residents of poorer neighbourhoods that stand to gain much from Turkey's construction boom, despite its discontents. So what is the nature of these areas of *gecekondu* (squatter) settlements, and how did their development become a political tool?

Squatter Rights: Kemalist City Planning and the Challenge of Gecekondu *Settlements*

During the early Turkish Republic (founded in 1923), illiteracy rates were as high as 90 per cent and the population was overwhelmingly rural, with 83 per cent of Turks living in the countryside.[1] In subsequent years, much effort went into modernising and Westernising the country with planning focused on strategies for urbanisation and industrialisation. This was specifically concentrated on the city of Ankara, which had been made the new capital and was the focal point of Turkey's strategy for rural-urban integration. The vision was to improve Turkey's social standards and create a new middle class.[2]

As it was now the centre of the new Turkish Republic, the city soon saw vast and rapid growth. Ankara's population in 1920 was as low as 20,000, but by 1927 this had increased more than threefold to 75,000. Just eight years later, the population reached six digits, standing at 123,000 in 1935.[3] Partly behind this rapid population increase were rail projects integrating Ankara with its rural surrounding areas, with the intention of connecting the Anatolian masses to their capital city. The government also facilitated programmes and projects for industrialisation in urban population centres. As a result, Anatolia was transformed, becoming increasingly urban. This was done in consultation with Western architects assisting in development schemes for the cities. Still, despite the rise of the urban population and its centralised administration, Turkey remained a predominantly rural country.[4]

It is in this context that Turkey saw a rise in *gecekondus*. While Turkey was ruled by the staunchly Kemalist CHP, until 1950, these unauthorised squatter settlements were barely tolerated. The government usually tried to demolish them or take measures to stop new ones from being built. 1949 saw the first law pertaining to such illegal housing construction, the Demolition of Illegally Built Structures Law No. 5431.

But the law was in vain. It did not prevent the building or increase the demolishment of illegal settlements, because during this period additional rural migrants found their way into Turkish cities. Housing for these new migrants was unaffordable. Instead they built their own homes illegally and soon new *gecekondu* settlements emerged. Thus urban growth continued throughout Turkey during this early process of industrialisation. Soon *gecekondus* became a fact of city life, and the government had no real option but to accept them.[5]

The 1950 general elections were a historic turning point for Turkey. The CHP, the party founded by Turkey's first head of state Mustafa Kemal Ataturk, lost and handed power to its rival, the moderately right-wing DP (Democrat Party). However, this did not stop Turkey's march towards greater industrialisation. If anything it intensified, with the DP removing trade barriers and concentrating its attention on public works programmes. It was also during this period that Turkey received Marshall Plan aid. Although designed to rebuild the economy and infrastructure of war-ravaged Europe, in Turkey Marshall aid also had the inadvertent effect of causing large redundancies in rural areas, as new tractor-based farming methods left hundreds of thousands, possibly millions, of fieldworkers jobless in the mid- to late 1950s.[6] One consequence of this was rural migration into the city, a development not opposed by the government at the time, which deemed it positive for the growth of industry. But the urban population continued to rise, as there were lower mortality rates and higher fertility levels. In 1950, Turkey's population stood at 21 million. Fifteen years later, it was 31 million. This in itself is a significant increase; however, it was in the cities that Turkey's population boom was particularly felt. In 1950, only 25 per cent of the country was urban-dwelling. By 1965 this figure had reached 35 per cent. This meant that Turkey's four largest cities had seen a 75 per cent population rise, as one in ten villagers had migrated to the city.[7] Many entered or built *gecekondu* residences.

During the 1960s, the government identified several key areas for addressing the *gecekondu* problem. These were the demolition of structures deemed to be sub-standard, prevention of further illegal building, and improvement of some existing housing.[8] In 1966 Gecekondu Law No. 775 was passed by parliament to tackle these issues, but it appears that the government had come to accept the presence of such illegally housed communities in Turkey's urban areas. This seems to be a result of the reality on the ground: by the mid- to late 1960s, 59 per cent of Ankara's population lived in such settlements. So did 45 per cent of Istanbul and 33 per cent of Izmir.[9] In recognition of Turkey's urban housing crisis, the government established the Ministry of Construction and Resettlement, which soon became, in effect, an urbanisation ministry. Metropolitan planning offices were also created, attempting to ensure that before a new settlement could be established, a plan had to be required, and that, upon approval, the costs of adequate infrastructure would be financed.[10]

However, these measures did not curb the proliferation of *gecekondus*. As there was a reduction of public land, new migrants from the countryside simply seized what was available and built, sometimes even on privately owned land. Others entered already existing *gecekondu* neighbourhoods and became tenants of other *gecekondu* residents who had built multiple homes in order to collect rent and make a profit.[11] By the 1970s, with one third of Turks living in *gecekondus* (the number was higher in the larger cities), amnesties were introduced to make some of the settlements legal.[12] Unable to prevent their growth or, often, demolish them, municipalities had no option but to provide *gecekondu* communities with utilities and services such as water and electricity. This simply served to increase their populations, and some *gecekondus* saw an increase in the size of their structures.[13]

In the *gecekondus*, which did not generally receive municipal services or access to utilities, residents had no option but to access these services illegally. Unwilling to demolish the settlements, the authorities again had little option but to try to contain the problem through further amnesties. One of the reasons for not dispersing these communities was that they were a large and growing population. The *gecekondu* represented millions of potential electoral supporters. Indeed, politicians courted their votes.[14] This was certainly the case in the 1970s, by which time half of the urban population in the majority of Turkish cities were from *gecekondus*, encouraging greater leniency from the vote-seeking government.[15]

One of the most devastating consequences of the nature of this urbanisation was in traffic and congestion. There were, of course, few developed roads in *gecekondu* areas, and the municipalities were unable to provide public transportation for the new and increasing population. One solution was the *dolmus* system. In essence, the *dolmus* are privately operated shared taxis, soon commonly used by commuters of a middle or low income. Local authorities began implementing public transportation along the lines of the *dolmus* routes.[16]

As urban planner Ilhan Tekeli explains, the *dolmus* system led to the "expansion of the city along intercity motorways, high-density inner-city development, and growth of the central business district toward high-income neighbourhoods." However, it had detrimental consequences for the functioning of the city. While the system was initially a useful and practical solution, it also had a negative impact, as public services remained substandard, traffic was horrendous, green areas disappeared and the landscape and identity of the city became unrecognisable.[17]

Courting Votes: Political Patrimonialism and the Gecekondus

In 1965, the Justice Party (AP) owed part of its electoral success to its appeals to and support from the urban poor.[18] Turkish historian Kemal Karpat observed that, in the 1965 and 1969 elections, it was the AP that received overwhelming support from *gecekondu* residents in Istanbul—this was a surprising development because, before migrating to the cities, many villagers had voted for the CHP.[19] Regardless, the AP soon turned word into deed. In 1966, it passed another *gecekondu* law, and launched the Bosphorus Bridge and beltway projects to connect the settlements with the city.[20]

The CHP did not give up on the *gecekondu* vote. In 1972, when Bulent Ecevit took over as party leader, he very much recognised the importance of the urban working-class vote, even guiding his party to a centre-left position. He forged strong ties with trade unions and courted *gecekondus*, promising to distribute land deeds to houses built before 1973. This strategy was rewarded when the CHP won the 1973 general election.[21]

However, it was not just elections that were affected by the *gecekondus*. Kemal Karpat argues that no other factor contributed more to social and political change and divisions than the expansion of *gecekondus*, to the extent that they even, albeit indirectly, caused political unrest.[22] This urban unrest, which plagued Turkish cities for over a decade, dates back to 1968. Turkish university students, many of whom were originally from rural areas, were experiencing anxieties over their cultural dislocation and alienation in the cities. They, like their fellow students across Europe, took to the streets in protest over their future prospects and job opportunities. This took place in the already volatile environment of Turkish campus politics.[23]

These tensions came to the fore when economic conditions deteriorated after the petrol crisis of 1973. The Turkish economy was on the verge of bankruptcy, and there were few public funds available for spending on the urban poor.[24] This was particularly devastating to *gecekondu* residents who were already the hardest hit by the economic meltdown, and feeling the pinch with shortages of basic commodities and foodstuffs. Far from their hopes of a better future when they migrated to the city, it was the urban poor who were suffering from the triple-digit inflation that occurred in 1979, from 15 per cent unemployment and industry only running on half capacity.[25]

It is in this context that Turkey's cities experienced gang warfare, political insurgency and brutal government crackdowns. An estimated 4,500 lives were lost in urban political conflict, in addition to the thousands wounded between 1976 and 1980, before the military finally intervened to restore order. *Gecekondus* were not only a hotbed for bloody violence between extreme left- and right-wing groups, but they also became recruiting grounds.[26] In Istanbul, a disproportionate number of politically motivated murders occurred in or nearby squatter settlements or districts.[27]

After the 1980 coup, the *gecekondus* were once again crucial to Turkey's political trajectory. Turkey was looking to open its economy to trade and the financial markets. The post-coup period ushered in an era of neo-liberal policies spearheaded by Prime Minister Turgut Ozal.[28] Always the astute politician, Ozal focused his attention on urban planning. He put into place Amnesty Laws Nos. 2805 and 2981 in 1983 and 1984, allowing for *gecekondu* land to be transferred into authorised urban land.[29] These laws also enabled additional construction in the settlements for up to four-storey apartment houses on plots that had already been legalised.[30] Ozal wanted to make the *gecekondus* more open to the market and to construction.[31] It is not surprising that by the early 1980s, the construction industry became, after textiles and clothing, Turkey's most important sector.[32]

In 1984, the Mass Housing Administration was established. Initially it was founded to meet the housing needs of low-income families. Also in 1984 there were two important reforms. One made metropolitan municipalities responsible for larger cities in their planning and control over urban areas. The second was the decentralisation of some administrative powers to local authorities, who were given responsibility over the planning and approval stages of housing developments.[33]

Also important to note is that from the late 1980s there was another increase in rural to urban migration, especially by people of Kurdish origin. This was a result of forced migrations from eastern and southeastern provinces because of insurgency and counterinsurgency between the state and the outlawed PKK. On the basis of national security, thousands of Kurdish villages were either emptied or destroyed.[34]

Notably, pro-Islamist parties maintained a support base hovering around the 12 per cent mark during the 1970s to the 1990s.[35] Particularly after the 1980 coup, political Islam enjoyed strong support among rural-origin migrants now living in *gecekondu* settlements, where there was an increase in religious gatherings during the 1990s. These *tariqats*, or religious organisations, established in low-income communities, created a considerable amount of public notice and added to the tensions and anxieties in urban areas.[36]

A significant source of support for political Islam was migrant dissatisfaction with the quality and efficiency of local services, as well as the neo-liberal trajectory of the 1980s. This was reflected in the 1994 local elections, which gave the Welfare Party a significantly increased share of the popular vote, to 19 per cent. It also gained the municipalities of Turkey's two most important cities, Ankara and Istanbul. Welfare was able to attract the votes of the urban poor by playing to their discontent with the policies enacted during the 1980s, which saw them marginalised in Turkish society.[37] In general elections the following year, the party saw continued success. It won almost 22 per cent of the vote, a result which translated into 158 seats out of 550 in parliament. Much of this success was due to the *gecekondu* vote; by this time *gecekondu* communities constituted 50 per cent of Istanbul, Izmir and Gaziantep and 60 per cent of Ankara.[38] Rather than appealing to the religious sentiments of *gecekondu* residents, the Welfare Party won popularity by meeting the needs of the urban poor, in the form of providing services and support.[39] As political scientist Ergun Ozbudun observes, Welfare politicians spoke of creating a "just order" that was "different from and superior to both capitalism and socialism," while at the same time condemning the economic system as a "slave system," with its ties to international financial institutions.[40]

Even Recep Tayyip Erdogan, Prime Minister until 2014 and a former Welfare Party mayor, played up his origins in a marginal and neglected Istanbul neighbourhood, the former *gecekondu* settlement of Kasımpaşa. This attracted considerable support from low-income households. During the religious month of Ramadan, Erdogan and his wife visited families living in *gecekondu* neighbourhoods, transmitting the message that he was one of them. Indeed, an important factor in the AKP's first general election victory in 2002 was the rhetoric and terminology it adopted in courting *gecekondu* voters.[41] With the patronage of the Welfare Party and later the AKP, residents of the *gecekondus* soon went from being on the periphery to representing the core of the city and its constituents.

Enter the AKP and the Boom in Gecekondu Housing and Redevelopment

From 1980 to the present day, Istanbul has been earmarked as the city to display Turkey as a major world economic player committed to neoliberalism. This became a particular priority of the AKP, which was attuned to the importance of the property market and the potential of urban areas to encourage economic growth. However, urban development and regeneration served a dual purpose. On one hand it would attract foreign investment and serve the global economic market. On the other it would encourage the growth of the construction industry for housing and residential projects as well as for offices and infrastructure.[42] The intended consequences were the enrichment and empowerment of *gecekondu* residents and a maintained patrimonial relationship between them and the AKP. There were both winners and losers in this arrangement, which also led to tensions between old and new inhabitants of Turkey's cities.

In 2004 and 2005, the Turkish parliament passed a series of laws that empowered urban municipalities, enabling them to initiate city projects in conjunction with the Mass Housing Administration.[43] The Mass Housing Administration itself was also granted the authority to build new housing and develop other construction projects. This gave central government more control over development. Soon the Mass Housing Administration's powers grew exponentially and it was able to control almost any urban development scheme. It could now alter existing plans, establish companies in the housing sector and give credit for transformation and restoration projects.[44] In addition to housing, the Administration's authority also included office space, schools, hospitals, prisons, mosques and shopping malls. It was only responsible to the prime minister, with little accountability in its finances and the quality of its building projects.[45]

Subsequently, the construction sector saw significant growth. Between 2002 and 2007, for example, the sector increased from 4.5 per cent of the country's labour market to 5.9 per cent. Meanwhile, the annual growth of the construction industry amounted to 22 per cent. In practical terms, this meant that there had been 43,430 new construction projects in 2002, but by 2006 this had ballooned to 114,204. In terms of floor area in buildings, in 2002 it was 36 million new square metres, but by 2007 it was 125 million.[46] In order to create such a boom in the construction industry, the AKP allowed for relaxation of the relevant legislation. In these same years, 2002–7, there were seventy-eight laws and ten by-laws passed either fully or partially related to construction in urban areas, plus an additional 198 legal arrangements, all of which contributed towards greater deregulation. This deregulation mostly gave additional autonomy to developers from both the private and public sectors, which enabled them to define the location and number of property investments. For example, the 2003 Law No. 4957 allowed the Ministry of Culture and Tourism to gain powers to develop tourist areas. The 2004 Law No. 5162 enabled the Mass Housing Administration to shift the authority to make plans for housing and tourism investments from the local to the national level, allowing it to fast-track the planning process.[47]

Other deregulation mechanisms included giving the Ministry of Environment and Urban Planning authority to bypass restrictive urban development legislation in planning land use, and the sale of public land for private development. The 2003 Law No. 4916 gave the minister of finance the ability to terminate licences on public property in order to sell it off; Laws 5005 and 52220 (2003 and 2004 respectively) expanded this power to include sales of schools and hospitals.[48] Law No. 5393 (2005) made municipalities responsible for decisions pertaining to urban development in relation to issues including earthquake protection, the preservation of historical or cultural structures and the building of commercial and industrial zones and housing.[49] The problem with such decentralisation was that laws were changed simply to justify large projects.[50] In reality, it was in neither the letter nor the spirit of the law.

The way in which *gecekondu* housing redevelopment usually worked was that property owners were allowed to live in the renewed project on the condition that they pay, in monthly instalments, the difference in value between their old home and the new property. The selling point for property owners was obtaining a house of higher value and formal ownership.[51] In some cases, entitlement deeds for the new property were sold off to real estate speculators, creating a market value for such documents.[52] Many *gecekondu* residents were real financial winners of the urban redevelopment projects, and duly grateful to the AKP. So too were the developers, who also became a support base for the party and constituted a new entrepreneurial class with close ties to the government.[53]

However, not everyone was a winner. In contrast with *gecekondu* owners, tenant residents were usually not offered compensation, and faced direct eviction. In the longer term, human geographer Ozan Karaman has pointed to two problems associated with such schemes. In Istanbul, demolitions in the predominantly Kurdish Ayazma-Tepeustu neighbourhoods began in 2007. Under the programme, homeowners were entitled to new apartments. However, despite the fifteen-year payment scheme that they were offered, and which most families agreed to, they soon realised that they would be unable to make such payments and instead sold their entitlement documents to speculators.[54] This was also the case of the rundown Sulukule area.[55] The threat of Article 3 of Expropriation Law No. 2942, which allowed for swift expropriation, was used to pressure *gecekondu* homeowners into signing up to the scheme rather than sell on their entitlement deeds.[56] Regardless, the fact is that many *gecekondu* residents did sell their deeds, and were grateful to the ruling party for the profit it brought them.

The construction boom and the development of the *gecekondu* areas caused tensions within the urban population. Citizens who defined themselves as true Istanbulites tended to blame the *gecekondus* for both the deterioration of and changes to the city.[57] They complained that, as the shantytowns were transformed and Istanbul was turned into a trademark city, the nature of the city's lifestyle, culture and quality of life also changed. The city became a commodity for those with money and disposable incomes. This was visible in the transformation of the *gecekondu* neighbourhoods, which were destroyed and replaced with modern and luxurious gated communities, often with swimming pools and even shopping malls, under the auspices of the Mass Housing Administration—which often did not consult the city's inhabitants, forced to learn of such developments from the media or through word of mouth.[58]

Urban Regeneration and the Gezi Park Protests

Important groups such as the Union of Chambers of Architects and Engineers vehemently opposed what they saw as the commoditisation of land in urban areas.[59] One important concern was the lack of citizen participation in the decision making process, with little to no consultation with residents about development plans and construction projects. This was even the case with infrastructural projects that were supposed to meet the needs of city residents, such as building houses and roads, as well as commercial enterprises that could transform neighbourhoods, such as shopping malls or new luxury apartments. However, it was the development in central public areas that really angered many people. This came to a head with the planned demolition of Gezi Park. Not only was there a complete lack of public consultation, but Gezi was also one of the last remaining green spaces in the city.

Istanbul's residents were also angered by the way in which the protests were brutally suppressed, an attempt to prevent them from having a say in the future of public and shared space in the city. This was especially the case as demolishing Gezi Park and the adjacent Ataturk Cultural Centre, two public spaces at the heart of the city, and replacing them with an Ottoman-style barracks, a shopping mall and perhaps a mosque, would have altered not only the city's landscape but also the nature of its identity. Plans to redevelop central squares and public parks threaten to alter the cultural character of an area, as well as depriving citizens of public green spaces.

There was an additional complication in the case of plans for Gezi Park and the central Taksim Square: the issue of identity. Although during the Ataturk period of the 1920s and 1930s, Istanbul was, to a certain extent, neglected in favour of Ankara, during the later republican period Taksim Square became increasingly important. It became a symbol of Turkey's modernisation. It was also the location of public events and celebrations as well as protests and public gatherings. It was the identifiable centre and therefore the most important part of Istanbul. The AKP even made plans for Taksim Square to become pedestrianised, despite lack of discussions with the local community, professional architects, urban planners and their respective associations. The Gezi Park scheme was criticised by many because it would replace a recreational area with a commercial one.[60]

Another controversial aspect of these plans was the popular association of Turkish ideology and identity with the history of the square. Kemalists saw Taksim Square as representative of the secular republican spirit. It differed from the narrow, Ottoman-like streets and passageways of older parts of Istanbul such as the famous Golden Horn. Instead, the large and open Taksim Square represented progressiveness and modernisation, an area where men and women could freely mix and interact. Turkish Islamic groups, meanwhile, saw Taksim Square and the surrounding area as problematic and desired to change it. In the 1990s, Prime Minister Necmettin Erbakan advocated plans to build a mosque in this central square.[61] Erbakan's Islamic party, the Welfare Party, was of course the AKP's predecessor. It is therefore not insignificant that rumours were circulating that not only was an imperial-style barracks to be built in place of Gezi Park, but also the Ataturk Cultural Centre in Taksim was to be replaced by a mosque. This departure from the secular Republic's tradition of distancing itself from its Ottoman and Islamic past was also evident in Erdogan's plan to build a giant mosque on the 885-foot hill of Camlica to the north of the city. Standing at 160,000 square feet, it would be seen from all areas of Istanbul.[62] Erdogan lent his support to both this project and a mosque in Taksim.[63] At the height of the Gezi protests, Erdogan insisted that plans for the mosque would go ahead.[64]

One might argue that the Gezi Park protests represented frustrated citizens attempting to reclaim their city. They were orchestrated to combat an urban regeneration policy that prioritised capital and big business over the rights of ordinary residents. In Gezi Park and Taksim Square, this was a battle between the police, and therefore the state, employing violence to prevent the gathering of citizens to protest and prevent changes to their public spaces.[65]

Mega Projects: Plans and Discontents

Turkey's recent development has not been limited to urban regeneration and construction. One of the most controversial policies of the AKP government, spearheaded by Erdogan, is the "crazy projects", a term that has been embraced and even used by the president himself. The word "crazy" refers to their sheer scale. It also signifies that such schemes are daring, and reflect the boldness of the AKP's political cadres in engaging in such feats of human ingenuity, to make Istanbul one of the world's greatest cities.

One such crazy project is the building of Kanal Istanbul, an artificial canal connecting the Black Sea at the city's north with the Sea of Marmara to the south. Announced by Erdogan in April 2011, the aim of this plan is to alleviate pressure on the heavily over-crowded Bosphorus strait that separates East from West, Europe from Asia. Istanbul remains Turkey's economic and cultural capital. Turkey is, of course, a world energy hub, with over 56,000 ships passing through the Bosphorus every year, carrying around 139 million tons of liquefied petroleum gas and an additional 3 million tons of chemicals.[66]

The logic behind Kanal Istanbul is not only to ease congestion and avoid a man-made ecological disaster that would threaten the lives of millions of the city's residents—such accidents have happened in the past including the deaths of twenty-nine sailors in 1994 when an oil tanker and cargo ship collided, and the 200,000 gallons of fuel discharged in 1999 when a tanker split. Kanal Istanbul is also intended to expand Turkey's transit potential. The canal would be located 45–50 kilometres west of Istanbul, between the Black Sea and the Marmara, to be completed by 2023. The scheme was hailed by Erdogan as an environmental project that would create a 150 metre-wide waterway, 25 metres in depth, allowing large vessels to pass through.[67]

The waterway would be 31 miles long, and Erdogan has said that it would outshine the Panama and Suez Canals.[68] It would have shopping and tourism facilities along its banks and could also include yacht marinas.[69] According to Erdogan and the Metropolitan Municipality, the project would cost US$10 billion,[70] a figure sure to skyrocket during development. It is also estimated that Kanal Istanbul would create around 2 to 2.5 million jobs—1 million during its construction and 1.5 million after its opening. It would contribute to the maintenance of Turkey's construction industry, which has consistently seen growth at around 4.2 per cent a year.[71] While full details of the Kanal Istanbul project are still sketchy, recent reports indicate that there are also plans for the development of a new town, which would have a population of around 500,000, a reduced figure from the 1.2 million originally intended, and no high-rises, with maximum six-storey buildings, designed in the Anatolian Turkic "Seljuk" style of the pre-Ottoman era.[72]

The second major planned project is a third airport for Istanbul. Initial construction has begun, and is planned to progress in stages. Its location, Arnavutkoy, in the northern part of the European side of the Bosphorus, is not too far from Silivri, which is close to the Kanal Istanbul site. The 6.5 million square-metre airport will boast four terminals, six runways, 165 boarding bridges and a capacity for 500 aeroplanes in total and 150 million passengers a year.[73] To put this into perspective, the airport will be six times the size of London's Heathrow.[74] Prime Minister Binali Yildirim, when he was minister of transportation, maritime affairs and communications, went so far as to comment that it would be visible from space. In May 2013, the Cengiz-Kolin-Limak-Mapa-Kalyon Consortium won the bid in a joint venture competing with three other bidders (seventeen groups had qualified to enter). From 2017, the winning consortium will pay the Turkish government €22.1 billion over twenty-five years.[75] Ground was broken in May 2014. Construction officially started on 1 May 2015 with the intention of completion by October 2017, to mark the anniversary of the founding of the Turkish Republic, and for the airport to be operational by 2018.[76]

Erdogan's other major crazy project is the third Istanbul bridge, known as the Yavuz Sultan Selim Bridge after Ottoman Sultan Selim the Grim, and its interconnecting motorways, costing around US$3 billion. The bridge began construction in 2013 and was opened to traffic on 26 August 2016. Meanwhile, plans have been made for a new three-level tunnel in Istanbul, for trains connected to the metro systems as well as automobiles. This new project was an important 2015 election pledge by the ruling party. Following the AKP's victory in November of that year, at the time of writing the plan looks likely to take hold.[77] Erdogan equally used a crazy project to boost his polling ahead of Turkey's first presidential election. A high-speed rail line to Ankara was opened on 25 July 2014, just in time for Erdogan to receive exposure ahead of the following month's vote. All of these transport links will, of course, feed into Istanbul's third airport.

While these projects are undoubtedly ambitious and, if successful, will no doubt benefit millions of Turks and guarantee Erdogan's place among Turkey's great state-builders, there are still highly significant obstacles. These mainly pertain to objections on environmental grounds and the potential ecological fallout. But, just as importantly, they also relate to the exclusive, non-consultative manner in which the projects have been planned, organised and executed. This has raised criticisms and objections from many Turks that the future direction of their fast-changing country has been decided for them, not by them.

One development that has caused particular concern, and another project completed months before elections—the local elections of March 2014—is the Marmaray, a metro tunnel under Istanbul's Bosphorus. Opened on 29 October 2013, the 1.4-kilometre tunnel cost £2.9 billion.[78] One reason for the delay was the discovery of a Byzantine-era port. This highlights the archaeological losses that these projects can inflict on a city as steeped in history as Istanbul. Thousands of artefacts and historical structures in Istanbul's old city have already been destroyed due to construction damage and shoddy restorations, as well as the changes to Istanbul's skyline.[79] The same goes for Istanbul's Golden Horn Metro Bridge, which was opened in February 2014 amidst complaints from some residents that it ruined the view of the historical Golden Horn peninsula.[80]

Critics also point out the huge cost of projects like the Marmaray, both to the state and to ordinary citizens who may get in their way. Opponents of the third airport plan point to the farmers who would lose their land. They were offered the equivalent of US$23 per square metre, just one tenth of the market value.[81] The question also remains of why the airport needs so much open space, while other airports with high passenger numbers require a far smaller area to function. Indeed, according to Candan Karlıtekin, a former executive board director of Turkish Airlines, the new airport is not even needed. Two extra runways at Istanbul's existing airports would make up the passenger numbers, without the ecological fallout (see below).[82] Some, such as CHP deputy Aykut Erdoglu, argue that far from being a financial benefit to Turkey, the third airport would actually be an €11 billion burden, as the government has issued financial guarantees to contractors if construction is delayed and if projected flight volumes are not reached.[83]

On top of this, there have been safety concerns about the mega projects. Despite claims that the Marmaray could withstand a level nine earthquake, it lacks an electronic security system to detect floods. Suleyman Solmaz of the Chamber of Architects and Engineers commented that the tunnel should not have been opened to the public in such conditions.[84] Kanal Istanbul has received similar criticism. Cemal Saydam of Hacettepe University and Etham Gonenc of Istanbul Technical University have warned that the project would leave the area smelling of hydrogen sulphide,[85] while Mikdat Kadioglu, professor of meteorology and disaster management, has pointed to the example of the Houston Canal, where small children living nearby experienced higher rates of leukaemia due to air pollution.

Aside from the human cost, the potential ecological effects of certain projects are vast. Kadioglu has warned that Kanal Istanbul might lead to the drying up of nearby lakes. Other experts have warned that its size will affect the oxygen content of the Sea of Marmara and the salt levels of the Black Sea, threatening fish migration patterns or even heralding their extinction.[86] The construction of the canal has also been criticised for lack of transparency, as plans remain a closely guarded secret. This is a common feature of the Istanbul mega projects: a survey conducted by Haluk Levent and Guven Dagistan of Galatasaray University found that residents in affected areas were largely unaware of the consequences of constructing a third bridge across the Bosphorus, and had not been given any detailed information.[87] Kanal Istanbul has been advanced from the top down, receiving disapproval from scientists and academics highlighting the potential global ecological fallout.[88]

Meanwhile, in the location currently earmarked for the third airport, there are over 2.5 million trees, of which 657,950 will need to be cut, with the remainder and additional trees planted or moved elsewhere.[89] If we just take the motorway from the third airport to the third bridge, now under construction, 18,500 acres of forestland will be destroyed.[90] The Turkish Foundation for Combating Soil Erosion released a report in March 2014 highlighting the environmental cost of such mega projects. It estimated that 8,715 hectares of forestland would be destroyed and air pollution increased, both of which would affect not only the city's population but also the migration of birds. The report also emphasised the damage the third bridge, Kanal Istanbul and the third airport would inflict not only on forest areas and agricultural land, but also on water resources, wildlife, creeks and streams.[91]

As Turkey has faced drought and water shortages in recent years, some experts such as Baran Bozoglu, President of the Chamber of Environmental Engineers, has said that the "crazy projects" threatened a further depletion of Turkey's water resources, arguing that seventy ponds and eight streams risk being depleted as a result of the third airport project, including Lake Terkos, which supplies water to Istanbul and Thrace.[92] This was a risk that the Environment and Urban Planning Ministry acknowledged, but it still concluded that there was no better place to build the airport.[93] Mikdat Kadioglu voiced similar concern about Kanal Istanbul, warning that the project might lead to the drying up of nearby lakes. Even before these projects are completed or realised, Turkey also has a significant air pollution problem. According to a study by the Environment and Urban Planning Ministry itself, seventy-nine of Turkey's eighty-one provinces have pollution issues, caused mainly by fuel usage in homes.[94] All in all, there is a very real fear that instead of benefiting Istanbul, the "crazy projects" would render the city uninhabitable in the near future.[95]

What has particularly angered some environmentalists are claims that although the authorities demolish green urban space, under the AKP many thousands of trees have been planted. Ankara-based environmental activist Tanju Gunduzalp says that this is not accurate, because the party includes in its numbers tress that have been planted in between motorways.[96] Environmental concerns cannot compete with the construction industry that drives the Turkish economy. Green space is just less of a priority.[97] This is despite environmental rights being enshrined in the Turkish constitution. Article 56 states that "everybody has the right to live in a healthy and balanced environment and that improving the environment, protecting the health of the environment, and protecting environment from pollution is the duty of both the state and the individual". This provision has been nullified by efforts to engage in neo-liberal policies and the facilitation of growth.[98]

While the Ministry of Environment, established in 1991, has passed laws and regulations, it is also the case that the state is reluctant to enforce environmental legislation effectively when it counters or risks economic growth. The EU accession process has played a part in this and represents something of a paradox. While EU membership holds incentives for environmental progress in Turkey, it is also economic performance and modernisation that makes EU accession so attractive. Ankara therefore supports projects that create jobs and expand the economy over environmental concerns.[99] Anyone who visits Turkey's major urban centres would be struck by the number of shopping malls in neighbourhoods throughout the city. Construction of a mall drives economic growth, which is then followed by consumption to supplement it. However, the proliferation of such shopping malls threatens the city centre where the public congregate, and the unique culture this produces.[100]

To make matters worse, the construction projects have also been affected by the corruption allegations of December 2013 and after. In reality, the large-scale accusations came as no real surprise. Documents from WikiLeaks had already indicated as much. Meanwhile Abdullatif Sener, a former deputy prime minister who has since left the AKP, stated to the authors of this volume one month before the investigation that the biggest problem facing Turkey is corruption, which now stands at its highest level in the history of the Republic, but the media has been incapacitated to report it.[101] These suspicions of corruption and nepotism highlight the lack of transparency in Turkey.[102]

Some executives from companies involved in the construction of the third bridge and airport were arrested or questioned by investigators of the corruption case over taking bribes and rigging bids in government tenders.[103] Some of those detained included Ali Agaoglu of the Agaoglu Group,[104] who is responsible for not quite a mega project but still a shockingly large urban residential and commercial project, Maslak 1453, which will consist of a twenty-four-towered residential compound with a shopping mall and commercial units. A second round-up, which was derailed after police refused to follow the prosecutors' orders, named Calik Holding, the company headed by Erdogan's son-in-law until January 2014, in the list of those wanted for questioning.[105] In all, the twenty-two people who were detained included members of three of Turkey's largest construction companies: Agaoglu, Emrullah Turanli and Osman Agca, all of which are known to be close to the government and were accused of illegal or irregular activities within the construction industry, such as making or receiving bribes. The investigation also touched Erdogan Bayraktar, then minister of environment and urban planning and before that chairman of the Mass Housing Administration.[106] His son, Abdullah Oguz Bayraktar, was detained, and Bayraktar was later obliged to resign. He even called on Erdogan to follow suit.

Several senior members of the Cengiz-Kolin-Limak-Mapa-Kalyon consortium, which won the tender to build Istanbul's third airport, were also investigated. The chair of Limak, Kolin board member Celal Kologlu and Kalyon executives Nihat Ozdemir, Orhan Cemal Kalyoncu and Omer Faruk Kalyoncu, all faced bribery charges.[107] This, of course, led AKP ministers such as Economy Minister Nihat Zeybekçi to call the investigation an attempt to derail Turkey's economic success and mega projects such as the new airport,[108] in other words an attack on the country's development and so on Turkey itself.[109] Accounting for nearly 17 per cent of national income,[110] the construction industry is the main driver of economic activity, and therefore of Turkey's GDP growth and domestic expenditure, mainly around Istanbul and Ankara with a spill-over effect on the rest of the economy. As we have seen with the *gecekondu* issue, construction not only drives the economy but is a source of electoral support for the AKP, because there has always been a housing crisis in Turkey, with not enough good-quality accommodation for the population.[111] However, the December 2013 corruption charges that implicated the highest echelons of power risk Turkey's international image, as well as its economic outlook for the future.[112]

Conclusion

Turkey's construction industry is important for economic growth, but it is vital for the success of the AKP. Not only do large-scale schemes such as the "crazy projects" maintain the construction industry while providing jobs, but they also connect the governing party to leading Turkish businesses. By the same token, the development of the *gecekondu* settlements is also a source of party patrimony, as many—though not all—residents reap financial benefits from urban regeneration on their land. As we know, this close relationship between government and business is not a new phenomenon; however, it has soared beyond any previously imagined heights under the AKP. What is worse, such urban projects, both residential and commercial, are going ahead with little consultation with either residents or, often, experts, who have very real concerns about the environmental and ecological consequences of the "mega projects". Worse still, the lack of transparency in commercial construction transactions has been highlighted by the 2013 corruption investigation. Instead of easing the public's concerns, the government has labelled this as an attack on the Turkish economy. For many citizens, though, it is their beloved cities that are being attacked, by unchecked urban construction.

6

WALTZING WITH OCALAN

TURKEY AND THE KURDISH PEACE PROCESS

Introduction

On 17 February 1999, Turkish television beamed images of Turkey's most wanted man, handcuffed, bound and showing signs of pain: the Kurdistan Workers' Party (PKK) leader, Abdullah Ocalan. He had been captured the day before by Turkish commando units as he was hiding in the Greek ambassador's residence in Nairobi, Kenya, after being forced to leave his base in Syria.[1] Soon he would be transported to the prison fortress of Imrali Island, which would become his home for over a decade, up to the time of writing. He faced trial and then life imprisonment after escaping the hangman's noose. His capture brought about a seismic shift in the shape of Turkey's Kurdish problem.

Under military tutelage, the way in which the Turkish state dealt with the Kurdish issue was through counterinsurgency. Political attempts to solve the problem were overshadowed by military means to fight the separatists. However, there have been attempts by the AKP to engage in a process of dialogue, on the understanding that the Kurdish problem cannot be solved by military means alone. The military particularly had a tendency to denigrate Kurdish aspirations. For example, recalling his time serving in Kurdish areas of south-east Turkey, retired four-star general Edip Baser believed that most Kurds did not harbour national aspirations; rather, Kurdish activism was due to the influence of Iraqi Kurd leader Masoud Barzani and of international powers.[2] Many Kurds would of course beg to differ.

Nevertheless, as we will see, despite both the optimism and furore that surrounded the negotiations with Ocalan and the PKK, in reality this political process was and still is at a very early stage. Even the AKP, although more attuned to the desires of the Kurds, still views the issue as a cultural problem rather than a national one. Perhaps paradoxically given this perspective, the AKP is also yet to recognise that there is no military solution to the conflict. Turkey has a long way to go before a meaningful solution is agreed to a problem that has plagued Turkey for many years.

Abdullah Ocalan and the Birth of the Modern Kurdish Struggle

In the period preceding Ocalan's capture in 1999, there had been little attempt to establish direct or indirect negotiating channels with the PKK. Security measures remained the default method of dealing with the Kurdish issue. Ocalan's impassioned first words after his capture ("I really love Turkey and Turkish people. My mother was Turkish. Sincerely, I will do all I can to be of service") were an indication that the Kurdish issue had taken on political dimensions, whilst simultaneously propelling him centre-stage as one of the most influential figures in Turkish politics.

Abdullah Ocalan, also known as "Apo" (Uncle in Kurdish), was born in the south-eastern Turkish village of Omerli, in the Halfeti district of Sanliurfa province. After graduating from high school and working at the Title Deeds Office in the predominantly Kurdish south-eastern city of Diyarbakir, he enrolled at Istanbul University's faculty of law. After just one year, he transferred to the prestigious Ankara Political Science Faculty.[3] Despite this, it appears that Ocalan, by his own admission, was not a particularly serious student. He was supposed to graduate in 1974, but the would-be Kurdish guerrilla leader did not complete his studies for an additional four years, supposedly a tactic to avoid being conscripted into the Turkish military. Instead Ocalan bided his time in libraries in a journey of self-discovery, reading about the history of the

Kurdish people. Initially, Ocalan says, he was conflicted about his ethnic identity. He recalled that "I fought within myself for a long time whether to be a Turk or a Kurd." Soon his answer was clear. He concluded that he should accept his Kurdish identity.[4] Ocalan's inner struggle was understandable. His first language, which he has always been more comfortable speaking, was Turkish.[5] Only later did Ocalan learn to speak a dialect of Kurdish.

What did Ocalan learn during his period of study and introspection? Supposedly it was the tragic history of his people. He would have read that, as early as the late nineteenth century, there had been conflagrations between Kurdish separatists and the central Ottoman administration. He would have studied the Kurdish predicament after the defeat of the Ottoman Empire in World War I, when the Western powers carved up the remains of the Empire to shape a new Middle East. This excluded Kurdistan, despite Kurdish self-determination being raised and in line with US President Woodrow Wilson's Fourteen Points, which sought to grant self-determination to the peoples in the region. Ocalan would have been all too aware that, under the terms of the 1920 Treaty of Sèvres, signed by the occupied Ottoman government, all of the Empire that would remain was a rump Turkish state in Anatolia, with territory in the eastern provinces allotted to an Armenian state, and Kurdish autonomy. However, this agreement was rejected by the emerging Turkish nationalist movement, united under the leadership of Mustafa Kemal Ataturk. The nationalists waged a war of independence that put an end to Kurdish and Armenian aspirations as well as defeating the Greeks in the West.[6] The new Turkish Republic was recognised under the Treaty of Lausanne (1923), which did away with the Treaty of Sèvres and led to international recognition of the Republic of Turkey. But the Kurdish question did not disappear with the official proclamation of the Republic that October.

The Caliphate had been the Islamic institution that united Kurds and Turks. With its abolition in 1924, the semblance of unity between Kurds and Turks had unravelled. At the same time, Ataturk developed an ethno-national ideology that sought to deny Kurdish and other identities and co-opt them into the state. Kurds were referred to as "Mountain Turks", traditional dress and the Kurdish language were banned and village names were changed to Turkish ones.[7] Ataturk stated that "Happy is whoever says 'I am a Turk'", a quotation that early Kemalists considered a reflection on the civic nature of Turkish identity: a Turk is a citizen who lives within the boundaries of the Turkish Republic. Meanwhile, language reform became a key cornerstone of Turkish identity, and speaking Turkish was a vehicle for becoming part of the Turkish nation. This was problematic for those who were reluctant to embrace this new identity and favoured the old;[8] and that was especially the case for the Kurds.

After the Caliphate was abandoned, a major rebellion was launched by Seyh Said, a Kurdish Sunni sheikh. Although it had religious overtones, it was also specifically a Kurdish uprising that expressed resentment of the new state's Turkish character and its attempts at forced assimilation.[9] This was in stark contrast to the Ottoman sultans, who had granted considerable autonomy to local leaders in return for loyalty to the Sublime Porte.[10] This uprising was a serious challenge to the Turkish state. At one point Seyh Said and his followers occupied one third of Kurdish Anatolia.[11] Not only was the revolt brutally suppressed, but also the south-east of Turkey remained under emergency law until the late 1930s. The Seyh Said uprising was not the only rebellion to be ruthlessly crushed. There were other revolts suppressed with a heavy hand, such as those in Agri in 1930 and in Dersim in 1938. Meanwhile, there were deportations of Kurdish groups and their resettlement in western provinces.[12] This was the tragic story of the Kurds in which the young Ocalan immersed himself as a young student in Ankara.

But it was not only Kurdish history that interested Ocalan. He read about and absorbed himself in the study of revolutionary activity and party organisation. By the time he was ready to complete his studies, he was also set to start his own revolutionary organisation. Ocalan and several other comrades founded the PKK in 1978 in the predominantly Kurdish city of Diyarbakir.[13] The new organisation's objectives were to reverse the wounds of history and establish a separate Kurdish state through a communist revolution.

Within two years, the organisation had killed 354 and injured 366 others, the majority not Turkish military personnel, but rather fellow Kurds labelled "fascist agents and local reactionaries".[14] The PKK's early activities did not go unnoticed by the Turkish authorities. In 1979, as the country was gripped by urban conflict and a general loss of authority which would lead to a coup the following year, Prime Minister Bulent Ecevit was criticised by the then opposition leader Suleyman Demirel on the basis that the state had lost its authority in the south-east to *Apoculer* or "Apo-ites", a reference to Ocalan's nickname.[15]

This led to a crackdown on PKK activities and in 1979 Ocalan fled to Syria. This was timely, as he left just ahead of the 1980 military coup, after which many PKK leaders also found refuge in Syria and particularly the Syrian-occupied Lebanese Bekaa Valley, where, between 1980 and 1984, Ocalan consolidated his leadership of the party as well as its structure. This was achieved with sometimes brutal methods against dissenters, including torture and execution.[16] Despite being active for several years, it was not until 1984 that the PKK established its military arm and launched hit-and-run guerrilla attacks from northern Iraq or Syria against Turkish forces, police and authorities in the Turkish south-east.[17]

However, Ocalan needed to address significant obstacles, the first of which was funding. The PKK involved itself in criminal activities. It took to robbing jewellery stores and drug trafficking in a similar vein to other revolutionary leftist groups at the time.[18] Indeed, a significant source of PKK fundraising was through organised crime, which over the years has been extensive. This has included an array of criminal activities from arms smuggling, drug trafficking and extortion to robbery, money laundering and even people smuggling.[19] The PKK has also received funding from sponsorship, at various points, by states antagonistic to Turkey, such as the Soviet Union, Iran and Syria,[20] the latter in particular seeing the PKK as a useful means of promoting Syrian territorial claims to the district of Hatay and of putting pressure on Turkey over water resources of the Euphrates river.[21] The PKK came to rely less on Syrian support as time went on and it made inroads within Kurdish society in Turkey, succeeding in recruiting new fighters.[22]

Part of the PKK's success was through its activities in Western Europe, especially after the 1980 military coup and the exodus of Kurdish migrant workers. Soon the PKK was able to create networks, branches and front organisations in Europe, particularly in Sweden and Germany, many of which published books, journals and articles in Kurdish and the major European languages. This was in addition to fundraising efforts and politicised cultural events and celebrations.[23]

A second obstacle that Ocalan needed to overcome was the tradi-tional organisation of Kurdish society, often structured along feudal lines. In order to meet this difficulty, Ocalan's struggle was not only against the Turkish state, but also against tribal associations and other socially conservative forces. He became committed to a social and political revolution among Kurdish communities, deeming this a pre-requisite for independence. As a result, PKK recruits initially came from marginal groups such as the peasantry and working classes, as well as "half-educated" youths who came from villages or small towns. Although underrepresented politically, these groups represented the majority of Kurds in Turkey.[24] It was for this reason that many of those who were attacked and targeted by the PKK were actually fellow Kurds. Ocalan needed not only to prove that his organisation was a powerful force to be reckoned with, but also to send a message to the Kurdish community at large that passive acceptance of the Turkish state was not an option. Many of the PKK's attacks on fellow Kurds were directed against the Village Guard, Kurdish militias that had been employed, financed and equipped by the state to combat the PKK. This was particularly so after 1985, when Prime Minister Ozal introduced the idea of using civilian militias from traditionally loyal Kurdish clans.[25] The fighting was brutal. It has been alleged that the PKK retali-ated against the Village Guard by killing not just armed men, but also entire families, including women and children.[26]

The Enduring Conflict

In all, Turkey fielded around 130,000 troops including special units in the south-east. At times they lost control of the region, not venturing out at night and retreating behind fortified positions.[27] From a military perspective, the PKK's activities were a significant burden on the Turkish state. By the late 1990s, over one third of the annual central government budget was spent on combating the PKK.[28]

In its attempt to repress the rebellion, the Turkish state closed down newspapers and periodicals, assassinated moderate Kurdish leaders, journalists and businessmen and orchestrated forced evacuations of villages in an attempt to deny the PKK bases for launching attacks.[29] Brutal measures were also adopted by Turkish law enforcement authorities, many of which have been documented by human rights organisations such as Human Rights Watch (HRW). For example, in 1997 HRW reported "widespread" torture and mistreatment of persons detained under anti-terror laws by the hands of the Anti-Terror Branch of the Security Directorate of Turkey's Ministry of the Interior, employing methods such as electrocutions, beating the soles of the feet, hanging by the arms in various positions, threats of sexual abuse, squeezing testicles or breasts as well as starving inmates or not allowing them to use toilet facilities.[30]

That was not all. In an earlier report in 1994, HRW had detailed forced evictions and home destruction suffered by the Kurdish population at the hands of the Turkish authorities, either for refusing to join the Village Guard system or because they were believed to have given food or shelter to PKK fighters.[31] In yet another HRW report, the agency identified that following the election of Suleyman Demirel as prime minister in November 1991, the rate of killings, torture and disappearances reached an "appalling rate" and noted that "Turkish security forces have attacked Kurdish cities in the south-east with increased ferocity" and that the government (as of 1992) had failed to investigate over 450 killings by death squad. The HRW report also detailed house raids in western Turkish cities such as Istanbul and Ankara with dozens of alleged terrorists shot and killed. In the south-east, protesters were dealt with through "shoot to kill" orders, with over 100 killed by police in demonstrations in 1992 alone.[32] All this did was provide further fertile recruiting ground for the PKK.[33]

One group that was exploited by the Turkish state to combat the PKK was Kurdish Hezbollah. This group emerged in the early 1990s in opposition to both the PKK and the state. Not to be confused with the Lebanese organisation of the same name, Hezbollah (as it is known in Turkey) was a uniquely Kurdish group that sought to create a Kurdish Islamic state. It received some sponsorship from Iran, which manipulated and sponsored both Kurdish Hezbollah and the PKK at different times.[34] These two groups engaged in conflict during the 1990s, and both committed human rights violations, including killings and torture. Kurdish Hezbollah was particularly severe.[35]

Sadettin Tantan, who was interior minister (1999–2001) in the pre-AKP coalition government, denies that the Turkish state had any hand in sponsoring Kurdish Hezbollah.[36] Even if this is so, Human Rights Watch and other such organisations have alleged that the Turkish authorities at least adopted a laissez-faire attitude towards the group, or even used it as a pawn in its battle against the PKK.[37] Ultimately the state would turn against the organisation in a series of battles fought brutally on both sides. Kurdish Hezbollah's swansong came in January 2000, after an armed battle against Turkish authorities at a house in the Istanbul neighbourhood of Beykoz.[38] Former Kurdish Hezbollah members who escaped conviction also contributed to the planning of the November 2003 al-Qaeda suicide attacks against the British consulate, the HSBC building and two Jewish synagogues in Istanbul, which left fifty-seven dead including British Consul General Roger Short.[39]

Kurdish Hezbollah would later regroup and launch a civilian political party, the Huda Party (Hur Dava Partisi), which campaigned in opposition to the secular Kurdish party of the day. The Huda Party claimed both Kurdish and traditional Islamic identity. It resented the equal brutality of the PKK and the government during the conflict and was angered by the PKK's hegemony in Kurdish politics. Unlike the secular PKK, the Huda Party advocated the idea that Kurds and Turks could work together through Islam to see their rights, such as education in the Kurdish language, respected.[40]

Under the leadership of coalition prime minister Tansu Ciller (1993–6), counterinsurgency operations intensified. What was known as the Castle Plan brought together government security agencies, drug traffickers and right-wing death squads in Kurdish areas.[41] In October 1993, Ciller held a press conference presenting a list of Kurdish artists, businessmen and other people who were helping the PKK, and added that she was going to eliminate the problem.[42] Soon there was a wave of kidnappings and assassinations in the south-east, where "special war" units were acting with impunity against the PKK while also engaging in drug trafficking, rape, blackmail and protection rackets.[43] Residents from hamlets and villages perceived to be pro-PKK were evicted, their crops and fields, if not their entire village, set ablaze, and their livestock machine-gunned as they watched.[44] In January 1994, almost 100 people were picked up individually by such squads, killed and buried somewhere along the road between Ankara and Istanbul.[45] The extent of the cooperation between ultranationalist paramilitary forces, the village guards, the security services and organised crime became clear after the Susurluk incident in 1996 (see Chapter 1), when leaders of these types of groups were found together when their car crashed. During this period, the height of the conflict, there were assassinations in the streets of south-eastern cities such as Diyarbakir on a daily basis. There were no witnesses, no reports and no prosecutions.[46]

Despite this extreme violence, the counterinsurgency did not end there. It was not until after Turkey and Syria signed the October 1998 Adana Protocol that the conflict abated; following Turkish mobilisation of troops on the border, Hafiz al-Asad agreed that he would no longer provide support for the PKK and would expel Ocalan, a development that helped lead to his capture.[47] After Ocalan was taken, he declared a ceasefire in 1999 and a formal end to the war several months later. Nevertheless, the violence did not totally subsist, and it has intensified and continued intermittingly to the present day, despite attempts at a peace process. In June 2004, the PKK resumed its activities. This was as the Iraq War was in full sway and the group claimed that the Turkish government was not returning its overtures for peace. In 2005, the PKK was allegedly responsible for a bomb at the Turkish resort of Kusadasi on the Aegean coast, which came days after another attack in the nearby popular resort of Cesme.[48]

These attacks were followed by yet another scandal, dubbed the Semdinli Affair after a town where a bookshop belonging to a former PKK member was bombed in November 2005, killing a passer-by. Supposedly the blast was made to look like a PKK attack; however, the perpetrators turned out to be a former PKK informer and two military officers, who were in possession of weapons and police and gendarmerie uniforms. This indicated that the attack was a false flag operation carried out by the military. The accused, though initially convicted, were subsequently released on the grounds that such cases had to be heard by a military court—this was before the constitutional reforms of 2010. The incident caused further unrest in other cities in the region, where stones were thrown at police stations and gendarmerie posts.[49]

2006 was also a violent year, with attacks claiming over 500 victims in cities such as Adana and Istanbul as well as resort towns such as Marmaris and Antalya.[50] Much of the violence was the result of a counterterrorism operation on 29 March 2006 that killed fourteen PKK operatives and led to demonstrations across south-east Turkey. The security clampdowns on the protests led to the deaths of fourteen demonstrators, mostly in Diyarbakir, the following day. Three children were left dead with hundreds detained and wounded. Protesters in Istanbul killed three women who were passing by and were hit by a petrol bomb. Further rallies took place in April 2006, leading to the detention of 200 children between the ages of twelve and eighteen, charged with illegal protests and aiding and abetting the PKK.[51]

In October 2006, the PKK declared a ceasefire, slowing the cycle of violence. However, this did not bring fighting to an end. Attacks and counter-attacks continued, with six people killed in Ankara on 22 May 2007 following a suicide bomb during rush hour at a shopping mall. Just ten days before, an explosion had left one person dead in the coastal city of Izmir. Then, on 7 October 2007, thirteen Turkish soldiers were ambushed and killed in Sirnak province near the Iraqi border, where the PKK was estimated to have 3,500 armed militants. On 17 October, the Turkish government was able to obtain parliamentary approval to launch cross-border raids into Iraq, with 40,000 troops at the ready. (This did not deter the PKK from killing twelve soldiers and capturing eight more on 21 October, provoking a Turkish counter-attack that killed thirty-two rebels.)[52]

On 24 October 2007, Turkish troops made a large-scale incursion into northern Iraq accompanied by F-16 fighter aircraft and helicopters to attack PKK bases. Over 650 militants were killed, along with forty-nine civilians. Turkish forces suffered 143 deaths in the ensuing armed conflict, which lasted until 2008.[53] In October 2009, tensions rose again when twenty-four PKK fighters were given a hero's welcome after they entered Turkey from the Habur border crossing in northern Iraq as part of an agreed amnesty.[54] Discussions in 2009 of attempts to grant Kurds greater rights did not prevent further tensions in 2010. Turkish police continued to detain Kurdish protesters as well as many members of the secular Kurdish party, the Peace and Democracy Party (BDP).[55]

After a short period of calm in August 2010, when Ocalan declared a ceasefire during the holy month of Ramadan, attacks continued. In October 2010, 153 people, including several elected mayors, human rights activists and political party members, were put on trial for assisting terrorism and for their membership of the Kurdistan Communities Union (KCK), the PKK's umbrella political movement (sometimes referred to as its urban wing). Violence even continued into 2011, when over 300 militants and 220 members of the security forces were reportedly killed in intermittent fighting.[56] In December 2011, thirty-five smugglers were killed, having been mistaken for terrorists during an airstrike. Finally, on 21 March 2013, Ocalan once again called for a ceasefire, then told his armed followers to leave Turkish territory. They heeded his call, and an estimated 2,000 PKK members left for northern Iraq as part of the peace process.[57] From 2013 to 2015, the Turkish state was in dialogue with the PKK in negotiations known as the Solution Process. The reasons for and ramifications of the decline of this short-lived process will be detailed in the pages below. But this was not the first time that there had been potential openings for dialogue.

It Takes Two to Tango: Past Failures in Potential Peace Openings

Before the most recent tentative talks, other Turkish leaders have tried and failed to stop the dispute. During the 1990s, there were several missed opportunities for Turkey and the PKK to reach some kind of accord. Instead, the conflict maintained its intensity.

One particular opportunity was in 1991, following Suleyman Demirel's election as prime minister and the defeat of Turgut Ozal, who then became president. This period saw the impact of the Gulf War and the subsequent refugee crisis in northern Iraq, which helped to humanise the Kurds' suffering in Turkish eyes.[58] Expectations were raised among Kurds after Ozal welcomed Kurdish autonomy in northern Iraq and Demirel recognised the urgency of the "Kurdish reality" along Turkey's eastern border. Another reason for optimism was that the presence of the Social Democratic Populist Party within Demirel's ruling coalition offered an alternative, purely political channel to the PKK for addressing Kurdish concerns. These circumstances, coupled with pressure from Jalal Talabani's Patriotic Union of Kurdistan (PUK),[59] culminated in the PKK unilaterally declaring a short-lived ceasefire in 1993. This led the security services, interpreting the cease-. fire as a sign of weakness, to believe—erroneously—that the PKK had been defeated.[60]

However, the possibility of some kind of reconciliation did not come to fruition. The reasons for the Turkish state's inability to capitalise on the moment were several. For one thing, there was mistrust between Prime Minister Demirel and President Ozal, with the former trying to undermine any initiatives by the latter. Meanwhile, the military, perhaps not fully briefing the political class on its activities, upped its game with mystery killings targeting members of the Kurdish community in 1992, after Demirel took office. The PKK upped the ante in response, launching attacks including a bomb in an Istanbul department store that killed eleven people.[61] Most importantly, the military and Demirel alike refused to accept the PKK's unilateral ceasefire as sincere, though it was a popular move among Kurds in the south-east. Worse still, Ozal, perhaps one of the Turkish politicians most open to some kind of a compromise,[62] died of a heart attack in April 1993.

Tansu Ciller, who became prime minister in 1993 when Demirel replaced Ozal as president, refused to confront the military on the Kurdish issue.[63] If anything, under Ciller the already brutal conflict intensified. In June 1993, the PKK attacked tourist areas in Turkey and targeted Turkish diplomatic missions in Europe. It even kidnapped European tourists vacationing in the Mediterranean resort city of Antalya, a move designed to undermine Turkey's burgeoning tourist industry as well as its international image.[64] The Turkish state was, to some extent, on the back foot. However, it soon gained the upper hand in 1995, after the military, especially commando and special police forces, received additional government funds for training and equipment, including additional helicopters. It was also able to mount incursions into northern Iraq with US consent and the permission of Iraqi Kurdish leader Masoud Barzani of the Kurdish Democratic Party. In Syria, on the other hand, the PKK remained entrenched,[65] and the Turkish armed forces' increased capacity did not encourage a non-military solution.

There were several other reasons why the 1991–3 period did not yield results in solving the Kurdish problem. As professor Philip Robins has pointed out, positive rhetoric from the Turkish government was not enough to reverse the enmity resulting from the under-development of the Kurdish south-east, alienated by poor public services and years of state repression. In addition, the military was still exerting influence over the Kurdish question behind the scenes.[66]

174

Meanwhile, Robins adds that there was political immaturity on the part of the Kurds, with members of the pro-Kurdish People's Labour Party determined to shun symbols of an ethnically Turkish state, the classic example being Leyla Zana taking her oath in Kurdish upon joining the National Assembly in November 1991.[67] According to Sedat Yurtdas, who was arrested along with Zana for saying the oath in Kurdish, they had acted for propaganda purposes. Party members committed other, smaller acts of defiance, such as wearing a visible handkerchief with the colours of the Kurdish flag in their breast pockets.[68] But Robins blames hardliners from both sides. The PKK insurgency continued despite the promising public debate on the crisis, while right-wing nationalist Turks were alarmed into action by the prospect of greater Kurdish rights. Matters came to a head during the New Year festival of Newroz in 1992; during this Kurdish holiday period, ninety-two died and 341 were injured, including two members of the security services while intervening to stop the celebrations.[69]

Too Hot to Trot: The Political Impact of Ocalan's Capture and the Peace Process

Another opportunity for peace manifested itself after Ocalan's capture in 1999. This development had already made an impact on Turkish politics and the general election of that year. Bulent Ecevit, who had been serving as caretaker prime minister of a minority government following the collapse of a series of coalitions since the 1995 elections, managed to lead his Democratic Left Party to victory, winning 22.6 per cent of the vote. This was not a clear leftward shift, though—the Nationalist Action Party, which had not passed the 10 per cent electoral threshold to enter parliament in 1995, this time obtained an 18.6 per cent vote share.[70]

Ocalan's trial started just after the 1999 elections. Many were surprised by what they perceived as the Kurdish leader's concern to spare his own life by offering some kind of reconciliation with his onetime enemies.[71] This was reflected in his first public appearance after his capture, when he reiterated his dedication to the service of the Turkish state, albeit by emphasising the need to end the Kurdish insurgency in return for real democratic rights. He stated, "You can hang me if you like, but let me solve the Kurdish problem first. You cannot do it without me".[72]

This did not spare Ocalan from his inevitable conviction. On 29 June 1999, he was sentenced to death on charges of treason.[73] However, this verdict was not implemented. On 3 October 2001, Turkey introduced a constitutional reform package designed to meet some of the EU's Copenhagen entry criteria. The reforms included restrictions on the death penalty, which would "not be imposed except in time of war, imminent threat of war and terrorist crimes."[74] Indeed, former prime minister Mesut Yilmaz was astute in his later comment that "the road to EU passes through Diyarbakir".[75] In 2002, additional EU-oriented reform packages were introduced which included the abolition of the death penalty and revisions to Turkey's anti-terror legislation,[76] as well as amendments to the procedural law enabling retrials of cases flagged by the European Court of Human Rights as carrying violations. This eventually led to the release of Kurdish members of parliament such as Leyla Zana, Selim Sadak, Hatip Dicle and Orhan Dogan.[77] While Ocalan's life was spared, his sentence was commuted to life imprisonment on the fortress-like Imrali Island, where he remains in virtual isolation.

The 2002 reform packages constituted under the AKP also allowed television broadcasting in Kurdish dialects including Zaza and Kirmanci. Meanwhile, the EU's decision to proceed with talks on Turkish accession on 17 December 2004 gave Ankara additional impetus to continue with reforms related to the Kurdish question. However, by the same token, Turkey put pressure on European governments to curtail the PKK's activities.[78] This, together with the change of attitude towards terrorist groups after the 9/11 attacks on the US, led to European nations cracking down on the PKK. In 2001, the UK placed the PKK on its list of terrorist groups, and was the first European country to do so. Soon after, in 2002, the EU followed suit.[79] This was a major blow to the credibility and legitimacy of the PKK and placed it on the wrong side of the War on Terror. There was no acknowledgement from Europe that the PKK represented many Kurds in Turkey. Instead, its status was reduced to that of a terrorist organisation.[80]

In fact, European pressure on the PKK did not stop there. When making contact with EU politicians, members of Kurdish parties in the Turkish parliament were urged to either disassociate themselves from the PKK or clarify the nature of their relationship with the armed group. PKK-affiliated organisations and sympathetic political parties devised compromise strategies to regain their lost political legitimacy, such as focusing on civil campaigns that aimed to secure Kurdish rights to educate children in their mother tongue and appealing for Ocalan to be recognised as a legitimate representative.[81]

The PKK's woes were unending in the post-9/11 period. Its legitimacy was weakened again after the invasion of Iraq in 2003 by the US and its coalition of the willing. The PKK found itself caught in the political crossfire, facing hardened public opinion in the region and internationally.[82] Moreover, with Iraq's Kurdish northern areas gaining autonomy, it was the Kurdistan Regional Government (KRG), rather than the PKK, that was seen as the central focus for many Kurds.[83] Indeed, the KRG's autonomy within a federalised but united Iraq put pressure on the PKK to water down its primary objective, from an independent Kurdistan by military means to self-governance in perhaps a confederalised Turkey.[84] The PKK had in fact been gravitating towards this position since the 1990s.

Following Ocalan's capture and imprisonment in 1999, there had been several internal changes to the functioning of the PKK. There were various reports of a power struggle between the PKK's European wing and armed units in the mountains in Turkey. However, the PKK soon regrouped under the confirmed leadership of Ocalan as president, despite his imprisonment. Ocalan then organised a temporary ten-member council to act on his behalf.[85] At first, this surprised many within official Turkish circles, who thought the PKK was a Stalinist-type organisation that would crumble once Ocalan was taken out of the equation. Not only was this not the case, but the PKK remained loyal to its founder, and his decisions, whether to intensify violence or declare a ceasefire, were obeyed. In November 2012, for example, Kurdish prisoners terminated a hunger strike when it had reached a critical sixty-eighth day as soon as Ocalan told them to.[86]

Despite the setbacks for the PKK in the post-9/11 period, Ocalan's decisions, actions and interventions once again made him a pivotal political player. He managed to capitalise on Turkey's EU accession hopes to spare his own life. Understanding that the tide was turning, he made a statement that called for the implementation of "true democracy" to solve the Kurdish problem on Turkey's existing borders.

This was clever, as it was compatible with both Ataturk's ambitions for a strong and united Turkey and entry into the EU.[87] Ocalan reminded his followers, "if they execute me, the EU candidacy, the economy and peace will all go down ... These all depend on my staying alive. I am a synthesis of values, not just a person. I represent democracy."[88] By the same token, Ocalan began to emphasise a confederal solution. In his vision, this "builds on the self-government of local communities and is organised in the form of open councils, town councils, local parliaments and larger congresses. The citizens are agents of this self-government, not state-based authorities."[89]

Another factor that enabled Ocalan to maintain his hold over the Kurdish movement was the success of Kurdish parties in elections. In 1999, the pro-Kurdish People's Democracy Party (HADEP) managed to garner 4.7 per cent of the vote, around 1.5 million votes in total. Despite this being below the 10 per cent threshold for parliamentary seats, it signified increased support for Kurdish-oriented parties in the south-eastern region. In the local elections of the same year, HADEP won in the major Kurdish population centres of Diyarbakir, Agri, Batman, Bingol, Hakkari, Siirt and Van, as well as nine other towns and twenty further districts.[90]

In the following elections in 2002, a new Kurdish party, the Democratic People's Party (DEHAP), ran after HADEP faced the possibility of closure (it was eventually banned by the Constitutional Court in 2003). DEHAP secured 6.2 per cent of the popular vote, again below the 10 per cent mark. Still, this was a significant increase. Two years later, in the 2004 local elections, DEHAP, as part of a coalition with several other small parties (while fighting a closure trial), obtained 5 per cent of the total popular vote, but won in five cities, thirty-one towns and thirty-three districts.[91]

These election successes made it almost unavoidable for Erdogan to become the first Turkish prime minister to formally acknowledge Turkey's Kurdish problem in August 2005, a move appreciated by many Kurds at the time.[92] This did not prevent the momentum that the Kurdish movement was enjoying. Not only did it see the release of Leyla Zana and her fellow imprisoned Kurdish parliamentarians, the BDP's predecessor, the DTP, founded in 2005, was able to circumvent the 10 per cent threshold in the 2007 general elections by running its candidates as independents. As a result, the party managed to send twenty-one deputies to parliament. There was a fly in the ointment, though—it was in these same elections that the AKP won in most of the predominantly Kurdish south-eastern cities.[93]

However, the AKP was unable to capitalise on this success. Soon Erdogan's initial popularity began to wane. There were widespread boycotts (ordered by the PKK) when Erdogan visited Diyarbakir in 2008. This was largely to do with Kurdish frustrations over the AKP's slow pace of reform. With the resulting strikes, public transportation did not run and the vast majority of the city's shops did not open.[94] This frustration made its mark during the March 2009 local elections. The AKP lost much support to the DTP, which waged an effective campaign that emphasised Kurdish identity. The DTP won ninety-nine municipalities in eastern Turkey as well as seats in nine provincial capitals.[95] This sent a clear message to the AKP: supplying goods and services was not enough for Kurds; their identity was more important.[96]

Asking the Devil to a Dance: State-Ocalan Peace Overtures under the AKP

Deciphering the nature of the Turkish-PKK talks is difficult, due to their secretive nature. However, some points can certainly be discerned. Organs of the state had been in contact with the PKK for years. There had been indirect contact with Ocalan between 1992 and 1993 through the back channel of the Iraqi PUK's Jalal Talabani, who had good relations with Prime Minister Ozal. In 1996 Prime Minister Erbakan sent untitled letters to Ocalan through intermediaries. This initiative came to naught after the "post-modern" military intervention the following year, but following the capture of Ocalan in 1999 military officials spoke to him during his incarceration until 2001. Between 2002 and 2005, a new team of military personnel began discussions with the Kurdish leader. This, however, was against the wishes of the general chief of staff, Hilmi Ozkok.[97]

After 2005, it was the National Intelligence Organisation that took over the Ocalan talks. This was an important development. The military was staunchly against talks with the PKK,[98] which at times once again involved Talabani as an intermediary. This time, the talks included not just Ocalan but also other leading PKK figures such as Sabri Ok, Zubeyir Aydar and Adem Uzun, as well as the Ministry of Foreign Affairs. The discussions were not confined to Imrali Island, but also took place in Europe and the Kandil mountains of Iraqi Kurdistan. One important development was the involvement of Murat Karayilan, a PKK leader based in Kandil, who sent a letter to Erdogan urging dialogue. This led to a deal, which was brokered with the involvement of National Intelligence chief Emre Taner, leading to thirty-four PKK fighters' return to Turkey in October 2009.[99] Initially, Erdogan tried to bypass any contact with Ocalan and instead attempted to direct discussions toward other Kurdish notables in the Kandil mountains and Europe, or even the BDP, which was founded in 2008 and came to replace the banned DTP. He would soon realise that, in order to come to any real agreement, Ocalan, who remained the most powerful leader of the Kurdish movement, simply could not be avoided.[100]

During the summer of 2009, as part of an attempt to bolster its handling of the Kurdish problem, the AKP launched its "Kurdish Opening" (Kurt acilimi).[101] After the government made this announcement, Ocalan, on 15 August 2009, unveiled his "road map" detailing his proposed solution to the Kurdish question.[102] He offered a ceasefire, which would replace the previously broken ceasefire of 2004. He urged the Turkish government to set up a "Truth and Reconciliation Commission". He also emphasised the need for legal and constitutional steps to be put in place to serve as a structured platform for the resolution of the conflict.[103]

This was a promising beginning. There were, however, a series of setbacks. One of them was the furore over the nature of the October 2009 victory parade for the returning thirty-four PKK militants, through the Habur border crossing with Iraq. The amnesty was designed as a confidence-building measure between the parties. However, any confidence was soon lost as the DTP and the PKK transformed the event into a show of power. As a result, many Turks looked upon the victory parade as an affront, or a terrorist victory parade, rather than a symbol of conciliatory politics. Under pressure, the AKP first broadened and then diluted its Kurdish initiative into a "Democratic Initiative" (demokratik acilim), which also focused on other minority social groups (Alevis, Romani Gypsies).[104] The government then confined its response to the Kurdish question to cultural and linguistic rights.[105]

It was in this context that Prime Minister Erdogan, in November 2009, called on parliament to support the initiative, stating: "It is wrong to call this problem only a Kurdish problem or only a democracy problem. The final aim is to reach national unity and brotherhood. It is a process of democracy".[106] This came as Interior Minister Besir Atalay unveiled to parliament the six first steps of the initiative, for promotion of democracy and economic development. These would include establishing an independent human rights institution; a commission to combat discrimination; a parliamentary ratification of the UN Convention Against Torture with a national preventative mechanism; an independent body tasked with receiving and investigating accusations of torture or mistreatment by the security forces; and the renaming of residential areas in line with demands from locals and political parties to be able to communicate in languages other than Turkish.[107] Some of these reforms were later made law in July 2010, notably with a reduction in the penalty for children accused of terror-related activities.[108] Others fell by the wayside.

At first the Kurdish opening was well received. This soon turned to doubt and even mistrust, with increasing numbers of Kurds believing it to be a move by the AKP to regain the voters it had lost during the 2009 local elections. Meanwhile, a US tour of the south-east revealed that what many Kurds wanted from the Turkish government was an end to military operations in the south-east, changes to the constitution enshrining Kurdish rights, wider use of the Kurdish language, and an amnesty for PKK fighters, with better conditions for Ocalan.[109] In December 2009, the DTP was banned as a result of its alleged association with the PKK, and over the course of the following months 1,400 members were arrested and 900 detained, provoking protests and violence in the south-east.[110]

Nevertheless, talks revived, this time with Hakan Fidan, who had good working relations with Erdogan, as the new head of National Intelligence. These talks, held between 2009 and 2011 most probably in Oslo, involved the PKK on one side and, on the other, a "state committee" and high-level bureaucrats from various ministries.[111] A foreign observer was present,[112] by some accounts the United Kingdom.[113] However, the talks collapsed after clashes between Turkish soldiers and the PKK in June 2011 left fourteen Turkish soldiers dead. The PKK blamed the Turkish military, claiming that the armed forces were continuing attacks.[114] Leaked tapes that appeared in the Turkish press at the time indicated that there had been at least five meetings in Oslo during these two years between Turkish and Kurdish officials, as well as several preparatory liaisons in between.[115] Meanwhile, the Kurdish Democratic Society Congress (DTK), close to both the PKK and the BDP, launched its plan for "democratic autonomy" in December 2010. By the end of the talks, the two sides had reached an agreement and drafted a protocol with terms of reference for further negotiations. In the wake of clashes in June 2011, however, the protocols that emerged from the talks were not signed by Erdogan, who apparently preferred to avoid proceeding to the next step. In later talks between Ocalan and the state, Ankara was again recalcitrant in going forward by turning the negotiations into an official framework for direct talks.[116]

Of course, this begs the question, what was written in this so-called protocol? According to details leaked to the press by the opposition CHP, some of the stipulations included the following: both sides would continue to negotiate and recognised the need to seek a permanent solution, as emphasised at talks in Oslo and on Imrali Island; the parties should negotiate over the names for the proposed Constitutional Council, Peace Council and Truth and Justice Commission, which were detailed in other documents drafted by Ocalan and presented at Imrali; Turkey would guarantee that two individuals representing the state (from National Intelligence, officially or unofficially) would visit Ocalan after the general elections of June 2011; those arrested in operations against the Kurdish umbrella unit, the KCK, would be released, and Kurdish members of the press as well as legal and political representatives of Kurdish people would cease to be intimidated; all military operations and movements were to cease until June 2011, when the two sides would meet again.[117]

Despite Erdogan not signing the protocol, it appears that talks continued between the Turkish state and the PKK. These remained an imperative as the ongoing civil war in Syria created a virtually autonomous Kurdish zone in the north of the country. Murat Karayilan, a senior commander of the PKK based in the Kandil mountains, sent a letter to *Taraf* newspaper explaining the reason for the increase in PKK violence.[118] Meanwhile, there was unrest in Turkey as Kurdish prisoners declared a hunger strike and over 100 members of the KCK were arrested and detained.[119] Kurdish parliamentary deputy Leyla Zana met Erdogan in July 2012, urging him to restart the peace process.[120] One month before, Bulent Arinc, deputy chairman of the AKP, had even commented that his government would consider moving Ocalan to house arrest if the PKK lay down its arms, following a call from Zana.[121]

Erdogan was soon obliged to admit that talks were taking place. In December 2012 Erdogan, in a television interview, stated that the government was in negotiations with the jailed Kurdish leader and that the talks concerned how the PKK could lay down its arms.[122] This new round of state talks with the PKK became known as the Solution Process. Over the next few months, members of the BDP, including its chairman Ahmet Turk, its co-chair (and later presidential candidate) Selahattin Demirtas and Ayla Akat Ata visited Ocalan in prison, perhaps acting as his liaisons. Some details of talks between Ocalan and BDP members were leaked to the press, although Erdogan and the government denied that these represented what was being discussed, and alleged that the leaks were an attempt to derail the talks.[123] Another setback was the murder of three female Kurdish activists in Paris in January 2013.[124]

Regardless, a breakthrough came in March 2013, after Ocalan's Kurdish New Year appeal for a ceasefire and for the PKK's disarmament and withdrawal from Turkey,[125] which soon led the PKK to lay down their arms and cross to the Kandil mountains of Iraq's autonomous Kurdistan Region. This response laid to rest any doubts about whether Ocalan was still in control of the Kurdish movement.[126] Soon after, on 4 April, the Turkish government announced a committee of "Wise Men", whose task was to discuss the peace process with the general public and promote the talks.[127]

According to Can Peker, a member of the Wise Men, this was the first time that different groups had come together and discussed the Kurdish question frankly and openly.[128] When the Wise Men reported back to Erdogan, they concluded that the Turkish public was ready for peace in all regions.[129] Finally, in September 2013, Erdogan announced another new democratic package aimed at resolving the Kurdish question. This included possible relaxations on the 10 per cent electoral threshold to allow Kurdish candidates to enter parliament as party members, rather than as independents. It also relaxed restrictions on the Kurdish language, allowing it to be taught in private (though not public) schools, and the use of Kurdish names for villages.[130]

However, for many Kurds the newly proposed package fell far short of expectations. It did not release all Kurdish activists (many of whom were journalists) or make the necessary changes to anti-terror law.[131] The BDP said that the measures were not enough to satisfy militants who had withdrawn from Turkish territory.[132] Changing the electoral threshold would also mean changing the electoral districts according to the package, making the concession almost null and void.[133] In any case, such issues would be addressed in a parliament that had been reduced to rubber-stamping AKP policies. As for lifting the ban on Kurdish letters, in many rallies in the south-east the ban was already being flouted.[134] The new package was also criticised on the basis that education in Kurdish would not be permitted in primary school, meaning that only after "a child passed through a Turkification process" could they learn Kurdish or their mother tongue. There were also no proposed changes to the constitution.[135]

Despite this disappointment, the most important development in the peace process to date occurred in July 2014, when the Turkish parliament passed a bill legalising official state talks with the PKK.[136] Previously, these had been conducted behind closed doors, as the PKK is designated a terrorist organisation. This bill could potentially authorise real and concrete discussions, paving the way for an official peace process. However, since violence erupted once more in 2015, this has become increasingly unrealistic. Meanwhile, among Kurds there remains serious dissatisfaction with the process.

Kurdish Attitudes and Discontent Regarding the Peace Process

Though the fallout and repercussions of the Syria conflict have been a significant factor in the recent spate of hostilities between Kurd and Turk, this was simply a spark that has ignited long-held suspicion of and discontent with the attempted peace process. What, then, have most Kurds in Turkey wanted from a peace process, and what has been the source of their disillusionment?

First and foremost, Kurds want to be taught in their mother tongue and have it recognised by the state as an official language. Kurds want to achieve democratic autonomy, whereby Kurds may elect their own governors in Kurdish regions and have Kurds within the public admin- istration—which would essentially mean a Kurdish canton, or a self- governing entity. Many also want the PKK and Ocalan to enter politi- cal life in Turkey, looking at Northern Ireland and Israel/Palestine as examples of political leaders being released as part of the peace pro- cess.[137] The desired position of Ocalan and the PKK at present appears to be that of a form of confederation.[138] Although the meaning of this is not entirely clear, it probably means local autonomy in local Kurdish municipalities, with more powers.[139]

Despite reforms initiated by the AKP in response to the Kurdish question, there have been significant delays and bureaucratic obstacles. These delays have reduced the effect of the reforms and created cyni- cism among many Kurds.[140] We've already seen this reflected in the boycott of Erdogan's visit to Diyarbakir in 2008 and Kurdish political parties' electoral defeats in the south-east region. Even the AKP's 2009 "Kurdish Opening" ran into trouble when the return of the thirty-four PKK fighters as part of a general amnesty was turned into a victory parade, angering many Turks.[141]

Confidence in the government had disintegrated among Kurds even before the upsurge of violence in 2015. According to Ertugrul Kurkcu, former co-chairman of the pro-Kurdish HDP, who spoke to the authors before violence reignited, "I don't see any Kurd who believes the sin- cerity of the government. Not from Ocalan himself to the lowest grass- roots … but the majority of Kurds are giving the talks a chance".[142] For many Kurds, there are still many outstanding questions that need to be addressed for the peace process to work and be meaningful. There is much anger over the arrests of members of the KCK in 2012, believed to be a ploy by the government for leverage in negotiations with Ocalan.[143] In fact, this incident shattered Kurdish trust in the govern- ment. Nearly every major Kurdish political figure had been arrested, with the exception of those in parliament, who have immunity.[144]

Meanwhile although poverty has decreased in the Kurdish regions, it is still the least developed part of the country. Unemployment aver- ages 50–60 per cent, there is still little industry, and employment is based on the social services. While Turkey's trade with the region is high and trade with Northern Iraq is expected at the time of writing to reach US$30 billion per annum, this has had almost no impact on Turkey's south-east.[145]

Of equal importance is the quest for justice and answers about extra-judicial killings and disappearances during the turbulent 1990s, which number in the thousands. Despite two investigations during the 1990s into state collusion over such killings, no one has been held accountable, and there is a lack of will to investigate high levels of state involvement in such acts.[146] What is truly required is a commission of inquiry to discover what happened in the eastern part of Turkey and prosecute those responsible.[147] Despite the AKP government confronting the military in the courts during the Ergenekon and Balyoz trials, no such challenge has been issued over the Kurdish issue. What many Kurds would like to see are prosecutions for human rights violations perpetrated by the military, the police services and JITEM, the Gendarmerie's counterterrorism and intelligence unit.[148] Any hope of such prosecutions was dealt a blow in November 2015, when a Turkish court acquitted eight JITEM members of unsolved murders in the Cizre region between 1993 and 1995.[149]

In 2009, there was a trial against retired colonel Cemal Temizoz, three former PKK members turned informers and three members of the "village guard" in Diyarbakir, who were accused of the killing and disappearance during the 1990s of twenty people in Cizre, Sırnak province.[150] JITEM was believed to be responsible for many of the arrests, executions and disappearances. However, there were significant problems with the trial, such as lengthy proceedings, witnesses retracting statements, threats to lawyers and witness intimidation, to name but a few.[151]

As Human Rights Watch asserts, in order for the problem to be tackled properly there needs to be a culture of full disclosure, investigations into the chain of command in such cases, witness protection provisions, prevention of the statute of limitations, governmental support for resources in such trials as well as accountability and a process for justice, truth and reconciliation. This is especially important as there are strong demands by the relatives of victims for the Turkish government to address past abuses.[152] Tahir Elci, head of the Diyarbakir Bar Association, who was shot dead in the crossfire of a gun battle in

November 2015, had before his death looked into such cases and had had to apply to the European Court of Human Rights in Strasbourg in order to obtain information for legal cases brought on behalf of families. In one case, Elci told the authors before his death that it took him ten years to fully investigate a claim, due to lack of cooperation from the authorities.[153] This was especially important as there have been attempts to excavate unregistered mass graves and burial sites, some of which were discovered in 2012.[154]

Although there have been decreases in human rights violations, there is still a lack of basic freedoms for Kurds such as expression, assembly and political organisation.[155] There are concerns about the internally displaced Kurds as a result of the Turkish state's war against the PKK. As Human Rights Watch notes, according to official figures 378,335 were left homeless and displaced because of the conflict, with the destruction of over 3,000 villages.[156] Despite the announcement of initiatives to assist the displaced, with a special agency and compensation through the Law on Compensation for Damage Arising from Terror and Combating Terror (Law No. 5233), such efforts have yet to materialise in a concrete manner. The maintenance of the village guard system and paramilitary attacks further complicate returns to villages, as the security situation is unstable.[157] Meanwhile, in Turkey's high-security "F-type" prisons, where individuals accused of crimes against the state are held, conditions have improved but still pose significant issues. Administrative detention is still practised, as are strip searches, beatings and detention in small cells with a lack of sunlight. Many prisons are overcrowded, while some prisoners are kept in isolation.[158] Some face difficulties in seeing doctors or going to hospitals for treatment.[159]

But perhaps the most significant obstacle to the peace process is the discrepancy between each side's approach to the problem. A common Kurdish critique is that, although the AKP has done the most to try to address the problem, the party still views the Kurdish question as a cultural issue rather than one of territory and national identity.[160] Indeed, the problem is one of power-sharing and nationality, the cultural and economic aspects being offshoots of the national question. Without dealing with the problem at its roots, the conflict will not be resolved.[161] However, the Turkish state does now recognise that it cannot maintain the status quo, given the regional and international ramifications.[162]

Another problem with the peace talks has been the lack of a third party mediator (although there have been outside observers). This was because Turkey opposed the idea, suspicious of international powers interfering in a problem it considered internal.[163] Be that as it may, the absence of an external mediator means that there is no one to push along the process when it reaches deadlock, or to arbitrate differences between the two parties.[164] Furthermore, the talks have resembled more a dialogue between two leaders following their own initiatives, Ocalan and Erdogan, than a coherent peace process structured by agreed frameworks and mechanisms.[165]

Regardless of these issues, with the transformation of the Kurdish campaign away from calls for independence, many Kurds now have hope for greater autonomy in Kurdish areas through empowered Kurdish municipalities.[166] The Gezi Park protests and the heavy-handed police reaction gave many Turks from Istanbul, Ankara, Izmir and other cities, who had never before experienced such force from the authorities, new sympathy for the Kurds. In fact, many protesters learned how to put up barricades and protect themselves from teargas from experienced Kurdish demonstrators. However, although Kurds were present at Gezi, the political party that represented them, the BDP, was not.[167] This indicates that the protests, which were in many respects a challenge to the AKP, were not something the Kurdish parties could accept, as only the AKP has made any inroads with the Kurdish process. Nevertheless, in the wake of the Gezi protests, the recently created pro-Kurdish HDP has gained prominence, on a platform of minority rights, greater democracy, gender equality and LGBT rights.[168] It stands as the sister party of the BDP, and slowly became its successor.

As the military has declined and the peace process has got underway, the era of extra-judicial killings has become increasingly rare and torture rates have reduced. However, there is a risk: as the AKP has grown in power, the police's capacity, scope and authority in the south-east have also increased.[169] Before the 2013 ceasefire broke down, Mehmet Kaya, president of the Diyarbakir Chamber of Commerce, commented that the moment was critical; if steps are not taken to advance the peace process, there is a real concern that the PKK may return to armed struggle.[170] The year 2012 was a warning point, when clashes between the PKK and security services claimed the lives of an estimated 1,000 people on both sides.[171] As we have seen, Kurds generally want an end to the military conflict—rather, they demand constitutional recognition of their rights, Kurdish "democratic" autonomy and the release of Ocalan.[172] But this has not been forthcoming. Ultimately, the peace process, still in its infancy, has not been strong enough to withstand the consequences of the Syria crisis, which has reignited the PKK's conflict with the Turkish state. The longer violence continues, the more intractable the situation will become.

The Decline of the Solution Process

By the end of 2014, the truce that had been in place since Ocalan's 2013 New Year appeal was all but shattered, replaced by a spiralling decline of the Solution Process into nothing short of all-out war. Despite the problems and discontent with the process, it was not just these, but also the developments in neighbouring Syria that were to shatter the fragile peace.

As Syria descended into civil war, Turkey found itself with multiple threats along its over 500-mile border to the south. Its once friend but now foe, Bashar al-Asad, was trying to reverse the fracturing of his own country, conducting fierce attacks against rebels, with support from Lebanon's Hezbollah and Russia, and allegedly unleashing chemical weapons, to the anger of the international community. Turkey has made no secret of its disdain for Asad, repeatedly calling for his ouster. However, by 2014, one of the most effective forces against the Asad regime was none other than the Islamic State in Iraq and Syria (ISIS), which, within the course of a year, spread through and conquered vast territories in both Syria and neighbouring Iraq. The rise of ISIS affected Turkey directly after forty-six Turks were captured by the group in Mosul, Iraq in June 2014. They were released only after Turkey itself reportedly released 180 members of the terrorist group.[173] Perhaps the most effective counter to ISIS in Syria are the Kurds, especially the Democratic Union Party (PYD) and its militia force, the People's Protection Units. However, Ankara views these groups with deep suspicion and hostility because of their deemed close associations with the PKK.

The Asad regime, the Kurds and ISIS represented three sides of a deadly triangle in Syria that has spelled danger for its neighbour and helped sound the death knell of the Kurdish-Turkish peace process. The three forces came to blows in the autumn of 2014, in the Syrian border city of Kobani and its environs. In September, ISIS laid siege to Kobani and its surrounding area. The majority of its inhabitants were of Kurdish origin. As the siege intensified over the following weeks and even months, the news was full of grave loss of life, human rights abuses and the increased velocity of bombardment of the Kurdish enclave, where the violence could be seen and heard from across the Turkish border.[174] Murmurs of Kurdish discontent in Turkey over Ankara's lack of action soon grew into a roar as events unfolded. Ocalan even declared that if the Kurds at Kobani were massacred the PKK-Turkey peace process would halt.[175] Kurdish citizens of Turkey watched helplessly as they witnessed the destruction (sometimes through binoculars), while thousands of Kurdish refugees fled Kobani en masse for the Turkish border. Teargas grenades and water cannons were used by protesters to hold them back.[176]

Soon riots and violent protests erupted in the Kurdish south-east of Turkey against the government's seeming unwillingness to take action against ISIS. By 7 October, at least twenty-two protesters had been killed and hundreds injured as demonstrators defied curfews imposed in at least six provinces and clashes took place in towns and cities such as Diyarbakir, Mus, Siirt and Batman.[177] Many protesters were angered that Turkey was not only failing to do enough to stop ISIS, but was also preventing Kurdish fighters from Turkey from crossing into Syria to help their kinsmen against the onslaught. Ankara only relented as far as allowing Kurdish fighters from the Iraqi Kurdistan Regional Government, an initial force of just 150, to enter.[178] President Erdogan added fuel to the fire with comments equating the Syrian Kurdish party, the PYD, with ISIS, informing reporters that "It is wrong to view them differently, we need to deal with them jointly".[179]

The Turkish state's inaction against ISIS was perceived by some as Ankara's reluctance to save its traditional enemy, the Kurds, from attack, even by ISIS, especially as a weakened Kurdish force could rebalance the power relations in peace talks between Ankara and the PKK.[180] Alternatively, perhaps Ankara underestimated the potential for Kobani to dislodge the peace process and was reluctant to engage ISIS if the stakes weren't too high, especially after Turkish hostages held by the group in Iraq had just been released. Regardless, the damage was done. Not only had the imprisoned Ocalan publicly stated that the peace process was hanging in the balance but so too had PKK military leaders on the ground, such as founding member Cemil Bayik from his base in the Kandil mountains on the Iraqi-Turkish border.[181] As protests in Turkey continued into November, with thousands marching in towns and cities such as Suruc and Diyarbakir, tensions had arisen between Turkey and the PKK. Soon they would boil over.

2015 was a year that saw sieges, arrests, airstrikes, curfews, terrorist attacks, roadside bombs, assassinations and a general return to violence reminiscent of the 1980s and '90s. In mid-October 2014, Turkish F-16s pounded Kurdish rebel positions inside Turkey, for the first time since the 2013 truce.[182] This strike came after members of the Turkish security service had been killed by unknown assailants;[183] such attacks against security personnel continued after the airstrikes. In an attempt to defuse tension in February 2015, Ocalan called again for the PKK to lay down its arms, in a statement read out by an HDP lawmaker in a press conference with Deputy Prime Minister Yalcin Akdogan. This came after members of the HDP had met members of the PKK at their headquarters in the Kandil mountains. The statement, which listed measures the government should take to support the peace process such as drafting a new constitution, was hailed by both HDP co-chair Selahattin Demirtas and Prime Minister Davutoglu.[184] Ocalan's message was reiterated ahead of Newroz (Kurdish New Year) celebrations in March. But even this was not enough to prevent the violence about to ensue.

One of the main sparks that set off the new round of hostilities came in June 2015. Just two days before general elections, twin blasts rocked an HDP campaign rally in Diyarbakir, killing four and wounding hundreds, just before Selahattin Demirtas was scheduled to speak. Despite calls for calm from Demirtas and Erdogan, and promises by Prime Minister Davutoglu to investigate the blasts, local youths remained on the site, protesting and throwing stones at police.[185] This was by no means the first time the HDP had been the target of violence on the campaign trail. There had already been scores of attacks including bombs at campaign offices and shots fired on campaign vehicles, which killed a driver.[186] These incidents came at a time when the stakes could not be higher. The HDP was seeking to pass the 10 per cent electoral threshold. If successful, it would gain representation as a party in Turkey's parliament, at the expense of the AKP's seats and therefore its ability to change the constitution.

The dust of the Diyarbakir bombings had barely settled when the south-east was rocked by another terrorist attack in July, this time in the district of Suruc near the Syrian border. Thirty-three people were killed after the youth wing of a leftist Kurdish-friendly political party was targeted by ISIS, most probably for its vocal support for the Kurds of Kobani.[187] Rallies were held across the country in support of the victims, condemning the government for its Syria policy and for not doing enough to help the Kurds across the border. Regardless, the bombing led to a wave of violence between the PKK and the Turkish state, with the PKK killing two police officers just days after the bombing, claiming this was in revenge for Suruc.[188] In the following weeks there was a spate of PKK attacks against the Turkish security services involving shootings, ambushes, land mines and even suicide bomb attacks or the use of rocket-propelled fire.[189] On one occasion, as many as eight Turkish soldiers were killed in a bomb attack in the south-eastern province of Siirt.[190]

In response, Turkish security forces increased operations in the area and killed eight PKK fighters in Hakkari.[191] The violence continued to escalate as Ankara became increasingly concerned about the growing strength and capabilities of the PKK. Not only was it increasingly popular in the south-east, but it was becoming more organised in the Kurdish areas of Iraq and Syria.[192] Over the course of July and August 2015, the conflict between the PKK and the Turkish state intensified to levels that had not been seen in well over a decade, pushing the peace process firmly onto the back burner.

Having joined the US-led international coalition against ISIS in July 2015, the Turkish air force launched a series of strikes against the terrorist organisation in Syria. However, Turkish engagements against ISIS targets were few and far between, compared with the air attacks against PKK bases in northern Iraq.[193] Indeed, the clampdown following the Suruc bombings targeted not only ISIS militants but also PKK fighters. At the end of July, Davutoglu announced that 590 suspected members of both organisations had been arrested.[194] More PKK targets were struck by Turkish jets in the following months. Some of the biggest attacks included a strike in September in south-east Turkey, a day after the PKK had killed sixteen Turkish soldiers. Just a couple of days later, on 8 September, fifteen police officers were killed in two bombings. Meanwhile, Turkish aircraft struck forty PKK targets.[195] In another operation in mid-September, around fifty-five PKK members were killed after warplanes bombed further targets in Turkey and Iraq.[196]

This upsurge of violence in the south-east took place at the same time as a second round of electoral campaigning, for the November re-run of the June 2015 general election, necessitated by the AKP's failure to find a suitable coalition partner. The pro-Kurdish HDP was under particular strain, especially after the 10 October 2015 Ankara twin bombings, which targeted an HDP election rally and claimed the lives of 102 civilians.[197] It was the worst terrorist attack in Turkey's history. ISIS was responsible (although there were some spurious claims that the PKK had been involved);[198] however, what concerned many was the conduct of the emergency services when treating the victims, many of whom were either Kurds or sympathetic towards the Kurdish struggle. Some were so angered that they even clashed with security services on the scene, only to be met with teargas.[199] The state also faced criticism over the lack of stringent security. Why, some asked, were AKP election rallies always secure, but not opposition party rallies?

The increase in violence was not limited to airstrikes and attacks on Turkish security services; it affected the day-to-day lives of ordinary Kurds in the south-east. Soon residents in some towns, cities and provinces such as Cizre began digging ditches and barricades in an effort to keep out Turkish security forces.[200] In twelve south-eastern cities, HDP local authorities went as far as declaring self-government.[201] In return, five Kurdish district majors and many activists were arrested.[202]

To overcome the barricades, the Turkish forces would often fire on PKK targets from great distances, causing civilian death and other collateral damage.[203] Raids against PKK targets had the same effect. Some cities and towns were under curfew for months on end, enduring a de facto siege. Businesses closed and quality of life deteriorated. According to the International Crisis Group, such actions in the south-east led to the displacement of 355,000 civilians, with over 250 non-combatants killed.[204] It was only a matter of time before the PKK would strike a Turkish target. This took place in mid-February 2016, when twenty-eight people, all but one of them military personnel, were killed in downtown Ankara after a car bomb exploded close to a military convoy.[205] The Kurdistan Freedom Falcons, an offshoot of the PKK, claimed responsibility. The group struck again the following month in the Kizilay area of Ankara, in a suicide bombing which took the lives of thirty-seven people.[206]

The violence of the 2015–16 period clearly derailed the nascent peace process and risked the conflict becoming even more intractable. This is especially the case since Turkey's parliament passed legislation in June 2016 requiring prime ministerial approval for prosecutors to charge generals with human rights violations, and Defence or Interior Ministry approval for cases against lower-ranking servicemen. In effect, this allowed the military to continue its counterinsurgency campaign with impunity.[207] This came six months after Erdogan declared that there would be no more talks with the PKK and that the state would instead "liquidate" PKK militants.[208]

As fighting intensified into 2016, leaving hundreds of security personnel and thousands of PKK militants dead,[209] the AKP government looked to take action on a political level against the pro-Kurdish HDP. In May 2016, Turkey's parliament passed a law to remove parliamentary immunity, paving the way for prosecution against HDP lawmakers on terror-related charges. Widely condemned internationally, the bill, which was signed into law by the president, was designed to side-line the HDP and to allow the ruling party to gain a majority in parliament so that it could change the constitution into a presidential system.[210] Its consequence has been to deny critics of the government's Kurdish policies a peaceful outlet to criticise the state within the country's democratic framework. Such action is bound to fuel more anger and resentment, dissipating hopes of a peaceful solution to the conflict.

There was a brief moment of renewed hope in 2016, after the failed 15 July coup. All political parties, including the HDP, expressed outrage against the attempted putsch. However, in contrast with the AKP's more conciliatory attitude towards the Kemalist CHP and the right-wing Nationalist Action Party, the HDP has not been included in the government's attempts to build a united front in the post-coup period.

For example, when Erdogan invited opposition leaders to a meeting with the prime minister on 25 July 2016, the HDP was neglected.[211] This was also the case with other political gatherings, including the 7 August rally in the Yenikapi neighbourhood of Istanbul, jointly attended by the major parties but with the exclusion of the HDP. When Erdogan made the gentlemanly gesture of withdrawing insult cases against opposition leaders, the HDP was again left out.[212] This was disappointing, marring a laudable attempt by the AKP at reconciliation between Turkey's bitterly opposed political parties, uniting at least on their shared condemnation of the attempted coup. In this sense, the exclusion of the HDP was a missed opportunity because, with its focus on the Kurdish question and a generally liberal orientation, the HDP's supporters had common cause in their opposition to an attempted putsch. The HDP was left alone to voice its condemnation of the coup, and of the political climate in which it took place as expressed by the party's co-chair Figen Yuksekdag.[213] In fact, the HDP has even called for the re-establishment of the Turkish-Kurdish peace talks, as conveyed by the party's other leader, Selahattin Demirtas; however, this has also gone unheeded by Erdogan and the AKP.[214]

Instead, violence in the south-east has continued. Viewing the military as weakened after the attempted coup and the ensuing purges, the PKK conducted a series of attacks on military bases towards the end of July that left scores of soldiers dead.[215] In one incident, the PKK attempted to storm a base in the Cukurca district of Hakkari, not too far from Turkey's border with Iraq. It was rebuffed, leaving thirty-five militants dead.[216] This increase in fighting, while the call for post-coup unity between Turk and Kurd has fallen on deaf ears, means that yet another opportunity for reconciliation has been wasted.

Conclusion

Even after many years of conflict, Ankara and the PKK are not currently engaged in a genuine peace process, let alone close to concluding one. The back channel discussions that have taken place between the two sides are nothing more than a prelude to the meaningful process now needed, in which terms and references are discussed going forward. Despite Turkey making significant inroads in solving the Kurdish question, there are still significant obstacles. Most problematic is the way in which the Kurdish issue is understood. Although light years ahead of the military and many ultranationalist Turks, who deem the problem a socio-economic challenge, the AKP has yet to fully appreciate that the Kurdish issue is a national question, rather than one associated with culture or democracy, although these too are important components. Yet the government does, at times, seem to understand that the Kurdish problem cannot be solved by military means alone. This is an important development.

In order to move forward, Turkey's politicians face many challenges. Turkish society needs to be ready to accept some Kurdish demands. Without such popular support, Erdogan may still be able to solve the Kurdish problem, but the political backlash would be such that he would be left with a Turkish problem instead.[217] If meaningful dialogue is to take place, many scars of the past years need to be healed; this would need to include investigating past misdeeds on the part of the state as well as mutually reciprocated confidence-building measures. Only then can the back channel dialogue develop into a promising peace process.

7

DAVUTOGLU'S RHYTHMIC DIPLOMACY

CLASSICAL CONCERT OR IMPROVISED JAZZ?

Introduction

For several decades, Turkey's foreign policy orientation was Western-looking, with its back turned to the Middle East. This was very much related to the outlook of the secular political elite, especially the military, which was then still the dominant political power. However, as the military's influence subsided in politics after the AKP's election in 2002, the AKP was able to develop and pursue a different global strategy, one that embraced Turkey's Middle Eastern neighbours, with some success. New trade links were forged, closer strategic relations were established and Turkey made its presence felt on the global stage. However, this policy shift was also highly problematic. Suspicions were raised among some traditional allies. Turkey's attempts to mediate between powers in the region, including in the Arab-Israeli conflict and the Iran nuclear crisis, were far from successful.

From the Arab uprisings in 2011 to the time of writing, Turkey's foreign policy has been marred by strategic misconceptions, aggressive rhetoric and a degree of hubris which would lead it to near-isolation by the end of 2015. Despite reconciliation with Israel and Russia, its only real allies in the region are Hamas, the Kurdistan Regional

Government and Qatar—a significant obstacle for future Turkish statespersons and diplomats to overcome. In the ideological underpinnings of its foreign policy, notably the "zero problems" goal, the AKP has confused ambition with strategy. And while it was able to navigate the difficult waters of the Middle East region for nearly a decade, the strategy crumbled after the Arab uprisings, leaving Turkey's foreign policy in a perilous state from which it is yet to recover.

Turkey and the EU: The End of the Affair?

Turkey's accession into the EU has been a major topic of debate ever since Turkey was announced as a candidate country for membership following the Helsinki European Council meeting of December 1999. Since the AKP came to power in 2002, Turkey's accession talks have been a top priority for the government.[1] The ruling party, especially during its first term (2002–7), has enthusiastically advocated membership, even successfully passing a number of domestic political reform packages with the intention of meeting EU criteria.[2]

The start of accession negotiations was an important moment in Turkish history, arguably a development that Turkey had been waiting for not least since the 1963 Ankara Agreement with the European Economic Community.[3] Even in 1996, the Turkish public was pleased about Turkey's Custom Union membership, so much so that in some cities countdown clocks were displayed to mark the time left for the free trade agreement between Turkey and Europe to come into effect.

Turkey becoming part of the EU was in tune with the vision of Mustafa Kemal Ataturk, the founder of modern Turkey,[4] with his pro-Western agenda. For the Turkish public, EU membership meant economic advancement, social freedom and the ability to travel, study and work within the EU. In 2004, according to the Eurobarometer surveys, almost 70 per cent of the Turkish public thought EU membership was good for Turkey.[5] On 3 October 2005, Turkey officially began membership talks. Turkey's then foreign minister, Abdullah Gul, gleefully broke the news to the Turkish public, exclaiming, "We have reached agreement. Turkey will be the only Muslim country in the EU."[6]

As we know, the EU reform process was fundamental to the AKP's restriction of civil-military relations, which led to the end of military tutelage. In addition, the AKP came to power following the financial crisis of 2001. The government's commitment to both the IMF stabilisation programme and the EU process was also in line with its efforts to boost the Turkish economy, a key factor in achieving political stability. For instance, in 2005, the EU-25 had a 38 per cent share in Turkey's total foreign direct investment inflows, and the government made serious efforts to improve its investment climate by promoting large-scale privatisation and eliminating legal obstacles.[7] Just as importantly, Turkish foreign policy toward the EU was shaped by the aftermath of parliament's decision not to allow US forces to use Turkish bases to invade Iraq in 2003. As Ziya Onis and Suhnan Yilmaz rightly point out, this development brought Turkey closer to the EU at the price of pulling Ankara away from Washington, even damaging US-Turkish relations.[8]

Soon, though, Ankara would fall out of love with the EU. One of the biggest challenges to Turkey's EU membership has been the Cyprus dispute. The AKP supported the Annan Plan, which proposed the reunification of the Turkish and Greek sides of the island. In an April 2004 referendum, 65 per cent of Turkish Cypriots voted in favour. However, almost three quarters of Greek Cypriots voted against. The Annan Plan was not to be. Instead, one month later, the Greek side of the island, the Republic of Cyprus, became a full EU member-state.

Negotiations with the EU soon began to decline. One year later, in 2006, the process was partially suspended over the Cyprus issue, after Ankara refused to open its ports and airports to Cyprus. Consequently, the EU put on hold eight of the thirty-five chapters of legislation required from Turkey before accession. For its part, Cyprus helped block another six chapters in 2009.[9] Not only did this scupper the negotiation process, according to foreign policy experts Philip Gordon and Omer Taspinar, it left Ankara with a sense of betrayal.[10]

There was also resistance to Turkish EU entry from several existing member-states. German chancellor Angela Merkel and the then French president, Nicolas Sarkozy, expressed their concerns in no uncertain terms.[11] In 2007, France attempted to block another five chapters.[12] Following the election of François Hollande as France's new president in 2012, Paris lifted its blockage and Hollande announced that France would not be the country to prevent the negotiation process from moving forward.[13] However, anti-Turkish sentiments in

Europe damaged the level of support and enthusiasm for EU member-ship in the eyes of the Turkish public. By spring 2006, the number of those holding the view that EU membership would be good for Turkey plummeted to 44 per cent.[14] Many believed that Islamophobia, the fear of Turkish migrants or Turkey's potential power within the EU's political structures were the real reasons for European scepticism regarding Turkish entry, not disappointment with Turkey's actual per-formance in the accession reform process or unfavourable predictions of its economic contribution.

In the November 2007 general elections, the AKP's vote share rose to 47 per cent. Soon the EU would lose its influence as an external power offering incentives for democratisation in Turkey.[15] Meanwhile, the EU's economic crisis since the end of 2009 obliged the AKP to look to other markets, which even stimulated Turkey's political engagement further afield—with Africa, Russia, China and, indeed, the Middle East.[16] As enthusiasm about EU entry wanes and accession appears unlikely in the near term, Turkey has attempted to diversify its foreign policy orientation.

Turkey's Very Own Kissinger

In 2001, a young professor from Istanbul's Beykent University pub-lished a book entitled *Strategic Depth (Stratejik Derinlik)*.[17] The mono-graph was based on the academic's PhD thesis, written as a student at Istanbul's prestigious Bogazici University. Following its release, the professor soon found himself at the centre of Turkey's corridors of power. First, he became Prime Minister Erdogan's chief foreign policy advisor, an elevated position that was previously less influential. Then, following Abdullah Gul's ascension to the presidency, he became Turkey's foreign minister. He then became Prime Minister, until May 2016, when, having fallen out with Erdogan, he was obliged to resign. The name of this academic is Ahmet Davutoglu. Gone were the copi-ous nights studying, writing and agonising in the Bogazici University library. Henry Kissinger once famously stated that "University politics are vicious precisely because the stakes are so small." Soon Davutoglu would be playing for the very highest stakes, changing the shape of Turkey's foreign relations for years to come.

Just like Kissinger, who also hailed from the ivory tower, Davutoglu would provide the blueprint for the AKP's foreign policy doctrine. In essence, Davutoglu's central claim in *Strategic Depth* was that Turkey, because of its Ottoman past as well as its shared culture, identity and religion with the Islamic world, could utilise its vital geostrategic location to enhance its standing in the world. Instead of viewing Turkey as a "wing state" of the West, because of its central position between Europe, the Middle East, the Black Sea and the Caucasus, Davutoglu argued that Turkey has the potential to be a "pivot state" in its surrounding regions.

If Turkey's geostrategic, cultural and economic assets were realised rather than suppressed, Davutoglu said, Turkey would be a significant international player. Turkey possesses hard power through its mighty military, but if soft power could also be utilised through trade and cultural initiatives, Turkish foreign policy could be pro-active, assertive and even a source for good in the world. But in order for this to be realised, Turkish foreign policy would have to break from its previous Western-oriented approach. Not that Davutoglu was advocating the breaking of good relations with the West. Rather, Turkey should use its strong links with North America, Europe and NATO to buttress its new relations with the Middle East and other regions, thus making Turkey a truly global power.

While Davutoglu was penning his thesis in the late 1990s, the Cold War had come to an end. During the Cold War period, the Republic of Turkey, built on the remnants of the Ottoman state after World War I, had consistently embarked on a Western-focused foreign policy. It viewed itself as a natural part of Europe. It was a staunch ally of the West and a pivotal NATO member-state. However, towards the end of the Cold War, Turkey began reassessing its position. Debates were taking place about Turkey's role in a changing world. Finishing his PhD in 1999, Davutoglu was writing as Turkey was becoming increasingly involved in Middle East affairs, by both choice and compulsion. Turkey's involvement in the First Gulf War, led by Prime Minister Ozal, was motivated by the need for Turkey to stay a relevant Western asset in the newly emerging world order.[18]

The Gulf crisis had serious economic and security repercussions for Turkey. This included a significant loss of revenue due to decreased energy exports by Saddam Hussein's Iraq. Turkey also faced a refugee crisis on its border, with Iraqi Kurds fleeing Saddam's reprisals. It was also during the late 1990s that Turkey's counterinsurgency campaign against the outlawed PKK was in full swing. And, in 1998, Turkey almost went to war with Syria because of Hafiz al-Asad's support for the PKK, including giving refuge to its leader, Abdullah Ocalan. While writing his thesis, Davutoglu was aware that Turkey was finding itself increasingly embroiled in the Middle East. Relations with Israel were at an all-time high as arms sales had surpassed the billion-dollar mark, and strategic cooperation and joint military exercises became common occurrences, raising alarm bells throughout the Muslim world. Davutoglu was also fully aware of the rising Anatolian business elite, who looked to the Middle East as a potential source of investment, trade and revenue.

Davutoglu continued to write his thesis while the Islamist Erbakan government was toppled following the military's ultimatum. Davutoglu must have been fully aware that Erbakan's anti-US and -EU policies, mixed with his embrace of leaders such as Colonel Qaddafi and Ayatollah Khatami and calls for an Islamic monetary fund, had angered the military establishment and contributed to their "post-modern" intervention in 1997. Erbakan's foreign policy failure was that his Islamic-oriented policies lacked coherence and an overarching doctrine that could be explained and justified in strategic terms. This was exactly the strength of *Strategic Depth*. What Davutoglu's ideas offered was not just a re-alignment of Turkish foreign policy, but a policy that could be defended and promoted for its strategic coherence. It was also timely, fitting with the AKP's domestic agenda, and would help propel Professor Davutoglu from near-obscurity to the centre of international attention in the Middle East.

Strategic Depth: Turkey's Hidden Asset

Davutoglu's ideas were adopted and implemented by the AKP government. Ankara's foreign policy from 2002 onwards was highly pro-active, seeking to ingratiate itself in the Middle East and embrace its neighbours. Davutoglu himself played a pivotal role, first as an advisor to Prime Minister Erdogan, then as minister of foreign affairs from May 2009 to

August 2014, and then as President Erdogan's first prime minister, until May 2016. Quite simply, he has been the architect of Turkey's foreign policy doctrine.[19] Before Davutoglu took up the post, the role of chief advisor on foreign affairs had been purely consultative—but Davutoglu's advice became a blueprint for the government's strategic thinking and foreign policy initiatives.[20] Under his influence, there was a marked change in both the rhetoric and practice of foreign policy, which developed a particular framework and vision.[21] Davutoglu's conception of "strategic depth" was particularly important, becoming the guiding principle behind the AKP's international outlook.

The Davutoglu doctrine was also influenced by neo-Ottomanism,[22] a concept used to describe Turkey's engagement in the Middle East. Forging ties with the region, which had largely been part of the Ottoman Empire in previous centuries, was not in itself new; other Turkish governments, such as those led by Ozal and Erbakan, had done the same.[23] However neo-Ottomanism goes further, taking the view that by embracing the Middle East, where Turkey has historical and cultural affinities with other states, Turkey can further enhance and influence the region.[24] This very idea is a significant break from traditional Turkish foreign policy, based on a Kemalist ideology that considered Turkey a Western nation and explicitly turned its back on the Middle Eastern past.[25]

By contrast, Davutoglu's thinking considers Islamic identity as a potential source of harmony with Turkey's Middle Eastern and Arab neighbours.[26] Meanwhile, Davutoglu also pays close attention to geopolitics. An important component of this strategy rests on the idea that Turkey's location offers serious advantages that should be utilised to greater effect. Davutoglu is interested in "choke points," areas that divide the warm seas of the world, where there is also a significant risk of intra-systemic competition.[27] According to Davutoglu, eight[28] of the world's sixteen most strategically important "choke points" are in Muslim countries and, if utilised correctly, offer strategic and geopolitical advantages.[29] Davutoglu believes that Turkey is the heir of the Ottoman Empire, which at one time unified much of the Muslim world. It is therefore Turkey that has the potential to be a trans-regional power with the ability to lead or even unify Muslim countries.[30]

Strategic depth rests on the idea that Turkey is situated in a very important geographical location and shares a common history with its surrounding regions. On the one hand is the heritage of the Ottoman Empire, and on the other is Turkey's location in various zones of influence—in Davutoglu's parlance, "historical depth" and "geographical depth" respectively.[31] In order to fully capitalise on these assets, Davutoglu believes that Turkey should therefore look back to its Ottoman past.[32] In his words, "We are a society with historical depth, and everything produced in historical depth, even if it is eclipsed at a certain conjuncture in time, may manifest itself again later".[33]

But, Davutoglu emphasises, it would be wrong for Turkey to concentrate on merely one country or region in its foreign policy trajectory, as this would risk over-reliance. Rather, equal weight should be given to all of Turkey's geographical regions. In other words, create a multi-directional foreign policy:[34]

> In terms of geography, Turkey occupies a unique space. As a large country in the midst of Afro-Euroasia's [sic] vast landmass, it may be defined as a central country with multiple regional identities that cannot be reduced to one unified character. Like Russia, Germany, Iran and Egypt, Turkey cannot be explained geographically or culturally by associating it with one single region. Turkey's diverse regional composition lends it the capability of manoeuvring in several regions simultaneously: in this sense, it controls an area of influence in its intermediate environs.[35]

To summarise, according to Davutoglu's perspective, Turkey should seek to link its past, present and future, as well as its geography, to enhance its global relations.[36] But this is not all. Davutoglu also believes that Turkey requires a five-point programme that will balance security and democracy, enabling Ankara to influence its environs; pursue a "zero-problem policy" towards its neighbours; develop relations in neighbouring regions and beyond; engage in a multi-dimensional foreign policy aiming for "complementation rather than competition"; and, what's more, engage in "rhythmic" diplomacy.[37] These five points, together with historical and geographical depth, certainly lend credence to one senior intelligence officer's comment to the authors that Davutoglu may be a good theoretician, but that does not mean his policies work in practice.[38] However, it is also debatable whether Davutoglu's ideas work even in theory.

As previously mentioned, during the initial stages of AKP rule, Turkey focused actively on the EU and its potential accession. The EU process assisted the AKP in presenting itself as a bridge between East and West. Although hesitant to portray itself as a model country for the Middle East to emulate, such suggestions did appear to please the AKP. For example, while holding the post of foreign minister, Abdullah Gul argued:

> The Turkish experience might serve as a source of inspiration for countries in the region. We have sought to achieve democracy, civil rights and liberties, respect for the rule of law, civil society, transparency, and gender equality. Our experience proves that national and spiritual values can be in perfect harmony with contemporary standards. [39]

Nevertheless, despite the benefits of its relations with the EU, Davutoglu believes that Turkey should also pay more attention to other parts of its regional neighbourhood; that is, the Middle East, the Balkans, and the Caucasus. [40] He feels that Turkey "should act as a central country, breaking away from a static and single-parameter policy, and becoming a problem solver by contributing to global and regional peace." [41] But the effectiveness of Turkey's regional engagement is highly questionable, as the Middle East arena has shown.

First Test: Iraq

Even before the AKP came to power, Turkey was very much aware of the security threat emanating from the Middle East. [42] Three of the "rogue states" identified by US President George W. Bush, Iraq, Iran and Syria, are Turkey's immediate neighbours, and were therefore a significant source of consternation for the then Turkish Prime Minister Bülent Ecevit (1999–2002). [43]

When the AKP entered office in 2002, the first test for the new government was the planned invasion of Iraq by a US-led coalition. There was splintered support for the use of Turkish bases for the transfer of US troops into Iraq, as the US had requested. The parliamentary opposition was even joined by ninety AKP deputies in rejecting a bill which would have granted the US such access. [44] The divisions within the AKP on this issue were not just about the ninety rogue parliamentarians. While soon-to-be prime minister Erdogan (who assumed office two weeks later) supported the pro-US bill, Davutoglu, his chief advisor at the time, was against it. [45]

The invasion of Iraq taught Ankara that its interests do not always match those of its most important ally and the world's greatest superpower. The US also saw Iraqi Kurds as an ally in the region,[46] much to Turkey's alarm. Following the Iraq War, much of Turkey's Middle East policy was shaped by this development and the need for Turkey to review its security interests because of the fluid situation on its border.[47] Iraq was, of course, an inescapable part of what Davutoglu considered Turkey's "geographical and historical depth", and constituted a challenge to overcome.[48]

Turkish concerns over Iraq were very much related to the possibility that the latter's post-World War II borders would change, leading to the establishment of a Kurdish state to Iraq's north that could become the PKK's base. This potential development led Turkey to search for new opportunities for security cooperation with its other regional neighbours.[49] As one of Erdogan's top advisors on foreign affairs at the time, Ibrahim Kalin, commented, "Turkey and its neighbours—Syria, Iraq and Iran—have reached a consensus" in their understanding of the efforts needed to prevent the establishment of a Kurdish state.[50] Indeed, in the first instance, Turkey looked for allies to meet the potential Kurdish threat. This would further distance Turkey from the US.

Because of its support for Hezbollah, Hamas and various Iraqi groups, Baathist Syria found itself on the wrong side of the "war on terror".[51] Ankara considered Washington's policy a threat to Turkish security.[52] From the AKP's perspective, alienating Syria would have the effect of destabilising the entire region, and it would be better for the US to engage diplomatically with Damascus.[53] This was certainly Turkey's choice of action; by 2007, Ankara had adopted a defensive policy to create a "security circle" through increased cooperation with regional countries.[54] The idea was that Turkey's own security was intrinsically linked to regional stability as a whole,[55] and that "the defence of Istanbul starts from Baghdad, Damascus and Sarajevo."[56]

The AKP focused its efforts on arbitrating in regional disputes while also developing stronger relations with its neighbours, namely Syria, Iraq and Iran.[57] This involved facilitating strategic cooperation meetings with these countries, which brought cabinet ministers and administration officials together to discuss regional matters on a bilateral basis.[58] Ankara also took the initiative to reduce tensions in the region by trying to mediate disputes between different parties, including conflicts between Syria and Israel, Hamas and Fatah, various Lebanese factions, and Iran and the West over Tehran's nuclear programme.[59]

The Root of All Evil

One of the most important factors behind Turkish foreign policy under the AKP has been the possibility of economic growth through trading and establishing business links with Middle Eastern nations. Davutoglu has gone as far as to call this a "primary driver".[60] Part of Turkey's "constructive engagement in its neighbourhood and beyond" has been economic engagement.[61] The emphasis on improving bilateral ties with neighbouring states has been achieved by focusing on economic and commercial relations.[62] Indeed, the AKP considers regional trade a "major synergy vehicle of continuous and sustainable development".[63]

Strengthening economic relations served another purpose, as Davutoglu saw such economic links as a means to solve regional problems and disputes in order to obtain "zero problems" with Turkey's neighbours.[64] The logic behind this is that economic integration could make political dialogue easier, subsequently stabilising the region and turning it into an area where goods and products would be able to move freely, from the south-eastern Turkish city of Kars all the way to the Atlantic.[65] It was this line of reasoning that led Ankara to lift visa restrictions and pen free trade agreements with regional countries.[66] In financial terms, this translated into increased economic turnover with Turkey's neighbours and new trade partners. Such agreements were first signed with Syria and Tunisia and then extended to Lebanon, Jordan, Egypt, and Morocco.[67] Trade volume increased significantly. For example, trade between Turkey and its neighbours stood at around US$12 billion in 2002, but this number would multiply to reach US$82 billion in 2008.[68] In the Arab world specifically, this number multiplied sixfold, from US$6.2 billion in 2002 to US$36 billion just six years later.[69] In total, Turkey's foreign trade was worth US$37 billion in 2002. By 2012, this figure had reached as high as US$153 billion.

Regardless, the EU remained Turkey's largest trade partner, and it was with this market that Ankara maintained a concerted effort to increase trade relations, especially exports, with Middle Eastern trade serving both to supplement Turkey's economic growth and to hedge against the effect of downturns and stagnation in the economies of North America and Europe.[70] Indeed, following the global economic meltdown of 2008, Turkey has strengthened its trade relations with its neighbours to the east, a policy that has received support from the Anatolian Tigers, a group that consists of the conservative bourgeoisie and a political support base for the AKP.

In fact, it has been under the AKP that these small- and medium-sized businesses have constituted a driving force in Turkey's foreign policy orientation; the number of such enterprises has increased from around 1.9 million in 2002 to over 3 million in 2013. With new markets in the Middle East to exploit, the success of these businesses has benefited Turkey domestically, especially in terms of employment. Between 2009 and 2011, joblessness decreased from 14.1 per cent to 9.8 per cent.[71] The unemployment rate in the south-eastern city Mardin is a case in point. In this border city with Syria, unemployment was as high as 17 per cent in 2008, but fell to 9.1 per cent in 2010.[72] Turkey's greater engagement with the Middle East, especially economically, has therefore served not only its foreign policy interests but its domestic agenda too.

Rolls Royce Ambitions but Rover Resources

One of the problems with strategic depth as a doctrinal basis for achieving "zero problem" foreign relations is its assumption that states within its vicinity will accept a greater Turkish influence, a supposition based on Turkey extending soft power and economic ties. However, in some cases this ideal did not materialise. Attempts to solve problems with one state or player may inflame tensions with others.

The biggest challenge to Turkey's new assertive foreign policy has been the Arab Spring. However, even before the uprisings, Turkey faced numerous setbacks in its attempt to gain prominence on the world stage. In some instances this was due to overreach. In others, it was the fact that just because Turkey sought "zero problems", other states remained concerned about Turkish dominance, even seeing Turkey's foreign policy as contrary to their own. They viewed Turkey's greater involvement in the region with suspicion or mistrust. So too did its traditional allies in the West. Turkey also had to face a doctrinal issue with the "zero problems" approach: it confused the strategy with the end goal. The idea of having no problems with states in its immediate neighbourhood is an aspiration, not a strategy in itself. The aspiration needed to be buttressed with a coherent plan and statecraft in order to fulfil the goal. However, under the AKP, "zero problems" was both the strategy and the goal. This doctrinal confusion led to a lack of depth within its foreign policy outlook that would affect Turkey's relations with its neighbours both before and after the Arab Spring.

For example, Turkey found that its attempts to reconcile its differences with Armenia were hampered. Signing a protocol with Armenia elicited opposition from Azerbaijan, and it became apparent that such an agreement would not be conducive to maintaining ties with the Turkic Republic, which was embroiled in a dispute with Armenia over its occupation of the Nagorno-Karabakh region. Indeed, within Armenia itself there were mixed feelings about rapprochement with Turkey, with the main opposition party favouring normalisation of relations but Tasnaksutyun, the left-wing nationalist party, opposing it, as did the Armenian Diaspora. Even within Turkey there was opposition from the Nationalist Action Party and the CHP, and the Armenian reconciliation became a highly divisive issue.[73] As we have seen, even Turkey's desire to end the Cyprus problem, which had caused difficulties with its EU accession hopes, ran into obstacles after the Annan Plan to reunite the country was rejected in a referendum in 2004 by 76 per cent of Greek Cypriots.[74]

It was the same story with Russia and South Ossetia. Despite closer ties between Turkey and Russia, in August 2008, Russia began to extensively inspect Turkish trucks with extra care, angered by Turkey's decision to allow European and US naval ships to pass through the Black Sea to Georgia during the South Ossetia crisis. Despite Russian foreign minister Sergey Lavrov's denial that Turkey was being singled out, a new customs procedure was put in place the following month,[75] even though Turkey had been limiting the passage of US warships precisely so as not to anger Russia.[76] Despite the resumption of normal diplomatic relations, during the height of the Syrian crisis in 2014, relations with Russia would reach new lows after Turkey downed a Russian fighter for entering its airspace.

As Ziya Onis attests, in the long term, such a multi-dimensional foreign policy, with no solid axis, has the potential to be counterproductive.[77] One of the main areas where this assertion has proved accurate has been the deterioration of Turkey's relations with Israel and its involvement in the Arab-Israeli conflict. Not only would Turkish-Israeli relations sink to an all-time low, this would also raise concerns about Turkey's foreign policy in Europe and the US. The 1990s saw a period of warming ties between Turkey and Israel, two of the region's superpowers. These ties became somewhat strained during the AKP's first term.[78] Turkey was increasingly uneasy about reports that retired Israeli military officers were training Kurdish peshmerga in 2005.[79] Even though in the next couple of years Turkey strengthened economic and diplomatic relations with the Kurdistan Regional Government, and saw its own Kurdish opening, the AKP also made allegations of Israeli support for Kurdish separatism. The National Intelligence Organisation had even suggested in a report that Israel was forging new ties with the PKK.[80] Meanwhile, eyebrows were raised when Erdogan called Israeli assassinations of Hamas leaders in 2004 "state terrorism".[81]

Still, Israeli-Turkish relations, although tense, were maintained. In addition to strong ties with Israel, Turkey had managed to gain influence and cultivate productive relationships with the Palestinian Authority. Even before the AKP came into office, Turkey was investing around US$10 million in Palestinian healthcare, tourism, agriculture, security, public administration and institutions.[82] Ankara was also part of the 1997 civilian observer mission, Temporary International Presence in Hebron, and, after the start of the Second (Al-Aqsa) Intifada in 2000, Turkey formed the Jerusalem Technical Committee to investigate whether Israeli excavations were harming the Temple Mount/Haram al-Sharif.[83] Turkey had also invested US$50 million in the Erez industrial park in the northern Gaza Strip in 2006.[84] Turkey was, therefore, in a position to be a useful mediator in the Israeli-Palestinian peace process.

However, Turkey was unable to turn this position into successful mediation. This was due to a miscalculation on Ankara's part in its relations with Hamas. Following the militant Palestinian faction's victory during the 2006 Palestinian elections, the Diplomatic Quartet (US, EU, UN and Russia) imposed conditions on the group before it would engage in official dialogue: first Hamas must recognise Israel, end violence and recognise past agreements. Turkey, insisting that the results of democratic elections should be respected, broke ranks with the international community's policy and made the fateful decision to host Hamas leader Khaled Mashal in February 2006.[85] From Ankara's perspective, Hamas had by all accounts freely and fairly won the elections, and the West's reluctance to engage with the group showed double standards.[86]

Ankara hoped that Mashal's tone could be moderated; instead, its invitation was seen as legitimising the group before the Quartet's and Israel's conditions had been met.[87] As a result, not only did Israel lose confidence in Turkey as an honest mediator, but serious concerns were raised in the West that Turkey's divergence with the international community was ideologically motivated; Ankara's engagement with Hamas enforced perceptions in some quarters that Turkey was not an ally, and could not and should not be trusted by the US or the EU.[88] The US criticised Turkey's conduct towards the visit as lacking clarity.[89] The move also angered Egypt, which saw Hamas as a threat. Ultimately, with this one blow, Turkey all but forfeited its role in the Israeli-Palestinian peace process.[90]

Still, there were hopes that Turkey could be an effective mediator in Israeli-Syrian discussions. Turkey had also cultivated strong ties with Bashar al-Asad. However, these expectations were soon abruptly dashed. Turkey found its ability to be a successful mediator and enjoy "zero problems" was hampered by events on the ground beyond its control. In this case, it was Israel's 2008 Operation Cast Lead, an onslaught against Hamas in Gaza after the latter increased its missile launching once a temporary ceasefire had come to an end. Israel's operation angered Turkey, which had felt that its mediation efforts were showing promise. Apparently, just prior to the operation the Israeli prime minister had been in Ankara, and Erdogan and Asad had been on the phone discussing points of contention.[91] This may have been so, but it must also be noted that despite mediating for many months, Turkey had been unable to conclude an agreement between Israel and Syria. Arguably, the only state capable of brokering such an agreement was the US, a world power with which Turkey was unable to compete, only able to offer a supporting role.

If this was not enough, Israel was further enraged by Turkey's actions after Iranian president Mahmoud Ahmadinejad visited Turkey in August 2008. Not only was Ahmadinejad the head of state of Hamas and Hezbollah's main supporter, but Jerusalem was vexed that its supposed ally had granted legitimacy to a man who had earlier elicited worldwide condemnation for his denial of the Holocaust and his call for Israel's destruction.[92] Although Israeli-Turkish relations were now at crisis point, soon they would sink even lower.

During Israel's 2008 Operation Cast Lead, Turkey, unlike countries such as Egypt, Jordan and Saudi Arabia, condemned Israel without even mentioning Hamas rocket fire into Israel (a pattern that would repeat itself in 2014, but this time with more vociferous and counterproductive rhetoric from Erdogan). Instead, Ankara declared Israeli actions a "crime against humanity".[93] During the crisis, Turkey even coordinated its position with Iran and hosted the secretary of Iran's supreme national security council, Saaed Jalili, who met with both Prime Minister Erdogan and President Gul.[94] Erdogan angrily stormed out of the 2008 Davos economic summit after publicly telling Israeli president Shimon Peres that Israel 'knows well how to kill'.[95] Turkey then excluded Israel from the Anatolian Eagle military exercise in October 2009. Both Italy and the US then withdrew from the exercise in protest. In the same month, Turkey and Syria announced that they would be expanding their joint military exercises.[96]

Turkish-Israeli ties continued to fray, especially after the Davos summit, but they would hit rock bottom after the Mavi Marmara Affair.[97] An ill-fated Turkish vessel, attempting to breach Israel's blockade of the Gaza Strip in 2010, was boarded in international waters as it approached the Gaza Strip by Israeli commandos, who killed nine Turkish citizens resisting the operation. Erdogan's comments after the affair that "the world now perceives the Star of David alongside the Swastika" eroded global sympathy with Turkey on this issue.[98] Turkey's ambassador to Israel was withdrawn after Israel refused to apologise.[99] Hostility escalated after Turkey highlighted the humanitarian disaster in Gaza, but it had turned a blind eye to crimes committed in Iran and Darfur,[100] inviting a charge of double standards.[101] From the perspective of the Turkish Foreign Ministry, the deaths of nine unarmed Turkish citizens in international waters was unacceptable. It marked a turning point, as Turkey had previously considered Israel an ally that it could criticise on its Palestinian policies.[102]

Nevertheless, Turkey's belligerence and antagonism towards Israel and its breaking of ranks over recognising Hamas would soon lead commentators to question whether Turkey was still a partner of the West. This would increasingly come to the fore over Turkey's warming relations with other Middle Eastern states. Israel issued an apology in 2013 for the deaths of Turkish citizens on board the Mavi Marmara and agreed to pay compensation to the families of the victims. Despite some reports of optimism after a preliminary agreement between the Israeli and Turkish governments was apparently made, full diplomatic ties were not restored at that time, owing to Ankara's insistence on its demand for the lifting of the siege of Gaza.[103] Even when relations were mended in June 2016, Turkey was unable to end Israel's blockade of Gaza. Instead it was agreed that Turkey could send aid to the nearby Israeli port of Ashdod, from where it would be sent to Gaza, and work on the strip's water, health and energy infrastructure. In return, Israel would pay compensation to the families of the Mavi Marmara victims, as indicated in 2013.[104]

Israel received by far the better deal. Now it was in a better position to export its natural gas through the more efficient and cost-effective route through Turkey. Ankara also agreed to stop aggressively attacking Israel in international fora such as the International Criminal Court (ICC) and to help Jerusalem retrieve four missing Israelis held in the Gaza Strip. Turkey also opened itself to charges that it had backtracked from its commitment not to restore ties until Israel ended its blockade, as Turkey's newly agreed contribution to Gaza was minimal; even before the deal was struck, Israel had been allowing aid to enter Gaza from Ashdod on an almost daily basis. One commentator went so far as to argue that Turkey would now be viewed as a paper tiger.[105] Turkey's agreement with Jerusalem was no doubt an attempt to reverse its increasing international isolation at a time of regional instability and a terrorist threat within its borders.

Turkey entered another diplomatic minefield in its relations with Iran. Not only did this further exacerbate tensions with Israel, but it also, like the Palestinian issue, put Turkey at odds with its traditional allies in the West. Much of this was related to closer cooperation over the energy and gas sector.[106] Overall, Turkey's close ties with Iran during the AKP's first term were worth an estimated US$4 billion by the end of 2005, a figure that would continue to increase in subsequent years. This included not only trade, but also security cooperation. In February 2006, the eleventh Iran-Turkey High Security Council meeting was held in Tehran.[107] Even during this early period, though, relations between Ankara and the Islamic Republic were not entirely smooth. Iran had cancelled a contract for a Turkish firm to run the Tehran airport, as well as a contract for Turkey to develop part of Iran's South Pars gas field.[108]

It was the Kurdish question that saw the warming of relations between Ankara and Tehran, with both facing separatist threats from the PKK and the Party of Free Life of Kurdistan respectively. This led to security exchanges and collaborations.[109] There was even a joint strike in the Kandil mountains against the PKK and its affiliates.[110] With the Kurdish question on the line as well as the opportunity to play a leading role on the world stage following its temporary membership of the UN Security Council in 2009–10, Ankara felt obliged to involve itself in the Iranian nuclear dispute. Turkey, along with Brazil, offered their own formula for solving the crisis, a nuclear fuel swap agreement that was more lenient than what the US and its European allies were proposing at the Security Council. The three parties signed the agreement in May 2010.[111] Turkish interference was not well received by the US, which had also brought the issue to the Security Council with the aim of passing a new resolution tightening sanctions.[112] Iran and Brazil voted against Resolution 1929, creating further distance between Turkey and the West in a matter of great importance to the latter.[113]

It did not help Ankara's case that in an interview Erdogan had dismissed concerns of Iran building a nuclear weapon as mere rumours,[114] at a time when Turkey's engagement with Iran was viewed by some as undermining the US and EU policy of isolating the Islamic state.[115] This was highlighted by Davutoglu's superfluous comment, after making the 2010 fuel deal, that sanctions against Iran were no longer necessary. This allowed both parties to blame Turkey for the failure of the process.[116] It certainly irked the US. One leaked diplomatic cable in early 2009 alleged that a joint Turkish-Iranian venture company to develop Iran's gas would enrich Erdogan's friends.[117]

Prior to this incident, the Iranian nuclear issue was hardly mentioned in Turkish-Iranian relations, but Ankara nevertheless saw fit to promote a position that significantly diverged from that of the EU and the US.[118] It appears that Turkey could not resist the opportunity of using its Security Council seat to gain influence on the world stage, perhaps in an ill-conceived attempt to bridge the differences between its new Iranian ally and its traditional allies in the West. However, not only did this fail and put strains on relations with the West, but Turkey's later foreign policy choices also increased tensions with the Islamic Republic, when the advantages of NATO membership obliged Turkey to allow the installation of NATO anti-missile radar on its territory. Tehran promptly criticised Ankara, despite Turkey's insistence that the radar was not to be deployed against Iran. This did not prevent Gen. Amir Ali Hajizadeh, a senior member of the Iranian Revolutionary Guards, from threatening to strike Turkey if the US or Israel attacked Iran.[119]

A further policy shift between Turkey and the West over Iran was highlighted in 2009, when fraudulent Iranian elections repressing the Green Movement of young Iranians demanding their vote be counted were condemned by the world, whereas Turkey was quick to recognise Ahmadinejad's re-election. Gul even visited Iran on a day when a Green Movement demonstration was set to take place. Davutoglu called the election crisis an internal Iranian matter, while AKP deputy Suat Kiniklioglu remarked that Turkey would not promote human rights and democracy the way the US does, but instead, would talk face to face behind closed doors. When asked if such issues would be discussed behind these doors, he replied, "it's not at the top of our agenda".[120] Turkey, which unlike Western countries shares a border with Iran, did not want to antagonise Tehran, an influential power in the region.[121]

Turkey's warming relations with Damascus were seen as similarly unhelpful in Washington. The Bush administration was trying to isolate the Asad regime for a myriad of reasons, including its possible role in ex-Lebanese prime minister Rafik Hariri's assassination and the belief that Syria was a safe haven for Iraqi Baathist officials as well as a transit route for jihadi militants entering Iraq to kill US troops. Washington also wanted to pressure Asad to make greater efforts to liberalise his regime.[122] Soon commentators were speculating that Turkey had to some extent joined the Iranian axis. Some in the US were even asking questions such as "who's losing Turkey?"[123] and why Turkey was "not acting like a NATO ally?" Even during the Obama administration (the first country Obama visited in the region was Turkey), in mid-2010 officials were still asking, "what happened?"[124]

One answer, according to a leaked US diplomatic cable, was that Ankara had "Rolls Royce ambitions but Rover resources", unable to compete with the US, EU and Russia in the region. Meanwhile its "neo-Ottoman" posturing required finding a constant underdog to sponsor.[125] Regardless, in addition to its domestic reforms, Turkey emphasised its multi-regional interests and strategic importance as a factor in negotiating with Brussels as an equal partner to gain EU membership.[126] But, as Piotr Zalewski notes, Turkey's foreign policy, once its greatest asset in its EU accession talks, is in danger of becoming its greatest liability.[127]

The Kurdish Question and Turkey's Foreign Policy

After the 2003 Iraq War, Turkey was hoping that Washington would take greater steps in combating the PKK. Ankara was increasingly taking the view that the US was not doing enough to protect Turkey's security concerns, but was instead supporting Kurdish independence in northern Iraq.[128] This anxiety was buttressed by the impression that Iraqi Kurdish leaders such as Talabani and Barzani, who supported the Iraq War, enjoyed leverage and influence in Washington at the expense of Turkey, whose support for the Iraqi Turkmen Front in northern Iraqi cities such as oil-rich Kirkuk—which Turkey insisted was a Turcoman city[129]—was alienating Ankara from Washington. There were also growing fears in Ankara that an annexation of Kirkuk by the Kurdistan Regional Government (KRG) would give the latter the financial capability to fund an independent Kurdish state.[130] Turkish commentator Soli Ozel argued that the basis for Turkey's later embrace of the KRG was a result of Erbil's success in hedging its bets ahead of the US withdrawal from Iraq, afraid that the Arabs would "eat them alive".[131]

In February 2008, Turkey launched a military operation to hunt down PKK militants that crossed into northern Iraq. This took place after consultations with both the KRG and the US. The KRG's recognition of Turkish security concerns and acceptance of the operation were in stark contrast to previous Turkish incursions into Iraqi Kurdish areas, such as the intervention of 1995. For Turkey, these gradually blossoming ties between Erbil and Ankara[132] came out of a realisation that its struggle against the PKK could not be won by military means alone, and that support from the KRG would be needed. Soon there were visits to Turkey by Iraqi Kurdish officials. Meanwhile, it was recognised that closer ties could lead to mutual benefit in other areas. Erbil, for its part, sought ties with Ankara as it would need to supply energy to the European market through Turkey. Turkey would also be required as an ally if the landlocked KRG ever faced a hostile Iran, or if relations with Shia-dominated Baghdad continued to sour.[133] Indeed, engaging with Kurds both at home and abroad has earned Ankara kudos. Its "dance" with Ocalan and the AKP's signs of intending to tackle the Kurdish question have been praised in nearly every visit that European leaders have made to Turkey.[134] The KRG has also lent support to Turkey's peace efforts with Ocalan.[135]

Ankara's ties with the KRG soon translated into financial reward. Iraq became Turkey's second largest export market in 2012, worth around US$10.8 billion, with projects worth US$3.5 billion. The new relationship with the KRG is perhaps one of the new Turkey's foreign policy success stories. Turkish firms now operate in northern Iraq in a vast range of different sectors, from construction to consumer goods. These business links have also helped to improve understanding between Ankara and Erbil.[136] However, even the warming Turkish-KRG ties have led to unforeseen problems. During the 2010 Iraqi elections, for example, Ankara's preferred prime ministerial candidate, Iyad Allawi, was beaten by Iran's favourite, Nuri al-Maliki.[137] Maliki, then prime minister of Iraq, called Turkey a hostile state in 2012. He even went as far as to claim that Ankara was meddling in Iraqi affairs and engineering sectarian fault lines.[138] This was despite Erdogan's visits to Iraq in March 2011, which had specifically been carefully planned to avoid such accusations. Erdogan visited Shia shrines, stopped over in Kurdish Erbil and delivered a speech in Baghdad's parliament, events designed to show that Turkey was committed to Iraqi unity.[139] Tensions with Iraq over the flow into each country from the Euphrates and Tigris rivers remains a problem, with Turkey increasing its own exploitation of these important water sources.[140]

It All Falls Down: Turkey and the Arab Spring

In late 2009, just months after the Green Movement in Iran was brutally suppressed, Ahmet Davutoglu penned an article in the *Turkish Policy Quarterly* that read:

> From our vantage point, there is a clear need to pursue a proactive diplomacy with the aim of strengthening prosperity, stability and security in a neighbourhood which spans the Balkans, the Caucasus and the Caspian basin, the Black Sea, the Eastern Mediterranean, the Middle East, from the Gulf to North Africa, not void of tension but also abundant with unfulfilled potential.[141]

The ink had barely dried before Turkey came to face its ultimate foreign policy challenge in the region: the Arab Spring.

The Arab uprisings that began in 2011 showed that, despite engaging in the Middle East, Turkey was still a relative newcomer to the region. Like the rest of the international community, the uprisings came as a surprise for Turkey. Nevertheless, throughout the turmoil Turkey tried to maintain the principles of the "zero problems" strategy, at the same time as adapting to the new dynamics.[142] In 2013 Davutoglu himself defined three "earthquakes" that affected Turkey's international system; one was the Arab Spring. Nevertheless, he argued, while some countries had been hesitant in the face of the uprisings, Turkey had adopted a "clear" and principled position—that Ankara's decision was to side with democratic change, supported by an "all-out" diplomatic effort to ensure that the transition to democracy would be smooth, unlike the experience of the Balkans during the 1990s.[143] Davutoglu also emphasised that Turkey had made every effort to fulfil these aims, especially in Syria, where it had campaigned against the conduct of the Asad regime. Turkey, he said, had taken the side of democracy from the inception of the uprisings.[144] However, this was hyperbole. In reality, it appears that Davutoglu, who had once described the need for Turkish foreign policy to engage in "rhythmic diplomacy", was now engaging less in a well-choreographed classical piece, and more in improvised jazz.

We should remember that, in explaining Turkish policy, Davutoglu later argued that when the AKP came to power in 2002 it had made promises for greater democracy, freedoms, a regime without tutelage, respect for the will of the people and anti-corruption. It was through this lens that he viewed the Arab Spring, as it emerged from similar demands by the people of the region. He added that these goals, in both Turkey and the Arab Middle East, were on the right side of the "flow of history".[145] Addressing critics who were asking what had happened to the "zero problems" approach, Davutoglu countered with the example of the Jasmine Revolution in Tunisia, retorting that intellectuals had not predicted the fall of Ben Ali, nor indeed of Mubarak, Qadaffi, or Saleh, and that although Turkey had taken a risk in taking a stand, this was the very nature of politics. He even pointed to the timing of Prime Minister Erdogan's speech to the Grand National Assembly, which called for Mubarak to leave office, as a key moment in the history of Turkish foreign policy, because Turkey then found itself in front of history rather than behind it.[146]

Leaving aside the highly problematic determinism of Davutoglu's thoughts over the "flow of history," in reality the Arab Spring caught Turkey off guard. Events in Tunisia, for example, happened too quickly for Turkey to form a meaningful response.[147] Meanwhile, Philip Robins has astutely noted that although Turkey may originally have had a "good Arab Spring", in light of the uprisings Turkey has shelved its "zero problems" policy to side with the Tunisian and Egyptian people.[148] Indeed, initially it appeared that Turkey was having a very good Arab Spring. It was even being hailed as a potential model for the region to follow after the uprisings. By the time Erdogan visited Egypt after the fall of Hosni Mubarak in September 2011, not only did he bring a large delegation of businessmen, but he was also greeted with cheers by masses of the Egyptian public.[149] The idea of Turkey as a model was even being discussed by Tunisia's Rachid Gannouci, co-founder of the Ennahda Party, and the grandson of Muslim Brotherhood founder Hassan al-Bana. Tariq Ramadan pointed to Turkey as a secular Muslim country, a democracy with a liberal market.[150]

However, this was as far as Turkey's success in the Arab Spring went. It was only able to take a stand in Tunisia and Egypt because it had negligible economic interests in these two countries, and in the case of Egypt, Turkey had a strained relationship with Mubarak anyway.[151] Turkey had little to lose in calling for him to resign.[152] Soon, the uprisings would reach regimes where Turkey had significant vested interests, and here its early successes stopped. Far from Davutoglu's argument that Turkey had

sided with democratic forces, in the case of Bahrain, Turkey had significant economic interests with the GCC and therefore found itself forced
to respect the security concerns of the Gulf States.[153] It made a measly
offer to mediate a resolution in Bahrain, appealing to Islamic sentiments
by stressing the importance of preventing another Karbala, a reference
to the battle in 680AD between the supporters of the Prophet's grandson, Hussein ibn Ali, and Yazid I over the rightful heir to the Caliphate,
which marked the beginnings of the Shia-Sunni split. Turkey reached out
to Shia leaders including al-Sistani of Basra; however, the GCC ignored
Turkey's attempt to mediate and crushed the revolt with Saudi intervention and without much further thought.[154]

Turkey also had an invested stake in the Qaddafi regime in Libya.
Turkey had an estimated $US23 billion in investments, especially from
its construction sector.[155] While intervention was being considered and
planned by NATO, which won the endorsement of the Arab League,
Ankara wavered. Instead of joining the anti-Qaddafi coalition, Turkish
leaders made telephone calls to the eccentric Libyan dictator in a futile
effort to find some kind of compromise and convince him to begin
democratic reforms.[156] All this did was give the impression that Turkey
was siding with a man who had awarded Erdogan the Qadaffi Prize for
human rights, rather than supporting the embattled and besieged
people of Benghazi. It was only after Turkish flags were burned in the
streets of Libya's second city and after Ankara's diplomatic overtures to
Qaddafi failed that Ankara finally fell into line and supported NATO
intervention.[157]

Meanwhile, Turkey was beginning to feel the financial pinch of the
post-Arab Spring world. Middle East exports in the first two months
of 2011, for example, saw a 21 per cent decrease in trade with Egypt.
This dropped by 38 per cent with Tunisia and 6 per cent with Libya.
Although there were increases with Iran, Saudi Arabia, Iraq and the
UAE,[158] these were countries relatively untouched by the uprisings. In
the case of Libya, there was a marked decline in terms of exports, from
US$146.445 million in January 2011 to as low as US$41.462 million
in May of the same year—a drop of almost US$105 million per month
within less than half a year. Before the uprising, some have estimated
that the level of Turkish investment projects in Libya had reached as
high as US$60 billion. In all, the economic fallout of the rebellion cost
Turkey as much as US$40 billion.[159]

To make matters worse, Turkey's policies towards Syria embroiled Ankara in competing interests between the US-supported Gulf states and the Iranian-led Shia camp supported by Iraq. Turkey attempted to pursue an activist policy against Asad while also navigating these regional divisions without losing popularity in the Arab world. This put Turkey in quite a quandary. If it were to simply return to traditional Kemalist foreign policy and support the Western approach, this would nullify its attempt to carve out a new foreign policy trajectory.[160] However, Turkey had a stake in Syria that was worth at least US$2.4 billion in trade, not to mention its joint cooperation arrangements against Kurdish separatists. When ties were strengthening between the two countries, Erdogan thought he had been able to make Asad listen to him and heed his advice, the elder statesman guiding the young ruler. Asad, on the other hand, thought he had tamed a once hostile Turkey on behalf of the Arab world.[161] In March 2011, Erdogan triumphantly announced that he had spoken to Asad and impressed upon him the need to implement social, economic and political reforms, even offering Turkish assistance.[162] This only angered both Syrian protesters and pro-change Arabs in the wider Middle East. It appeared that Turkey, the so-called post-Spring model, was siding with an Arab dictator.[163] Ankara now faced a difficult decision—either adopt a restrained approach or call for Asad's removal. Erdogan now chose the latter.

Believing Asad's downfall was imminent and not wanting to be seen as reluctant as in Libya, Turkey's campaign against Asad was also an attempt to create a sphere of influence in this newly emerging Middle East.[164] Also, since the Obama administration was viewed as leading from behind in Libya, Turkish opposition to Asad was also an attempt for Ankara to lead from the front. However this was a miscalculation. Unlike Qaddafi, Asad held on to power and Turkey was powerless to remove the stubborn Syrian dictator.[165]

In June 2011, Erdogan stated publicly that Asad had not made good on his promises to reform. Erdogan appeared to be personally angered by the apparent affront.[166] Indeed, while Syria had been the key to Turkey's Middle East opening during the early AKP years, the Asad regime was now becoming Turkey's most difficult challenge.[167] Not only did Turkey have a stake in the Syrian unrest because of refugee influx and decreased security, highlighted by the deaths of forty-three people in twin bombings in the border town of Reyhanli, but there was also the possibility of the PKK using Syria as a base for activism, and the risk of a sectarian war that would destabilise the whole region.[168] Turkey hosted the Free Syrian Army and called for a safe zone or buffer zone, and it has been reported that Turkey turned a blind eye to arms flowing to the Syrian opposition.[169] There was even talk of direct Turkish intervention. The Syrian quagmire also created friction with Iran, which supported the Asad regime, with Saudi Arabia, which was willing to support Salafi groups, and with Russia, which has continued to support Asad throughout the turmoil. Indeed, in Syria and the wider Arab world, Turkey has seen the limitations of its regional influence and "zero problems" policy.[170] Quite frankly, achieving "zero problems" was simply not within Turkey's grasp, and remains an unrealistic utopian vision.

Turkey's woes in the Middle East have not ceased since the Arab Spring. Ankara's burgeoning ties with the Muslim Brotherhood government of Egypt led by Mohammed Morsi failed to read the feeling of the Egyptian street, which was manipulated by the military. After Morsi was forced from office and put on trial, with his supporters massacred in the streets in the summer of 2013, Erdogan strongly condemned the "coup", perhaps more passionately than any other world leader, and went on to criticise the West's lack of condemnation.[171] Relations with Egypt have not recovered. Erdogan even went so far as to call the military chief-turned-president, Gen. Abdul Fattah al-Sissi, a "tyrant".[172] Soon both countries recalled their ambassadors.

Turkish policy-makers denied the domestic implications of its position towards the military intervention in Egypt;[173] however, it seems likely that concerns about the perceived validity of military interference in politics were a motivating factor. But there were some unintended consequences. Although Turkey maintained good relations with the Gulf States, there was a significant difference of opinion regarding Morsi's ouster, putting Turkey in a policy zone in opposition to the Gulf States as well as Jordan.[174] One saving grace was the development of closer ties between Turkey and Qatar, with Ankara announcing the establishment of its first overseas military base in the Gulf kingdom; troops were first deployed in April 2016.[175] This rapprochement was a result of Ankara and Doha's similar positions on Hamas and on supporting rebel groups in Syria, as well as attempts at forging a closer alliance with Saudi Arabia.[176] However, such relations are still at a tentative early stage.

If that were not enough, following Israel's Operation Protective Edge in 2014 against Hamas's tunnel infrastructure and rocket launching facilities in Gaza, Turkey was virtually alone in Europe and the Middle East, excepting Qatar, in siding with Hamas. Turkey and Qatar's attempt at brokering a ceasefire did not work. Instead, Turkey drew international condemnation after Erdogan said that Israel's operation, which claimed the lives of over 2,000 Gaza residents, was more barbaric than Hitler, upsetting Jewish and Western sensibilities. In a dangerous turn of events, he then called on Turkey's tiny and vulnerable Jewish community to condemn Israel's actions.[177] Once again, Turkey found itself at odds with many Middle Eastern states and its traditional Western allies, whose silence over the destruction of Gaza was striking.

Times Are Critical

Today, Turkey finds itself increasingly isolated in the region just as it faces one of the biggest threats to the Middle East state system, the rise of ISIS. This organisation, spurned by al-Qaeda and condemned the world over for its shocking brutality, has made vast advances in Iraq and, despite loss of territory in 2016, threatens a deepening humanitarian and existential crisis for regional countries to which Turkey is not immune. Not only has there been a further influx of refugees fleeing ISIS terror, but when Mosul was captured, so too were Turkish hostages, including workers and diplomats.[178] Turkey found itself powerless and under heavy international pressure to stem the tide of foreign jihadists crossing its border into Syria.[179] Turkey was only able to join the international coalition against ISIS in August 2015 after it had allegedly freed hundreds of ISIS-affiliated prisoners in exchange for its captured diplomatic personnel in Mosul, who were released on 20 September 2014. It was even alleged that British jihadists were among those released, to London's consternation.[180]

The spread of ISIS and the ongoing crisis in Syria have proved to be Turkey's biggest foreign policy challenge since World War II. Not only has the civil war in Syria had domestic repercussions within Turkey, both in the form of increased Kurdish militancy and terrorism by a

PKK emboldened by Kurdish gains in Syria's Kurdish Rojava area, but Turkey has also had to deal with the threat of home-grown ISIS terrorists, who have set up splinter cells within the country. Turkey has been the victim of a wave of ISIS atrocities such as the shocking airport gun and bomb attack of 28 June 2015, which claimed at least forty-one victims and wreaked havoc on Turkey's ailing tourism sector,[181] and the March 2016 Istanbul suicide bombing that killed four (three Israelis and an Iranian) and injured dozens on the popular Istiklal Avenue.[182] This followed another attack in Istanbul's touristic old city, two months prior, which had killed ten German tourists and was considered the worst attack on German nationals in thirteen years.[183] These attacks, though horrific in themselves and leaving the city reeling, paled in comparison with the 2015 Ankara bombings that massacred around 103 civilians at the HDP's co-hosted rally, the worst terrorist attack in Turkey's history.[184]

Turkey's policies on the Syrian crisis, and the Arab uprisings in general, have done untold damage to its foreign relations with neighbours near and far. On 24 November 2015, Turkey downed a Russian SU-24 fighter jet that had strayed into its territory along the border with Syria, after it had apparently ignored repeated warnings to leave Turkish airspace. This caused a major rift in Turkish-Russian relations, with Russian president Vladimir Putin publicly condemning Turkey. He called the shooting of the plane a "stab in the back delivered by the accomplices of terrorists" and warned of "serious consequences.[185] Russia imposed sanctions on Turkish products and visa requirements on Turkish visitors, while stopping Russian tour operators and travel agents from selling holidays or package tours to Turkey.[186] The strain in ties between Ankara and Moscow reached such proportions that, when a Russian military vessel passed through the Bosphorus, a Russian soldier was pictured aiming a rocket launcher ready to fire.[187] The increased tensions with Russia caused Turkey's NATO allies to wince. Far from siding staunchly with its NATO ally, US president Barack Obama urged dialogue and "discourage[d] any kind of escalation".[188] In some European quarters, there was anger that Turkey had provoked the Russian bear. The tabloid press in the United Kingdom, for example, ran headlines intimating that Turkey was provoking a third world war.[189]

Perhaps the most damaging aspect of Turkey's fallout with Russia has been in its proxy war in Syria, where the two countries are on distinctly different sides. However, Turkey is in a more fragile position than Russia, owing to Ankara's opposition to the People's Protection Units due to their links with the PKK and its hold over Kurdish enclaves in Syria's north. Since the 2015 crisis between Russia and Turkey, Moscow has lent its support to the Kurdish groups, who have been happy to receive backing from either Russia or the US-led coalition.[190] Just as Turkey reconciled with Israel in the face of increased isolation, President Erdogan was obliged to apologise to Putin for the downing of the jet, in order for relations to normalise. As the BBC put it, in this particular battle of wills "it looks like Mr Erdogan blinked first".[191]

Meanwhile, Turkey's continued opposition to working with the Syrian Kurds, such as its insistence that neither the PYG nor the PYD be represented in international fora such as the Geneva meetings on the future of Syria, has created a continued gap between Turkey and its European and US allies.[192] In August 2015, there was further upset in the Western foreign policy community when Turkey, having finally decided to join coalition airstrikes against ISIS, also hit PKK targets in Iraq, in a better concerted effort and in much greater number.[193]

Turkey has had to deal with the financial, social and cultural strains of having up to 2.7 million Syrian refugees, the majority residing in the largest cities rather than in refugee camps close to the border.[194] The Syrian refugee crisis has cost Turkey billions of dollars, but without Ankara receiving credit for settling and absorbing those seeking support and shelter. Instead, Turkey is continually in the spotlight for the hundreds of thousands of refugees seeking a new life in Europe from Turkey, or for foreign jihadists entering Europe from Syria through its territory.

In March 2016, Turkey and the EU settled an agreement for dealing with the refugee crisis. However, many within Europe were surprised by Turkey's demands during the negotiating process. Not only was Ankara requesting billions of euros for its efforts, but it was also demanding the speeding up of Turkey's EU accession process and visa-free travel for Turks within the Schengen zone. Some European leaders, such as French president François Hollande, even expressed opposition to the plan, and, like Austria, France took this opportunity to state that Turkey could never join the EU.[195] Rather than the basis for stronger cooperation between Europe and Turkey, Ankara now faces the risk that the refugee crisis may plunge Turkish-EU relations to even greater depths of mistrust and hostility.

Another Fine Mess: The Post-July 2016 Military Coup

The attempted military coup of 15–16 July 2016 has had a significant impact on Turkey's foreign relations. One immediate consequence was that flights from the Incirlik airbase, used by the international coalition against ISIS, were temporarily suspended and for several days required generators to maintain power, hampering the coalition's ability to operate over Iraq and Syria.[196] The putsch and its aftermath, reflecting as it has a certain turbulence within Turkish politics, have also called into question Turkey's stability as an ally not only against ISIS but for NATO more generally. And, with purges and arrests of its leading officers, the potency and capabilities of the military as an effective fighting body are now in question. As journalist Burak Bekdil explained, with 44 per cent of the senior command structure removed, "Organizational weaknesses and operational vulnerabilities will be inevitable, especially at a time when the military must fight a multitude of asymmetrical wars inside and outside Turkey".[197]

In addition to the inevitable decline of Turkey's military preparedness, bilateral relations with traditional Western allies have reached a low ebb. Concerned with the nature of the post-putsch crackdown, US and European leaders have urged Erdogan and the ruling AKP not to turn the aftermath into a witch-hunt against its opposition and to respect fundamental freedoms. For Europe, the possibility of reinstating capital punishment, abolished in Turkey in 2004 but sought by a vocal group of protesters in the immediate aftermath of the attempted coup, has also been a source of particular concern in the West, especially after President Erdogan refused to rule it out. German foreign minister Frank-Walter Steinmeier commented in a very frank manner that the reintroduction of the death penalty would be the end of Turkey's EU accession process. The Austrian chancellor, Christian Kern, went further, calling for Europe to scrap the accession process following the post-coup purges.[198] Such tensions also highlight Europe's concerns over Turkey's terror laws, which pushed back Turks receiving visa-free travel to Europe in return for the March 2016 refugee deal.

Germany has warned the EU that it should not be "blackmailed" after Turkish foreign minister Mevlut Cavusoglu demanded that visa requirements be dropped by October 2016.[199]

The response to European criticism from President Erdogan and the AKP government has been a mixture of both anger and outrage. In their eyes, Europe has failed to condemn the coup attempt or to acknowledge its severity. Erdogan was quick to point out that no European or US leaders visited Turkey in the immediate aftermath of the putsch, despite it claiming the lives of 238 Turkish citizens. He was also angry at EU foreign policy chief Federica Mogherini's comments condemning the crackdown, claiming double standards and lack of empathy (what if Italy's parliament had been bombed, he asked), going on to comment that Europe had sided with the coup plotters.[200] Turkey's EU minister, Omer Celik, echoed Erdogan's comments, arguing that the West's criticism had drifted into anti-Turkish sentiment.[201]

Another source of tension between Turkey and its traditional allies was the accusation of US involvement in the coup plot. Labour Minister Suleyman Soylu had intimated that the United States was behind the whole thing.[202] Secretary of State John Kerry, who would later visit Turkey to ease tensions, denied this as "utterly false", warning that such allegations from Turkish officials would negatively affect bilateral relations. While reiterating his and Obama's support for the Turkish government, Kerry went on to caution against the crackdown and even suggest that Turkey's membership of NATO would be in jeopardy if the rule of law were not maintained in the post-putsch period.[203] This did not stop Erdogan from accusing the West of taking sides and claiming that the putsch had been "scripted" by "foreign forces".[204] Meanwhile, the US joint chiefs of staff chairman, Gen. Joseph Dunford, was obliged to deny allegations circulated in the pro-government Turkish press that—among other US-orchestrated conspiracies— retired US generals had been involved in the coup.[205]

The most determining factor in the post-putsch decay in US-Turkish relations has been Turkey's demand that the US extradite Fetullah Gulen, whom Ankara alleges is the mastermind behind the coup and who resides in the United States.[206] Washington has stated that it requires an official extradition request, which it has not yet received, as well as tangible evidence of Gulen's involvement. Thus far, US officials have not been convinced of the evidence provided by Turkish officials, and it has even been reported that the more Turkish officials publicly demand Gulen's extradition, the less likely it is to happen.[207] Nevertheless, a Turkish court has issued an arrest warrant for the exiled preacher for his alleged role in the coup attempt.[208] Fetullah Gulen's continued residence in Pennsylvania is bound to continue straining relations, as is Turkish disappointment that US and other Western officials did not offer enough support during the attempted coup. Turkey has feigned stronger relations with Moscow, with Erdogan meeting Putin in August 2016. Whether this will lead to a real strengthening of ties between Moscow and Ankara remains to be seen; either way, Turkey's international status is tenuous at best, with old but stable alliances looking increasingly fragile.

Conclusion

The decline of the military in politics under the AKP created space for new thinking about the direction and focus of Turkish foreign policy and Turkey's place in the world. The architect of the new trajectory was Ahmet Davutoglu, using his doctrine of strategic depth to steer Ankara toward greater relations with the Middle East as Erdogan's foreign policy advisor, then as foreign minister and, until May 2016, as prime minister. While there was certainly some logic in Davutoglu's thinking, and while Ankara can boast of several foreign policy successes, especially its relations with the Kurdistan Regional Government, Turkey's turning away from the Western-centric approach of the past has been troublesome to say the least. Relations with Turkey's traditional allies, unsure of this new direction, have suffered. The fallout with Israel has had multiple consequences. Turkey has been unable to position itself as an effective mediator in regional disputes, including its own. More importantly, the Arab uprisings from 2011 and especially the Syrian Civil War have highlighted a significant lacuna in the "zero problems" policy approach, confusing the ultimate goal with the strategy for achieving it. Soon, a series of foreign policy missteps were to leave Turkey vulnerable, especially in the Middle East, with no real friends except for the KRG, Hamas and Qatar, and many dangerous foes.

CONCLUSION

After another election victory, this time winning almost 52 per cent of the vote, Recep Tayyip Erdogan became in August 2014 the first popularly elected president in the history of the Turkish Republic. In his victory speech, Erdogan vowed to lead Turkey into a "new era of social reconciliation by leaving old disputes in the Old Turkey." He also called on the public to "mobilise our energy for New Turkey".[1] These were the right words for the occasion.

Erdogan is correct that old disputes need to be settled and resolved before Turkey can truly fulfil its unlimited potential. Some of these old scars are remnants from many years of military tutelage; others are from the AKP's first and second terms. However, Erdogan's reference to "old disputes" is very telling. While it is correct that the vestiges of the military-secular elite that once dominated Turkey have to be incorporated within the system in order for Turkey to progress, some of its disputes are not old but new. The AKP has only recently become embroiled in a feud with its one-time fellow travellers, the Gulen movement, leading to an attempted coup in July 2016. This is a wound that, one assumes, will not be healed anytime soon.

Meanwhile, many Turks are angered by the serious problems within Turkish politics, which must be addressed. Indeed, as this book has highlighted, Turkey's democratic system of government has many weaknesses. It has become aggressively majoritarian, and fixing this ill should be the priority for the government moving forward. The potential of the new Turkey can only be realised through the strengthening of its democracy. This is especially important after the AKP's election victory in November 2015 and its efforts to create a new, constitution-ally enshrined presidential system in the post-putsch coup environ-ment. What the AKP and Erdogan want from such a system is not yet entirely clear. However, what Turkey requires is the strengthening of its democratic institutions and governance.

What this volume has shown is that, in the post-military age, Turkey desperately needs to fix its political climate. This would include not only tolerance and consensus politics, but also greater accountability on the part of elected officials and transparency in how they conduct their business. It would involve a fight against corruption, and openness in decisions that affect the lives of millions of people. Also needed is a reinforcement of Turkey's delicate and fragile system of checks and balances, with a clear separation of powers.

That said, we have also seen that Turkey has a long way to go before it realises its full democratic potential. Yes, the armed forces are now confined to the barracks. This is a positive development and was a long time coming. But the process has been explosive. The confusion sur-rounding alleged and real coup plots and "deep state" networks has not only shocked many Turks, but polarised them as well. It certainly did not help that, at the same time as the government became embroiled in a dispute with the Gulen movement, which was believed to domi-nate the judiciary, the court convictions of many military personnel were discredited.

Many Turks are now suspicious of the AKP and its majoritarian style of governance. There are serious concerns that free speech has been eroded, as well as freedom of assembly and peaceful protest. The Gezi Park movement is a case in point. Many asked why such heavy-handed police measures were used against people protesting governmental plans for a shared public space. Many Turks also want their concerns over large-scale development and public projects to receive politicians' attention and for the government to offer an extended period of public consultations before engaging in schemes that would transform the lives of millions, especially where there are potential ecological and environmental ramifications.

It is of concern not only to Turks but also to the international com-munity that the Turkish public cannot exercise the right to protest without being beaten or sprayed with teargas by the police. Turkey is a young and dynamic society. Members of its burgeoning middle class expect their rights to be respected and for the state not to interfere in their private lives. Many Turks, old and young, will not tolerate a government that uses authoritarian measures to stifle their freedom. This includes restrictions on online fora and social media. The risk of not respecting such freedoms is further polarisation and protest. Turkey has a vibrant civil society and an intelligent, well-educated population that wants to be included, if not tolerated and respected, despite having lifestyles or views different from those of the current ruling elite. If such political inclusion were realised, it would be a mark of a strong and confident country.

No freedom of expression has been more stifled in Turkey than that of the press. Its powerlessness to report stories that criticise the government is a serious concern both inside and outside Turkey. Put quite simply, Turkey cannot be a real democratic society when scores of its journalists languish behind bars. Not only is bullying the press embarrassing for a self-identifying democratic state, but it also displays a lack of understanding of the depth of democracy on the part of those who are leading the country. A free and open press is not a threat to the state; it is an asset. Restrictions on journalism run counter to the spirit of democracy, as does governmental support for tenders and contracts exclusively with owners of media outlets supportive of government policies.

This brings us to the very important problem of government accountability, especially in Turkey's urban development projects. Highly contentious in itself, the construction industry not only drives the Turkish economy, but is also an important factor in support for and opposition to the AKP. However, the perception that the government may, carte blanche, engage in such projects without any transparency or due process is shared by many, not just the party's political opponents. When citizens' quality of life is affected or threatened by drastic changes to their surroundings, they want the right to voice concern and to be consulted.

The government's reaction to the corruption allegations of December 2013—a crackdown on the Gulen movement and its "parallel structures" within the state—addressed only one half of the problem: subversive elements within government institutions. The other half is lack of transparency and the authoritative manner of the ruling party. For any government, corruption is a threat to its very legitimacy as well as to the state itself; no one should be above the law, including presidents, generals, prime ministers, teachers, doctors or even postal workers. The best way of dealing with corruption allegations is to investigate them, regardless of their source.

The future of the new Turkey rests very much on the reconciliation process between Turk and Kurd. The Kurdish conflict has taken a heavy toll on Turkey, in the form of human life, the economy and social cohesion. The decline of the military and of its hard-line approach to the Kurdish question has not led to successful resolution of the issue. The challenge for the government of the new Turkey is to recognise that the Kurdish question is more than just a cultural or socioeconomic problem; it is also a national issue. To address the problem from its root cause will take much political courage. It will be a long process, one that Turkey is only now beginning. However, failing to find this solution risks returning to the bloodshed and war that hampered Turkey's growth and development at the height of the conflict in the 1980s and 1990s. Unfortunately, Turkey appears to be heading in that dangerous direction, with its major population centres, Istanbul and Ankara, falling victim to multiple terrorist attacks.

Meanwhile, Turkey is facing a crisis in its foreign policy. Currently, Turkey is increasingly isolated in the Middle East, a region that, on the one hand, has been a foreign policy priority for the AKP, and, on the other, is now the source of Turkey's main strategic threats. When military dominance of foreign policy direction first came to an end, "strategic depth" and "zero problems" were interesting and innovative doctrines. In some cases, they were successful. However, in others, Turkey's foreign relations have suffered. Far from experiencing zero problems, Turkey's relations with Israel, a regional and nuclear superpower, have soured. Even with the recent reconciliation, it is highly unlikely that ties between Ankara and Jerusalem will reach the same strategic level as during the 1990s. Turkey's involvement in the Iranian nuclear issue has also backfired. As the Arab Spring turns into a long winter with the rise of ISIS in Iraq and Syria, Turkey faces its biggest threat close to its borders, spilling over with a spate of terrorist atrocities. But Turkey now has a demoralised military, lacks friends in the region and faces suspicion from the West over its conduct.

CONCLUSION

In the days and weeks that followed the July 2016 attempted coup, there was an outpouring of nationalist and patriotic sentiment from nearly all corners of society, reflecting general outrage at the putsch and support for Turkey's democracy. Turkish flags were hung not only in public areas and from government buildings, but also in private homes, vehicles and offices. Billboards, instead of featuring advertising, displayed the Turkish flag, with slogans such as "Hakimiyet Milletindir" (The Nation is Sovereign) and "Biz milletiz Turkiyeyi darbeye terore yedirmeyiz" (We are the nation and we won't let the coup or terror take over the nation). Such messages of solidarity with the government and the democratic system were displayed everywhere imaginable, including on car bumpers, on billboards and stuck on top of *Cosmopolitan* magazine. Such sentiments reflected both a sense of genuine outrage and reluctance to appear unpatriotic. Perhaps there was even an element of fear, given the post-coup purge among government workers and agencies. In contrast, largely absent were demands for answers as to why, and in exactly what way, the AKP had been so close in the past to the Gulen movement, accused by the government itself of being behind the attempted coup. This has revealed a political climate of impunity, in which public officials remain unanswerable to the electorate. The fact that the president and the ruling party are former bedfellows of a movement that they themselves accuse of attempting a military takeover calls into question the competency of elected government officials. At minimum, they owe the Turkish public a detailed explanation of how and why they were "duped" for so long, as well as an independent public inquiry as to the nature of AKP-Gulenist relations until the falling out of 2013.

Still, there has been a certain degree of hope to the climate of solidarity and the manoeuvring for political consensus on the part of President Erdogan and the AKP. For example, on 29 July 2016, Erdogan announced that he would drop all court cases against those who had insulted him (some 2,000).[2] Several days later, Prime Minister Yildirim did the same.[3] The opposition CHP leader Kilicdaroglu, hailing the president's move as "elegant", reciprocated.[4]

However, despite what looked to be a positive new direction in Turkish politics, there were and continue to be alarm bells signalling that this state of affairs may not last. The government's newfound conciliatory attitude has not extended to the Kurdish-oriented HDP, which won over 10.5 per cent of the popular vote in the November 2015 general elections. And some of the decrees passed by the AKP under emergency rule, such as the restructuring of the military under the Defence Ministry's jurisdiction, indicate the party's desire to transfer such powers to the president at a later stage. Regardless of the conciliatory gestures of the moment, any changes to the constitution will touch on the fault lines between the AKP and opposition parties, including the CHP, all of whom are wary of amendments that would give the presidency too much power. There also remain serious concerns about the extent of the government crackdown. In other words, once real, substantive changes are initiated, the current solidarity between parties will prove short-lived. Opposition leader Kilicdaroglu has already warned that "The state should not be governed by anger and revenge" and that the culprits of the putsch should be tried "lawfully with the understanding of abiding by the rule of law".[5]

If, while Erdogan and the AKP rule through emergency law, there are further crackdowns and heavy-handed measures that could alter the nature of Turkish politics, the opposition's patience will wear thin. Reports of attacks against Turkey's Alevi minority, which constitutes between 10 and 25 per cent of the country, represent another worrying development that threatens the post-putsch spirit of shared patriotism.[6] Indeed, after the dust has settled, Turkey will still face the problems of 14 July 2016: the Kurdish question, the nature of the future constitution, troubled neighbourhood policies and international relations, identity politics, secular-religious divides and majoritarian-style politics. One can only hope that the post-putsch period could usher in a new consensus-based politics—though judging by Turkey's troubled political history, this is highly doubtful. The obstacles facing the new Turkey have not dissipated since the end of military tutelage.

However, Turkey has only recently entered a post-military age. The challenges are great, but if it rises to meet them, the new Turkey may be vibrant, dynamic, modern, inclusive, democratic and strong.

NOTES

INTRODUCTION

1. Interview with Ali Bayramoglu, columnist for *Yeni Safak*, Istanbul, 6 November 2013.
2. Interview with Nihat Ali Ozcan, security analyst at the Economic Policy Research Foundation of Turkey (TEPAV), Ankara, 7 November 2013.
3. Interview with Gareth Jenkins, Senior Associate Fellow at the Silk Road Studies Program and regular commentator in *Turkey Analyst*, Istanbul, 10 November 2013.
4. Ibid.
5. Interview with Ilhan Cihaner, CHP deputy and former public prosecutor (1994–2011), Ankara, 17 February 2014.
6. Interview with Gareth Jenkins, Istanbul, 10 November 2013.
7. Interview with Nedim Sener, journalist for *Posta*, Istanbul, 24 February 2014.
8. Interview with Tahir Elci, head of Diyarbakir Bar Association, Diyarbakir, 18 February 2014.
9. Interview with Ilhan Cihaner, CHP deputy and former Public Prosecutor (1994–2011), Ankara, 17 February 2014.
10. Interview with Nedim Sener, Istanbul, 24 February 2014.
11. Interview with Mevlut Cavusoglu, Minister of Foreign Affairs, Ankara, 20 February 2014.
12. Asli Aydintasbas, "The good, the bad and the Gülenists", European Council on Foreign Relations, 23 September 2016, http://www.ecfr.eu/publications/summary/the_good_the_bad_and_the_gulenists7131?utm_content=buffer1ae15&utm_medium=social&utm_source=twitter.com&utm_campaign=buffer#a2 (last visited 27/09/2016).
13. *Hurriyet Daily News*, 3 August 2016.

14. Interview with Ekmeleddin Ihsanoglu, MHP deputy and joint CHP and CHP candidate in the 2014 presidential election, Istanbul, 21 December 2015.
15. Iren Ozgur, "Arabesk Music in Turkey in the 1990s and Changes in National Demography, Politics, and Identity", *Turkish Studies*, Vol. 7, No. 2, 175–190, June 2006, p. 180.

1. THE GENERAL'S LAST SIGH

1. *Hurriyet Daily News*, 5 July 2013.
2. Umit Cizre and Joshua Walker, "Conceiving the New Turkey After Ergenekon", *The International Spectator: Italian Journal of International Affairs*, Vol. 45, No. 1, 89, p. 93; Aylin Guney and Petek Karatekelioglu, "Turkey's EU Candidacy and Civil-Military Relations: Challenges and Prospects", *Armed Forces and Society*, Vol. 31, No. 3, Spring 2005, pp. 441–3; Umit Cizre, "Problems of Democratic Governance of Civil-Military Relations in Turkey and the European Enlargement Zone", *European Journal of Political Research*, Vol. 43, No. 1, January 2004, p. 108.
3. Ali L. Karaosmanoglu, "Civil-Military Relations", Metin Heper and Sabri Sayari (eds), *The Routledge Handbook of Modern Turkey* (New York: Routledge, 2012), p. 150.
4. Yaprak Gursoy, "The changing role of the military in Turkish politics: democratization through coup plots?", *Democratization*, Vol. 19, No. 4, 2012, p. 741.
5. William Hale, *Turkish Politics and the Military* (London and New York: Routledge, 1994), p. 311.
6. Gursoy, "The changing role of the military in Turkish politics", p. 741.
7. Ozgur Mutlu Ulus, *The Army and the Radical Left in Turkey: Military Coups, Socialist Revolution and Kemalism*, (London: I.B. Tauris, 2011).
8. Feroz Ahmad, *The Making of Modern Turkey* (London: Routledge, 1993), pp. 124–5.
9. Ibid., p. 313.
10. Umit Cizre Sakallioglu, "The Anatomy of the Turkish Military's Political Autonomy", *Comparative Politics*, Vol. 29, No. 2, January 1997, p. 158.
11. Translated by Gareth Jenkins, "Continuity and Change: Prospects for Civil-Military Relations in Turkey", *International Affairs*, Vol. 83, No. 2, 2007, pp. 342–3.
12. Hale, *Turkish Politics and the Military*, p. 315.
13. Sakallioglu, "The Anatomy of the Turkish Military's Political Autonomy", pp. 156–7.

14. Jenkins, "Continuity and Change: Prospects for Civil-Military Relations in Turkey", p. 344.
15. Sakallioglu, "The Anatomy of the Turkish Military's Political Autonomy", p. 158.
16. *The New York Times*, 1 March 1997; *Milliyet*, 1 March 1997.
17. Cengiz Candar, "Post-Modern Darbe", *Sabah*, 27 June 1997.
18. Kerem Oktem, *Angry Nation: Turkey Since 1989* (Halifax: Fenwood, 2011), pp. 106–7.
19. *The Washington Post*, 4 March 1997.
20. *Turkish Daily News*, 19 June 1997; *Los Angeles Times*, 19 June 1997; *Milliyet*, 19 March 1997.
21. *The Times*, 28 February 1997; *Milliyet*, 3 March 1997.
22. Oktem, *Angry Nation*, p. 106.
23. *The Times*, 28 February 1997.
24. *BBC News*, 17 January 1998; *Washington Post*, 17 January 1998; *Milliyet*, 17 January 1998.
25. *The Guardian*, 23 June 2001.
26. Ergun Ozbudun, *The Constitutional System of Turkey: 1876 to the Present* (New York: Palgrave Macmillan, 2011), pp. 62–4, 74–6, 129–38.
27. Quoted in Umit Cizre-Sakalliogly and Menderes Cinar, "Turkey 2002: Kemalism, Islamism, and Politics in the Light of the February 28 Process", *The South Atlantic Quarterly*, Vol. 102, No. 2/3, Spring/Summer 2003, p. 326.
28. Soner Cagaptay, "The November 2002 Elections and Turkey's New Political Era", *MERIA Journal*, Vol. 6, No. 4, December 2002.
29. Interview with Nimet Bas, former minister for women and family affairs, former minister of national education and head of the Parliamentary Commission to Investigate Military Coups, Istanbul, 10 November 2013.
30. *The Washington Post*, 11 December 1999; *Hurriyet*, 11 December 1999.
31. *The Washington Post*, 4 August 2002; *Hurriyet*, 2 August 2002.
32. Council of the European Union, "Copenhagen European Council, 12 and 13 December: Presidency Conclusions", Brussels, 29 January 2003, Polgen 84, 15917/02.
33. *The Times*, 17 December 2004; *The Times*, 18 December 2004; *Hurriyet*, 18 December 2004.
34. *The Independent*, 4 December 2002.
35. *The Daily Telegraph*, 31 July 2003; *Sabah*, 31 July 2003; *The Times*, 31 July 2003; *Hurriyet*, 30 July 2003.
36. Mehmet Bardakci, "Coup Plots and the Transformation of Civil-Military Relations in Turkey under AKP Rule," *Turkish Studies*, Vol. 14, No. 3, 2003, pp. 413–15.

37. European Commission, "Regular Report on Turkey's Progress Towards Accession", Brussels, 9 October 2002, SEC (2002) 1412.

38. European Commission, "Regular Report on Turkey's Progress Towards Accession", Brussels, 6 October 2004, SEC (2004) 1201.

39. European Commission, "Turkey: 2005 Progress Report", Brussels, 9 November 2005, SEC (2005) 1426.

40. Aylin Guney and Petek Karatekellioglu, "Turkey's EU Candidacy and Civil-Military Relations: Challenges and Prospects," *Armed Forces and Society*, Vol. 31, No. 3, Spring 2005, p. 446.

41. Interview with Edip Baser, former deputy chief of the general staff, Istanbul, 6 November 2013.

42. Ibid.

43. Ibid.

44. Jenkins, "Continuity and Change", p. 339.

45. Interview with Gareth Jenkins, Senior Associate Fellow at the Silk Road Studies Program and regular commentator in *Turkey Analyst*, Istanbul, 10 November 2013; also see, Metin Heper, "Civil-Military Relations in Turkey: Toward a Liberal Model?", *Turkish Studies*, Vol. 12, No. 2, June 2011.

46. Interview with Nihat Ali Ozcan, retired major in the TSK and security expert at the Ankara-based Economic Policy Research Foundation of Turkey (TEPAV), Ankara, 7 November 2013.

47. Interview with Gareth Jenkins, Istanbul, 10 November 2013.

48. Metin Heper, "The Justice and Development Party Government and the Military in Turkey," *Turkish Studies*, Vol. 6, No. 2, June 2005, p. 217. However, it is worth noting that Ozkok accused the then prime minister, Abdullah Gul, of encouraging anti-secular activities after Gul questioned the military's decision to expel several officers for engaging in Islamist activities and for discussing women's right to wear headscarves in state-owned buildings. See *The Independent*, 10 January 2003; *Cumhuriyet*, 10 January 2013; *The Guardian*, 10 January 2003; *Milliyet*, 10 January 2013.

49. Heper, "The Justice and Development Party Goverment and the Military in Turkey", p. 218.

50. Ibid., p. 219.

51. Interview with Nihat Ali Ozcan, Ankara, 7 November 2013.

52. Alper Gormus, *Imaj ve Hakikat: Bir Kuvvet Komutaninin Kaleminden Turk Ordusu*, (Istanbul: Etkilesim, 2012), pp. 203–44.

53. Heper, "The AKP Government and the Military in Turkey", p. 224.

54. *The Independent*, 1 May 2003; *Cumhuriyet*, 24 April 2003.

55. Jenkins, "Continuity and Change", p. 350.

56. *The Guardian*, 27 May 2003; *Cumhuriyet*, 23 May 2003.

57. *Washington Post*, 27 May 2003; *Cumhuriyet*, 27 May 2003.

58. Ambassador W. Robert Pearson, "Ankara: Turkey's Deep State", Wikileaks, Cable: 03ANKARA4544, 21 July 2003, https://wikileaks. org/cable/2003/07/03ankara4544.html (last visited 12/08/2014).

59. Jenkins, "Continuity and Change", p. 351.

60. Interview with Gareth Jenkins, Istanbul, 10 November 2013.

61. Ambassador W. Robert Pearson, "Ankara: Turkey's Deep State", Wikileaks, Cable: 02ANKARA 8252, 15 November 2002, https:// wikileaks.org/cable/2002/11/02ankara8252.html (last visited 12/08/2014).

62. Ambassador W. Robert Pearson, "Ankara: Defining the Republic of Turkey: General Staff and Government Struggle with Themselves and Each Other", Wikileaks, Cable: 03ANKARA3694, 6 June 2003, https://wikileaks.org/cable/2003/06/03ankara3694.html (last visited 12/08/2014).

63. On occasions Ozkok did hold his ground against the AKP without prompting. After AKP deputy Fehmi Husrev Kutlu complained about portraits of Ataturk in parliament in December 2003, Ozkok issued a statement backing a military officer who had attacked Kutlu's complaint. See Jenkins, "Continuity and Change", p. 350.

64. Interview with Gareth Jenkins, Istanbul, 10 November 2013.

65. Interview with Edip Baser, Istanbul, 6 November 2013. (Baser said this was only a hunch, as he had retired in 2002. However, his suspicions appear to be corroborated in the diaries (known in Turkey as the "coup diaries") of Ozden Ornek, the commander of the Turkish Naval Forces, which were later published as a book entitled *Gormus, Imaj ve Hakikat*, p. 244.

66. Ambassador Ross Wilson, "Ankara: Turks of Two Minds on the Military's Intervention," Wikileaks, Cable: 07ANKARA1071, 7 May 2007, https://wikileaks.org/cable/2007/05/07ankara1071.html (last visited 12/08/2014).

67. Ambassador Ross Wilson, "Ankara: Talk Tough from Turkey's Generals: Reading Between the Lines," Wikileaks, Cable: 06ANKARA5922, 13 October 2006, https://wikileaks.org/cable/2006/10/06ankara 5922.html (last visited 12/08/2014); *The Times*, 1 May 2007.

68. Oktem, *Angry Nation*, pp. 151–2.

69. *The New York Times*, 29 April 2007; *Cumhuriyet*, 28 April 2007.

70. *The New York Times*, 15 April 2007; *BBC News*, 29 April 2007; *The Independent*, 30 April 2007; *Cumhuriyet*, 29 April 2007; *Cumhuriyet*, 30 April 2007.

71. *The Washington Times*, 25 April 2007; *Sabah*, 24 April 2007.

72. Ozbudun, *The Constitutional System of Turkey*, p. 74.

73. "Excerpts of Turkish army statement," *BBC News*; *Sabah*, 28 April 2007.

74. Ambassador Ross Wilson, "Ankara: Perspectives on the Turkish Military's Political Gambit," Wikileaks, Cable: 07ANKARA1070, 7 May 2007, https://wikileaks.org/cable/2007/07/07ankara1070.html (last visited 12/08/2014).

75. *BBC News*, 28 April 2007; *Turkish Daily News*, 4 May 2007; *Sabah*, 28 April 2007. Omer Taspinar notes that the US response was delayed; see Omer Taspinar, "The Old Turks' Revolt: When Radical Secularism Threatens Democracy," *Foreign Affairs*, Vol. 86, No. 6, November/December 2007, p. 129.

76. Oktem, *Angry Nation*, p. 153; *BBC News*, 1 May 2007; Ozbudun, *The Constitutional System of Turkey*, p. 75.

77. Ozbudun, *The Constitutional System of Turkey*, p. 75.

78. *The Guardian*, 28 August 2007; *The Daily Telegraph*, 29 August 2007; *Hurriyet*, 28 August 2007.

79. Soner Cagaptay, H. Akin Unver, and Hale Arifagaoglu, "Will the Turkish Constitutional Court Ban the AKP?", Washington Institute of Near East Policy, PolicyWatch 1355, 19 March 2008.

80. Ambassador Ross Wilson, "Ankara: Turkey's New CHOD: General Ilker Basbug," Wikileaks, Cable: 08ANKARA1392, 4 August 2008, https://wikileaks.org/cable/2008/08/08ankara1392.html (last visited 12/08/2014).

81. *Spiegel Online*, 30 July 2008; *The Guardian*, 31 July 2008; *Hurriyet*, 30 July 2008.

82. Interview with Nimet Bas, Istanbul, 10 November 2013.

83. Ambassador James Jeffrey, "Ankara: Ergenekon: As the Power Pendulum Swings," Wikileaks, Cable: 09ANKARA368, 12 March 2009, https://wikileaks.org/cable/2009/03/09ankara368.html (last visited 12/08/2014).

84. *Turkish Daily News*, 19 September 1997.

85. *The Globe and the Mail*, 15 November 1996.

86. *The Washington Post*, 1 January 1997.

87. Interview with Gareth Jenkins, Istanbul, 10 November 2013.

88. Gareth Jenkins, "Between Fact and Fantasy: Turkey's Ergenekon Investigation," *Silk Road Paper 2009*, Central Asia-Caucasus Institute: Silk Road Studies Program, August 2009, p. 37.

89. Ibid., pp. 37–8.

90. *Anatolia News Agency*, Ankara, 23 January 2008.

91. *Associated Press International*, 26 January 2008; *Hurriyet*, 26 January 2008.

92. *Agence France Presse*, 21 March 2008, Ilhan Selcuk ve Doğu Perinçek Göz Altında, *Hurriyet*, 21 March 2008.

93. Interview with Nimet Bas, Istanbul, 10 November 2013.

94. However, he claims these really were purely a training exercise. Interview with Edip Baser, Istanbul, 6 November 2013; interview with Nihat Ali Ozcan, Ankara, 7 November 2013.

95. Ibid.

96. *Agence France Presse*, 21 March 2008.

97. *BBC Monitoring Europe*, 30 January 2008, taken from NTV, Istanbul, 30 January 2008.

98. *BBC News*, 4 February 2008.

99. *Associated Press International*, 26 January 2008; *Hurriyet*, 26 January 2008.

100. *Agence France Presse*, 30 March 2008.

101. Interview with Ilhan Cihaner, CHP deputy and former public prosecutor (2007–11), Ankara, 17 February 2014.

102. Ibid.

103. *Observer*, 4 May 2008.

104. Interview with Ilhan Cihaner, Ankara, 17 February 2014.

105. Interview with Celal Ulgen, lawyer for many of the accused in the Ergenekon and Balyoz cases, Istanbul, 6 November 2013; interview with Ilhan Cihaner, Ankara, 17 February 2014.

106. Interview with Celal Ulgen, Istanbul, 6 November 2013; interview with Gareth Jenkins, Istanbul, 10 November 2013; interview with Ilhan Cihaner, Ankara, 17 February 2014.

107. Ambassador Ross Wilson, "Ankara: Turkey: More Arrested in Ergenekon Investigation," Wikileaks, Cable: 08ANKARA1701, 24 September 2008, https://wikileaks.org/cable/2008/09/08ankara1701.html (last visited 12/08/2014).

108. *CNN.com*, 1 July 2008.

109. *The Guardian*, 15 July 2008; *Sabah*, 14 July 2008.

110. *The New York Times*, 15 July 2008.

111. *The Globe and the Mail*, 15 July 2008. In 2015, the Workers' Party changed its name to "Patriotic Party" (Vatan Partisi).

112. *Anatolia Agency*, 20 October 2008; *The Guardian*, 20 October 2008.

113. *The Guardian*, 9 January 2009; *Hurriyet*, 8 January 2009.

114. *The Irish Times*, 23 January 2009; "16 Ilde 39 Gozalti," *Bianet*, 22 January 2009.

115. Ibid.

116. Ibid.

117. *The New York Times*, 18 April 2009; *Sabah*, 13 April 2009.

118. *The Independent*, 21 July 2009.

119. Ibid.

120. *The Times*, 7 August 2009.

121. *The Guardian*, 23 February 2010; *Taraf*, 20 January 2010.

122. *The New York Times*, 23 February 2010.

123. *The New York Times*, 25 February 2010.

124. *The New York Times*, 26 February 2010.

125. US Embassy in Ankara, 25 January 2010, "Ankara: Turkish Military Takes a Pounding with 'Sledgehammer'", Wikileaks, Cable: 10ANKARA120. https://wikileaks.org/cable/2010/03/10ankara120. html (last visited 12/08/2014).

126. Ambassador James Jeffrey, "Ankara: Largest Wave of Military Detentions to Date Poses Questions: What Next in Military-AKP Clash?", Wikileaks, Cable: 10ANKARA294, 23 February 2010, https://wikileaks.org/cable/2010/02/10ankara294.html (last visited 12/08/2014).

127. *The Washington Post*, 6 January 2012; *Hurriyet*, 6 January 2012.

128. *The Times*, 28 March 2012.

129. *The Times*, 22 September 2012; *Hurriyet*, 21 September 2012.

130. *The Daily Telegraph*, 6 August 2013; *The Guardian*, 6 August 2013.

131. *BBC News*, 7 March 2014.

132. *Hurriyet Daily News*, 10 March 2014.

133. Interview with Irem Cicek, lawyer of Dursun Cicik, Istanbul, 24 February 2014.

134. Interview with Gareth Jenkins, Istanbul, 10 November 2013; *The Economist*, 6 June 2012.

135. For the most comprehensive critical account of the Ergenekon investigation, see Jenkins, "Between Fact and Fantasy".

136. *BBC News*, 21 April 2016.

137. *Daily Sabah*, 19 June 2014.

138. *Hurriyet Daily News*, 31 March 2015.

139. *Wall Street Journal*, 30 July 2011.

140. *Hurriyet Daily News*, 13 January 2015; *Hurriyet Daily News*, 29 May 2015.

141. Recep Tayyip Erdogan, "Speech at Turkish Military Academy" (Harp Akademileri Komutanlığı'nı Ziyaretleri Vesilesiyle Yaptıkları Konuşma), Ankara: Presidency of the Republic of Turkey, 19 March 2015, http://www.tccb.gov.tr/konusmalar/353/29807/harp-akademileri-komutanligini-ziyaretleri-vesilesiyle-yaptiklari-konusma.html (last visited 26/02/2016); Recep Tayyip Erdogan, "President Erdoğan's Address to Mukhtars at the 3rd Meeting of Municipal Headmen" (Üçüncü Muhtarlar Toplantısı'nda Yaptıkları Konuşma), Ankara: Presidency of the Republic of Turkey, 24 February 2015, http://www.tccb.gov.tr/konusmalar/353/2997/ucuncu-muhtarlar-toplantisinda-yaptiklari-konusma.html (last visited 26/02/2016).

142. Yalcin Akdogan, "Ellerinde nur mu var, topuz mu?", *Star Gazetesi*, 24 December 2013.
143. Emre Peker, "Turkey's Military Moves Against Coup Cases as Judiciary Fights Government," *Wall Sreet Journal*, 3 January 2014; *Hurriyet Daily News*, 26 December 2014.
144. *Hurriyet Daily News*, 8 January 2014.
145. *Zaman*, 13 April 2015.
146. *Haberturk*, 22 February 2015.
147. Cengiz Aktar, "The truth about Operation Shah Euphrates," *Al Jazeera*, 23 February 2015.
148. *Haberturk*, 22 February 2015.
149. *Halk TV*, 5 March 2015; Cengiz Aktar, "The truth about Operation Shah Euphrates," *Al Jazeera*, 23 February 2015; *Cumhuriyet*, 22 February 2015; *Zaman* 23 February 2015.
150. *WorldBulletin.net*, "Turkish opposition criticizes gov't over Shah Firat operation", 24 February 2015.
151. *Anatolian Agency*, 24 February 2015.
152. *Today's Zaman*, 22 July 2015; *Cumhuriyet*, 22 July 2015; *Reuters*, 22 July 2015. Later in August a local group, Apocu Fedailer (Fedayeen of Apo), claimed responsibility. *Hurriyet Daily News*, 7 August 2015.
153. *The Guardian*, 28 July 2015.
154. *T24*, 19 August 2015.
155. Edward Luttwak, *Coup d'État: A Practical Handbook*, (Harmondsworth: Penguin Books, 1969), p. 58.
156. Ibid., pp. 61–85.
157. Ibid., pp. 89–104, 110.
158. Ibid., pp. 114–15.
159. Dani Roderik, "Turkey's Baffling Coup," *Project Syndicate*, 17 July 2016; Steven A. Cook, *The Washington Post*, 16 July 2016.
160. Luttwak, *Coup d'État*, pp. 118–22.
161. Ibid., pp. 112–28.
162. Ibid., pp. 128–30.
163. Ibid., pp. 157–8.
164. Interview with Ismail Hakki Pekin, former head of Turkey's General Staff Intelligence Department and deputy chair of the Vatan Party, Ankara, 22 July 2016.
165. Zack Beauchamp, "Why Turkey's Coup Failed, according to an Expert", interview with Naunihal Singh, *Vox World*, 16 July 2016.
166. Simon A. Waldman, "The military's last stand: what went wrong for Turkey's Coup Plotters?" *The Globe and Mail*, 16 July 2016.
167. Steven A. Cook, "Turkey has had lots of coups. Here's why this one failed," *Washington Post*, 16 July 2016.

168. Luttwak, *Coup d'État*, pp. 30–2.

169. Ibid., pp. 36–7.

170. Interview with Ismail Mesut Sezgin, director at the Centre for Hizmet Studies, Ankara, 8 August 2016.

171. *The Guardian*, 16 July 2016; Fetullah Gulen, "Fethullah Gulen: I Condemn All Threats to Turkey's Democracy", *The New York Times*, 25 July 2016.

172. Patrick Kingsley, "Turkey detains 6,000 over coup attempt as Erdogan vows to 'clean state of virus'", *The Guardian*, 17 July 2016.

173. Asli Aydintasbas, "The good, the bad and the Gülenists", European Council on Foreign Relations, 23 September 2016, http://www.ecfr. eu/publications/summary/the_good_the_bad_and_the_gulenists 7131?utm_content=buffer1ae15&utm_medium=social&utm_source= twitter.com&utm_campaign=buffer#a2 (last visited 27/09/2016).

174. Aaron Stein, "Inside a Failed Coup and Turkey's Fragmented Military", *War on the Rocks*, 20 July 2016.

175. Claire Berlinski, "Who Planned Turkey's Coup?", *City Journal*, 20 July 2016.

176. Stein, "Inside a Failed Coup and Turkey's Fragmented Military".

177. Kadri Gursel, "Turkey's failed coup reveals 'army within an army'", *Al-Monitor*, 22 July 2016.

178. Interview with Ismail Hakki Pekin, Ankara, 22 July 2016.

179. *Financial Times*, 2 August 2016; *Hurriyet Daily News*, 31 July 2016.

180. *The Guardian*, 31 July 2016.

181. Interview with Ismail Hakki Pekin, Ankara, 22 July 2016.

182. Interview with Abdullatif Sener, former AKP deputy prime minister (2002–7), Ankara, 8 November 2013.

2. THE IRRESISTIBLE RISE OF THE AKP

1. Omer Taspinar, "Turkey: The New Model?", Robin Wright (ed.), *The Islamists Are Coming: Who They Really Are*, The United States Institute of Peace, April 2012, pp. 127–37.

2. Interview with Ali Bayramoglu, columnist for *Yeni Safak*, Istanbul, 6 November 2013.

3. Fulya Atacan, "Explaining Religious Politics at the Crossroad: AKP-SP," *Turkish Studies*, Vol. 6, No. 2, June 2005, pp. 187–99; Mustafa Sen, "Transformation of Turkish Islamism and the Rise of the Justice and Development Party", *Turkish Studies*, Vol. 11, No. 1, May 2010, pp. 62–3.

4. Ahmet Yildiz, "Politico-Religious Discourse of Political Islam in Turkey: The Parties of National Outlook," *The Muslim World*, Vol. 93, No. 2, April 2003, pp. 188–90.

5. Ibid.

6. Interview with Rifat Bali, author and expert on the history of the Jews in Turkey, Istanbul, 4 November 2013.

7. Interview with Sevket Kazan, former justice minister, Welfare Party (1974, 1997–8) and Felicity Party, Ankara, 17 February 2014.

8. Pinar Tank, "Political Islam in Turkey: A State of Controlled Secularity", *Turkish Studies*, Vol. 6, No. 1, March 2005, p. 7.

9. Atacan, "Explaining Religious Politics at the Crossroads," pp. 187–8.

10. M. Hakan Yavuz, *Islamic Political Identity in Turkey* (Oxford: Oxford University Press, 2003) p. 70.

11. Hugh Poulton, *The Top Hat, the Grey Wolf and the Crescent: Turkish Nationalism and the Turkish Republic* (London: Hurst, 1997) p. 179.

12. Anat Lapidot, "Islamic Activism in Turkey Since the 1980 Military Takeover", *Terrorism and Political Violence*, Vol. 8, No. 2, 1996, p. 68.

13. Poulton, *The Top Hat*, pp. 179–80.

14. Lapidot, "Islamic Activism in Turkey Since the 1980 Military Takeover", p. 69.

15. Tank, "Political Islam in Turkey", p. 5; Constitution of the Republic of Turkey, Article 24, p. 11.

16. Poulton, *The Top Hat*, pp. 183–4.

17. Bennaz Toprak, *Islam and Political Development in Turkey* (Leiden: EJ Brill, 1981), p. 47.

18. Thomas W. Smith, "Between Allah and Ataturk: Liberal Islam in Turkey," *The International Journal of Human Rights*, Vol. 9, No. 3, 2005, p. 313.

19. Poulton, *The Top Hat*, p. 184.

20. Ibid., pp. 184–6.

21. Sam Kaplan, "Din-U Devlet All Over Again? The Politics of Military Secularism in Turkey Following the 1980 Coup," *International Journal of Middle East Studies*, Vol. 34, No. 1, February 2002, p. 114.

22. Yavuz, *Islamic Political Identity in Turkey*, p. 75.

23. Smith, "Between Allah and Ataturk," p. 313.

24. Lapidot, "Islamic Activism in Turkey Since the 1980 Military Takeover", p. 68.

25. Sencer Ayata, "Patronage, Party, and State: The Politicization of Islam in Turkey", *Middle East Journal*, Vol. 50, No. 1, Winter 1996, p. 43.

26. Ibid.

27. Yavuz, *Islamic Political Identity in Turkey*, p. 64.

28. Ibid., p. 65.

29. Ayata, "Patronage, Party, and State", p. 44.

30. Ibid., p. 44.

31. Turkish Parliament Archives, "Türkiye Cumhuriyeti Milletvekili Genel Seçimleri 1995 Yılı Genel Seçimlerinde Partilerin Aldıkları Oylar ve

Oranları", http://www.tbmm.gov.tr/develop/owa/secimler.secimdeki_partiler?p_secim_yili=1995 (last visited 19/10/2013).

32. *Milliyet*, 9 July 1996.
33. Ayata, "Patronage, Party, and State", p. 52.
34. Metin Heper, "Islam and Democracy in Turkey: Toward a Reconciliation?", *Middle East Journal*, Vol. 51, No. 1, Winter 1997, p. 35.
35. Tank, "Political Islam in Turkey", pp. 9–10.
36. Binnaz Toprak, "Islam and Democracy in Turkey", *Turkish Studies*, Vol. 6, No. 2, 2005, p. 172.
37. NTV, 14 May 2000.
38. Sebnem Gumuscu and Deniz Sert, "The Power of the Devout Bourgeoisie: The Case of the Justice and Development Party in Turkey", *Middle Eastern Studies*, 2009, Vol. 45, No. 6, 2009, p. 963.
39. Gareth Jenkins, "Muslim Democrats in Turkey?", *Survival*, Vol. 45, No. 1, Spring 2003, p. 49.
40. Interview with Rifat Bali, Istanbul, 4 November 2013.
41. Gumuscu and Sert, "The Power of the Devout Bourgeoisie", p. 962.
42. *The New York Times*, 10 March 2003.
43. *The Washington Post*, 11 September 2010.
44. *The New York Times*, 28 March 2014.
45. Yalcin Akdogan, *AK Parti ve Muhafazakar Demokrasi* (Ankara: Alfa Yayinlari, 2004), pp. 15–16.
46. Gumuscu and Sert, "The Power of the Devout Bourgeoisie", p. 957.
47. Jenkins, "Muslim Democrats in Turkey?", pp. 53–4.
48. AKP Programme, undated, see http://www.akparti.org.tr/site/akparti/parti-programi#bolum (last visited 29/09/2014).
49. See Erdogan's opening speech in *International Symposium on Conservatism and Democracy* (Ankara: AK Parti Yayınları, 2004), p. 11.
50. AKP Programme.
51. *Al Arabiya*, 14 September 2011.
52. *Hurriyet*, 10 January 2004.
53. Ergun Ozbudun, "From Political Islam to Conservative Democracy: The Case of the Justice and Development Party in Turkey," *South European Society and Politics*, Vol. 11, No. 3–4, September–December 2006, p. 546.
54. Gamze Cavdar, "Islamist *New Thinking* in Turkey: A Model for Political Learning?", *Political Science Quarterly*, Vol. 121, No. 3, 2006, p. 481.
55. Jenkins, "Muslim Democrats in Turkey?", pp. 53–4. The first female MP to wear a headscarf entered parliament in October 2013.
56. Ibid.
57. Zeyneb Cagliyan–Icener, "The Justice and Development Party's

Conception of 'Conservative Democracy': Invention or Reinterpretation?", *Turkish Studies*, Vol. 10, No. 4, 2009, p. 606.

58. Meliha B. Altunisik, "The Possibilities and Limits of Turkey's Soft Power", *Insight Turkey*, Vol. 10, No. 2, 2008, p. 44.

59. Lerna Yanik, "The Metamorphosis of Metaphors of Vision: 'Bridging' Turkey's Location, Role and Identity After the End of the Cold War", *Geopolitics*, Vol. 14, No. 3, 2009, p. 534.

60. Yalcin Akdogan, *AK Parti ve Muhafazakar Demokrasi*, (Ankara: Alfa Yayınları, 2004), pp. 15–16.

61. Soner Cagaptay, "The November 2002 Elections and Turkey's New Political Era," *MERIA Journal*, Vol. 6, No. 4, December 2002.

62. Sultan Tepe, "Turkey's AKP: A Model 'Muslim-Democratic' Party?", *Journal of Democracy*, Vol. 16, No. 3, July 2005, p. 71.

63. *The Daily Telegraph*, 5 November 2002; Mustafa Sen, "Transformation of Turkish Islamism and the Rise of the Justice and Development Party", *Turkish Studies*, Vol. 11, No. 1, May 2010, p. 59.

64. Michel Garfinkiel, "Is Turkey Lost?", *Commentary*, March 2007.

65. Nicole Pope and Hugh Pope, *Turkey Unveiled: A History of Modern Turkey* (New York: Overlook, 2004), p. 350.

66. Hasan Turunc, "Islamist or Democrat? The AKP's Search for Identity in Turkish Politics," *Journal of Contemporary European Studies*, Vol. 15, No. 1, 2007, p. 84.

67. Ozbudun "From Political Islam to Conservative Democracy", p, 546.

68. Jenkins, "Muslim Democrats in Turkey?", p. 55.

69. Feroz Ahmad, *Turkey: The Quest for Identity*, (Oxford: Oneworld, 2003), pp. 181–2.

70. Gulen Movement, "Brief History of the Gulen Movement," undated, http://www.gulenmovement.us/gulen-movement/brief-history-of-gulen-movement (last visited 27/09/2014).

71. Interview with Ilhan Cihaner, Ankara, 17 February 2014.

72. Interview with Ihsan Yilmaz, a self-declared Gulen follower who teaches at the Gulenist Fatih University, Istanbul, 15 February 2014.

73. *The Daily Telegraph*, 9 October 2015.

74. Interview with Bulent Kenes, former editor-in-chief of *Today's Zaman*, Istanbul, 24 February 2014.

75. Interview with Nedim Sener, journalist for *Posta*, Istanbul, 24 February 2014.

76. Ibid.

77. Elisabeth Ozdalga, "The Hidden Arab. A Critical Reading of the Notion of Turkish Islam", *Middle Eastern Studies*, Vol. 42, No. 4, July 2006, p. 559.

78. M. Hakan Yavuz, "Towards an Islamic Liberalism? The Nurcu Movement

and Fethullah Gülen", *Middle East Journal*, Vol. 53, No. 4, Autumn, 1999, pp. 584–6; David Tittenson, *The House of Service, The Gulen Movement and Islam's Third Way*, (Oxford: Oxford University Press, 2014), pp. 174–5.

79. Ibid., p. 593.
80. Interview with Etyem Mahcupyan, columnist for *Aksam*, Istanbul, 5 November 2013.
81. Berrin Koyuncu Lorasdagi, "The Prospects and Pitfalls of Religious Nationalist Movement in Turkey: The Case of the Gülen Movement", *Middle Eastern Studies*, Vol. 46, No. 2, 2010, p. 224.
82. Joshua D. Hendrick, "Globalization, Islamic activism, and passive revolution in Turkey: the case of Fethullah Gülen", *Journal of Power*, Vol. 2, No. 3, December 2009, p. 346.
83. Interview with Bulent Kenes, Istanbul, 24 February 2014.
84. Joshua D. Hendrick, "Media Wars and the Gülen Factor in the New Turkey", *Middle East Report 260*, Fall 2011, p. 44.
85. Interview with Bulent Kenes, Istanbul, 24 February 2014.
86. Istar B. Gozaydın, "The Fethullah Gülen movement and politics in Turkey: a chance for democratization or a Trojan horse?", *Democratization*, Vol. 16, No. 6, 2009, pp. 1216–19.
87. Ibid.
88. Gareth Jenkins, "AKP Forming Closer Links with the Gulen Movement," *Eurasia Daily Monitor*, Vol. 4, No. 217, 21 November 2007.
89. Interview with Ihsan Yilmaz, Istanbul, 15 February 2014.
90. Ahmet T. Kuru, "Changing perspectives on Islamism and secularism in Turkey: The Gülen Movement and the AK Party," Greg Barton, Paul Weller, Ihsan Yilmaz (eds), *Muslim World in Transition: Contributions of the Gülen Movement*, (London: Bloomsbury, 2013), p. 150.
91. Jenkins, "AKP Forming Closer Links with the Gulen Movement".
92. Interview with Bulent Kenes, Istanbul, 24 February 2014.
93. Kuru, "Changing perspectives on Islamism and secularism in Turkey," p. 147.
94. Interview with Irfan Guvendi, deputy head of MUSIAD, Ankara Branch, Ankara, 21 February 2014.
95. Gözaydın, "The Fethullah Gülen movement and politics in Turkey", p. 1219.
96. Interview with Sadettin Tantan, former interior minister (1999–2001), Istanbul, 15 February 2014.
97. Hendrick, "Globalization, Islamic activism", p. 351.
98. Ibid.
99. Altay Atli, "Businessmen as Diplomats: The Role of Business Associations in Turkey's Foreign Economic Policy", *Insight Turkey*, Vol. 13, No. 1, 2011, p. 116.

100. Kamil Yılmaz, "The Emergence and Rise of Conservative Elite in Turkey", *Insight Turkey*, Vol. 11, No. 2, 2009, p. 121.
101. Sevket Pamuk, "Globalization, Industrialisation and Changing Politics in Turkey", *New Perspective on Turkey*, No. 38, 2008, p. 268. Anatolian centres of industry include Konya, Yozgat, Denizli, Çorum, Aksaray and Gaziantep provinces.
102. Interview with Irfan Guvendi, Ankara, 21 February 2014.
103. Ayse Bugra, "Class, Culture and State: An Analysis of Interest Representation by Two Turkish Business Associations", *International Journal of Middle East Studies*, Vol. 30, No. 4, November 1998, pp. 521–39.
104. Ayse Bugra and Osman Savaskan, "Yerel Sanayi ve Bugünün Türkiyesi'nde İş Dünyası", *Toplum Bilim*, No. 118, 2010, pp. 94–6.
105. Gumuscu and Sert, "The Power of the Devout Bourgeoisie", p. 963.
106. Ahmet Insel, "The AKP and Normalizing Democracy in Turkey", *The South Atlantic Quarterly*, Vol. 102, No. 2/3, Spring/Summer 2003, pp. 297–8.
107. Gumuscu and Sert, "The Power of the Devout Bourgeoisie", p. 964.
108. Refet S. Gürkaynak and Selin Sayek Böke, *İktidarın Ekonomi Politiği: AKP Döneminde Türkiye Ekonomisi*, Birikim Dergisi, December 2013, p. 64.
109. Turkish Statistical Institute, http://www.officialstatistics.gov.tr (last visited 27/09/2016).
110. Huzur ve İstikrarla Türkiye'nin Yol Haritası, "November 1, 2015 Elections, Party Manifesto", p. 123, https://www.akparti.org.tr/site/haberler/iste-ak-partinin-secim-beyannamesi/78619#1 (last visited 13/10/2016).
111. TOBB Economic Report 2008, http://www.tobb.org.tr/Documents/yayinlar/ekonomik%20rapor.pdf (last visited 31/03/2016), p. 15.
112. *Hurriyet*, 10 May 2008.
113. IMF, "Turkey: Concluding Statement of the 2014 Article IV Mission," press release, 24 September 2014.
114. *The Economist*, 1 August 2015.
115. "Payback time! Emerging markets and the rising dollar," *Global Economy Watch, PWG*, May 2015, http://www.pwc.com/gx/en/issues/economy/global-economy-watch/emerging-markets-and-rising-dollar.html (last visited 31/03/2016).
116. IMF, "Staff Report For the 3024 Article IV Consultation," 3 November 2014, http://www.imf.org/external/pubs/ft/scr/2014/cr14329.pdf (last visited 31/03/2016).
117. *Hurriyet Daily News*, 11 January 2016.
118. Dani Rodrik, *Turkish economic myths*, 16 April 2015, http://rodrik.

typepad.com/dani_rodriks_weblog/2015/04/turkish-economic-myths.html (last visited 31/03/2016).

119. Daniel Dombey, "Turkey posts larger-than-expected deficit of $65bn," *Financial Times*, 13 February 2013.

120. Selva Tor, "Büyük resmin küçük adamı: Sarraf," *Al Jazeera Turk*, 25 March 2016.

121. "Türkiye'nin Altın Üretimi, Tüketimi, İthalatı ve İhracatı," 23 January 2013, http://www.mahfiegilmez.com/2012/10/turkiyenin-altn-uretimi-tuketimi.html (last visited 31/03/2016).

122. *Hurriyet Daily News*, 23 March 2016.

123. OECD, "Economic Policy Reforms 2013: Going for Growth," Paris: OECD Publishing, 2013, p. 252.

124. *Reuters*, 9 March 2015.

125. Interview with an executive board member of The Union of Chambers and Commodity Exchanges of Turkey (TOBB), 11 December 2015, Istanbul.

126. Interview with Bahadir Kaleagasi, international coordinator, TUSIAD, Istanbul, 22 December 2015.

127. Interview with Ali Bayramoglu, columnist for *Yeni Safak*, Istanbul, 6 November 2013.

128. Gumuscu and Sert, "The Power of the Devout Bourgeoisie", p. 960.

129. Interview with Nihat Ali Ozcan, Ankara, 7 November 2013.

130. Interview with Umut Guner, general coordinator of KAOS GL, Ankara, 7 November 2013.

131. Interview with Erdal Tanas Karagol, professor at Yildirim Beyazit University and SETA economy expert, Ankara, 17 February 2014.

132. *BBC News*, "Excerpts of Turkish army statement," 28 April 2007.

133. *The Washington Post*, 29 August 2007.

134. Soner Cagaptay, H. Akin Unver, and Hale Arifagaoglu, "Will the Turkish Constitutional Court Ban the AKP?", Washington Institute of Near East Policy, Policy Watch 1355, 19 March 2008.

135. *Spiegel Online*, 30 July 2008; *The Guardian*, 31 July 2008.

136. Ersin Kalaycıoglu, "Kulturkampf in Turkey: The Constitutional Referendum of 12 September 2010", *South European Society and Politics*, Vol. 17, No. 1, 2012, p. 5.

137. Ibid. Also see Ozbudun, *The Constitutional System of Turkey*, pp. 147–9.

138. *Anadolu Agency*, 26 April 2013.

139. *BBC News*, 24 May 2013.

140. *Today's Zaman*, 29 September 2013.

141. *The New York Times*, 7 November 2013.

142. *BBC News*, 9 September 2004.

143. *BBC News*, 30 May 2016.
144. Cem Baslevent and Ali T. Akcura, "Micro Evidence on Inter-Party Vote Movements in Turkey: Who Voted for AKP in 2002?", Munich Personal RePEc Archive Paper, No. 11683, November 2008, p. 5.
145. Cagaptay, "The November 2002 Elections", pp. 42–3.
146. Taspinar, "Turkey: The New Model?".
147. Mustafa Akyol, "Turkey's Liberal Divide", *Al-Monitor*, 11 August 2012.
148. Ozlem Terzi, *The Influence of the European Union on Turkish Foreign Policy* (Surrey: Ashgate, 2010), p. 33.
149. *The New York Times*, 19 June 2013.
150. *Today's Zaman*, 24 July 2013.
151. *Today's Zaman*, 6 June 2013.
152. *Hurriyet Daily News*, 2 April 2013.
153. *Today's Zaman*, 11 October 2007.
154. Soner Cagaptay, "Turkey's Local Elections: Liberal Middle-Class Voters Abandon AKP", Washington Institute of Near East Policy: Policywatch #1500, 30 March 2009.
155. Interview with Ali Bayramoglu, columnist for *Yeni Safak*, Istanbul, 6 November 2013.
156. *BBC News*, 25 December 2013.
157. Eight months later, the charges against Erdogan's son and the others were dismissed as baseless by the office of the chief prosecutor in Istanbul. *Hurriyet Daily News*, 1 September 2014.
158. *The Economist*, 11 January 2014.
159. Interview with Hikmet Sami Turk, former Democratic Left Party justice minister (1999–2002) and defence minister (1999), London (by telephone), 7 January 2014.
160. Interview with Mevlut Cavusoglu, Minister of Foreign Affairs, Ankara, 20 February 2014.
161. Interview with Ihsan Yilmaz, Istanbul, 15 February 2014; *Wall Street Journal*, 4 June 2010.
162. Interview with Bulent Kenes, Istanbul, 24 February 2014.
163. Ibid.
164. Generally these investigations are referred to as "probes" because they were shut down in their early stages.
165. Interview with Irfan Guvendi, Ankara, 21 February 2014.
166. Ambassador Eric Edelman, "Ankara: Erdogan and the AKP Party After Two Years in Power: Trying to Get a Grip on Themselves, on Turkey, on Europe," Wikileaks, Cable: 04ANKARA7211, 30 December 2004, https://wikileaks.org/cable/2004/12/04ANKARA7211.html (last visited 12/08/2014).
167. Steven A. Cook, "Emperor Erdogan," *Politico*, 3 February 2015.

168. Interview with Ergun Ozbudun, professor of constitutional law, Istanbul Sehir University, Istanbul, 21 December 2015.

169. *BBC.com*, 14 November 2014.

170. Fehim Tastekin, "Shadow government set up in Erdogan's white palace," *Al Monitor*, 11 December 2014.

171. *Today's Zaman*, 5 July 2015.

172. OSCE, Office for Democratic Institutions and Human Rights, International Election Observation Mission, "Republic of Turkey— Parliamentary Elections, 7 June 2015, Statement of Preliminary Findings and Conclusions," Ankara, 8 June 2015.

173. "Ruling AK Party unveils manifesto for June elections," AK Parti, 15 April 2015, https://www.akparti.org.tr/english/haberler/ruling-ak-party-unveils-manifesto-for-june-elections/73321#1 (last visited 26/02/2016).

174. *Milliyet*, 6 February 2015; *Cumhuriyet*, 31 July 2015; *Diken*, 6 September 2015.

175. For a complete breakdown of the election tally and voting districts, see *Hurriyet Daily News*, "Turkish General Elections 215", http://www.hurriyetdailynews.com/election/default.html (last visited 10/08/2015).

176. *Sozcu*, 14 June 2015.

177. *Vatan Gazetesi*, 21 August 2015; *Milliyet*, 19 August 2015.

178. *Hurriyet Daily News*, "Turkish-style presidential system needed, Erdoğan repeats," 27 February 2015.

179. Levent Köker, "AK Party election manifesto fails to meet expectations," *Today's Zaman*, 19 April 2015.

180. Ibid.

181. AFP, "Turkish deputy prime minister says women should not laugh out loud", *The Guardian*, 29 July 2014.

3. ERDOGAN'S WAY: TURKEY'S MAJORITARIANISM AND ITS DISCONTENTS

1. Alexis de Tocqueville, *Democracy in America*, various editions.

2. Fareed Zakaria, "The Rise of the Illiberal Democracy", *Foreign Affairs*, Vol. 76, No. 6, Nov/Dec 1997, pp. 22–6.

3. Ibid., p. 28.

4. *The Economist*, "Turkey's Troubles: Democrat or Sultan," 8 June 2013.

5. *Today's Zaman*, 16 June 2013.

6. *Today's Zaman*, 5 June 2013.

7. *Reuters*, 2 June 2013.

8. *Hurriyet Daily News*, 4 May 2013.

9. Mehdi Hasan, "In Turkey the right to free speech is being lost", *The Guardian*, 10 June 2012.

10. Semih Idiz, "Erdogan Denies He is a King", *Al-Monitor*, 31 May 2013.

11. Mustafa Akyol, "Is Erdogan a Democrat?", *The New York Times*, 1 November 2013.

12. Interview with Etyem Mahcupyan, Istanbul, 5 November 2013.

13. Interview with Ali Bayramoglu, columnist for *Yeni Safak*, Istanbul, 6 November 2013.

14. Freedom House, *Freedom in the World 2012: Turkey*, http://www.freedomhouse.org/report/freedom-world/2012/turkey#.VCyE0ld Cxtw (last visited 01/10/2014); *Hurriyet Daily News*, 29 November 2009.

15. Interview with Abdullatif Sener, Ankara, 8 November 2013.

16. Digdem Soyaltin, "Turkish Court of Accounts in Crisis: An Urgent Problem, Yet Not a Main Concern?", Centre for Policy and Research on Turkey, 19 December 2013; European Commission, "Turkey 2012 Progress Report, Brussels", 10 October 2012, SWD(2012) 336 final.

17. *Today's Zaman*, 13 October 2013.

18. *The Observer*, 1 June 2013.

19. Sina Aksin, *Turkey: From Empire to Revolutionary Republic* (New York: New York University Press, 2007), p. 269.

20. This is a method, named after mathematician Victor D'Hondt, which calculates seat allocations in proportion to the popular vote. The alternative method is the Sainte-Lague method. For an easy-to-read explanation, see Douglas J. Amy, *Behind the Ballot Box: A Citizen's Guide to Voting Systems* (Westport: Praeger, 2000).

22. Serap Yazici, "UPDATE: A Guide to Turkish Public Law and Legal Research", *Global Lex*, May/June 2012, http://www.nyulawglobal.org/globalex/turkey1.htm#laws (last visited 30/11/2013).

23. Interview with Aykan Erdemir, CHP deputy, Ankara, 20 February 2014.

24. Support for Improvement in Governance and Management (SIGMA), "The Administrative Capacity of the Turkish Grand National Assembly", SIGMA Peer Review Report, August 2010, p. 7.

25. Ibid.

26. Gareth Jenkins, "The Politics of Personality: Erdogan's Irascible Authoritarianism", *Turkish Analyst*, 13 February 2009.

27. Interview with Abdullatif Sener, Ankara, 8 November 2013.

28. *The Guardian*, 5 May 2016.

29. *The Telegraph*, 19 May 2016; *Hurriyet Daily News*, 19 May 2016.

30. Hakan Yavuz, *Secularism and Muslim Democracy in Turkey* (Cambridge: Cambridge University Press, 2009), p. 98.

31. Morton Abramowitz and Henry J. Barkey, "Turkey's Political Revolution", *Wall Street Journal*, 22 March 2010.

32. Interview with Etyem Mahcupyan, Istanbul, 5 November 2013.

33. Jenkins, "The Politics of Personality".

34. Yavuz, *Secularism and Muslim Democracy in Turkey*, p. 130.

35. *BBC News*, 3 June 2005.

36. *Hurriyet Daily News*, 10 June 2013.

37. *BBC News*, 10 August 2014.

38. Interview with Ekmeleddin Ihsanoglu, Nationalist Action Party deputy and candidate in the 2014 presidential election, Istanbul, 21 December 2015.

39. See, for example, Demirtas's sarcastic speech on TRT insinuating unfair coverage: *Today's Zaman*, 4 August 2014. Media restrictions were highlighted as a source of concern by the OSCE; see OSCE, Office for Democratic Institutions and Human Rights, "Republic of Turkey: Presidential Elections, 10 August 2014," OSCE/ODIHR Needs Assessment Mission Report, 7–9 May 2014, pp. 8–10.

40. Article 175, Constitution of the Republic of Turkey, pp. 104–5.

41. Article 101, Constitution of the Republic of Turkey, p. 49.

42. *Hurriyet Daily News*, 6 February 2015.

43. OSCE, "Republic of Turkey: Presidential Elections, 10 August 2014," p. 4.

44. *Today's Zaman*, 9 March 2015; *The Guardian*, 19 January 2015; *Reuters*, 19 January 2015; *Hurriyet Daily News*, 27 March 2015.

45. Ismail Aksel, *Turkish Judicial System Bodies, Duties and Officials* (Ankara: Ministry of Justice, Department for Strategy Development, Ankara), 2013, p. 10.

46. Ibid.

47. Interview with Nimet Bas, Istanbul, 10 November 2013.

48. Gunes Murat Tezcur, "Judicial Activism in Perilous Times: The Turkish Case", *Law & Society Review*, Vol. 43, No. 2, June 2009, p. 310.

49. *Radikal*, 10 February 2006.

50. *Al Jazeera*, 17 May 2006.

51. *Hurriyet*, 18 May 2006.

52. *DW Turkish*, 17 May 2006.

53. *BBC News*, 29 April 2007.

54. *Zaman*, 9 March 2013.

55. Interview with Nimet Bas, Istanbul, 10 November 2013; "Excerpts of Turkish army statement," *BBC News*, 28 April 2007.

56. *The Guardian*, 2 May 2007.

57. Taha Akyol, "Cumhurbaskani ve Hukuk," *Hurriyet*, 27 June 2014.

58. Interview with Sami Selcuk, former first president of the Court of Cassation until 2002, Ankara, 8 November 2013.

59. Interview with Ilhan Cihaner, Ankara, 17 February 2014.
60. Interview with Etyem Mahcupyan, Istanbul, 5 November 2013.
61. *The Economist*, 13 September 2010.
62. Ergun Ozbudun, "AKP at the Crossroads: Erdoğan's Majoritarian Drift", *South European Society and Politics*, Vol. 19, No. 2, 2014, p. 156.
63. Interview with Osman Can, former Constitutional Court reporter (2002–2010) and AKP Central Executive Committee member, Istanbul, 6 November 2013.
64. Interview with Ozturk Turkdogan, president of the Human Rights Association, Ankara, 7 November 2013.
65. Interview with Sami Selcuk, Ankara, 8 November 2013.
66. Ozbudun, "AKP at the Crossroads", p. 156.
67. Ibid.
68. Interview with Mevlut Cavusoglu, Ankara, 20 February 2014.
69. *Hurriyet Daily News*, 21 January 2014.
70. Interview with Ilhan Cihaner, Ankara, 17 February 2014.
71. *Hurriyet Daily News*, 15 February 2014.
72. Human Rights Watch, *Turkey: President Should Veto Judiciary Law*, 21 February 2014, https://www.hrw.org/news/2014/02/21/turkey-president-should-veto-judiciary-law (last visited 07/09/2016).
73. Tulin Daloglu, "Turkey's top court upholds separation of powers," *Al Monitor*, 11 April 2014.
74. Interview with Osman Can, Istanbul, 6 November 2013.
75. *The New York Times*, 29 May 2007.
76. Soner Cagaptay and Ruya Perincek, "No Women, No Europe", *Hurriyet Daily News*, 20 January 2010.
77. Interview with Osman Can, Istanbul, 6 November 2013.
78. Interview with Abdullatif Sener, Ankara, 8 November 2013.
79. *BBC News*, 17 July 2016; *Hurriyet*, 17 July 2016; *The New York Times*, 17 July 2016.
80. *The Guardian*, 20 July 2016; *Haberturk*, 19 July 2016.
81. *BBC News*, 21 July 2016; *The Guardian*, 21 July 2016; *BBC Turkce*, 21 July 2016; *Hurriyet*, 21 July 2016.
82. *The Independent*, 30 July 2016; *Hurriyet*, 30 July 2016.
83. Josh Keller, Iaryna Mykhyalyshyn and Safak Timur, "The Scale of Turkey's Purge is Nearly Unprecedented", *The New York Times*, 2 August 2016.
84. *The National*, 3 August 2016; *Reuters*, 2 August 2016; *Hurriyet*, 2 August 2016.
85. *Hurriyet Daily News*, 23 July 2016; *Anatolian Agency*, 23 July 2016.
86. Amnesty International, "Turkey: Independent monitors must be allowed to access detainees amid torture allegations," 24 July 2016, https://

www.amnesty.org/en/latest/news/2016/07/turkey-independent-monitors-must-be-allowed-to-access-detainees-amid-torture-allegations/ (last visited 07/09/2016).

87. *The Guardian*, 18 July 2016.

88. *BBC News*, 21 July 2016.

89. *CNN.com*, 26 July 2016; *Sabah*, 24 July 2016.

90. *US News and World Report*, 26 July 2016; *Cumhuriyet*, 25 July 2016.

91. *Hurriyet Daily News*, 31 July 2016; *Sabah*, 27 July 2016.

92. *Hurriyet Daily News*, 28 July 2016; *Birgun*, 30 July 2016.

93. *Bloomberg*, 17 July 2016; *IHA*, 16 July 2016.

94. Bilgic and Kafkaslı, 2013; Ergun Ozbudun, "AKP at the Crossroads: Erdoğan's Majoritarian Drift," *South European Society and Politics*, Vol. 19, No. 2, 2014, p. 157.

95. Nilufer Gole, "Gezi—Anatomy of a Public Square Movement," *Insight Turkey*, Vol. 15, No. 3, 2013, pp. 8–11.

96. *Konda*, "Gezi Report: Public Perceptions of the 'Gezi Protests'. Who were the people at Gezi Park?", 5 June 2014.

97. Coskun Tastan, "The Gezi Park Protests in Turkey: A Qualitative Field Research," *Insight Turkey*, Vol. 15, No. 3, 2013, pp. 28–31.

98. Interview with "Ozgur", member of the Besiktas *Carsi*, Istanbul, 5 November 2013.

99. Ibid.

100. Interview with Alper Sen of the Video Documentation Collective, Istanbul, 23 February 2014.

101. *Konda*, "Gezi Report," p. 20.

102. Interview with Hamit Demir, actor and activist, Istanbul, 24 February 2014.

103. Interview with Tanju Gunduzalp, editor-in-chief of *Solfasol*, an Ankara-based environmental magazine, Ankara, 21 February 2014; *Konda*, "Gezi Report," pp. 18–20.

104. Interview with Umut Guner, Ankara, 7 November 2013.

105. *Reuters*, 15 April 2014.

106. *Hurriyet Daily News*, 7 March 2010.

107. Interview with Umut Guner, Ankara, 7 November 2013.

108. Interview with Ihsan Eliacik, group leader and public face of the anti-capitalist Muslims, Istanbul, 25 February 2014.

109. Interview with Ali Arikan, general secretary of the Alevi Culture Associations, 20 February 2014.

110. Fırat Bozcalı and Çagrı Yoltar, "A Look at Gezi Park from Turkey's Kurdistan Hot Spots," *Cultural Anthropology*, 31 October 2013, https://culanth.org/fieldsights/396-a-look-at-gezi-park-from-turkey-s-kurdistan (last visited 07/09/2016).

111. Interview with Tanju Gunduzalp, Ankara, 21 February 2014.

112. Istanbul Doctors Association, "Biber Gazi Silah Olarak Kullaniliyor," press release, 28 January 2014.

113. *Al Jazeera*, 19 January 2014.

114. *Hurriyet Diuly News*, 25 December 2014; *Sunday's Zaman*, 13 January 2015; Constanze Letsch, "A Year After the Protests, Gezi Park Nurtures the Seeds of a New Turkey", *The Guardian*, 29 May 2014.

115. *FT.com*, 27 March 2015.

116. *DefenceWorld.net*, 25 September 2015.

117. Tayfun Atay, "Reflections on the Gezi Park incident," *Insight Turkey*, Vol. 15, No. 3, 2013, pp. 39–44.

118. Kemal Kirisci, "Turkey Protests: Are the Youth at Gezi Park a New Actor in Turkish Democracy?" Brookings Institute: Up Front, 13 June 2013.

119. *Konda*, "Gezi Report," pp. 8–12.

120. Ibid., pp. 20–21.

121. Burak Kadercan, "The Gezi Park Protests illustrate the fall of the military as a political actor in Turkey," London School of Economics: European Politics and Policy, 18 October 2013.

122. Saul Bellow, *To Jerusalem and Back: A Personal Account* (London: Penguin Classics, 2008; originally published 1976).

123. Interview with Ceren Kener, columnist for *Turkiye* with over 66,000 Twitter followers, Istanbul, 5 November 2013.

124. *Today's Zaman*, 7 May 2012; Homi Kharas, *The Emerging Middle Class in Developing Countries*, Paris: OECD, January 2010.

125. CIA, "The World Factbook: Turkey," https://www.cia.gov/library/publications/the-world-factbook/geos/tu.html (last visited 01/10/2014).

126. Index Mundi, "Turkey Demographics Profile 2014," http://www.indexmundi.com/turkey/demographics_profile.html (last visited 27/09/2014).

127. Statista, "Turkey: degree of urbanization from 2002 to 2012," http://www.statista.com/statistics/255487/urbanization-in-turkey/ (last visited 27/09/2014).

128. Web Index 2014 data, http://thewebindex.org/data/?indicator=INDEX&country=ALL (last visited 24/01/2016).

129. Turkish Statistical Institute, "Information and Communication Technology (ICT) Usage Survey on Households and Individuals, 2015", Press Release, No. 18660, 18 August 2015.

130. Karin Alexander, "Social media's role in Turkey's dissent", *New Internationalist Blog*, 4 July 2013, http://newint.org/blog/2013/07/04/social-media-turkey/ (last visited 08/03/2014).

131. "Information and Communication Technology (ICT) Usage Survey on Households and Individuals, 2015", Press Release, No. 18660, 18 August 2015; Comscore, "It's a Social World: Top 10 Need-to-Knows About Social Networking and Where It's Headed", 21 December 2011, http://www.comscore.com/Insights/Presentations-and-Whitepapers/2011/it_is_a_social_world_top_10_need-to-knows_about_social_networking (last visited 02/10/2014); Esra Dogramaci and Damian Radcliffe, "How Turkey Uses its Media", Digital News Report 2015, Reuters Institute for the Study of Journalism, 23 October 2015.

132. Comscore, "It's a Social World".

133. Ibid.

134. Interview with Ceren Kener, Istanbul, 5 November 2013.

135. Al Jazeera, 22 March 2014.

136. BBC News, 4 June 2013.

137. Interview with Ceren Kener, Istanbul, 5 November 2013.

138. Alex Kantrowitz, "Social Media And Istanbul's Protests: Four Things You Need To Know", Forbes, 19 June 2013.

139. Pablo Barberá and Megan Metzger, "A Breakout Role for Twitter? Extensive Use of Social Media in the Absence of Traditional Media by Turks in Turkish in Taksim Square Protests", The Monkey Cage, 1 June 2013, http://themonkeycage.org/2013/06/01/a-breakout-role-for-twitter-extensive-use-of-social-media-in-the-absence-of-traditional-media-by-turks-in-turkish-in-taksim-square-protests (last visited 08/03/2014).

140. Kantrowitz, "Social Media And Istanbul's Protests".

141. Interview with Alper Sen, Istanbul, 23 February 2014.

142. Interview with Dr. Ozden Sener, Chairman of the Ankara Association of Medicine, Ankara, 22 February 2014.

143. Alex Kantrowitz, "The Secret Behind The Turkish Protesters' Social Media Mastery", PBS Media Shift, 1 July 2013, http://www.pbs.org/mediashift/2013/07/the-secret-behind-the-turkish-protesters-social-media-mastery (last visited 09/03/2014).

144. The Guardian, 3 June 2013.

145. The Guardian, 5 June 2013.

146. Reuters, 26 June 2013.

147. Interview with Ertugrul Kurkcu, HDP deputy and former co-chair, Ankara, 9 November 2013.

148. Interview with Mevlut Cavusoglu, Ankara, 20 February 2014.

149. Interview with Ceren Kener, Istanbul, 5 November 2013.

150. Wall Street Journal, 16 September 2013.

151. Barin Kayaaoglu, "Turkey's AKP Mobilizes Twitter Army for Elections", Al-Monitor, 18 September 2013.

152. Emre Kizilkaya, "AKP's Social Media Wars", *Al-Monitor*, 14 November 2013.

153. Such instances are plentiful, but for just a few examples see *The Daily Telegraph*, 25 February 2015; *Hurriyet Daily News*, 13 March 2015; *The Guardian*, 17 June 2015.

154. Stephen Starr, "Turkey's Twitter Problem", *Global Post*, 30 June 2013, http://www.globalpost.com/dispatch/news/regions/europe/turkey/130629/turkey-twitter-facebook-social-media-erdogan-taksim-bbc-turkce (last visited 08/03/2014).

155. Baruk Ozcetin, "Between Representation and Participation: Political Twitter Use in Turkey", 1st International Symposium on Media Studies, Antalya, Turkey: 2013, p. 591.

156. *Today's Zaman*, 22 August 2015.

157. *Hurriyet*, 30 June 2015.

158. *Diken*, 16 June 2015.

159. "Turkey: End Prosecutions for Insulting the President," *Human Rights Watch*, 29 April 2015, https://www.hrw.org/news/2015/04/29/turkey-end-prosecutions-insulting-president (last visited 07/09/2016).

160. *Zaman*, 14 March 2015.

161. Ed Finn, "Power of social media: Erdogan's smart use of a smartphone," *CNN.com*, 18 July 2016; Uptin Saiidi, "For someone who doesn't like social media, Erdogan used it effectively to put down a coup," *CNBC*, 18 July 2016; Sam Schechner, "Erdogan Embraces Social Media to Repel Coup Attempt in U-Turn", *Wall Street Journal*, 17 July 2016.

162. For a detailed analysis, see Pinar Tremblay, "How Erdogan used the power of the mosques against coup attempt," *Al-Monitor*, 25 July 2016; *Yeni Şafak*, 15 July 2016.

163. Ibid.

164. Interview with Levent Cicek, former head of the youth wing of the Heart of Ottoman, Ankara, 21 July 2016.

165. *Haaretz*, 1 June 2013; *Hurriyet*, 30 July 2013.

166. *Hurriyet Daily News*, 17 July 2016.

167. *Hurriyet Daily News*, 7 February 2015.

168. *Daily Sabah*, 9 March 2015.

169. *Al Jazeera*, 22 March 2013.

170. M.K. Kaya, "The Return of Hakan Fidan to MİT is the Sign of a Power Struggle," *Turkish Analyst*, Vol 8, No. 5, 11 March 2015.

171. *Al-Monitor*, "Amberin Zaman, Turkey spy chief's resignation: power play or family feud?", 13 February 2015.

172. *Vatan*, 8 February 2015.

173. M.K. Kaya, "The Return of Hakan Fidan to MİT is the Sign of a Power Struggle".

174. *NTV.com*, 5 June 2013; *Milliyet*, 1 June 2013.

175. *Haberturk*, 10 September 2015.

176. *Milliyet*, 21 January 2012.

177. Ahmet Sever, *Abdullah Gül ile 12 Yıl: Yaşadım, Gördüm*, Yazdım Dogan Kitap, 30. Baskı, Istanbul, pp. 140, 170.

178. *The New York Times*, 22 May 2016.

179. Nur Bilge Crisis, "Dismantling Turkey: The Will of the People?", Birol Yesilada and Barry Rubin (eds), *Islamisation of Turkey under the AKP* (London: Routledge, 2011), p. 43.

4. BREAKING THE NEWS

1. Rasit Kaya and Barıs Cakmur, "Politics and the Mass Media in Turkey," *Turkish Studies*, Vol. 11, No. 4, 2010, p. 523; Metin Heper and Tanel Demirel, "The Press and the Consolidation of Democracy in Turkey", *Middle Eastern Studies*, Vol. 32, No. 2, April 1996, p. 111.

2. Constitution of the Republic of Turkey, Chapter 2, Article 26, pp. 12–13; European Convention on Human Rights, Article 10.

3. Constitution of the Republic of Turkey, Article 28, pp. 13–14.

4. *The New York Times*, 13 November 1983.

5. Lois Whitman and Thomas Froncek, *Paying the Price: Freedom of Expression in Turkey* (New York: Human Rights Watch, 1989), p. 14.

6. Ibid., pp. 15–16.

7. Ibid., p. 17.

8. The text of Penal Code 301 can be found in "Turkish Penal Code, Part 3," 26 September 2004, available at http://www.tbmm.gov.tr/kanunlar/k5237.html (last visited 27/09/2014).

9. Dink was prosecuted for violating the article on three occasions. Human Rights Watch, *Turkey: Outspoken Turkish-Armenian Journalist Murdered*, 20 January 2007.

10. *Today's Zaman*, 2 May 2008.

11. Murat Akser and Banu Baybars-Hawks, "Media and Democracy in Turkey: Toward a Model of Neoliberal Media Autocracy," *Middle East Journal of Culture and Communication*, Vol. 5, No. 3, 2012, p. 304.

12. Kaya and Cakmur, "Politics and the Mass Media in Turkey", p. 530.

13. Ibid.

14. Andrew Finkel, "Who Guards the Turkish Press? A Perspective on Press Corruption in Turkey", *Journal of International Affairs*, Vol. 54, No. 1, Fall 2000, p. 154.

15. Kaya and Cakmur, "Politics and the Mass Media in Turkey", p. 530.

16. Heper and Demirel, "The Press and the Consolidation of Democracy in Turkey", p. 112.

17. *Milliyet*, 1 March 2012.
18. Heper and Demirel, "The Press and the Consolidation of Democracy in Turkey", p. 112.
19. Kaya and Cakmur, "Politics and the Mass Media in Turkey," p. 530.
20. Sevket Kazan, *28 Subat Postmodern Bir Darbenin Anatomisi* (Ankara: MGV Yayinlan, Ankara, 2013); Interview with Sevket Kazan, Ankara, 17 February 2014.
21. *The Economist*, 14 February 2002.
22. *Zaman*, 25 February 2006.
23. Finkel, "Who Guards the Turkish Press?" p. 156; Aylin Sagtur Mutlu, "Cassettes that Shook a Country," *Eurasia News*, 31 December 1998.
24. Interview with Nedim Sener, journalist for *Posta*, Istanbul, 24 February 2014.
25. Gareth Jenkins, "A House Divided Against Itself: The Deteriorating State of Media Freedom in Turkey," *Turkey Analyst*, Vol. 5, No. 3, 6 February 2012, p. 2.
26. Akser and Baybars-Hawks, "Toward a Model of Neoliberal Media Autocracy", *Middle East Journal of Culture and Communications*, 5 (2012), p. 302.
27. Kaya and Cakmur, "Politics and the Mass Media in Turkey", p. 530; Ceren Sozeri, "The political economy of the media and its impact on freedom of expression," Carmen Rodrigues, Antonio Avalos, Hakan Yılmaz and Ana I. Planet, (eds), *Turkey's Democratisation Process* (London: Routledge, 2014), p. 401.
28. Jenkins, "A House Divided Against Itself", p. 2.
29. Human Rights Watch, *The Kurds of Turkey: Killings, Disappearances and Torture*, New York, March 1993.
30. Ibid., p. 2.
31. Interview with a veteran journalist reporting from south-east Turkey, Diyarbakir, 18 February 2014.
32. *Hurriyet*, 27 August 2011; *The Economist*, 3 March 2011.
33. Kaya and Çakmur, "Politics and the Mass Media in Turkey", p. 531.
34. Interview with Abdullatif Sener, Ankara, 8 November 2013.
35. Interview with Nuray Mert, columnist for the *Hurriyet Daily News*, Istanbul, 4 November 2013.
36. Jenkins, "A House Divided Against Itself," p. 4.
37. Ayse Bugra and Osman Savaskan, *New Capitalism In Turkey: The Relationship between Politics, Religion and Business* (Cheltenham: Edward Elgar, 2014), p. 98.
38. Jenkins, "A House Divided Against Itself", p. 3.
39. Bugra and Savaskan, *New Capitalism In Turkey*, p. 90.
40. *Zaman*, 5 October 2008.

41. *The Economist*, 14 December 2013.

42. Bugra and Savaskan, *New Capitalism In Turkey*, p. 90; *Wall Street Journal Turkish*, 13 January 2014.

43. *Financial Times*, 8 September 2009.

44. Kaya and Çakmur, "Politics and the Mass Media in Turkey," p. 532.

45. Interview with Abdullatif Sener, Ankara, 8 November 2013.

46. *Yeni Safak*, 7 December 2008.

47. *Milliyet*, 8 September 2009.

48. *Milliyet*, 6 September 2008.

49. Jenkins, "A House Divided Against Itself", p. 4.

50. Orhan Kemal Cengiz, "European Court Presses Erdogan on Free Speech," *Al-Monitor*, 25 July 2013.

51. Gulseren Adakli, "Capital and Capitalists in Turkey, media capital and ultra-cross media ownership", *Perspective: Political Analyses and Commentary*, Issue 8, April 2004, p. 20.

52. Ibid.

53. *Sozcu*, 28 May 2014.

54. *Hurriyet*, 20 December 2013.

55. *Today's Zaman*, 31 January 2014.

56. *Hurriyet*, 1 February 2014. It later said this was a mistake.

57. Adakli, "Capital and Capitalists in Turkey", p. 20.

58. Ibid., p. 21.

59. *Today's Zaman*, 2 March 2014.

60. Cengiz Candar, "The Erdogan tapes," *Al Monitor*, 27 February 2014.

61. *Sozcu*, 14 January 2014; *Yeni Akit*, 3 May 2014.

62. Jenkins, "A House Divided Against Itself", p. 3.

63. Ibid.

64. *Reuters*, 4 August 2014.

65. *Today's Zaman*, 4 August 2014.

66. *Today's Zaman*, 5 June 2015.

67. European Commission, "Turkey: 2013 Progress Report," Brussels, 16 October 2013, SWD (2013) 417, final, p. 33.

68. OSCE, Office for Democratic Institutions and Human Rights, Limited Election Observation Mission, "Republic of Turkey, Presidential Election, 10 August 2014: Interim Report," 31 July 2014.

69. Interview with Nedim Sener, Istanbul, 24 February 2014; *Dogan News Agency*, 5 February 2014.

70. Akser and Baybars-Hawks, "Media and Democracy in Turkey", p. 307.

71. Ibid., p. 309.

72. Reporters Without Borders for Press Freedom, "Number of journalists convicted in Ergenekon trial rises to 20", 7 August 2013.

73. *BBC News*, "Egemen Bagis—Turkish Minister for EU Affairs", *Hardtalk* http://www.bbc.co.uk/programmes/b01cpfr3 (last visited 6/09.2014).

74. *Hurriyet Daily News*, 6 March 2011.
75. *Hurriyet Daily News*, 16 November 2011; Pen International, "PEN International applauds the publication of seized manuscript as Turkish writers rally around imprisoned journalist," 18 November 2011, http://www.pen-international.org/newsitems/pen-international-applauds-the-publication-of-seized-manuscript-as-turkish-writers-rally-around-imprisoned-journalist/?print=print (last visited 27/09/2014).
76. *Hurriyet Daily News*, 8 March 2011.
77. *Daily Sabah*, 9 July 2014.
78. *Today's Zaman*, 8 July 2014.
79. Aksera and Baybars-Hawks, "Media and Democracy in Turkey", p. 309.
80. Committee to Protect Journalists, *Turkey's Press Freedom Crisis: The Dark Days of Jailing Journalists and Criminalizing Dissent*, New York, October 2012, pp. 8, 13–14.
81. Alya Albayrak, "Turkish Colonel, Journalist Fired Over Kurdish Killings", *Wall Street Journal* blog, "Emerging Europe," 9 January 2012, http://blogs.wsj.com/emergingeurope/2012/01/09/turkish-colonel-journalist-fired-over-kurdish-killings/ (last visited 07/09/2014).
82. *The Guardian*, 24 March 2013.
83. Interview with Ali Bayramoglu, Istanbul, 6 November 2013.
84. Interview with Abdullatif Sener, Ankara, 8 November 2013.
85. Dexter Filkins, "Letter From Turkey: The Deep State", *The New Yorker*, 12 March 2012.
86. *The Economist*, 7 August 2014.
87. *The Telegraph*, 8 August 2014.
88. Committee to Protect Journalists, *Turkey's Press Freedom Crisis*, pp. 11–12.
89. Interview with Ihsan Yilmaz, Istanbul, 15 February 2014.
90. Interview with Nuray Mert, Istanbul, 4 November 2013.
91. Committee to Protect Journalists, *Turkey's Press Freedom Crisis*, pp. 7, 20–25.
92. Freedom House, *Democracy in Crisis: Corruption, Media, and Power in Turkey*, Freedom House Special Report, New York, 2014, p. 8.
93. *The New York Times*, "Editorial: Dark Clouds Over Turkey," 22 May 2015; *The New York Times*, 28 May 2015. For the *Hurriyet's* response to Erdogan's accusations see *Hurriyet Daily News*, "Hürriyet's address to the Turkish president", 19 May 2015.
94. *Today's Zaman*, 6 June 2015.
95. *The Guardian*, "Editorial: The Guardian view on President Erdogan's lies: an apology would be welcome," 9 June 2015.
96. *T24*, 6 January 2015.
97. *BBC Turkish*, 31 August 2015.
98. *Hurriyet*, 19 December 2014.

99. *The New York Times*, 4 March 2016; *The Guardian*, 6 March 2016.

100. *Hurriyet*, 9 April 2015.

101. Constanze Letsch, "Turkish journalists face secret trial for revealing arms deliveries to Syria", *The Guardian*, 25 March 2016, https://www.theguardian.com/world/2016/mar/25/turkish-journalists-can-dundar-erdem-gul-secret-trial-revealing-arms-deliveries-syria (last visited 07/09/2016).

102. *The Guardian*, 6 February 2014. This was later amended to make it obligatory for the TIB to send its decision to a court within twenty-four hours, which would also have to make a decision within twenty-four hours; otherwise the TIB's block would become void, *Hurriyet Daily News*, 18 February 2014.

103. *Reuters*, 18 February 2014.

104. *Hurriyet Daily News*, 18 February 2014.

105. *BBC News*, 8 February 2014; *BBC News*, 23 February 2014.

106. *Reuters*, 19 February 2014.

107. Reporters Without Borders for Freedom of Information, *Enemies of the Internet 2014*, 12 March 2014.

108. Freedom House, *Freedom on the Net 2013: A Global Assessment of Internet and Digital Media*, 3 October 2013, pp. 719–21; NTV, 20 September 2013.

109. *Open Net Initiative*, "Turkey," 18 December 2010, https://opennet.net/research/profiles/turkey (last visited 15/04/2014).

110. Ibid.

111. Yaman Akdeniz, "Report of the OSCE Representative on Freedom of the Media on Turkey and Internet Censorship", *Organization for Security and Co-operation in Europe*, The Representative on Freedom of the Media, 2010, pp. 4, 8.

112. Ibid.

113. *Freedom on the Net 2013*, p. 723.

114. Ibid.

115. European Commission, "Turkey 2010 Progress Report," Brussels, 9 November 2010, SEC(2010) 1327, pp. 21, 56.

116. Reporters Without Borders for Freedom of Information, *Countries Under Surveillance: Turkey*, 12 March 2011, http://en.rsf.org/turkey-turkey-11–03–2011,39758.html (last visited 27/09/2014). For further details see EU progress reports such as European Commission, "Turkey 2011 Progress Report," Brussels, 12 October 2011, SEC(2011) 1201 final, p. 27; European Commission, "Turkey 2012 Progress Report," Brussels, 10 October 2012, SWD(2012) 336 final, p. 22; European Commission, "Turkey 2013 Progress Report," Brussels, 16 October 2013, SWD(2013) 417 final, p. 52.

117. *The Guardian*, 11 June 2010.

118. *Hurriyet Daily News*, 19 December 2012.

119. *CNN Turkish*, 30 October 2010.

120. *Today's Zaman*, 6 March 2014.

121. *Reuters*, 20 March 2014.

122. *BBC News*, 21 March 2014.

123. *The Guardian*, 21 March 2014; *BBC News*, 21 March 2014; *Al Jazeera*, 22 March 2014.

124. Amnesty International, "Turkey should immediately reverse its 'draconian' Twitter ban", press release, 21 March 2014.

125. *Hurriyet Daily News*, 22 March 2014.

126. *Reuters*, 21 March 2014.

127. Interview with Yaman Akdeniz, associate professor of human rights law and Internet activist, Istanbul Bilgi University, London, 21 March 2014.

128. *BBC News*, 3 April 2014.

129. *Reuters*, 6 April 2015; *The Telegraph*, 2 April 2015.

130. *The Independent*, 10 October 2015.

5. URBAN PLANNING, DEVELOPMENT AND THE POLITICS OF THE *GECEKONDU*

1. Halil I. Tas & Dale R. Lightfoot, "Gecekondu Settlements in Turkey: Rural-Urban Migration in the Developing European Periphery", *Journal of Geography*, Vol. 104, No. 6, 2005, p. 264.

2. Ilhan Tekeli, "Cities in Modern Turkey", *Urban Age*, Istanbul, November 2009, p. 1.

3. Zeynep Kezer, "Contesting Urban Space in Early Republican Ankara", *Journal of Architectural Education*, Vol. 52, No. 1, 1998, p. 11; Rusen Keles, *Eski Ankara'da bir Sehir Tipolojiri* (Ankara: Ankara Universitesi Siyasal Bilgiler Fakultesi Yayinlari, 1971), p. 5.

4. Munevver Ozge Balta and Feral Eke, "Spatial Reflection of Urban Planning in Metropolitan Areas and Urban Rent; a Case Study of Cayyolu, Ankara", *European Planning Studies*, Vol. 19, No. 10, October 2011, p. 1822.

5. Neslihan Demirtas, *Social Spatialization in a Turkish Squatter Settlement: The Dualism of Strategy and Tactic Reconsidered* (Frankfurt: Lang, Europäische Hochschulschriften, 2009) p. 80.

6. Tas and Lightfoot, "Gecekondu Settlements in Turkey", p. 266.

7. Iren Ozgur, "Arabesk Music in Turkey in the 1990s and Changes in National Demography, Politics, and Identity", *Turkish Studies*, Vol. 7, No. 2, 175–190, June 2006, pp. 178–9.

8. Demirtas, *Social Spatialization in a Turkish Squatter Settlement*, p. 80.

9. Ayse Bugra, "The Immoral Economy of Housing in Turkey," *International Journal of Urban and Regional Research*, Vol. XXII, No. 2, June 1998, p. 307.

10. Ilhan Tekeli, "Cities in Modern Turkey," p. 2.

11. Pinar Turker-Devecigil, "Urban Transformation Projects as a Model to Transform Gecekondu Areas in Turkey: The Example of Dikmen Valley—Ankara", *International Journal of Housing Policy*, Vol. 5, No. 2, 2005, p. 214.

12. Asuman Turkun, "Urban Regeneration and Hegemonic Power Relationships", *International Planning Studies*, Vol. 16, No. 1, 2011, p. 63.

13. Ibid.; Sabri Sayari and Bruce Hoffman, "Urbanisation and insurgency: The Turkish case, 1976–1980", *Small Wars and Insurgencies*, Vol. 5, No. 2, 1994, p. 165.

14. Ibid.

15. Josef Leitmann and Deniz Baharoglu, "Reaching Turkey's spontaneous settlements: The institutional dimension of infrastructure provision", *International Planning Studies*, Vol. 4, No. 2, 1999, p. 196.

16. Ilhan Tekeli, "Cities in Modern Turkey," *Urban Age*, Cities Programme, London School of Economics, November 2009, p. 3.

17. Ibid., p. 3.

18. S. Ilgu Ozler, "Politics of the Gecekondu in Turkey: The political choices of urban squatters in national Elections", *Turkish Studies*, Vol. 1, No. 2, Autumn 2000, p. 44.

19. Kemal Karpat, *The Gecekondu* (New York: Cambridge University Press, 1976), p. 211.

20. Ibid.

21. Ergun Ozbudun, "Turkey", Myron Weiner and Ergun Ozbudun (eds), *Competitive Elections in Developing Countries*, (North Carolina: Duke University Press, 1987), p. 347.

22. Kemal Karpat, "Turkish Democracy at Impasse: Ideology, Party Politics, and the Third Military Intervention", *International Journal of Turkish Studies*, Vol. 2, No. 1, Summer-Spring 1988, p. 18.

23. Sayari and Hoffman, "Urbanisation and insurgency: The Turkish case, 1976–1980," p. 166.

24. Ibid., p. 165.

25. Ibid., p. 166.

26. Ibid., p. 171.

27. John Duncan Powell, "Peasant Society and Clientelist Politics," *American Political Science Review*, Vol. 64, No. 2, June 1970, p. 412.

28. Neslihan Demirtas and Seher Sen, "Varos identity: The redefinition of low income settlements in Turkey," *Middle Eastern Studies*, Vol. 43, No. 1, 2007, p. 90.

29. Leitmann and Baharoglu, "Reaching Turkey's spontaneous settlements", p. 197.
30. Demirtas, *Social Spatialization in a Turkish Squatter Settlement*, p. 90.
31. Ibid.
32. Turkun, "Urban Regeneration and Hegemonic Power Relationships", p. 64.
33. Balta and Eke, "Spatial Reflection of Urban Planning in Metropolitan Areas and Urban Rent", p. 1822.
34. Turkun, "Urban Regeneration and Hegemonic Power Relationships", p. 64.
35. Ozler, "Politics of the Gecekondu in Turkey," p. 52.
36. Demirtas and Sen, "Varos identity," p. 97.
37. Ibid., pp. 96–7.
38. Tas and Lightfoot, "Gecekondu Settlements in Turkey," p. 67.
39. Ozler, "Politics of the Gecekondu in Turkey," p. 53.
40. Ergun Ozbudun, "Turkey: How Far from Consolidation?", *Journal of Democracy*, Vol. 7, No. 3, 1996, p. 134.
41. Demirtas and Sen, "Varos Identity", pp. 97–8.
42. Ayda Eraydin and Tuna Tasan-Kok, "State Response to Contemporary Urban Movements in Turkey: A Critical Overview of State Entrepreneurialism and Authoritarian Interventions", *Antipode*, Vol. 46, No. 1, 2014, p. 118.
43. Ozan Karaman, "Urban Pulse: (Re)Making Space for Globalization in Istanbul", *Urban Geography*, Vol. 29, No. 6, 2008, p. 519.
44. Eraydin and Tasan-Kok, "State Response to Contemporary Urban Movements in Turkey", p. 119; Turkun, "Urban Regeneration and Hegemonic Power Relationships", p. 69.
45. Erbatur Cavusoglu and Julia Strutz, "We'll come and Demolish Your House!: The role of spatial (re)-production in the neoliberal hegemonic politics of Turkey," Ismet Akca, Ahmet Berken and Baris Alp Ozden, *Turkey Reframed* (London: Pluto Press, 2014), p. 147.
46. Osman Balaban, "The negative effects of construction boom on urban planning and environment in Turkey: Unraveling the role of the public sector", *Habitat International*, Vol. 36, No. 1, January 2012, p. 29.
47. Ibid., pp. 30–1.
48. Ibid., pp. 31–2.
49. Turkun, "Urban Regeneration and Hegemonic Power Relationships," p. 66.
50. Ibid., p. 62.
51. Ozan Karaman, "Resisting urban renewal in Istanbul", *Urban Geography*, Vol. 35, No. 2, March 2014, p. 297.
52. Ibid., p. 299.

53. Eraydin and Tasan-Kok, "State Response to Contemporary Urban Movements in Turkey", p. 119.

54. Karaman, "Urban Pulse", p. 522.

55. Ibid., pp. 522–3.

56. Turkun, "Urban Regeneration and Hegemonic Power Relationships," p. 67.

57. Demirtas and Sen, "*Varos* Identity", p. 93.

58. Gulcen Erdi Lelandais, "Citizenship, minorities and the struggle for a right to the city in Istanbul," *Citizenship Studies*, Vol. 17, No. 6–7, 2013, p. 822.

59. Eraydin and Tasan-Kok, "State Response to Contemporary Urban Movements in Turkey", p. 120.

60. Murat Gul, John Dee and Cahide Nur Cunuk, "Istanbul's Taksim Square and Gezi Park: The Place of Protest and the Ideology of Place," *Journal of Architecture and Urbanism*, Vol. 38, No. 1, 2014, p. 68.

61. Ibid., p. 68.

62. Daniel Donbey, "Erdogan's grand ambitions for Istanbul", *Washington Post*, 31 August 2012.

63. *Hurriyet Daily News*, 29 November 2012; *Bloomberg*, 28 November 2012.

64. *Hurriyet Daily News*, 2 June 2012.

65. Mehmet Baris Kuymulu, "Reclaiming the right to the city: Reflections on the urban uprisings in Turkey", *City*, Vol. 17, No. 3, 2013, p. 275.

66. *The Guardian*, 27 April 2011.

67. *Today's Zaman*, 27 April 2011.

68. *BBC News*, 27 April 2011.

69. *Today's Zaman*, 5 July 2013.

70. *Turkey Review*, "Turkish Lexicon", 30 June 2011.

71. *Today's Zaman*, 28 April 2011.

72. *Hurriyet Daily News*, 24 February 2015; *Daily Sabah*, 24 March 2015.

73. *Daily Sabah*, 6 June 2014.

74. Alexander Christie-Miller, "Erdogan's Grand Construction Projects are Tearing Istanbul Apart," *Newsweek*, 31 July 2014.

75. *Wall Street Journal*, 3 May 2013; *Hurriyet Daily News*, 3 May 2013.

76. *Today's Zaman*, 4 July 2015.

77. *Daily Sabah*, 13 November 2015.

78. *The Independent*, 29 October 2013.

79. Cumali Onal, "Istanbul's historical peninsula disappearing", *Today's Zaman*, 3 March 2014.

80. Paul Benjamin, "Istanbul's recent rapid transit projects remain areas of contention", *Today's Zaman*, 23 February 2014.

81. *Agence France Presse*, 28 March 2014.

82. Fatma Disli Zibak, "Istanbul becoming uninhabitable with mega construction projects", *Today's Zaman*, 30 May 2013.

83. *Today's Zaman*, 18 October 2015.

84. *The New York Times*, 30 October 2013.

85. *Hurriyet Daily News*, 24 February 2015.

86. Gila Benmayor, "Kanal İstanbul, at all costs", *Hurriyet Daily News*, 21 May 2013.

87. Gurhan Savgi, "Istanbul residents deceived over construction of third bridge", *Today's Zaman*, 6 April 2014.

88. Gurhan Savgi, "Either Kanal Istanbul project or Istanbul must be sacrificed", *Today's Zaman*, 9 February 2014.

89. *Hurriyet Daily News*, 3 May 2013; *The Journal of Turkish Weekly*, 18 July 2015.

90. *Agence France Presse*, 28 March 2014.

91. *Env.net*, "TEMA Foundation announced its Report on Istanbul Projects", 26 March 2014, http://www.env-net.org/tema-foundation-announced-its-report-on-istanbul-projects/# (last visited 11/04/2014).

92. *Today's Zaman*, 31 July 2014.

93. Christie-Miller, "Erdogan's Grand Construction Projects are Tearing Istanbul Apart".

94. *Hurriyet Daily News*.

95. Zibak, "Istanbul becoming uninhabitable with mega construction projects".

96. Interview with Tanju Gunduzalp, Ankara, 21 February 2014.

97. Ibid.

98. Leila M. Harris and Mine Islar, "Commodification and Environmental Governance", Yildiz Atasoy (ed.), *Global Economic Crisis and the Politics of Diversity*, (New York: Palgrave Macmillan, 2014), p. 54; Article 56, Constitution of the Republic of Turkey, p. 26.

99. Hande Paker, Fikret Adaman, Zeynep Kadirbeyoglu and Begum Ozkaynak, "Environmental Organisations in Turkey: Engaging the State and Capital," *Environmental Politics*, Vol. 22, No. 5, 2013, p. 763.

100. Interview with Tanju Gunduzalp, Ankara, 21 February 2014.

101. Interview with Abdullatif Sener, Ankara, 8 November 2013.

102. Interview with Mustafa Sonmez, Istanbul-based economist, Istanbul, 24 February 2014.

103. Mehul Srivastava and Benjamin Harvey, "The Edifice Complex Driving Turkey's Scandal", *Bloomberg Business Week*, 9 January 2014.

104. *Today's Zaman*, 29 December 2013.

105. Srivastava and Harvey, "The Edifice Complex Driving Turkey's Scandal".

106. Kadri Gursel, "Crackdown shatters AKP 'anti-corruption' taboo", *Al-Monitor*, 19 December 2013.

107. *Hurriyet Daily News*, 13 March 2014.
108. *Hurriyet Daily News*, 13 March 2014.
109. Interview with Mevlut Cavusoglu, Minister of Foreign Affairs, Ankara, 20 February 2014.
110. Mustafa Sonmez, "Construction again the hope of the economy in 2016", *Hurriyet Daily News*, 29 February 2016.
111. Interview with Erdal Tanas Karagol, Ankara, 17 February 2014.
112. Interview Mustafa Sonmez, Istanbul, 24 February 2014.

6. WALTZING WITH OCALAN: TURKEY AND THE KURDISH PEACE PROCESS

1. *The Washington Post*, 18 February 1999.
2. Interview with Edip Baser, Istanbul, 6 November 2013.
3. Fehmi Koru, "Too many questions, but not enough answers", *Turkish Daily News*, 8 June 1999.
4. Abdullah Ocalan, "We Are Fighting Turks Everywhere," *Middle East Quarterly*, Vol. 5, No. 2, June 1998, pp. 79–85.
5. Andrew Mango, *Turkey and the War on Terror: For Forty Years we Fought Alone* (London: Routledge, 2005), p. 32.
6. Dogu Ergil, "The Kurdish Question in Turkey", *Journal of Democracy*, Vol. 11, No. 3, July 2000, p. 124.
7. Philip Robins, "The Overlord State: Turkish Policy and the Kurdish Issue", *International Affairs*, Vol. 69, No. 3, October 1993, pp. 660–1; John Bulloch and Harvey Morris, *No Friends but the Mountains: The Tragic History of the Kurds* (London: Viking, 1992), p. 172.
8. Svante E. Cornell, "The Land of Many Crossroads: The Kurdish Question in Turkish Politics," *Orbis* 45, no. 1, Winter 2001, p. 34.
9. Henry J. Barkey, "The Struggles of 'Strong' State," *Journal of International Affairs*, Vol. 51, No. 1, Fall 2000, p. 91.
10. Dogu Ergil, "The Kurdish Question in Turkey", p. 124.
11. Robins, "The Overlord State", p. 660.
12. Ergil, "The Kurdish Question in Turkey", p. 125.
13. Ali Kemal Ozcan, *Turkey's Kurds: A theoretical analysis of the PKK and Abdullah Ocalan* (London: Routledge, 2006), p. 97.
14. Mango, *Turkey and the War on Terror*, p. 34.
15. Ibid.
16. Nur Bilge Criss, "The Nature of PKK Terrorism in Turkey", *Studies in Conflict and Terrorism*, Vol. 18, No. 1, 1995, p. 19.
17. Eunyoung Kim and Minwoo Yun, "What Works? Countermeasures to Terrorism: A Case Study of PKK," *International Journal of Comparative and Applied Criminal Justice*, Vol. 32, No. 1, Spring 2008, p. 69.

18. Criss, "The Nature of PKK Terrorism in Turkey," pp. 18–19.
19. Interview with Edip Baser, Istanbul, 6 November 2013. For a comprehensive analysis of the PKK's revenue from its involvement in organised crime see Mitchell P. Roth and Murat Sever, "The Kurdish Workers' Party (PKK) as Criminal Syndicate: Funding Terrorism Through Organised Crime, A Case Study", *Studies in Conflict and Terrorism*, Vol. 30, No. 10, 2007, pp. 901–20.
20. Bulloch and Morris, *No Friends but the Mountains*, p. 168.
21. Mango, *Turkey and the War on Terror*, pp. 35–7.
22. Henri J. Barkey, "Turkey's Kurdish Dilemma, *Survival*, Vol. 35, No. 4, Winter 1993, p. 52.
23. Martin van Bruinessen, "Between Guerrilla War and Political Murder: The Workers' Party of Kurdistan", *Middle East Report* No. 153, July–August 1988.
24. Merella Galletti, "The Kurdish Issue in Turkey", *The International Spectator: Italian Journal of International Affairs*, Vol. 34, No. 1, Jan-March 1999, p. 124; van Bruinessen, "Between Guerrilla War and Political Murder".
25. Robins, "The Overlord State", p. 664.
26. Criss, "PKK Terrorism in Turkey", p. 19.
27. Barkey, "Turkey's Kurdish Dilemma", p. 52.
28. Nimet Beriker-Atiyas, "The Kurdish Conflict in Turkey: Issues, Parties and Prospects," *Security Dialogue*, Vol. 28, No. 4, April 2011, p. 441.
29. Barkey, "Turkey's Kurdish Dilemma", p. 56.
30. Human Rights Watch, *Turkey: Torture and Mistreatment in Pre-Trial Detention by Anti-Terror Police*, Vol. 9, No. 4 (D), March 1997.
31. Human Rights Watch, *Turkey: Forced Displacement of Ethnic Kurds from South-eastern Turkey*, Vol. 6, No. 12 October 1994.
32. Human Rights Watch, "The Kurds of Turkey: Killings, Disappearances and Torture".
33. Ramazan Aras, "State sovereignty and the politics of fear: Ethnography of political violence and the Kurdish struggle in Turkey," Cengiz Gunes, and Welat Zeydanlioglu (eds), *The Kurdish Question in Turkey: New perspectives on violence, representation and reconciliation* (London: Routledge, 2014), p. 95.
34. Interview with Sadettin Tantan, Istanbul, 15 February 2014.
35. Interview with Abdurrahim Ay, head of Diyarbakir branch of Mazlumder (Organisation of Human Rights and Solidarity for Oppressed People), Diyarbakir, 19 February 2014.
36. Interview with Sadettin Tantan, Istanbul, 15 February 2014.
37. Human Rights Watch, *What is Turkey's Hizbullah? 16 February 2000*; Bulent Aras and Gokhan Bacik, "The Mystery of Turkish Hizballah",

Middle East Policy, Vol. IX, No. 2, June 2002, pp. 153–5; Suleyman Ozoren, "Turkish Hizballah (Hizbullah): A Case Study of Radical Terrorism", *Turkish Weekly*, 1 December 2004.

38. John T. Nugent, Jr, "The Defeat of Turkish Hizballah as a Model for Counter-Terrorism Strategy", *MERIA Journal*, Vol. 8, No. 1, March 2004.

39. Interview with Sadettin Tantan, Istanbul, 15 February 2014.

40. Interview with Hussein Yilmaz, deputy head of the Huda Party, Diyarbakir, 19 February 2014.

41. *The New York Times*, 30 January 1998.

42. *The New York Times*, 6 April 1997.

43. Kendal Nezan, "Turkey's pivotal role in the international drug trade", *Le Monde Diplomatique*, July 1998.

44. Stephen Kinzer, *Crescent and Star: Turkey Between Two Worlds* (New York: Farrar, 2008), pp. 118–19.

45. Nezan, "Turkey's pivotal role in the international drug trade".

46. Interview with a veteran journalist reporting from south-east Turkey, Diyarbakir, 18 February 2014.

47. Soner Cagaptay, "The End of Pax Adana", *Hurriyet Daily News*, 25 August 2012.

48. *BBC News*, 16 July 2005.

49. Oktem, *Angry Nation*, pp. 141–2.

50. *GlobalSecurity.org*, "Kongra-Gel, Kurdistan Freedom and Democracy Congress (KADEK), Kurdistan Workers' Party (PKK), http://www.globalsecurity.org/military/world/para/pkk.htm (last visited 26/05/2014).

51. Oktem, *Angry Nation*, pp. 142–3.

52. *GlobalSecurity.org*, "Kongra-Gel, KADEK, PKK".

53. Ibid.

54. *Hurriyet Daily News*, 22 October 2009.

55. *GlobalSecurity.org*, "Kongra-Gel, KADEK, PKK".

56. Matt Dupee, "Turkish military offensive against the PKK beset by errant airstrike", *Longwarjournal.org*, 29 December 2011.

57. Ibid.

58. Henri J. Barkey and Graham E. Fuller, "Turkey's Kurdish Question: Critical Turning Points and Missed Opportunities," *Middle East Journal*, Vol. 51, No. 1, Winter 1997, p. 74.

59. Ibid., p. 68.

60. Michael M. Gunter, *The Kurds and the Future of Turkey* (New York: St. Martin's Press, 1997), p. 77.

61. Barkey and Fuller, "Turkey's Kurdish Question", pp. 69–70; Ergil, "The Kurdish Question in Turkey", p. 126.

NOTES   pp. [174–178]

62. Gunter, *The Kurds and the Future of Turkey*, p. 77.
63. Barkey and Fuller, "Turkey's Kurdish Question", pp. 70–1.
64. Barkey, "Turkey's Kurdish Dilemma," p. 54.
65. Ergil, "The Kurdish Question in Turkey", pp. 127–8.
66. Robins, "The Overlord State", p. 666.
67. Ibid., p. 667.
68. Interview with Sedat Yurtdas, former deputy for the People's Labour Party, Diyarbakir, 18 February 2014.
69. Robins, "The Overlord State", p. 667.
70. *BBC Turkish*, 18 April 1999.
71. *BBC News*, 4 June 1999.
72. *The Guardian*, 1 June 1999.
73. *BBC News*, 29 June 1999.
74. William Hale, "Human Rights, the European Union and the Turkish Accession Process," *Turkish Studies*, Vol. 4, No. 1, 2003, p. 119.
75. *Sabah*, 17 December 1999.
76. Meltem Muftuler Bac, "Turkey's Political Reforms and the Impact of the European Union", *South European Society and Politics*, Vol. 10, No. 1, 2005, p. 24.
77. Firat Cengiz and Lars Hoffmann, *Rethinking Conditionality: Turkey's EU Accession and the Kurdish Question*, TILEC Discussion Paper, 12 March 2012, p. 14.
78. Michael Gunter, *The Kurds Ascending. The Evolving Solution to the Kurdish Problem in Iraq and Turkey* (New York: Palgrave Macmillan, 2008), p. 61.
79. Marlies Casier, "Designated Terrorists: The Kurdistan Workers' Party and its Struggle to (Re)Gain Political Legitimacy", *Mediterranean Politics*, Vol. 15, No. 3, 2010, p. 393.
80. Ibid., p. 403.
81. Ibid., p. 405.
82. A.H. Akkaya and J. Jongerden, "The PKK in the 2000s: Continuity through breaks?", M. Casier & J. Jongerden, J. (eds), *Nationalisms and politics in Turkey: political Islam, Kemalism and the Kurdish issue* (London: Routledge, 2011), p. 154.
83. Ibid.
84. Interview with Seydi Firat, former PKK member and current general secretary of the Democratic Society Congress (DTK), Diyarbakir, 19 February 2014.
85. Michael Gunter, "The continuing Kurdish problem in Turkey after Ocalan's capture," *Third World Quarterly*, Vol. 21, No 5, 2000, p. 851.
86. NTV/MSNBC, 18 November 2012.
87. Gunter, "The continuing Kurdish problem in Turkey", p. 854.
88. Ibid.

89. Akkaya, and Jongerden, "The PKK in the 2000s," p. 153.
90. *Turkish Daily News*, 29 April 1999.
91. *BBC News*, 29 September 2003; Cengiz Gunes, *The Kurdish National Movement in Turkey: From protest to resistance* (New York: Routledge, 2012), p. 167.
92. Stephen F. Larrabee and Gonul Tol, "Turkey's Kurdish Challenge", *Survival Global Politics and Strategy*, Vol. 53, No. 4, 2011, p. 146.
93. Banu Eligur, "The Changing Face of Turkish Politics: Turkey's July 2007 Parliamentary Elections", *Middle East Brief No. 22*, Crown Center for Middle East Studies, Brandeis University, November 2007; Vahap Coskun, "Election in south-east and eastern Anatolia", *Today's Zaman*, 13 June 2011.
94. Larrabee and Tol, "Turkey's Kurdish Challenge", p. 146.
95. *Bianet*, 12 December 2009.
96. Larrabee and Tol, "Turkey's Kurdish Challenge", p. 146.
97. Cengiz Candar, "'Leaving the Mountain': How may the PKK lay down arms? Freeing the Kurdish Question from Violence," Turkiye Ekonomik ve Sosyal Etudler Vakfi (TESEV), March 2012, p. 58.
98. Interview with a retired senior officer from the intelligence service, Turkey, 10 September 2014.
99. Ibid., p. 58.
100. Interview with Sedat Yurtdas, Diyarbakir, 18 February 2014.
101. Cengiz Candar succinctly quipped that the "opening" was "an enigma […] for every party concerned or involved". Cengiz Candar, "The Kurdish Question: The Reasons and Fortunes of the 'Opening'", *Insight Turkey*, Vol. 11, No. 4, 2009, p. 16.
102. Abdullah Ocalan, "The Road Map to Democratization of Turkey and Solution to the Kurdish Question," *PKK Online*, 15 August 2009, http://www.pkkonline.com/en/index.php?sys=article&artID=123 (last visited 07/09/2014).
103. Ibid.
104. Marlies, "Designated Terrorists," p. 400.
105. Interview with a retired senior officer from the intelligence service, Turkey, 10 September 2014.
106. *Hurriyet Daily News*, 13 November 2009.
107. Ibid.
108. *Today's Zaman*, 23 July 2010.
109. Ambassador James Jeffrey, 9 October 2009, "Ankara: Growing Pessimism Among Kurds in South-east About 'The Opening'", Wikileaks, Cable: 09ANKARA1468, https://wikileaks.org/cable/2009/10/09ankara1468.html (last visited 12/08/2014). Also see Ambassador James Jeffrey, 9 December 2009, "Ankara: South-east

Perspective: Kurdish Opening Burried Under Self-Interest and Insincerity," Wikileaks, Cable: 09ANKARA1749. https://wikileaks. org/cable/2009/12/09ankara1749.html (last visited 12/08/2014).

110. *eKurd,Net*, 15 February 2011; *Al Jazeera*, 13 December 2009; *BBC News*, 11 December 2009.

111. Candar, "'Leaving the Mountain'", pp. 58–59.

112. Interview with Seydi Firat, former PKK member and current general secretary of the Democratic Society Congress (DTK), Diyarbakir, 19 February 2014.

113. International Crisis Group, "Turkey: The PKK and a Kurdish Settlement," *Crisis Group Europe Report N°219*, 11 September 2012.

114. *BBC News*, 21 March 2013.

115. *Taraf*, 14 September 2011.

116. Interview with Seydi Firat, former PKK member and current general secretary of the Democratic Society Congress (DTK), Diyarbakir, 19 February 2014.

117. *Today's Zaman*, 18 September 2012.

118. *Today's Zaman*, 11 October 2011.

119. *Today's Zaman*, 13 February 2013. They were finally all released by July 2014.

120. *Hurriyet Daily News*, 1 July 2012.

121. *Hurriyet Daily News*, 15 June 2012.

122. *The Guardian*, 31 December 2012.

123. *Milliyet*, 28 February 2013; Cengiz Candar, "Ocalan Signals Openness to Talks With Turkey on Kurdish Issue", *Al-Monitor*, 3 March 2013.

124. *The Guardian*, 10 January 2013.

125. *Wall Street Journal*, 25 April 2013.

126. Interview with Mehmet Kaya, president of the Diyarbakir Chamber of Commerce, Istanbul, 15 February 2014.

127. *Today's Zaman*, 3 April 2013.

128. Interview with Can Peker, member of Wise Men Committee, former executive member of TUSIAD, Chairman of TESEV, Istanbul, 24 February 2014.

129. Interview with Ozturk Turkdogan, Ankara, 7 November 2013.

130. *The New York Times*, 30 September 2013.

131. Yavuz Baydar, "Erdogan's Democracy Package Gets Cool Reception", *Al-Monitor*, 30 September 2013; interview with Ertugrul Kurkcu, Ankara, 9 November 2013.

132. *Reuters*, 30 September 2013.

133. Interview with Ertugrul Kurkcu, Ankara, 9 November 2013.

134. Ibid.; Gareth Jenkins, "The Democratization Package and Erdogan's Hall of Mirrors", *The Turkey Analyst*, Vol. 6, No. 8, 9 October 2013.

135. Interview with Ertugrul Kurkcu, Ankara, 9 November 2013.
136. *Al Jazeera*, 10 July 2014; DW.de, 10 July 2014.
137. Interview with Seydi Firat, Diyarbakir, 19 February 2014.
138. Interview with Ertugrul Kurkcu, Ankara, 9 November 2013.
139. Interview with Sedat Yurtdas, Diyarbakir, 18 February 2014.
140. Larrabee and Tol, "Turkey's Kurdish Challenge", p. 146.
141. Ibid., p. 147; Casier, "Designated Terrorists," p. 398.
142. Interview with Ertugrul Kurkcu, Ankara, 9 November 2013; similar sentiments were expressed in our interview with Seydi Firat, Diyarbakir, 19 February 2014.
143. Interview with Mehmet Kaya, Istanbul, 15 February 2014; interview with Ozturk Turkdogan, Ankara, 7 November 2013.
144. Interview with Seydi Firat, Diyarbakir, 19 February 2014.
145. Interview with Mehmet Kaya, 15 February 2014.
146. Human Rights Watch, *Time For Justice: Ending Impunity for Killings and Disappearances in 1990s Turkey*, 3 September 2012, pp. 1–2.
147. Interview with Mehmet Kaya, Istanbul, 15 February 2014; interview with Seydi Firat, Diyarbakir, 19 February 2014.
148. Interview with Seydi Firat, Diyarbakir, 19 February 2014.
149. *Hurriyet Daily News*, 6 November 2015.
150. Human Rights Watc, *Time For Justice*, pp. 1–2.
151. Ibid., pp. 2–3.
152. Ibid., pp. 18–19.
153. Interview with Tahir Elci, head of the Diyarbakir Bar Association, Diyarbakir, 18 February 2014.
154. Human Rights Watch, *Time For Justice*, pp. 56–9.
155. Interview with Ozturk Turkdogan, Ankara, 7 November 2013.
156. Human Rights Watch, *Still Critical: Prospects in 2005 for Internally Displaced Kurds in Turkey*, Vol. 17, No. 2(D), March 2005, pp. 5–6.
157. Ibid., pp. 10–11.
158. Interview with Ozturk Turkdogan, Ankara, 7 November 2013.
159. Interview with Abdurrahim Ay, Diyarbakir, 19 February 2014.
160. Interview with Mehmet Kaya, 15 February 2014.
161. Interview with Sedat Yurtdas, Diyarbakir, 18 February 2014.
162. Interview with Seydi Firat, Diyarbakir, 19 February 2014.
163. Interview with Mehmet Kaya, 15 February 2014.
164. Interview with Sedat Yurtdas, Diyarbakir, 18 February 2014.
165. Ibid.; interview with Mehmet Kaya, Istanbul, 15 February 2014.
166. Interview with Sedat Yurtdas, Diyarbakir, 18 February 2014.
167. Ibid.; interview with Umut Guner, Ankara, 7 November 2013.
168. Interview with Ertugrul Kurkcu, Ankara, 9 November 2013.
169. Ibid.

170. Interview with Mehmet Kaya, Istanbul, 15 February 2014.
171. Interview with Tahir Elci, head of the Diyarbakir Bar Association, Diyarbakir, 18 February 2014.
172. Interview with Mehmet Kaya, Istanbul, 15 February 2014.
173. *The Guardian*, 6 October 2014.
174. *The Independent*, 18 September 2014; *The Guardian*, 4 October 2014; *The New York Times*, 10 October 2014.
175. *The Guardian*, 2 October 2014.
176. *The Guardian*, 4 October 2014.
177. *Reuters*, 8 October 2014; *The Independent*, 7 October 2014; Patrick Cockburn, "Isis in Kobani: Turkey ignores Kurdish fury as militants close in on capturing the town", *The Independent*, 9 October 2014.
178. Ilhan Tanir, "Komabi and Kurdish Nationalism in Turkey", Carnegie Endowment for International Peace, 6 November 2014; *Daily Sabah*, 3 December 2014.
179. *The Guardian*, 8 October 2014.
180. Interview with Garo Paylan, HDP deputy, Istanbul, 20 December 2015.
181. *Reuters*, 11 October 2014.
182. *The Independent*, 14 October 2014.
183. Guney Yildiz, "Turkey-PKK Peace Process at 'Turning Point'", *BBC News*, 12 November 2014.
184. *The Telegraph*, 28 February 2015.
185. *Daily Sabah*, 5 June 2015.
186. *The Guardian*, 5 June 2015; *Today's Zaman*, 6 June 2015.
187. *The New York Times*, 20 July 2015; *Hurriyet Daily News*, 14 August 2015.
188. *BBC News*, 22 July 2015.
189. *Today's Zaman*, 8 August 2015; *Reuters*, 2 August 2015; *Daily Sabah*, 10 August 2015.
190. *BBC News*, 19 August 2015.
191. *Yeni Safak*, 20 August 2015.
192. Interview with Garo Paylan, HDP deputy, Istanbul, 20 December 2015.
193. *Observer*, 25 July 2015.
194. *BBC News*, 26 July 2015.
195. *Wall Street Journal*, 7 September 2015; *Reuters*, 8 September 2015.
196. *Al Jazeera*, 19 September 2015.
197. *BBC News*, 17 October 2015; *The Guardian*, 11 October 2015; *Al Jazeera*, 10 October 2015.
198. *The Guardian*, 11 October 2015.
199. Ibid.; *The Independent*, 10 October 2015.

200. *BBC.com*, 10 September 2015; *Rudaw*, 20 November 2015.

201. *T24*, 20 August 2015; *BBC.com*, 29 December 2015.

202. *Hurriyet Daily News*, 20 August 2015.

203. Interview with Garo Paylan, HDP deputy, Istanbul, 20 December 2015.

204. Crisis Group Europe, "The Human Cost of the PKK Conflict in Turkey: the Case of Sur," *Crisis Group Europe Briefing No. 80*, Diyarbakir/Istanbul/Brussels, 17 March 2016, p. 3.

205. *The Guardian*, 17 February 2016.

206. *BBC News*, 17 March 2016.

207. *Wall Street Journal*, 12 June 2016.

208. *Hurriyet Daily News*, 20 January 2016.

209. *Aljazeera.com*, 5 April 2016.

210. *Reuters*, 20 May 2016; *Parliament Magazine*, 7 June 2016.

211. *Rudaw*, 25 July 2016; *Hurriyet*, 25 July 2016.

212. *Hurriyet Daily News*, 1 August 2016; *BBC Turkce*, 29 July 2016.

213. *Hurriyet Daily News*, 19 July 2016; *Haberturk*, 19 July 2016.

214. *Hurriyet Daily News*, 26 July 2016; *Gerçek Gundem*, 23 July 2016.

215. *Hurriyet Daily News*, 28 July 2016; *Hurriyet Daily News*, 31 July 2016; *Daily Sabah*, 30 July 2016.

216. *BBC News*, 30 July 2016; *Al Jazeera Turk*, 29 July 2016.

217. Interview with a retired senior officer from the intelligence service, Turkey, 10 September 2014.

7. DAVUTOGLU'S RHYTHMIC DIPLOMACY: CLASSICAL CONCERT OR IMPROVISED JAZZ?

1. 58th Government Programme, presented by Prime Minister Abdullah Gul at the Turkish Parliament, 24 November 2002, p. 17, https://www.akparti.org.tr/upload/documents/58inci-hukumet-programi.pdf (last visited 31/03/2016).

2. For reforms in Turkey, see Gamze Avcı, "The Justice and Development Party and the EU: Political Pragmatism in a Changing Environment", *South European Politics and Society*, 16(3), 409–421, 2011; Erhan Dogan "The historical and discoursive roots of the Justice and Development Party's EU stance", *Turkish Studies*, vol. 6, no. 3, 2005, pp. 421–437.

3. European Commission's Website, "Enlargement, EU-Turkey Relations," http://ec.europa.eu/enlargement/candidate-countries/turkey/eu_turkey_relations_en.htm (last visited 31/03/2016).

4. Nathalie Tocci (2005), "Europeanization in Turkey: Trigger or Anchor for Reform?", *South European Society and Politics*, 10, 1, p. 75.

5. Eurobarometer, "Eurobarometer 63: Public Opinion in the European Union," National Report, Executive Summary Turkey, Spring 2005, p. 5.

6. Nicholas Watt, "Europe embraces Turkey as diplomatic deadlock is broken," *The Guardian*, 4 October 2005.

7. Ziya Oniş and Caner Bakır, "Turkey's Political Economy in the Age of Financial Globalization: The Significance of the EU Anchor," *South European Society and Politics*, 12:2, 2007, p. 158.

8. Ziya Onis and Suhnaz Yilmaz, "The Turkey-EU-US Triangle in Perspective: Transformation or Continuity?", *Middle East Journal*, Vol. 59, No. 2, "Changing Geopolitics" (Spring 2005), p. 279.

9. Turkish Foreign Ministry, "Turkey-EU Relations", http://www.mfa.gov.tr/relations-between-turkey-and-the-european-union.en.mfa (last visited 31/03/2016).

10. For a useful discussion of the rising Euroscepticism and anti-Western sentiments in Turkey from around 2005 onwards, see Philip Gordon and Omer Taspinar, "Turkey on the Brink," *The Washington Quarterly*, Vol. 29, No. 3 (Summer 2006), p. 63.

11. For EU's opposition to Turkey, see Meltem Muftuler-Bac "Turkey's Accession to the European Union: The Impact of the EU's Internal Dynamics," *International Studies Perspectives* (2008) 9, 201–19.

12. William Hale (2011), "Human Rights and Turkey's EU Accession Process: Internal and External Dynamics," 2005–10, *South European Society and Politics*, 16:2, p. 327.

13. *DW Turkish*, 27 January 2014.

14. Eurobarometer, "Eurobarometer 67: Public Opinion in the European Union", Spring 2007, National Report, Executive Summary, Turkey, p. 2.

15. Senem Aydın-Düzgit (2012), "No Crisis, No Change: The Third AKP Victory in the June 2011 Parliamentary Elections in Turkey," *South European Society and Politics*, 17:2, p. 330.

16. Omer Taspinar, *Turkey: The New Model?*, April 2012, Washington DC: The Woodrow Wilson Center.

17. Ahmet Davutoglu, *Stratejik Derinlik/Türkiye'nin Uluslararası Konumu* (The Strategic Depth: The Turkish International Location), (Istanbul: Kure Yayınları, 2001).

18. Graham E. Fuller, *The New Turkish Republic: Turkey as a Pivotal State in the Muslim World* (Washington DC: United States Institute of Peace Press, 2008), pp. 98–100.

19. Bulent Aras, "Davutoğlu Era in Turkish Foreign Policy", *SETA Publications*, Vol. 32, May 2009, p. 3.

20. Alexander Murinson, "The Strategic Depth Doctrine of Turkish Foreign Policy", *Modern Eastern Studies*, Vol 42, No. 6, 2006, p. 947.

21. Aras, "Davutoğlu Era in Turkish Foreign Policy," p. 3.

22. For more information about the concept of neo-Ottomanism, see

Philip Robins, "Turkish Foreign Policy Since 2002: Between a Post-Islamist Government and a Kemalist State", *International Affairs*, Vol. C. LXXXIII, No. 1, 2007, pp. 289–304; Hakan Yavuz, "Turkish identity and foreign policy in flux: The rise of Neo-Ottomanism", *Middle East Critique*, Vol. 7, No. 12, 1998.

23. Adam Szymanski, "Turkish Foreign Policy in 2007–2009: Continuity or Change?", *Polish Quarterly of International Affairs*, Vol. 19 No. 2, 2009, p. 3.

24. Aras, "Davutoğlu Era in Turkish Foreign Policy", p. 4.

25. Murinson, "The Strategic Depth Doctrine of Turkish Foreign Policy", p. 947.

26. Ahmet Davutoğlu, "Medeniyetin Ben İdraki (Self-Cognition of Civilizations)", *Divan*, Vol. 1, 1997, p. 1.

27. Ahmet Davutoglu, "The Clash of Interest: An Explanation of the World (Dis)order", *Perceptions: Journal of International Affairs*, Vol. 2, No. 4, December 1997–February 1998, p. 1.

28. These are the Suez Canal, Bab el-Mandep (exit from the Red Sea), the Strait of Hormuz (exit from the Persian Gulf), the Strait of Malacca (between the Malay Peninsula and Sumatra), the Sunda Strait (between Sumatra and Java), the Lombok Strait (between Bali and Mataram), the Bosphorus and Dardanelles (exit from the Black Sea), which are under full control of Muslim countries, and the Strait of Gibraltar, which separates a Muslim state (Morocco) and a European state (Spain).

29. Davutoglu, "The Clash of Interest," p. 2.

30. Joshua Walker, "Introduction: The Sources of Turkish Grand Strategy-Strategic Depth and Zero-Problems in Context", *Turkey's Global Strategy*, LSE Publications, 2011, p. 7.

31. Davutoglu, *Stratejik Derinlik*, p. 9.

32. Murinson, "The Strategic Depth Doctrine of Turkish Foreign Policy", p. 952.

33. In an interview with A. Davutoglu, "The power Turkey does not use is that of Strategic Depth", *The Turkish Daily News*, 15 June 2010.

34. Davutoglu, *Stratejik Derinlik*, pp. 142, 501.

35. Ahmet Davutoglu, "Turkey's New Foreign Policy", *Insight Turkey*, Vol. 10, No. 1, 2008, p. 78.

36. Ibid., pp. 79–83.

37. Ibid., p. 80.

38. Interview with a retired senior officer from the intelligence service, Turkey, 10 September 2014.

39. Abdullah Gul, "Turkey's Role in a Changing Middle East Environment", *Mediterranean Quarterly*, Vol. 15, No. 1, 2004, p. 6.

40. Ahmet Davutoglu, "Turkey's Central Role," *Hurriyet Daily News*, 4 May 2009.

41. Ahmet Davutoglu, "Türkiye Merkez Ulke Olmalı" ("Turkey should be the centre country"), *Radikal*, 26 February 2004.

42. Bulent Aras and Rabia Karakaya Polat, "From Conflict to Cooperation: Desecuritization of Turkey's Relations with Syria and Iran", *Security Dialogue*, Vol. 39, No. 5, 2008, p. 510.

43. Meliha B. Altunisik and Ozlem Tur, "From Distant Neighbors to Partners? Changing Syrian–Turkish Relations", *Security Dialogue*, Vol. 37, No. 2, 2006, p. 240.

44. *Hurriyet*, 2 March 2003.

45. Murinson, "The Strategic Depth Doctrine of Turkish Foreign Policy," p. 956.

46. Oguzlu, "The Middle Easternization of Turkey's Foreign Policy", p. 8.

47. Nuri Yesilyurt and Atay Akdevilioglu, "Türkiye'nin Ortadoğu Politikası (Turkey's Middle East Policy)", in Bulent Duru, Ilhan Uzgel et al. (eds), *AKP Kitabı (AKP Book)*, (Istanbul: Phoenix, 2010), p. 387; Tarık Oguzlu, "The Middle Easternization of Turkey's Foreign Policy: Does Turkey Dissociate from the West?", *Turkish Studies*, Vol. 9, No. 1, 2008, p. 5.

48. Sabah Kardas, "Turkey and the Iraq Crisis: JDP Between Identity and Interest", in M. Hakan Yavuz (ed.), *The Emergence of a New Turkey*, (Salt Lake City: The University of Utah Press, 2006), p. 319.

49. Gencer Ozcan. "The Changing Role of Turkey's Military in Foreign Policy Making," *UNISCI Discussion Papers*, no. 23, May 2010, p. 23.

50. Interview with Ibrahim Kalin, President Recep Tayyip Erdogan's top foreign policy advisor, Ankara, 14 July 2011.

51. Altunisik and Tur, "From Distant Neighbors to Partners?", p. 239.

52. Steven A. Cook and Elizabeth Sherwood-Randall, "Generating Momentum for a New Era in US-Turkey Relations", *Council of Foreign Relations Press*, June 2006, p. 33.

53. Address by R. T. Erdogan, "Democracy in the Middle East, Pluralism in Europe: Turkish View" in Harvard University, Kennedy School of Government, 30 January 2003, available on http://belfercenter.ksg. harvard.edu/files/erdogan-%20harvard%20prepared%20remarks.pdf (last visited 29/09/2014).

54. Ibid.

55. Interview with Bulent Aras, former head of Center for Strategic Research at Turkish Foreign Ministry, Ankara, 23 July 2011.

56. Interview with Ibrahim Kalin, Ankara, 14 July 2011.

57. Volker Peters, "Turkey's Role in the Middle East: An Outsider's Perspective", *Insight Turkey*, Vol. 12, No. 4, 2010, p. 2.

58. Kadri Kaan Renda, "Turkey's Neighborhood Policy: An Emerging Complex Interdependence?", *Insight Turkey*, Vol. 13, No. 1, 2011, p. 99.
59. Peters, "Turkey's Role in the Middle East", p. 2.
60. *Turkishtime*, interview with A. Davutoglu, "Is Dunyasi Artık Dispolitikanin Onculerinden (Business World is In the Front Line of Foreign Policy)", April–May 2004.
61. Ahmet Davutoglu, "Turkish Foreign Policy and the EU in 2010", *Turkish Policy Quarterly*, Vol. 8, No. 3, Fall 2009, p. 13.
62. Altay Atli, "Businessman as Diplomats: The Role of Business Associations in Turkey's Foreign Policy", *Insight Turkey*, Vol. 13, No. 1, 2011, p. 116.
63. *Haber* 7, 27 June 2007.
64. Davutoglu, "The Clash of Interests", p. 40.
65. Kemal Kirişçi, "Turkey's 'Demonstrative Effect' and the Transformation of the Middle East", *Insight Turkey*, Vol. 14, No. 2, 2011, p. 48.
66. *Today's Zaman*, 13 February 2011.
67. Turkey signed free trade agreements with these Middle Eastern countries under the European Union's Euro-Med process.
68. Turkish Statistical Institute, "Foreign Trade Statistics," http://www.turkstat.gov.tr/PreTablo.do?tb_id=12&ust_id=4 (last visited 05/10/2013).
69. Ibid.
70. Meliha B. Altuniskik and Lenore G. Martin, "Making Sense of Turkish Foreign Policy in the Middle East under AKP", *Turkish Studies*, Vol. 12, No. 4, December 2011, p. 581.
71. Interview with Can Peker, member of Wise Men Committee, former executive member of TUSIAD, chairman of TESEV, Istanbul, 24 February 2014; Index Mundi, "Turkey Unemployment Rate," http://www.indexmundi.com/g/g.aspx?c=tu&v=74 (last visited 27/09/2014).
72. Altunisik and Martin, "Making sense of Turkish foreign policy," p. 582.
73. Bulent Aras and Hakan Fidan, "Turkey and Eurasia: Frontiers of a New Geographic Imagination", *New Perspectives on Turkey*, No. 40, 2009, pp. 206–7.
74. *The New York Times*, 25 April 2004.
75. Aras and Fidan, "Turkey and Eurasia", No. 40, 2009, p. 212.
76. Saban Kardas, "Turkey: Redrawing the Middle East Map: Or Building Sandcastles?", *Middle East Policy*, Vol. 17, No. 1, Spring 2010, p. 116.
77. Ziya Onis, "Multiple Faces of the 'New' Turkish Foreign Policy: Underlying Dynamics and a Critique", *GLODEM Working Paper Series*, April 2010, pp. 3–4.
78. On the evolution of ties between Israel and Turkey see Ofra Bengio, *The Turkish-Israeli Relationship: Changing Ties of Middle East Outsiders* (New

York: Palgrave Macmillan, 2004), pp. 103–126; Efraim Inbar, *The Israeli-Turkish Entente* (London: King's College Mediterranean Studies, 2001).

79. *Today's Zaman*, 5 December 2005; Banu Eligur, "Crisis in Turkish-Israeli Relations (December 2008–June 2011): From Partnership to Emnity," *Middle Eastern Studies*, Vol. 48, No. 4, May 2012, p. 431.

80. Eligur, "Crisis in Turkish-Israeli Relations", p. 433.

81. *The Guardian*, 4 June 2004.

82. Meliha Benli Altunisik, "The Possibilities and Limits of Turkey's Soft Power in the Middle East", *Insight Turkey*, Vol. 10, No. 2, 2008, p. 51.

83. Ibid.

84. *The New York Times*, 3 January 2006.

85. *Los Angeles Times*, 17 February 2006.

86. Interview with Mevlut Cavusoglu, Ankara, 20 February 2014.

87. Altunisik, "The Possibilities and Limits of Turkey's Soft Power", p. 52.

88. Cook and Sherwood-Randall, "Generating Momentum for a New Era in U.S.-Turkey Relations", p. 23.

89. Ambassador Ross Wilson, 17 February 2006, "Ankara: Turkey's Message to Hamas," Wikileaks, Cable: 06ANKARA765. https://wikileaks.org/cable/2006/02/06ankara765.html (last visited 12/08/2014).

90. Steven A. Cook, "Turkey's War at Home", *Survival: Global Politics and Strategy*, Vol. 51, No. 5, September 2009, p. 114.

91. Herb Keinon, "Assad: Olmert okayed Golan deal before Gaza Op", *Jerusalem Post*, 18 March 2009.

92. *Reuters*, 13 August 2008; Eligur, "Crisis in Turkish-Israeli Relations", p. 433.

93. Washington Institute for Near East Policy, "In His Own Words: Erdogan on Israel, Hamas, and the Gaza Conflict," PolicyWatch #1475, 11 February 2009.

94. Eligur, "Crisis in Turkish-Israeli Relations", p. 436.

95. *The New York Times*, 29 January 2009.

96. Eligur, "Crisis in Turkish-Israeli Relations", p. 442.

97. Taha Ozhan, "Turkey, Israel and the US in the Wake of the Gaza Flotilla Crisis", *Insight Turkey*, Vol. 12, No. 3, 2010.

98. Piotr Zalewski, "The Self-Appointed Superpower: Turkey Goes it Alone", *World Policy Journal*, Vol. 27, No. 4, Winter 2010/2011, p. 100.

99. *BBC News*, 2 September 2011. Turkey would have to wait until March 2013 to receive an apology from Israeli Prime Minister Benjamin Netanyahu.

100. Eligur, "Crisis in Turkish-Israeli Relations", pp. 433–5.

101. Zalewski, "The Self-Appointed Superpower", p. 100.

102. Interview with Omer Onhon, deputy undersecretary of the Turkish Ministry of Foreign Affairs, Ankara, 8 November 2013.

103. *Haaretz*, 22 March 2015; *Haaretz*, 17 December 2015; *The Daily Telegraph*, 17 December 2015; *Reuters*, 15 February 2016.

104. *Washington Post*, 27 June 2016; *CNN.com*, 27 June 2016.

105. *Reuters*, 27 June 2016; *Financial Times*, 27 June 2016; *YnetNews*, 27 June 2016; Avi Issacharoff, "For Hamas, lousy deal exposes Turkey as a paper tiger", *Times of Israel*, 27 June 2016.

106. Daphne McCurdy, "Turkish-Iranian Relations: When Opposites Attract", *Turkish Policy Quarterly*, Vol. 51, No. 3, 2008; Bill Park, *Modern Turkey: People, state and foreign policy in a globalized world* (London: Routledge, 2012), p. 114.

107. Cook and Sherwood-Randall, "Generating Momentum for a New Era in U.S.-Turkey Relations", p. 20.

108. Altuniskik and Martin, "Making Sense of Turkish Foreign Policy", p. 581.

109. William Hale, *Turkish Foreign Policy since 1774* (London: Routledge, 2013), pp. 241–2.

110. Nathalie Tocci and Joshua W. Walker, "From Confrontation to Engagement: Turkey and the Middle East", Ronald H. Linden et al (eds), *Turkey and its Neighbors: Foreign Relations in Transition* (Boulder: Lynne Reinner, 2012), p. 37.

111. *The Guardian*, 17 May 2010.

112. Stephen Kinzer, "Iran's Nuclear Deal", *The Guardian*, 17 May 2010.

113. *Washington Post*, 10 June 2010.

114. *BBC News*, interview with Erdogan, 16 March 2010.

115. Altuniskik and Martin, "Making Sense of Turkish Foreign Policy", p. 572; Gregory L. Schulte, "Why Turkey Cannot Abstain on Iran's Nuclear Violations", *Turkish Policy Quarterly*, Vol. 8, No. 4, 2009–20.

116. Cenap Cakmak and Gokhan Guneysu, "Turkish-American Relations During Obama Era: Unfulfilled Expectations", *Turkish Studies*, Vol. 14, No. 2, June 2013, p. 196.

117. Ambassador James Jeffrey, "Ankara: Deals with Iran Benefit PM Erdogan's Friends," 27 February 2009, Wikileaks, Cable: 09ANKARA321, http://www.wikileaks.org/cable/2009/02/09ANKARA321.html (last visited 16/08/2014).

118. Kadir Ustun, "Turkey's Iran Policy: Between Diplomacy and Sanctions", *Insight Turkey*, Vol. 12, No. 3, 2010; Altuniskik and Martin, "Making Sense of Turkish Foreign Policy", p. 574.

119. Ariel Cohen, "Obama's Best Friend? The Alarming Evolution of US-Turkish Relations", *Middle East Security and Policy Studies*, No. 10, The Begin-Sadat Center for Strategic Studies, May 2013, p. 25.

120. Zalewski, "The Self-Appointed Superpower", p. 100.

121. Interview with Omer Onhon, Ankara, 8 November 2013.
122. Cook and Sherwood-Randall, "Generating Momentum for a New Era in U.S.-Turkey Relations", p. 19; Kirisci claims that Turkey played an important role in persuading Asad to give up a suspect in the Hariri murder. See Kemal Kirisci, *Turkey's Foreign Policy in Turbulent Times*, (Paris: European Union Institute for Security Studies EUISS), Chailot Paper 92, 2006, p. 78.
123. Nicholas Danforth, "Ideology and Pragmatism in Turkish Foreign Policy: From Ataturk to the AKP", *Turkish Policy Quarterly*, Vol. 7, No. 3, Fall 2008, p. 91.
124. Steven A. Cook, "The USA, Turkey and the Middle East: Continuities, Challenges and Opportunities", *Turkish Studies*, Vol. 12, No. 4, December 2011, p. 717.
125. Ambassador James Jeffrey, "Ankara: What Lies Beneath Ankara's New Foreign Policy," 20 January 2010, Wikileaks, Cable: 10ANKARA87, http://www.wikileaks.org/cable/2010/01/10ANKARA87.html (last visited 16/08/2014).
126. Kardas, "Turkey: Redrawing the Middle East Map or Building Sandcastles?", p. 132.
127. Zalewski, "The Self-Appointed Superpower", p. 102.
128. Cook and Sherwood-Randall, "Generating Momentum for a New Era in U.S.-Turkey Relations", pp. 10–12.
129. Ibid.
130. Larrabee, "Turkey's New Geopolitics", p. 163.
131. Zalewski, "The Self-Appointed Superpower," p. 100.
132. Kemal Kirisci, "The transformation of Turkish foreign policy: The rise of the trading state", *New Perspectives on Turkey*, No. 40, 2009, pp. 30, 40–41, 47.
133. Larrabee, "Turkey's New Geopolitics", p. 162.
134. Interview with Mevlut Cavusoglu, Ankara, 20 February 2014.
135. Interview with Minister Falah Mustafa, head of Foreign Relations Department, Kurdistan Regional Government, London, 10 April 2014.
136. Ibid.
137. Altuniskik and Martin, "Making Sense of Turkish Foreign Policy in the Middle East", p. 583.
138. Cohen, "Obama's Best Friend?", p. 32.
139. Henri J. Barkey, "Turkey and Iraq: The making of a partnership," *Turkish Studies*, Vol. 12, No. 4, December 2011, p. 663.
140. Ibid.
141. Davutoglu, "Turkish Foreign Policy and the EU in 2010," p. 13.
142. Interview with Omer Onhon, Ankara, 8 November 2013.

143. Ahmet Davutoglu, "The Three Major Earthquakes in the International System and Turkey", *The International Spectator*, Vol. 48, No. 2, June 2013, pp. 5–6.

144. Ibid.

145. Ibid.

146. Ibid.

147. Henri J. Barkey, "Turkish-Iranian Competition after the Arab Spring", *Survival: Global Politics and Strategy*, Vol. 54, No. 6, November 2012, p. 150.

148. Philip Robins, "Turkey's 'double gravity' predicament: the foreign policy of a newly activist power", *International Affairs*, Vol. 82, No. 2, 2013, pp. 390–1; also see Omar Taspinar, "Turkey's Strategic Vision and Syria," *The Washington Quarterly*, Vol. 35, No. 3, Summer 2012, p. 135.

149. Taspinar, "Turkey's Strategic Vision and Syria," p. 135.

150. Kirisci, "Turkey's "Demonstrative Effect", p. 34.

151. Robins, "Turkey's 'double gravity' predicament", pp. 390–1.

152. Barkey, "Turkish-Iranian Competition after the Arab Spring", p. 150.

153. Taspinar, "Turkey's Strategic Vision and Syria," p. 136.

154. Ibid.

155. *Today's Zaman*, 22 February 2011.

156. Hale, *Turkish Foreign Policy since 1774*, p. 244.

157. Robins, "Turkey's 'double gravity' predicament", pp. 391–2.

158. Ozlem Tur, "Economic Relations with the Middle East Under the AKP—Trade, Business Community and Reintegration with Neighboring Zones", *Turkish Studies*, Vol. 12, No. 4, December 2011, p. 598.

159. Ibid.

160. Robins, "Turkey's 'double gravity' predicament: the foreign policy of a newly activist power", pp. 392–3.

161. Ibid., p. 394.

162. Taspinar, "Turkey's Strategic Vision and Syria," p. 137.

163. Ibid.

164. Robins, "Turkey's 'double gravity' predicament: the foreign policy of a newly activist power", pp. 394–5.

165. Ibid.

166. Taspinar, "Turkey's Strategic Vision and Syria," p. 137.

167. Erol Cebeci and Kadir Ustun, "The Syrian Quagmire: What's Holding Turkey Back?", *Insight Turkey*, Vol. 14, No. 2, 2012, pp. 15–16.

168. Ibid., p. 16.

169. Ibid., p. 17.

170. Taspinar, "Turkey's Strategic Vision and Syria," p. 138.

171. *Financial Times*, 5 July 2013; Mustafa Akyol, "Turkey Condemns Egypt's Coup", *Al-Monitor*, 21 August 2013.

172. Herb Keinon, "Erdogan slams Egypt's Sisi as 'tyrant' over Cairo policy toward Hamas", *The Jerusalem Post*, 18 July 2014.

173. Interview with Omer Onhon, Ankara, 8 November 2013.

174. Ibid.

175. *Reuters*, "Seeing shared threats, Turkey sets up military base in Qatar", 28 April 2016, http://www.reuters.com/article/us-qatar-turkey-military-idUSKCN0XP2IT (last visited 07/09/2016).

176. Olivier Decottignies and Soner Cagaptay, "Turkey's New Base in Qatar," *Washington Institute for Near East Policy*, PolicyWatch 2545, 11 January 2016; *The Guardian*, 12 April 2016.

177. *Haaretz*, 28 July 2014; *The Independent*, 20 July 2014.

178. *The Guardian*, 11 June 2014.

179. *The Guardian*, 24 August 2014; *Hurriyet Daily News*, 24 August 2014; *Daily Sabah*, 2 September 2014; Semih Idiz, "Turkey under pressure over Jihadists on border," *Al-Monitor*, 24 January 2014.

180. *The Guardian*, 6 October 2014.

181. *The Guardian*, 29 June 2016; *BBC News*, 29 June 2016.

182. *The New York Times*, 19 March 2016.

183. *CNN.com*, 13 January 2016.

184. *CNN.com*, 12 October 2015.

185. *Reuters*, 24 November 2015; *BBC News*, 24 November 2015; *The New York Times*, 24 November 2015.

186. *BBC News*, 28 November 2015.

187. *Reuters*, 6 December 2015.

188. *The New York Times*, 24 November 2015.

189. *The Daily Mirror*, 13 February 2016; *The Express*, 15 February 2016.

190. For instance see Ariel Ben Solomon, "Analysis: Russia, US Compete to Ally with Kurds in ISIS Fight", *Jerusalem Post*, 9 February 2016; L. Todd Wood, "Russia supporting Kurdish groups in Syria to Turkey's detriment", *Washingtom Times*, 8 February 2016; *Reuters*, 17 February 2016.

191. *BBC News*, 2 July 2016.

192. Cengiz Candar, "Under pressure from Turkey, UN excludes PYD from Syria talks", *Al-Monitor*, 29 January 2016.

193. *Observer*, 25 July 2015.

194. For a detailed breakdown of Syrian refugees per country, see UNHCR. "Syria Regional Refugee Response, Inter-agency information sharing portal," undated, http://data.unhcr.org/syrianrefugees/country.php?id=224 (last visited 21/03/2016).

195. *FT.com*, 7 March 2016; *The New York Times*, 7 March 2016; *Reuters*,

7 March 2016; *Hurriyet Daily News*, 7 March 2016; Mark Mardell, "Turkey had European Union over a barrel", *BBC News*, 17 March 2016.

196. Thomas Gibbons-Neff, "How the U.S. Military scrambled in Turkey to keep working during the coup attempt," *Washington Post*, 2 August 2016.

197. Burak Bekdil, "The Turkish Army: Twice a loser," *Hurriyet Daily News*, 3 August 2016.

198. *The Daily Telegraph*, 4 August 2016.

199. *The Daily Telegraph*, 1 August 2016.

200. *Anadolu Agency*, 2 August 2016; *BBC Turkce*, 2 August 2016.

201. *Anadolu Agency*, 4 August 2016.

202. *Hurriyet Daily News*, 17 July 2016; *Zaman*, 16 July 2016.

203. *The Independent*, 18 July 2016; *ABCNews*, 17 July 2016; *The New York Times*, 17 July 2016.

204. *Washington Times*, 2 August 2016; *TRT Haber*, 2 August 2016.

205. *Hurriyet Daily News*, 27 July 2016.

206. *Hurriyet Daily News*, 2 August 2016.

207. *Wall Street Journal*, 4 August 2016.

208. *The Guardian*, 4 August 2016; *Milliyet*, 4 August 2016.

CONCLUSION

1. *Hurriyet Daily News*, 10 August 2014.

2. *BBC News*, 30 July 2016.

3. *Hurriyet Daily News*, 4 August 2016.

4. *Hurriyet Daily News*, 31 July 2016.

5. Zia Weisse, "Allegations of torture in Turkey as rule of law erodes," *Politico EU*, 25 July 2016.

6. *Hurriyet Daily News*, 18 July 2016.

BIBLIOGRAPHY

Interviews

Yaman Akdeniz, Associate Professor of Human Rights Law and Internet Activist, Istanbul Bilgi University, London 21 March 2014.

Bulent Aras, former head of the Centre for Strategic Research at the Turkish Foreign Ministry, Ankara, 23 July 2011.

Ali Arikan, General Secretary of the Alevi Culture Association, 20 February 2014.

Abdurrahim Ay, head of Diyarbakir Branch of Mazlumder (Organisation of Human Rights and Solidarity for Oppressed People), Diyarbakir, 19 February 2014.

Rifat Bali, author and expert on the history of the Jews in Turkey, Istanbul, 4 November 2013.

Nimet Bas, former Minister for Women and Family Affairs, and former Minister of National Education, Head of the Parliamentary Commission to Investigate Military Coups, Istanbul, 10 November 2013.

Edip Baser, former Deputy Chief of General Staff until 2005, Istanbul, 6 November 2013.

Ali Bayramoglu, columnist for *Yenisafak*, Istanbul, 6 November 2013.

Osman Can, former Constitutional Court reporter (2002–10) and the AKP's Central Executive Committee member, Istanbul, 6 November 2013.

Mevlut Cavusoglu, Minister of Foreign Affairs, Ankara, 20 February 2014.

Irem Cicek, lawyer of Dursun Cicik, Istanbul, 24 February 2014.

Levent Cicek, former head of the youth wing of the Heart of Ottoman, Ankara, 21 July 2016.

Ilhan Cihaner, CHP deputy and former Public Prosecutor (2007–2011), Ankara, 17 February 2014.

Hamit Demir, actor and activist, Istanbul, 24 February 2014.

Tahir Elci, head of Diyarbakir Bar Association, Diyarbakir, 18 February 2014.

BIBLIOGRAPHY

Ihsan Eliacik, group leader and public face of the Anti-Capitalist Muslims, Istanbul, 25 February 2014.

Aykan Erdemir, deputy for the People's Republican Party (CHP), Ankara, 20 February 2014.

Seydi Firat, former PKK member and current General Secretary of the Democratic Society Congress (DTK), Diyarbakir, 19 February 2014.

Tanju Gunduzalp, Editor-in-Chief of *Solfasol*, Ankara-based environmental magazine, Ankara, 21 February 2014.

Umut Guner, General Coordinator of KAOS GL, Ankara-based LGBT organisation, Ankara, 7 November 2013.

Irfan Guvendi, Deputy Head of MUSIAD, Ankara Branch, Ankara, 21 February 2014.

Ekmeleddin Ihsanoglu, MHP deputy and joint CHP and CHP candidate in the 2014 presidential election, Istanbul, 21 December 2015.

Gareth Jenkins, Senior Associate Fellow at the Silk Road Studies Program and regular commentator for *Turkey Analyst*, Istanbul, 10 November 2013.

Bahadir Kaleagasi, International Coordinator, TUSIAD, Istanbul, 22 December 2015.

Ibrahim Kalin, Turkish President Recep Tayyip Erdogan's top foreign policy advisor, Ankara, 14 July 2011.

Erdal Tanas Karagol, Professor at Yildirim Beyazit University and SETA economy expert, Ankara, 17 February 2014.

Mehmet Kaya, President of the Diyarbakir Chamber of Commerce, Istanbul, 15 February 2014.

Sevket Kazan, former Justice Minister, Welfare Party (1974, 1997–8) and Sadet Party, Ankara, 17 February 2014.

Ceren Kener, columnist for *Turkıye*, Istanbul, 5 November 2013.

Bulent Kenes, former Editor-in-Chief of *Today's Zaman*, Istanbul, 24 February 2014.

Ertugrul Kurkcu, deputy and former co-chairman of the People's Democratic Party (HDP), Ankara, 9 November 2013.

Etyem Mahcupyan, columnist for *Aksam*, Istanbul, 5 November 2013.

Nuray Mert, columnist for *Hurriyet Daily News*, Istanbul, 4 November 2013.

Falah Mustafa, Minister and Head of Foreign Relations Department, Kurdistan Regional Government, London, 10 April 2014.

Omer Onhon, Deputy Undersecretary of the Turkish Ministry of Foreign Affairs, Ankara, 8 November 2013.

Ergun Ozbudun, Professor of Constitutional Law, Istanbul Sehir University, Istanbul, 21 December 2015.

Nihat Ali Ozcan, retired Major in the Turkish armed forces, security expert at the Ankara-based Economic Policy Research Foundation of Turkey (TEPAV), Ankara, 7 November 2013.

BIBLIOGRAPHY

Garo Paylan, HDP Deputy, Istanbul, 20 December 2015.

Can Peker, Member of Wise Men Committee, former Executive Member of TUSIAD, Chairman of TESEV, Istanbul, 24 February 2014.

Ismail Hakki Pekin, former head of Turkey's General Staff Intelligence Department and Deputy Chair of Vatan Party, Ankara, 22 July 2016.

Sami Selcuk, former First President of the Court of Cassation until 2002, Ankara, 8 November 2013.

Alper Sen, Video Documentation Collective, Istanbul, 23 February 2014.

Abdullatif Sener, former Deputy Prime Minister (2002–7), Ankara, 8 November 2013.

Nedim Sener, journalist for *Posta*, Istanbul, 24 February 2014.

Ozden Sener, Chairman of the Ankara Association of Medicine, Ankara, 22 February 2014.

Ismail Mesut Sezgin, Director at the Centre for Hizmet Studies, Ankara, 8 August 2016.

Mustafa Sonmez, Istanbul-based *Economist*, Istanbul, 24 February 2014.

Sadettin Tantan, former Interior Minister (1999–2001), Istanbul, 15 February 2014.

Hikmet Sami Turk, former DSP Justice Minister (1999–2002) and Defence Minister (1999), London (by telephone), 7 January 2014.

Ozturk Turkdogan, President of Human Rights Association, Ankara, 7 November 2013.

Celal Ulgen, lawyer for many of the accused in the Ergenekon and Balyoz trials, Istanbul, 6 November 2013.

Husseyin Yilmaz, Deputy Head of the Huda Party, Diyarbakir, 19 February 2014.

Ihsan Yilmaz, a self-declared Gulen follower who teaches at the Gulenist Fatih University, Istanbul, 15 February 2014.

Sedat Yurtdas, former Deputy for the People's Labor Party (HEP), Diyarbakir, 18 February 2014.

Several of our interviewees expressed a wish to remain anonymous. In respect for their wishes, they have been cited as follows:

"Ozgur ", member of the Besiktas Carsi, Istanbul, 5 November 2013.

Executive Board Member of the Union of Chambers and Commodity Exchanges of Turkey (TOBB), Istanbul, 11 December 2015.

Retired senior officer from the intelligence service, Turkey, 10 September 2014.

Veteran journalist reporting from south-east Turkey, Diyarbakir, 18 February 2014.

Documents and Official Publications / Reports

AKP, "International Symposium on Conservatism and Democracy" (Ankara: AK Parti Yayınları, 2004).

BIBLIOGRAPHY

Constitution of the Republic of Turkey, Ankara, 1982.

Council of the European Union, "Copenhagen European Council, 12 and 13 December: Presidency Conclusions", Brussels, 29 January 2003, Polgen 84, 15917/02.

European Commission, "Regular Report on Turkey's Progress Towards Accession", Brussels, 9 October 2002, SEC (2002) 1412.

European Commission, "Regular Report on Turkey's Progress Towards Accession", Brussels, 6 October 2004, SEC (2004) 1201.

European Commission, "Turkey: 2005 Progress Report", Brussels, 9 November 2005, SEC (2005) 1426.

European Commission, "Turkey 2011 Progress Report", Brussels, 12 October 2011, SEC (2011) 1201 final.

European Commission, "Turkey 2012 Progress Report", Brussels, 10 October 2012, SWD (2012) 336 final.

European Commission, "Turkey 2013 Progress Report", Brussels, 16 October 2013, SWD (2013) 417 final.

IMF, "Staff Report For the 3024 Article IV Consultation", 3 November 2014, http://www.imf.org/external/pubs/ft/scr/2014/cr14329.pdf (last visited 31/03/2016).

KONDA, "Gezi Report: Public Perceptions of the 'Gezi Protests'. Who were the people at Gezi Park?", 5 June 2014.

OECD, "Economic Policy Reforms 2013: Going for Growth", Paris, 2013.

OSCE, Office for Democratic Institutions and Human Rights, Limited Election Observation Mission, Republic of Turkey, "Presidential Election, 10 August 2014: Interim Report", Ankara, 31 July 2014.

————, Office for Democratic Institutions and Human Rights, International Election

Observation Mission, "Republic of Turkey—Parliamentary Elections, 7 June 2015, Statement of Preliminary Findings and Conclusions", Ankara, 8 June 2015.

Turkish Parliament Archives, "Türkiye Cumhuriyeti Milletvekili Genel Seçimleri 1995 Yılı Genel Seçimlerinde Partilerin Aldıkları Oylar ve Oranları", http://www.tbmm.gov.tr/develop/owa/secimler.secimdeki_partiler?p_secim_yili=1995 (last visited 19/10/2013).

Turkish Penal Code, Part 3, 26 September 2004, available at http://www.tbmm.gov.tr/kanunlar/k5237.html (last visited 27/09/2014).

Turkish Statistical Institute, "Foreign Trade Statistics", http://www.turkstat.gov.tr/PreTablo.do?alt_id=1046 (last visited 28/09/2016).

Wikileaks, Cablegate

Cable: 02Ankara8252
Cable: 03Ankara3694

BIBLIOGRAPHY

Cable: 03Ankara4544
Cable: 04ANKARA7211
Cable: 06Ankara5922
Cable: 06Ankara765
Cable: 07Ankara1070
Cable: 07Ankara1071
Cable: 08Ankara1392
Cable: 08Ankara1701
Cable: 09ANKARA321
Cable: 09Ankara368
Cable: 09Ankara1468
Cable: 09Ankara1749
Cable: 10ANKARA87
Cable: 10Ankara120
Cable: 10Ankara294

Newspapers and News Sources

Agence France Presse
Al Arabiya
Al Jazeera
Al-Monitor
Anatolian News Agency
Associated Press International
BBC Monitoring Europe
BBC News
Bianet
Bloomberg News
Bloomberg Business Week
CNN.com
Cumhuriyet
Daily Sabah
Daily Telegraph
Diken
DW Turkish
The Economist
eKurd.net
Financial Times
Forbes
German Times
Global Post
The Globe and the Mail
The Guardian

BIBLIOGRAPHY

Haaretz
Haberturk
HalkTV
Hurriyet
Hurriyet Daily News (formerly *Turkish Daily News*)
The Independent
The Irish Times
Jerusalem Post
Le Monde diplomatique
Los Angeles Times
Milliyet
The Monkey Cage
MSNBC
The New York Times
Newsweek
NTV
The Observer
Radikal
Politico
Reuters
Sabah
Sozcu
Star
Spiegel Online
Taraf
Today's Zaman
The Times
Turkey Review
T24
Vatan
Vox World
The Wall Street Journal
The Wall Street Journal Blog
The Wall Street Journal Turkish
Washington Post
Worldbulletin
Yeni Akit
Yeni Safak
Zaman

Press Releases

Amnesty International, "Turkey should immediately reverse its 'draconian' Twitter ban", 21 March 2014.

294

BIBLIOGRAPHY

Amnesty International, "Turkey: Independent monitors must be allowed to access detainees amid torture allegations", 24 July 2016.

Human Rights Watch, "What is Turkey's Hizbullah?", 16 February 2000.

Human Rights Watch, "Turkey: Outspoken Turkish-Armenian Journalist Murdered", 20 January 2007.

————, "Turkey: President Should Veto Judiciary Law", 21 February 2014.

————, "Turkey: End Prosecutions for Insulting the President", 29 April 2015.

IMF Turkey, "Concluding Statement of the 2014 Article IV Mission", 24 September 2014.

Istanbul Doctors Association, "Biber Gazi Silah Olarak Kullaniliyor", 28 January 2014.

PEN International, "PEN International applauds the publication of seized manuscript as Turkish writers rally around imprisoned journalist", 18 November 2011, http://www.pen-international.org/newsitems/pen-international-applauds-the-publication-of-seized-manuscript-as-turkish-writers-rally-around-imprisoned-journalist/?print=print (last visited 27/09/2014).

Presidency of the Republic of Turkey, "President Erdoğan Address to Mukhtars at the 3rd Meeting of Municipal Headmen, (Üçüncü Muhtarlar Toplantısı'nda Yaptıkları Konuşma)", 24 February 2015, http://www.tccb.gov.tr/konusmalar/353/2997/ucuncu-muhtarlar-toplantisinda-yaptiklari-konusma.html (last visited 26/02/2016).

Presidency of Republic of Turkey, "Recep Tayyip Erdogan, Speech at Turkish Military Academy (Harp Akademileri Komutanlığı'nı Ziyaretleri Vesilesiyle Yaptıkları Konuşma)", 19 March 2015, http://www.tccb.gov.tr/konusma-lar/353/29807/harp-akademileri-komutanligini-ziyaretleri-vesilesiyle-yaptiklari-konusma.html (last visited 26/02/2016).

Reporters Without Borders for Press Freedom, "Number of journalists convicted in Ergenekon trial rises to 20", 7 August 2013.

Online Sources

AKP, "58th Government Programme, presented by Prime Minister Abdullah Gül at the Turkish Parliament", 24 November 2002, https://www.akparti.org.tr/upload/documents/58inci-hukumet-programi.pdf (last visited 26/03/2016).

————, "AK Parti Programme", undated, http://www.akparti.org.tr/site/akparti/parti-programi#bolum (last visited 29/09/2014).

————, "Huzur ve İstikrarla Türkiye'nin Yol Haritası, November 1, 2015 Elections, Party Manifesto", https://www.akparti.org.tr/site/haberler/iste-ak-partinin-secim-beyannamesi/78619#1 (last visited 03/01/2016).

————, "Ruling AK Party unveils manifesto for June elections", 15 April

BIBLIOGRAPHY

2015, https://www.akparti.org.tr/english/haberler/ruling-ak-party-unveils-manifesto-for-june-elections/73321#1 (last visited 26/02/2016).

CIA, "The World Factbook: Turkey", https://www.cia.gov/library/publications/the-world-factbook/geos/tu.html (last visited 01/10/2014).

ComScore, "It's a Social World: Top 10 Need-to-Knows About Social Networking and Where It's Headed", 21 December 2011, http://www.comscore.com/Insights/Presentations-and-Whitepapers/2011/it_is_a_social_world_top_10_need-to-knows_about_social_networking (last visited 02/10/2014).

Dani Rodrik, "Turkish Economic Myths", 16 April 2015, http://rodrik.typepad.com/dani_rodriks_weblog/2015/04/turkish-economic-myths.html (last visited 31/03/2016).

ENV.net, "TEMA Foundation announced its Report on Istanbul Projects", 26 March 2014, http://www.env-net.org/tema-foundation-announced-its-report-on-istanbul-projects/# (last visited 11/04/2014).

European Commission, "Eurobarometer 63: Public Opinion in the European Union, National Report, Executive Summary Turkey", Spring 2005, http://ec.europa.eu/public_opinion/archives/eb/eb63/eb63_exec_tr.pdf (last visited 01/04/2016).

———, "Eurobarometer 67: Public Opinion in the European Union, National Report, Executive Summary, Turkey", Spring 2007, http://ec.europa.eu/public_opinion/archives/eb/eb67/eb67_tr_exec.pdf (last visited 01/04/2016).

———, "Enlargement, EU Turkey Relations", http://ec.europa.eu/enlargement/candidate-countries/turkey/eu_turkey_relations_en.htm (last visited 31/03/2016).

GlobalSecurity.org, "Kongra-Gel; Kurdistan Freedom and Democracy Congress (KADEK); Kurdistan Workers' Party (PKK)", http://www.globalsecurity.org/military/world/para/pkk.htm (last visited 26/05/2014).

Gulen Movement, "Brief History of the Gulen Movement", undated, http://www.gulenmovement.us/gulen-movement/brief-history-of-gulen-movement (last visited 27/09/2014).

Index Mundi, "Turkey Demographics Profile 2014", http://www.indexmundi.com/turkey/demographics_profile.html (last visited 27/09/2014).

———, "Turkey Unemployment Rate", http://www.indexmundi.com/g/g.aspx?c=tu&v=74 (last visited 27/09/2014).

Magfi Egilmez, "Türkiye'nin Altın Üretimi, Tüketimi, İthalatı ve İhracatı ", 23 January 2013, http://www.mahfiegilmez.com/2012/10/turkiyenin-altn-uretimi-tuketimi.html (last visited 31/03/2016).

Open Net Initiative, "Turkey", 18 December 2010, https://opennet.net/research/profiles/turkey (last visited 15/04/2014).

PWG, "Payback time! Emerging markets and the rising dollar", Global

BIBLIOGRAPHY

Economy Watch, May 2015, http://www.pwc.com/gx/en/issues/economy/global-economy-watch/emerging-markets-and-rising-dollar.html (last visited 31/03/2016).

Recep Tayyip Erdogan, "Democracy in the Middle East, Pluralism in Europe: Turkish View", address at Harvard University, Kennedy School of Government, 30 January 2003, http://belfercenter.ksg.harvard.edu/files/erdogan-%20harvard%20prepared%20remarks.pdf (last visited 29/09/2014).

Statista, "Turkey: degree of urbanization from 2002 to 2012", http://www.statista.com/statistics/255487/urbanization-in-turkey/ (last visited 27/09/2014).

TOBB, "Economic Report 2008", http://www.tobb.org.tr/Documents/yayinlar/ekonomik%20rapor.pdf (last visited 31/03/2016), p. 15.

Turkish Statistical Institute, http://www.turkstat.gov.tr/Start.do (last visited 28/09/2016).

UNHCR, "Syria Regional Refugee Response, inter-agency information sharing portal", undated, http://data.unhcr.org/syrianrefugees/country.php?id=224 (last visited 21/03/2016).

Books, Journal Articles and Papers

Jacob Abdai, "Israel and Turkey: From Covert to Overt Relations", *Journal of Conflict Studies*, Vol. XV, No. 2, 1995.

Morton Abramowitz and Henri Barkey, "Turkey's Transformers: The AKP Sees Big", *Foreign Affairs*, Vol. 88, No. 6, November/December 2009.

———, "Turkey's Political Revolution", *Wall Street Journal*, 22 March 2010.

Gulseren Adakli, "Capital and Capitalists in Turkey: Media capital and ultra-cross media ownership", *Perspective: Political Analyses and Commentary*, Issue 8, April 2004.

Feroz Ahmad, *The Making of Modern Turkey* (London: Routledge, 1993).

———, *Turkey: The Quest for Identity*, (Oxford: Oneworld, 2003).

Ismet Akca, Ahmet Berken and Baris Alp Ozden, *Turkey Reframed* (London and New York: Pluto Press, 2014).

Yaman Akdeniz, "Report of the OSCE Representative on Freedom of the Media on Turkey and Internet Censorship", Organization for Security and Co-operation in Europe, Representative on Freedom of the Media, 2010.

Yalcın Akdogan, *AK Parti ve Muhafazakar Demokrasi*, (Ankara: Alfa Yayınları, 2004).

———, "Ellerinde nur mu var, topuz mu?", *Star Gazetesi*, 24 December 2013.

H. Akkaya, and J. Jongerden, "The PKK in the 2000s: Continuity through breaks?" M. Casier & J. Jongerden, J. (Eds) *Nationalisms and Politics in Turkey: Political Islam, Kemalism and the Kurdish issue* (London: Routledge, 2011).

BIBLIOGRAPHY

Ismail Aksel, *Turkish Judicial System Bodies, Duties and Officials*, (Ankara: Ministry of Justice, Department for Strategy Development, 2013).

Murat Akser and Banu Baybars-Hawks, "Media and Democracy in Turkey: Toward a Model of Neoliberal Media Autocracy ", *Middle East Journal of Culture and Communication*, Vol. 5, No. 3, 2012.

Sina Aksin, *Turkey: From Empire to Revolutionary Republic* (New York: New York University Press, 2007).

Kenan Aksu (Ed.), *Turkey: A Regional Power in the Making* (Newcastle: Cambridge Scholars, 2013).

Cengiz Aktar, "The truth about Operation Shah Euphrates ", *Al Jazeera*, 23 February 2015.

Mustafa Akyol, "Turkey's Liberal Divide", *Al-Monitor*, 11 August 2012.

———, "Turkey Condemns Egypt's Coup", *Al-Monitor*, 21 August 2013.

———, "Is Erdogan a Democrat?", *The New York Times*, 1 November 2013.

Taha Akyol, "Cumhurbaskani ve Hukuk ", *Hurriyet*, 27 June 2014.

Alya Albayrak, "Turkish Colonel, Journalist Fired Over Kurdish Killings", *The Wall Street Journal Blog*, Emerging Europe, 9 January 2012, http://blogs. wsj.com/emergingeurope/2012/01/09/turkish-colonel-journalist-fired-over-kurdish-killings (last visited 13/10/2016).

Karin Alexander, "Social media's role in Turkey's dissent", *New Internationalist Blog*, 4 July 2013, http://newint.org/blog/2013/07/04/social-media-turkey (last visited 13/10/2016).

Hakan Altinay, "Turkey's Soft Power: An Unpolished Gem or an Elusive Mirage?" *Insight Turkey*, Vol. 10, No. 2, 2008.

Benli Meliha Altunisik, "The Turkish Model and Democratization in the Middle East", *Arab Studies Quarterly*, Vol. 27. No. 1/2, Winter/Spring, 2005.

———, "The Possibilities and Limits of Turkey's Soft Power", *Insight Turkey*, Vol. 10, No. 2, 2008.

Benli Meliha Altunisik and Lenore G. Martin, "Making Sense of Turkish Foreign Policy in the Middle East under AKP", *Turkish Studies*, Vol. 12, No. 4, December 2011.

Benli Meliha Altunisik and Ozlem Tur, *Turkey: Challenges of Continuity and Change* (London: Routledge, 2005).

———, "From Distant Neighbors to Partners? Changing Syrian–Turkish Relations", *Security Dialogue*, Vol. 37, No. 2, 2006.

Douglas J. Amy, *Behind the Ballot Box: A Citizen's Guide to Voting Systems* (Westport, CT: Praeger, 2000).

Ramazan Ara, *The Formation of Kurdishness in Turkey: Political Violence, Fear and Pain* (London: Routledge, 2014).

Bulent Aras, "Davutoğlu Era in Turkish Foreign Policy", *SETA Publications*, Vol: 32, May, 2009.

BIBLIOGRAPHY

Bulent Aras and Gokhan Bacik, 'The Mystery of Turkish Hizballah', *Middle East Policy,Vol. IX, No. 2, June 2002*.

Bulent Aras and Hakan Fidan, "Turkey and Eurasia: Frontiers of a New Geogrpahic Imagination", *New Perspectives on Turkey*, No. 40, 2009.

Bulent Aras and Rabia Karakaya Polat, "From Conflict to Cooperation: Desecuritization of Turkey's Relations with Syria and Iran", *Security Dialogue,* Vol. 39, No. 5, 2008.

Ramazan Aras, "State sovereignty and the politics of fear: ethnography of political violence and the Kurdish struggle in Turkey ", in Cengiz Gunes, and Welat Zeydanlioglu (Eds), *The Kurdish Question in Turkey: New perspectives on violence, representation and reconciliation* (London: Routledge, 2014).

Fulya Atacan, "Explaining Religious Politics at the Crossroad: AKP-SP ", *Turkish Studies,* Vol. 6, No. 2, June 2005.

Yildiz Atasoy (ed.), *Global Economic Crisis and the Politics of Diversity*, (New York: Palgrave Macmillan, 2014).

Tayfun Atay, "Reflections on the Gezi Park incident ", *Insight Turkey*, Vol. 15, No. 3, 2013.

Altay Atli, "Businessman as Diplomats: The Role of Business Associations in Turkey's Foreign Policy", *Insight Turkey,* Vol. 13, No. 1, 2011.

Gamze Avcı, "The Justice and Development Party and the EU: Political Pragmatism in a Changing Environment", *South European Politics and Society*, 16(3), 2011.

Sencer Ayata, "Patronage, Party, and State: The Politicization of Islam in Turkey", *Middle East Journal,* Vol. 50, No. 1, Winter 1996.

Meltem Muftuler Bac, "Turkey's Political Reforms and the Impact of the European Union", *South European Society and Politics,* Vol. 10, No. 1, 2005.

————, "Turkey's Accession to the European Union: The Impact of the EU's Internal Dynamics ", *International Studies Perspectives*, 9, 2008

Osman Balaban, "The negative effects of construction boom on urban planning and environment in Turkey: Unraveling the role of the public sector", *Habitat International,* Vol. 36, No. 1, January 2012.

Pablo Barbera and Megan Metzger, "A Breakout Role for Twitter? Extensive Use of Social Media in the Absence of Traditional Media by Turks in Turkish in Taksim Square Protests", *The Monkey Cage*, 1 June 2013, http://themon-keycage.org/2013/06/01/a-breakout-role-for-twitter-extensive-use-of-social-media-in-the-absence-of-traditional-media-by-turks-in-turkish-in-taksim-square-protests (last visited 28/09/2016).

Mehmet Bardakci, "Coup Plots and the Transformation of Civil–Military Relations in Turkey under AKP Rule ", *Turkish Studies*, 14:3, 2003, pp. 413–15.

Henri J. Barkey, "Turkey's Kurdish Dilemma, *Survival,* Vol. 35, No. 4, Winter 1993.

BIBLIOGRAPHY

————, "The Struggles of a 'Strong' State ", *Journal of International Affairs*, Vol. 51, No. 1, Fall 2000.

————, "Turkey and Iraq: The making of a partnership ", *Turkish Studies*, Vol. 12, No. 4, December 2011.

————, "Turkish-Iranian Competition after the Arab Spring", *Survival: Global Politics and Strategy*, Vol. 54, No. 6, November 2012.

————(Ed.), *Reluctant Neighbour: Turkey's Role in the Middle East* (Washington DC: US Institute of Peace Press, 1996).

Henri J. Barkey and Graham E. Fuller, "Turkey's Kurdish Question: Critical Turning Points and Missed Opportunities ", *Middle East Journal*, Vol. 51, No. 1, Winter 1997.

Greg Barton, Paul Weller, Ihsan Yilmaz (eds), *Muslim World in Transition: Contributions of the Gülen Movement* (London: Bloomsbury, 2013).

Cem Baslevent and Ali T. Akcura, "Micro Evidence on Inter-Party Vote Movements in Turkey: Who Voted for AKP in 2002?", Munich Personal RePEc Archive Paper, No. 11683, November 2008.

Yavuz Baydar, "Erdogan's Democracy Package Gets Cool Reception", *Al-Monitor*, 30 September 2013.

Burak Bekdil, "The Turkish Army: Twice a loser ", *Hurriyet Daily News*, 3 August 2016.

Christopher de Bellaigue, *Rebel Land: Among Turkey's Forgotten People* (London: Bloomsbury, 2009).

Ofra Bengio, *The Turkish-Israeli Relationship: Changing Ties of Middle East Outsiders* (New York: Palgrave Macmillan, 2004).

————, "Altercating Interests and Orientations between Israel and Turkey: A View from Israel", *Insight Turkey*, Vol. 11, No. 2, 2009.

Paul Benjamin, "Istanbul's recent rapid transit projects remain areas of contention", *Today's Zaman*, 23 February 2014.

Gila Benmayor, "Kanal İstanbul, at all costs", *Hurriyet Daily News*, 21 May 2013.

Nimet Beriker-Atiyas, "The Kurdish Conflict in Turkey: Issues, Parties and Prospects ", *Security Dialogue*, Vol. 28, No. 4, April 2011.

Claire Berlinski, "Who Planned Turkey's Coup?", *City Journal*, 20 July 2016.

Pinar Bilgin, "Turkey's changing security discourses: The challenge of globalization", *European Journal of Political Research*, Vol. 44, No. 1, 2005.

Mirela Bogdani, *Turkey and the Dilemma of EU Accession: When Religion meets Politics* (London: I.B. Tauris, 2011).

Suha Bolukbasi, "Behind the Turkish-Israeli Alliance", *Journal of Palestine Studies*, Vol. 29, No. 1, 1999.

Rahman G. Bonab, "Turkey's Emerging Role as a Mediator on Iran's Nuclear Activities", *Insight Turkey*, Vol. 11, No. 3, 2009.

Yucel Bozdaglioglu, *Turkish Foreign Policy and Turkish Identity: A Constructivist Approach* (New York: Routledge, 2003).

BIBLIOGRAPHY

Ayse Bugra, "The Immoral Economy of Housing in Turkey", *International Journal of Urban and Regional Research*, Vol. XXII, No. 2, June 1998.

————, "Class, Culture and State: An Analysis of Interest Representation by Two Turkish Business Associations", *International Journal of Middle East Studies*, Vol. 30, No. 4, November 1998.

Ayse Bugra and Osman Savaskan, "Yerel Sanayi ve Bugünün Türkiyesi'nde İş Dünyası", *Toplum Bilim*, No. 118, 2010.

————, *New Capitalism In Turkey: The Relationship Between Politics, Religion and Business* (Cheltenham: Edward Elgar, 2014).

John Bulloch and Harvey Morris, *No Friends but the Mountains: The Tragic History of the Kurds* (London: Viking, 1992).

Soner Cagaptay, "The November 2002 Elections and Turkey's New Political Era", *MERIA Journal*, Vol. 6, No. 4, December 2002.

————, "Turkey's Local Elections: Liberal Middle-Class Voters Abandon AKP", *Washington Institute of Near East Policy: Policywatch #1500*, 30 March 2009.

————, "The End of Pax Adana", *Hurriyet Daily News*, 25 August 2012.

Soner Cagaptay, H. Akin Unver, and Hale Arifagaoglu, "Will the Turkish Constitutional Court Ban the AKP?", Washington Institute of Near East Policy, Policy Watch 1355, 19 March 2008.

Soner Cagaptay and Rüya Perincek, "No Women, No Europe", *Hurriyet Daily News*, 20 January 2010.

Zeyneb Çagliyan–Içener, "The Justice and Development Party's Conception of 'Conservative Democracy': Invention or Reinterpretation?", *Turkish Studies*, Vol. 10, No. 4, 2009.

Rusen Cakir, "The Kurdish Political Movement and the 'Democratic Opening'", *Insight Turkey*, Vol. 12, No. 2, 2010.

Cenap Cakmak and Gokhan Guneysu, "Turkish-American Relations During the Obama Era: Unfulfilled Expectations", *Turkish Studies*, Vol. 14, No. 2, June 2013.

Cengiz Candar, "The Kurdish Question: The Reasons and Fortunes of the 'Opening'", *Insight Turkey*, Vol. 11, No. 4, 2009.

————, "'Leaving the Mountain': How may the PKK lay down arms? Freeing the Kurdish Question from Violence ", Turkiye Ekonomik ve Sosyal Etudler Vakfi (TESEV), March 2012.

————, "Ocalan Signals Openness to Talks With Turkey on Kurdish Issue", *Al-Monitor*, 3 March 2013.

————, "The Erdogan tapes ", *Al Monitor*, 27 February 2014.

————, "Under pressure from Turkey, UN excludes PYD from Syria talks", *Al-Monitor*, 29 January 2016.

Ali Carkoglu, "Turkey's November 2002 Elections: A New Beginning?", *MERIA Journal*, Vol. 6, No. 4, 2002.

BIBLIOGRAPHY

Ali Carkoglu and Ersin Kalaycioglu, *Turkish Democracy Today: Elections, Protest and Stability in an Islamic Society* (London: I.B. Tauris, 2007).

Marlies Casier, "Designated Terrorists: The Kurdistan Workers' Party and its Struggle to (Re)Gain Political Legitimacy", *Mediterranean Politics*, Vol. 15, No. 3, 2010.

M. Casier and J. Jongerden (Eds), *Nationalisms and politics in Turkey: Political Islam, Kemalism and the Kurdish issue* (London: Routledge, 2011),

Gamze Cavdar, "Islamist *New Thinking* in Turkey: A model for Political Learning?", *Political Science Quarterly*, Vol. 121, No. 3, 2006.

Erbatur Cavusoglu and Julia Strutz, "We'll come and Demolish Your House!: The role of spatial (Re)-Production in the neoliberal hegemonic politics of Turkey ", Ismet Akca, Ahmet Berken and Baris Alp Ozden, *Turkey Reframed* (London: Pluto Press, 2014).

Erol Cebeci and Kadir Ustun, "The Syrian Quagmire: What's Holding Turkey Back?", *Insight Turkey*, Vol. 14, No. 2, 2012.

Firat Cengiz and Lars Hoffmann, *Rethinking Conditionality: Turkey's EU Accession and the Kurdish Question*, TILEC Discussion Paper, 12 March 2012.

Orhan Kemal Cengiz, "European Court Presses Erdogan on Free Speech ", *Al-Monitor*, 25 July 2013.

Gokhan Cetinsaya, "Essential Friends and Natural Enemies: The Historic Roots of Turkish-Iranian Relations", *MERIA Journal*, Vol. 7, No. 3, 2003.

Alexander Christie-Miller, "Erdogan's Grand Construction Projects are Tearing Istanbul Apart ", *Newsweek*, 31 July 2014.

Umit Cizre, "Demythologizing the National Security Concept: The Case of Turkey", *Middle East Journal*, Vol. 57, No. 2, 2003.

————, "Problems of Democratic Governance of Civil-Military Relations in Turkey and the European Enlargement Zone", *European Journal of Political Research*, Vol. 43, No. 1, January 2004.

————, "The Emergence of the Government's Perspective on the Kurdish Issue", *Insight Turkey*, Vol. 11, No. 4, 2009.

Committee to Protect Journalists, "Turkey's Press Freedom Crisis: The Dark Days of Jailing Journalists and Criminalizing Dissent", New York, October 2012.

Patrick Cockburn, "Isis in Kobani: Turkey ignores Kurdish fury as militants close in on capturing the town", *The Independent*, 9 October 2014.

Ariel Cohen, "Obama's Best Friend? The Alarming Evolution of US-Turkish Relations", *Middle East Security and Policy Studies*, No. 10, The Begin-Sadat Center for Strategic Studies, May 2013.

Steven A. Cook, *Ruling But Not Governing: The Military and Political Development in Egypt, Algeria, and Turkey* (Baltimore, MD: Johns Hopkins University Press, 2007).

————, "Turkey's War at Home", *Survival: Global Politics and Strategy*, Vol. 51, No. 5, September 2009.

BIBLIOGRAPHY

————, "The USA, Turkey and the Middle East: Continuities, Challenges and Opportunities", *Turkish Studies*, Vol. 12, No. 4, December 2011.

————, "Emperor Erdogan ", *Politico*, 3 Februray 2015.

————, "Turkey has had lots of coups: Here's why this one failed", *Washington Post*, 16 July 2016.

Steven A. Cook and Elizabeth Sherwood-Randall, "Generating Momentum for a New Era in US-Turkey Relations", *Council of Foreign Relations Press*, June 2006.

Erik Cornell, *Turkey in the 21ˢᵗ Century: Opportunities, Challenges, Threats* (Richmond: Curzon, 2001).

Svante E. Cornell, "The Land of Many Crossroads: The Kurdish Question in Turkish Politics", *Orbis* 45, no. 1, Winter 2001.

Vahap Coskun, "Election in southeast and eastern Anatolia", *Today's Zaman*, 13 June 2011.

Nur Bilge Criss, "The Nature of PKK Terrorism in Turkey", *Studies in Conflict and Terrorism*, Vol. 18, No. 1, 1995.

Tulin Daloglu, "Turkey's top court upholds separation of powers", *Al Monitor*, 11 April 2014.

Nicholas Danforth, "Ideology and Pragmatism in Turkish Foreign Policy: From Ataturk to the AKP", *Turkish Policy Quarterly*, Vol. 7, No. 3, Fall 2008.

Ahmet Davutoglu, "Medeniyetin Ben İdraki (Self-Cognition of Civilizations)", *Divan*, Vol. 1, 1997.

————, "The Clash of Interest: An Explanation of the World (Dis)Order", *Perceptions: Journal of International Affairs*, Vol. 2, No. 4, December 1997 to February 1998.

————, *Stratejik Derinlik / Türkiye'nin Uluslararası Konumu (The Strategic Depth: The Turkish International Location)* (Istanbul: Kure Yayınları, 2001).

————, "Türkiye Merkez Ülke Olmalı" ("Turkey should be the centre country"), *Radikal*, 26 February 2004.

————, "Turkey's Central Role", *Hurriyet Daily News*, May 4, 2009.

————, "Turkish Foreign Policy and the EU in 2010", *Turkish Policy Quarterly*, Vol. 8, No. 3, Fall 2009.

————, "The Three major Earthquakes in the International System and Turkey", *The International Spectator*, Vol. 48, No. 2, June 2013.

Olivier Decottignies and Soner Cagaptay, "Turkey's New Base in Qatar ", *Washington Institute for Near East Policy*, PolicyWatch 2545, 11 January 2016.

Neslihan Demirtas, *Social Spatialization in a Turkish Squatter Settlement: The Dualism of Strategy and Tactic Reconsidered* (Frankfurt: Lang, Europäische Hochschulschriften, 2009).

Neslihan Demirtas and Seher Sen, "Varos identity: The redefinition of low income settlements in Turkey", *Middle Eastern Studies*, Vol. 43, No. 1, 2007.

Thomas Diez and Barry Rubin, "The European Union and Turkey", *Survival*, Vol. 41, No. 1, 1999.

BIBLIOGRAPHY

William J. Dobson, *The Dictator's Learning Curve: Inside the Global Battle for Democracy* (London: Harvill Secker, 2012).

Erhan Dogan, "The Historical and Discoursive Roots of the Justice and Development Party's EU Stance", *Turkish Studies*, Vol. 6, No. 3, 2005.

Daniel Dombey, "Erdogan's grand ambitions for Istanbul", *Washington Post*, 31 August 2012.

——, "Turkey posts larger-than-expected deficit of $65bn", *Financial Times*, 13 Februray 2013.

Bulent Duru and Ilhan Uzgel (et al. eds), *AKP Kitabı (AKP Book)*, (Istanbul: Phoenix, 2010).

Senem Aydın-Duzgit, "No Crisis, No Change: The Third AKP Victory in the June 2011 Parliamentary Elections in Turkey", *South European Society and Politics*, 17:2, 2012.

Helen Rose Ebaugh, *The Gulen Movement: A Sociological Analysis of a Civic Movement Rooted in Moderate Islam* (Dordrecht: Springer, 2010).

Vera Eccarius-Kelly, *The Militant Kurds: A Duel Strategy for Freedom* (Santa Barbara: Praeger, 2011).

Mine Eder, "Implementing Economic Criteria of EU Membership: How Difficult is it for Turkey?", *Turkish Studies*, Vol. 4, No. 1, 2003.

Banu Eligur, "The Changing Face of Turkish Politics: Turkey's July 2007 Parliamentary Elections", *Middle East Brief No. 22: Crown Center for Middle East Studies, Brandeis University*, November 2007.

——, "Crisis in Turkish-Israeli Relations (December 2008–June 2011): From Partnership to Emnity ", *Middle Eastern Studies*, Vol. 48, No. 4, May 2012, p. 431.

Ayda Eraydin and Tuna Tasan-Kok, "State Response to Contemporary Urban Movements in Turkey: A Critical Overview of State Entrepreneurialism and Authoritarian Interventions", *Antipode*, Vol. 46, No. 1, 2014.

Dogu Ergil, "The Kurdish Question in Turkey", *Journal of Democracy*, Vol. 11, No. 3, July 2000.

Tahire Erman and E. Goker, "Alevi Politics in Contemporary Turkey", *Middle Eastern Studies*, Vol. 36, No. 4, 2000.

Dexter Filkins, "Letter From Turkey: The Deep State", *The New Yorker*, 12 March 2012.

Carter Vaughn Findley, *The Turks in World History* (Oxford: Oxford University Press, 2005).

Andrew Finkel, "Who Guards the Turkish Press? A Perspective on Press Corruption in Turkey", *Journal of International Affairs*, No. 54, No. 1, Fall 2000.

Ed Finn, "Power of social media: Erdogan's smart use of a smartphone", *CNN. com*, 18 July 2016.

Freedom House, *Freedom in the World 2012*: Turkey, http://www.freedomhouse.org/report/freedom-world/2012/turkey#.VCyE0ldCxtw (last visited 01/10/2014).

————, *Freedom on the Net 2013: A Global Assessment of Internet and Digital Media*, 3 October 2013.

————, *Democracy in Crisis: Corruption, Media, and Power in Turkey*, Freedom House Special Report, New York, 2014

Graham E. Fuller, *The New Turkish Republic: Turkey as a Pivotal State in the Muslim World* (Washington DC: United States Institute of Peace Press, 2008).

Graham E. Fuller and Ian O. Lesser, et al, *Turkey's New Geopolitics: From the Balkans to Western China* (Boulder: Westview, 1993).

Merella Galletti, "The Kurdish Issue in Turkey", The *International Spectator: Italian Journal of International Affairs*, Vol. 34, No. 1, Jan-March 1999.

Thomas Gibbons-Neff, "How the U.S. Military scrambled in Turkey to keep working during the coup attempt ", *Washington Post*, 2 August 2016.

Ayla Gol, *Turkey facing east: Islam, modernity and foreign policy* (Manchester: Manchester University Press, 2013).

Nilufer Gole, "Gezi—Anatomy of a Public Square Movement", *Insight Turkey*, Vol. 15, No. 3, 2013.

Vecdi Gonul, "Turkey-NATO Relations and NATO's New Strategic Concept", *Turkish Policy Quarterly*, Vol. 9, No. 1, 2010.

Philip Gordon and Omer Taspinar, "Turkey on the Brink", *The Washington Quarterly*, Vol. 29, No. 3 (Summer 2006).

Alper Gormus, *Imaj ve Hakikat: Bir Kuvvet Komutaninin Kaleminden Turk Ordusu*, (Istanbul: Etkilesim, 2012).

Jurgen Gottschlich, "The New Sultan of Turkey?", *German Times*, April 2010.

Istar B. Gozaydın, "The Fethullah Gülen movement and politics in Turkey: a chance for democratization or a Trojan horse?", *Democratization*, Vol. 16, No. 6, 2009.

Anna Grabolle-Celiker, *Kurdish Life in Contemporary Turkey: Migration, Gender and Ethnic Identity* (London: I.B. Tauris, 2013).

Ioannis N. Grigoriadis, *Trials of Europeanization: Turkish Political Culture and the European Union* (New York: Palgrave Macmillan, 2009).

Abdullah Gül, "Turkey's Role in a Changing Middle East Environment", *Mediterranean Quarterly*, Vol. 15, No. 1, 2004.

Murat Gul, John Dee and Cahide Nur Cunuk, "Istanbul's Taksim Square and Gezi Park: The Place of Protest and the Ideology of Place", *Journal of Architecture and Urbanism*, Vol. 38, No. 1, 2014.

Fethullah Gulen, "Fethullah Gulen: I Condemn All Threats to Turkey's Democracy", *New York Times*, 25 July 2016.

Sebnem Gumuscu and Deniz Sert, "The Power of the Devout Bourgeoisie: The Case of the Justice and Development Party in Turkey", *Middle Eastern Studies*, 2009, Vol. 45, No. 6, 2009.

BIBLIOGRAPHY

Cengiz Gunes, *The Kurdish National Movement in Turkey: From protest to resistance* (New York: Routledge, 2012).

Cengiz Gunes and Weal Zeydanlioglu (Eds), *The Kurdish Quesiton in Turkey: New perspectives on violence, representation and reconciliation* (London: Routledge, 2014).

Aylin Guney and Petek Karatekelioglu, "Turkey's EU Candidacy and Civil-Military Relations: Challenges and Prospects", *Armed Forces and Society*, 31, No. 3, 2005.

Michael M. Gunter, *The Kurds and the Future of Turkey* (New York: St. Martin's Press, 1997).

————, "The continuing Kurdish problem in Turkey after Ocalan's capture ", *Third World Quarterly*, Vol. 21, No 5, 2000.

————, *The Kurds Ascending: The Evolving Solution to the Kurdish Problem in Iraq and Turkey* (Basingstoke: Palgrave Macmillan, 2007).

Gulistan Gurbey and Ferhad Ibrahim, *The Kurdish Conflict in Turkey: Obstacles and Chances for Peace and Democracy* (New York: St Martin's Press, 2000).

Refet S. Gürkaynak and Selin Sayek Böke, "İktidarın Ekonomi Politiği: AKP Döneminde Türkiye Ekonomisi", *Birikim Dergisi*, December 2013.

Michel Gurfinkiel, "Is Turkey Lost?", *Commentary*, March 2007.

Kadri Gursel, "Crackdown shatters AKP 'anti-corruption' taboo", *Al-Monitor*, 19 December 2013.

————, "Turkey's failed coup reveals 'army within an army'", *Al-Monitor*, 22 July 2016.

Yaprak Gursoy, "The changing role of the military in Turkish politics: democratization through coup plots?", *Democratization*, Vol. 19, No. 4, 2012.

William Hale, *Turkish Politics and the Military*, (London and New York: Routledge, 1994).

————, "Human Rights, the European Union and the Turkish Accession Process ", *Turkish Studies*, Vol. 4, No. 1, 2003.

————, *Turkey, the US and Iraq* (London: Saqi, 2007).

————, *Turkish Foreign Policy since 1774* (London: Routledge, 2013).

Leila M. Harris and Mine Islar, "Commodification and Environmental Governance", Yildiz Atasoy (ed.), *Global Economic Crisis and the Politics of Diversity*, (New York: Palgrave Macmillan, 2014).

Mehdi Hasan, "In Turkey the right to free speech is being lost", *The Guardian*, 10 June 2012.

Cemalettin Hasimi, "Mapping the Pathways: Public Perceptions and the Kurdish Question", *Insight Turkey*, Vol. 11, No. 4, 2009.

Joshua D. Hendrick, "Globalization, Islamic activism, and passive revolution in Turkey: the case of Fethullah Gülen", *Journal of Power*, Vol. 2, No. 3, December 2009.

————, "Media Wars and the Gülen Factor in the New Turkey", *Middle East Report 260*, Fall 2011.

Metin Heper, "Islam and Democracy in Turkey: Toward a Reconciliation?", *Middle East Journal*, Vol. 51, No. 1, Winter 1997.

————, "The AKP Government and the Military in Turkey ", *Turkish Studies*, Vol. 6, No. 2, June 2005.

————, "Civil-Military Relations in Turkey: Toward a Liberal Model?", *Turkish Studies*, Vol. 12, No. 2, June 2011.

Metin Heper and Tanel Demirel, "The Press and the Consolidation of Democracy in Turkey", *Middle Eastern Studies*, Vol. 32, No. 2, April 1996.

Metin Heper and Sabri Sayari (eds), *The Routledge Handbook of Modern Turkey*, (New York and Oxon: Routledge, 2012).

Human Rights Watch, *The Kurds of Turkey: Killings, Disappearances and Torture*, New York, March 1993.

————, *Turkey: Forced Displacement of Ethnic Kurds from Southeastern Turkey*, Vol. 6, No. 12, October 1994.

————, *Turkey: Torture and Mistreatment in Pre-trail Detention by Anti-Terror Police*, Vol. 9, No. 4 (D), March 1997.

————, *Still Critical: Prospects in 2005 for Internally Displaced Kurds in Turkey*, Vol. 17, No. 2 (D), March 2005.

————, *Time For Justice: Ending Impunity for Killings and Disappearances in 1990s Turkey*, 3 September 2012.

————, *Turkey: Forced Displacement of Ethnic Kurds from Southeastern Turkey*, Vol. 6, No. 12, October 1994.

Semih Idiz, "Erdogan Denies He is a King", *Al-Monitor*, 31 May 2013.

————, "Turkey under pressure over Jihadists on border ", *Al-Monitor*, 24 January 2014.

Efraim Inbar, *The Israeli-Turkish Entente* (London: King's College Mediterranean Studies, 2001).

Ahmet Insel, "The AKP and Normalizing Democracy in Turkey", *The South Atlantic Quarterly*, Vol. 102, No. 2/3, Spring/Summer 2003.

International Crisis Group, "Turkey: The PKK and a Kurdish Settlement ", *Crisis Group Europe Report N°219*, 11 September 2012.

————, "The Human Cost of the PKK Conflict in Turkey: the Case of Sur ", *Crisis Group Eurpe Briefing No. 80*, Diyarbakir/Istanbul/Brussels, 17 March 2016.

Avi Issacharoff, "For Hamas, lousy deal exposes Turkey as a paper tiger", *Times of Israel*, 27 June 2016.

Gareth Jenkins, *Context and Circumstance: The Turkish Military and Politics*, Adelphi Papers 337 (London: International Institute for Strategic Studies, 2001).

————, "Muslim Democrats in Turkey?", *Survival*, Vol. 45, No. 1, Spring 2003.

———, "Continuity and Change: Prospects for Civil-Military Relations in Turkey", *International Affairs*, Vol. 83, No. 2, 2007.

———, "AKP Forming Closer Links with the Gulen Movement", *Eurasia Daily Monitor*, Volume: 4 Issue: 217, 21 November 2007.

———, "The Politics of Personality: Erdogan's Irascible Authoritarianism", *Turkish Analyst*, 13 February 2009.

———, "Between Fact and Fantasy: Turkey's Ergenekon Investigation", *Silk Road Paper 2009*, Central Asia-Caucasus Institute: Silk Road Studies Program, August 2009.

———, "A House Divided Against Itself: The Deteriorating State of Media Freedom In Turkey", *Turkey Analyst*, Vol. 5, No. 3, 6 February 2012.

———, "The Democratization Package and Erdogan's Hall of Mirrors", *Turkey Analyst*, Vol. 6, No. 8, 9 October 2013.

Dietrich Jung, "Turkey and the Arab World: Historical Narratives and New Political Realities", *Mediterranean Politics*, Vol. 10, No. 1, 2005.

Dietrich Jung and Wolfgang Piccoli, *Turkey at the Crossroads: Ottoman Legacies and the Greater Middle East* (London: Zed Books, 2001).

Burak Kadercan, "The Gezi Park Protests illustrate the fall of the military as a political actor in Turkey", *London School of Economics: European Politics and Policy*, 18 October 2013.

Ersin Kalaycioglu, "Elections and Party Preferences in Turkey: Changes and Continuities in the 1990s", *Comparative Political Studies*, Vol. 27, No. 4, 1994.

———, "*Kulturkampf* in Turkey: The Constitutional Referendum of 12 September 2010", *South European Society and Politics*, Vol. 17, No. 1, 2012.

Alper Kaliber and Nathalie Tocci, "Civil Society and the Transformation of Turkey's Kurdish Question", *Security Dialogue*, Vol. 41, No. 2, 2010.

Ibrahim Kalin, "Debating Turkey and the Middle East: The Dawn of a New Geopolitical Imagination?", *Insight Turkey*, Vol. 11, No. 1, 2009.

Alex Kantrowitz, "The Secret Behind The Turkish Protesters' Social Media Mastery", *PBS Media Shift*, 1 July 2013, http://www.pbs.org/media-shift/2013/07/the-secret-behind-the-turkish-protesters-social-media-mastery (last visited 28/09/2016).

———, "Social Media And Istanbul's Protests: Four Things You Need To Know", *Forbes*, 19 June 2013.

Sam Kaplan, "Din-U Devlet All Over Again? The Politics of Military Secularism in Turkey Following the 1980 Coup", *International Journal of Middle East Studies*, Vol. 34, No. 1, February 2002.

Ozan Karaman, "Urban Pulse: (Re)Making Space for Globalization in Istanbul", *Urban Geography*, Vol. 29, No. 6, 2008.

————, "Resisting urban renewal in Istanbul", *Urban Geography*, Vol. 35, No. 2, March 2014.

Ali L. Karaosmanoglu, "Civil-Military Relations", in Metin Heper and Sabri Sayari (eds), *The Routledge Handbook of Modern Turkey* (New York: Routledge, 2012).

————, "The Evolution of the National Security Culture and the Military in Turkey", *Columbia University Journal of International Affairs*, Vol. 54, No. 1, 2000.

Sabah Kardas, "Turkey and the Iraq Crisis: JDP Between Identity and Interest", in H. Yavuz (ed), *The Emergence of a New Turkey* (Salt Lake City, UT: University of Utah Press, 2006).

————, "Turkey: Redrawing the Middle East Map: Or Building Sandcastles?", *Middle East Policy*, Vol. 17, No. 1, Spring 2010.

Kemal H. Karpat, *The Gecekondu* (New York: Cambridge University Press, 1976).

————, "Turkish Democracy at Impasse: Ideology, Party Politics, and the Third Military Intervention", *International Journal of Turkish Studies*, Vol. 2, No. 1, Summer-Spring 1988.

————, *Studies on Turkish Politics and Society* (Leiden: Koninklikje Brill, 2004).

Riva Kastoryano (Ed.), *Turkey between Nationalism and Globalisation* (London: Routledge, 2013).

Merve Kavakci, "Turkey's Test with its Deep State", *Mediterranean Quarterly*, Vol. 20, No. 4, 2009.

M.K. Kaya, "The Return of Hakan Fidan to MIT is the Sign of a Power Struggle", *Turkish Analyst*, Vol. 8, No. 5, 2015.

Serder Kaya, "The Rise and Decline of the Turkish 'Deep State': The Ergenekon Case", *Insight Turkey*, Vol. 11, No. 4, 2009.

Raşit Kaya and Barış Çakmur, "Politics and the Mass Media in Turkey ", *Turkish Studies*, Vol. 11, No. 4, 2010.

Barin Kayaoglu, "Turkey's AKP Mobilizes Twitter Army for Elections", *Al-Monitor*, 18 September 2013.

Sevket Kazan, *28 Subat Postmodern Bir Darbenin Anatomisi*, (Ankara: MGV Yayinlan, Ankara, 2013).

Herb Keinon, "Assad: Olmert okayed Golan deal before Gaza op", *Jerusalem Post*, 18 March 2009.

Herb Keinon, "Erdogan slams Egypt's Sisi as 'tyrant' over Cairo policy toward Hamas", *Jerusalem Post*, 18 July 2014.

Rusen Keles, *Eski Ankara'da bir Sehir Tipolojiri* (Ankara: Ankara Universitesi Siyasal Bilgiler Fakultesi Yayinlari, 1971).

Josh Keller, Iaryna Mykhyalyshyn and Safak Timur, "The Scale of Turkey's Purge is Nearly Unprecedented", *The New York Times*, 2 August 2016.

BIBLIOGRAPHY

E. Fuat Keyman (Ed.), *Remaking Turkey: Globalization, Alternative Modernities and Democracy* (Lanham, MD: Lexington, 2007).

Zeynep Kezer. "Contesting Urban Space in Early Republican Ankara", *Journal of Architectural Education*, Vol. 52, No. 1, 1998.

Eunyoung Kim and Minwoo Yun, "What Works? Countermeasures to Terrorism: A Case Study of PKK ", *International Journal of Comparative and Applied Criminal Justice*, Vol. 32, No. 1, Spring 2008.

Stephen Kinzer, *Crescent and Star: Turkey Between Two Worlds* (New York: Farrar, 2008).

———, "Iran's Nuclear Deal", The Guardian, 17 May 2010.

Kemal Kirisci, *Turkey's Foreign Policy in Turbulent Times*, (Paris: European Union Institute for Security Studies EUISS), Chailot Paper 92, 2006.

———, "The Transformation of Turkish Foreign Policy: The Rise of the Trading State", *New Perspectives on Turkey*, Vol. 40, 2009.

———, "Turkey's 'Demonstrative Effect' and the Transformation of the Middle East", *Insight Turkey*, Vol. 14, No. 2, 2011.

———, "Turkey Protests: Are the Youth at Gezi Park a New Actor in Turkish Democracy?", *Brookings Institute: Up Front*, 13 June 2013.

Kemal Kirisci and Gareth M. Winrow, *The Kurdish Question and Turkey: An Example of a Trans-State Ethnic Conflict* (London: Frank Cass, 1997).

Emre Kizilkaya, "AKP's Social Media Wars", *Al-Monitor*, 14 November 2013.

Levent Koker, "AK Party election manifesto fails to meet expectations", *Today's Zaman*, 19 April 2015.

Fehmi Koru, "Too many questions, but not enough answers", *Turkish Daily News*, 8 June 1999.

Talha Kose, "The AKP and the 'Alevi Opening': Understanding the Dynamics of the Rapprochement", *Insight Turkey*, Vol. 12, No. 2, 2010.

Paul Kubicek, "The European Union and Grassroots Democratization in Turkey", *Turkish Studies*, Vol. 6, No. 3, 2005.

Mehmet Baris Kuymulu, "Reclaiming the right to the city: Reflections on the urban uprisings in Turkey", *City*, Vol. 17, No. 3, 2013.

Ahmet Kuzu and Alfred Stepan, *Democracy, Islam and Secularism in Turkey* (New York: Columbia University Press, 2012).

Anat Lapidot, "Islamic Activism in Turkey Since the 1980 Military Takeover", *Terrorism and Political Violence*, Vol. 8, No. 2, 1996.

Stephen F Larrabee, "Turkey Rediscovers the Middle East", *Foreign Affairs*, Vol. 84, No. 4, July/August 2007.

Stephen F. Larrabee and Ian O. Lesser, *Turkish Foreign Policy in an Age of Uncertainty* (Washington DC: Rand, 2003).

Stephen F. Larrabee and Gonul Tol, "Turkey's Kurdish Challenge", *Survival Global Politics and Strategy*, Vol. 53, No. 4, 2011.

Josef Leitmann and Deniz Baharoglu, "Reaching Turkey's spontaneous settlements: The institutional dimension of infrastructure provision", *International Planning Studies*, Vol. 4, No. 2, 1999.

Gulcen Erdi Lelandais, "Citizenship, minorities and the struggle for a right to the city in Istanbul ", *Citizenship Studies*, Vol. 17, No. 6–7, 2013.

Ian O. Lesser, "Turkey and the United States and the Delusion of Geopolitics", *Survival*, Vol. 48, No. 3, 2006.

Ronald H. Linden et al (Eds), *Turkey and its Neighbors: Foreign Relations in Transition* (Boulder, CO: Lynne Rienner, 2012).

Berrin Koyuncu Lorasdagi, "The Prospects and Pitfalls of Religious Nationalist Movement in Turkey: The Case of the Gülen Movement", *Middle Eastern Studies*, Vol. 46, No. 2, 2010.

Asa Lundgren, *The Unwelcome Neighbour: Turkey's Kurdish Policy* (London, I.B. Tauris, 2007).

Edward Luttwak, *Coup d'État: A Practical Handbook* (Harmondsworth: Penguin Books, 1969).

Andrew Mango, *Turkey: The Challenge of a New Role* (Westport, CT: Praeger, 1994).

———, *Turkey and the War on Terror: For Forty Years we Fought Alone* (London: Routledge, 2005).

Mark Mardell, "Turkey had European Union over a barrel", *BBC News*, 17 March 2016.

Daphne McCurdy, "Turkish-Iranian Relations: When Opposites Attract", *Turkish Policy Quarterly*, Vol. 51, No. 3, 2008.

David McDowall, *A Modern History of the Kurds* (London: I.B. Tauris, 1996).

Linda Michaud-Emin, "The Restructuring of the Military High Command in the Seventh Harmonization Package and its Ramifications for Civil-Military Relations in Turkey", *Turkish Studies*, Vol. 8, No. 1, 2007.

Chris Morris, *The New Turkey* (London: Granta Books, 2005).

Alexander Murinson, "The Strategic Depth Doctrine of Turkish Foreign Policy", *Modern Eastern Studies*, Vol 42, No. 6, 2006.

Aylin Sagtur Mutlu, "Cassettes that Shook a Country ", *Eurasia News*, 31 December 1998.

Kendal Nezan, "Turkey's pivotal role in the international drug trade", *Le Monde diplomatique*, July 1998.

Narli Nilufer, "Civil-military relations in Turkey", *Turkish Studies*, Vol. 1, No. 1, 2000.

John T. Nugent, Jr., "The Defeat of Turkish Hizballah as a Model for Counter-Terrorism Strategy", *MERIA Journal*, Vol. 8, No. 1, March 2004.

Abdullah Ocalan, "We Are Fighting Turks Everywhere ", *Middle East Quarterly*, Vol. 5, No. 2, June 1998.

———, "The Road Map to Democratization of Turkey and Solution to the

BIBLIOGRAPHY

Kurdish Question ", *PKK Online*, 15 August 2009, http://www.pkkonline. com/en/index.php?sys=article&artID=123 (last visited 13/10/2016).

Tarık Oguzlu, "The Middle Easternization of Turkey's Foreign Policy: Does Turkey Dissociate from the West?", *Turkish Studies*, Vol. 9, No. 1, 2008.

Kerem Oktem, *Angry Nation: Turkey Since 1989* (Halifax: Fenwood, 2011).

Robert Olsen, *The Kurdish Movement in the 1990s: Its Impact on Turkey and the Middle East* (Lexington, KY: University Press of Kentucky, 1996).

Cumali Onal, "Istanbul's historical peninsula disappearing", *Today's Zaman*, 3 March 2014.

Ziya Onis, "Turkey-EU Relations: Beyond the Current Stalemate", *Insight Turkey*, Vol. 10, No. 4, 2008.

————, "Beyond the 2001 Financial Crisis: The Political Economy of the New Phase of Neoliberal Restructuring in Turkey", *Review of International Political Economy*, Vol. 16, No. 3, 2009.

————, "Multiple Faces of the 'New' Turkish Foreign Policy: Underlying Dynamics and a Critique", *GLODEM Working Paper Series*, April 2010.

Ziya Onis and Caner Bakır, "Turkey's Political Economy in the Age of Financial Globalization: The Significance of the EU Anchor", *South European Society and Politics*, 12:2, 2007.

Ziya Onis and Suhnaz Yilmaz, "The Turkey-EU-US Triangle in Perspective: Transformation or Continuity?", *Middle East Journal*, Vol. 59, No. 2, Changing Geopolitics (Spring 2005).

Ergun Ozbudun, "Turkey", in Myron Weiner and Ergun Ozbudun (eds), *Competitive Elections in Developing Countries*, (Durham, NC: Duke University Press, 1987).

————, "Turkey: How Far from Consolidation?", *Journal of Democracy*, Vol. 7, No. 3, 1996.

————, "From Political Islam to Conservative Democracy: The Case of the Justice and Development Party in Turkey ", *South European Society and Politics*, Vol. 11, No. 3–4, September–December 2006.

————, *The Constitutional System of Turkey: 1876 to the Present* (New York: Palgrave Macmillan, 2011).

————, *Party Politics and Social Cleavages in Turkey*, (Boulder: Lynne Reinner Publishers, 2013).

————, "AKP at the Crossroads: Erdoğan's Majoritarian Drift", *South European Society and Politics*, Vol. 19, No. 2, 2014.

Gencer Ozcan, "The Changing Role of Turkey's Military in Foreign Policy Making ", *UNISCI Discussion Papers*, no. 23, May 2010.

Ali Kemal Ozcan, *Turkey's Kurds: A theoretical analysis of the PKK and Abdullah Ocalan* (London: Routledge, 2006).

Baruk Ozcetin, "Between Representation and Participation: Political Twitter Use in Turkey", *1st International Symposium on Media Studies*, Antalya, 2013.

BIBLIOGRAPHY

Elisabeth Ozdalga, "The Hidden Arab. A Critical Reading of the Notion of Turkish Islam", *Middle Eastern Studies*, Vol. 42, No. 4, July 2006.

Munevver Ozge Balta and Feral Eke, "Spatial Reflection of Urban Planning in Metropolitan Areas and Urban Rent; a Case Study of Cayyolu, Ankara", *European Planning Studies*, Vol. 19, No. 10, October 2011.

Iren Ozgur, "Arabesk Music in Turkey in the 1990s and Changes in National Demography, Politics, and Identity", *Turkish Studies*, Vol. 7, No. 2, June 2006.

Taha Ozhan, "Turkey, Israel and the US in the Wake of the Gaza Flotilla Crisis", *Insight Turkey*, Vol. 12, No. 3, 2010.

Taha Ozhan and Hatem Ete, "A New Agenda for the Kurdish Question", *Insight Turkey*, Vol. 11, No. 1, 2009.

S. Ilgu Ozler, "Politics of the Gecekondu in Turkey: The political choices of urban squatters in national elections", *Turkish Studies*, Vol. 1, No. 2, Autumn 2000.

Suleyman Ozoren, "Turkish Hizballah (Hizbullah): A Case Study of Radical Terrorism", *Turkish Weekly*, 1 December 2004.

Hande Paker, Fikret Adaman, Zeynep Kadirbeyoglu and Begum Ozkaynak, "Environmental Organisations in Turkey: Engaging the State and Capital ", *Environmental Politics*, Vol. 22, No. 5, 2013.

Sevket Pamuk, "Globalisation, Industrialisation and Changing Politics in Turkey", *New Perspective on Turkey*, No. 38, 2008.

Bill Park, "Strategic Location, Political Dislocation: Turkey, the United States, and Northern Iraq", *Middle East Review of International Relations*, Vol. 7, No. 2 (2003).

————, "Turkey's Policy Towards Northern Iraq: Problems and Prospects", Adelphi Papers 371, International Institute for Strategic Studies, 2005.

————, "The Fetullah Gulen Movement", *MERIA Journal*, Vol. 12, No. 3, 2008.

————, *Modern Turkey: People, state and foreign policy in a globalised world* (London: Routledge, 2012).

Mark R. Parris, "Starting Over: US-Turkish Relations in the Post-Iraq Era", *Turkish Policy Quarterly*, Vol. 3, No. 1, 2003.

Ruairi Patterson, "Rising Nationalism and the EU Accession Process", *Turkish Policy Quarterly*, Vol. 7, No. 1, 2008.

Emre Peker, "Turkey's Military Moves Against Coup Cases as Judiciary Fights Government", *The Wall Street Journal*, 3 January 2014.

Volker Peters, "Turkey's Role in the Middle East: An Outsider's Perspective", *Insight Turkey*, Vol. 12, No. 4, 2010.

Nicole Pope and Hugh Pope, *Turkey Unveiled: A History of Modern Turkey* (New York: Overlook, 2004).

BIBLIOGRAPHY

Hugh Poulton, *Top Hat, Grey Wolf and Crescent: Turkish Nationalism and the Turkish Republic* (London: Hurst, 1997).

John Duncan Powell, "Peasant Society and Clientelist Politics ", *American Political Science Review*, Vol. 64, No. 2, June 1970.

Angel Rabasa and Stephen F. Larrabee, *The Rise of Political Islam in Turkey* (Washington DC: RAND Corporation, 2008).

Kadri Kaan Renda, "Turkey's Neighborhood Policy: An Emerging Complex Interdependence?", *Insight Turkey*, Vol. 13, No. 1, 2011.

Reporters Without Borders for Freedom of Information, "Countries Under Surveillance: Turkey", 12 March 2011, http://en.rsf.org/turkey-turkey-11–03–2011,39758.html (last visited 27/09/2014).

————, "Enemies of the Internet 2014", 12 March 2014.

Philip Robins, "The Overlord State: Turkish Policy and the Kurdish Issue", *International Affairs*, Vol. 69, No. 3, October 1993.

————, "Turkish Foreign Policy Under Erbakan", *Survival*, Vol. 39, No. 2 (1997).

————, *Suits and Uniforms: Turkish Foreign Policy Since the Cold War* (London: Hurst, 2003).

————, "Turkish Foreign Policy Since 2002: Between a Post-Islamist Government and a Kemalist State", *International Affairs*, Vol. C.LXXXIII, No. 1, 2007.

————, "Turkey's 'double gravity' predicament: the foreign policy of a newly activist power", *International Affairs*, Vol. 82, No. 2, 2013.

Dani Roderik, "Turkey's Baffling Coup ", *Project Syndicate*, 17 July 2016; Steven A. Cook, *Washington Post*, 16 July 2016.

Carmen Rodrigues, Antonio Avalos, Hakan Yılmaz and Ana I. Planet (Eds), *Turkey's Democratisation Process* (London: Routledge, 2014).

David Romano, *The Kurdish National Movement: Opportunity, Mobilization and Identity* (Cambridge: Cambridge University Press, 2006).

Mitchell P. Roth and Murat Sever, "The Kurdish Workers Party (PKK) as Criminal Syndicate: Funding Terrorism Through Organised Crime, A Case Study", *Studies in Conflict and Terrorism*, Vol. 30, No. 10, 2007.

Eric Rouleau, "Turkey's Dream of Democracy", *Foreign Affairs*, Vol. 79, No. 6, November/December 2006.

Barry Rubin and Kemal Kirisci (eds), *Turkey in World Politics: An Emerging Multiregional Power* (Boulder, CO: Lynne Rienner, 2001).

Michael Rubin, "Green Money, Islamist Politics in Turkey", *Middle East Quarterly*, Vol. XII, No. 1, 2005.

————, "A Comedy of Errors: American-Turkish Diplomacy and the Iraq War", *Turkish Policy Quarterly*, Vol. 4, No. 1, 2005.

Uptin Saiidi, "For someone who doesn't like social media, Erdogan used it effectively to put down coup ", *CNBC*, 18 July 2016;

BIBLIOGRAPHY

Nil S. Satana, "Civil-Military Relations in Europe, the Middle East and Turkey", *Turkish Studies*, Vol. 12, No. 2, June 2011.

Gurhan Savgi, "Istanbul residents deceived over construction of third bridge", *Today's Zaman*, 6 April 2014.

————, "Either Kanal İstanbul project or İstanbul must be sacrificed", *Today's Zaman*, 9 February 2014.

Sabri Sayari and Bruce Hoffman, "Urbanisation and insurgency: The Turkish case, 1976–1980", *Small Wars and Insurgencies*, Vol. 5, No. 2, 1994.

Sam Schechner, "Erdogan Embraces Social Media to Repel Coup Attempt in U-Turn", *The Wall Street Journal*, 17 July 2016.

Gregory L. Schulte, "Why Turkey Cannot Abstain on Iran's Nuclear Violations", *Turkish Policy Quarterly*, Vol. 8, No. 4, 2009–10.

Mustafa Sen, "Transformation of Turkish Islamism and the Rise of the Justice and Development Party", *Turkish Studies*, Vol. 11, No. 1, May 2010.

Ahmet Sever, *Abdullah Gül ile 12 Yıl: Yaşadım, Gördüm*, Yazdım Dogan Kitap, 30. Baskı, Istanbul, 2015.

David Shankland, *The Alevis in Turkey: The Emergence of a Secular Islamic Tradition* (London: Routledge, 2003).

Rachel Sharon-Krespin, "Fetullah Gulen's Grand Ambition: Turkey's Islamist Danger", *Middle East Quarterly*, Vol. XVI, No. 1, 2009.

SIGMA, "The Administrative Capacity of the Turkish Grand National Assembly", Support for Improvement in Governance and Management (SIGMA) Peer Review Report, August 2010.

Sefa Simsek, "The Transformation of Civil Society in Turkey: From Quantity to Quality", *Turkish Studies*, Vol. 5, No. 3, 2004.

Thomas W. Smith, "Between Allah and Ataturk: Liberal Islam in Turkey ", *The International Journal of Human Rights*, Vol. 9, No. 3, 2005.

Ariel Ben Solomon, "Analysis: Russia, US Compete to ally with Kurds in ISIS fight", *Jerusalem Post*, 9 February 2016.

Murat Somer, "Turkey's Kurdish Conflict: Changing Context, and Domestic and Regional Implications", *Middle East Journal*, Vol. 58, No. 2, 2004.

Mustafa Sonmez, "Construction again the hope of the economy in 2016", *Hurriyet Daily News*, 29 February 2016.

Gul Sosay, "Delegation and Accountability: Independent Regulatory Agencies in Turkey", *Turkish Studies*, Vol. 10, No. 3, 2009.

Digdem Soyaltin, "Turkish Court of Accounts in Crisis: An Urgent Problem, yet not a Main Concern?", Centre for Policy and Research on Turkey, 19 December 2013.

Ceren Sozeri, "The political economy of the media and its impact on freedom of expression ", in Carmen Rodrigues, Antonio Avalos, Hakan Yılmaz and Ana I. Planet, (Eds), *Turkey's Democratisation Process* (London: Routledge, 2014).

BIBLIOGRAPHY

Mehul Srivastava and Benjamin Harvey, "The Edifice Complex Driving Turkey's Scandal", *Bloomberg BusinessWeek*, 9 January 2014.

Stephen Starr, "Turkey's Twitter Problem", *Global Post*, 30 June 2013, http://www.globalpost.com/dispatch/news/regions/europe/turkey/130629/turkey-twitter-facebook-social-media-erdogan-taksim-bbc-turkce (last visited 28/09/2016).

Aaron Stein, "Inside a Failed Coup and Turkey's Fragmented Military", *War on the Rocks*, 20 July 2016.

Norman Stone, *Turkey: A Short History* (London: Thames and Hudson, 2010).

Necdet Subasi, "The Alevi Opening: Concept, Strategy and Process", *Insight Turkey*, Vol. 12, No. 2, 2010.

Adam Szymanski, "Turkish Foreign Policy in 2007–2009: Continuity or Change?", *Polish Quarterly of International Affairs*, Vol. 19 No. 2, 2009.

Ilhan Tanir, "Komabi and Kurdish Nationalism in Turkey", Carnegie Endowment for International Peace, 6 November 2014.

Pinar Tank, "Political Islam in Turkey: A State of Controlled Secularity", *Turkish Studies*, Vol. 6, No. 1, March 2005.

Halil I. Tas & Dale R. Lightfoot, "Gecekondu Settlements in Turkey: Rural-Urban Migration in the Developing European Periphery", *Journal of Geography*, Vol. 104, No. 6, 2005.

Omer Taspinar, "The Old Turks' Revolt: When Radical Secularism Threatens Democracy", *Foreign Affairs*, Vol. 86, No. 6, November/December 2007.

———, "Turkey's Strategic Vision and Syria", *The Washington Quarterly*, Vol. 35, No. 3, Summer 2012.

———, "Turkey: The New Model", Robin Wright (Ed.), *The Islamists Are Coming: Who They Really Are* (Washington, DC: The United States Institute of Peace, April 2012).

———, *Turkey: The New Model?*, April 2012, The Woodrow Wilson Center.

Coskun Tastan, "The Gezi Park Protests in Turkey: A Qualitative Field Research", *Insight Turkey*, Vol. 15, No. 3, 2013.

Fehim Tastekin, "Shadow government set up in Erdogan's white palace", *Al Monitor*, 11 December 2014.

Ilhan Tekeli, "Cities in Modern Turkey", Urban Age, Cities Programme, London School of Economics, November 2009.

Sultan Tepe, "Turkey's AKP: A Model 'Muslim-Democratic' Party?", *Journal of Democracy*, Vol. 16, No. 3, July 2005.

Ozlem Terzi, *The Influence of the European Union on Turkish Foreign Policy* (Surrey: Ashgate, 2010).

Guneş Murat Tezcur, "Judicial Activism in Perilous Times: The Turkish Case", *Law & Society Review*, Vol. 43, No. 2, June 2009.

David Tittenson, *The House of Service, The Gulen Movement and Islam's Third Way*, (Oxford: Oxford University Press, 2014).

BIBLIOGRAPHY

Nathalie Tocci, "Europeanization in Turkey: Trigger or Anchor for Reform?", *South European Society and Politics*, Vol. 10, No. 1, 2005.

Nathalie Tocci and Joshua W. Walker, "From Confrontation to Engagement: Turkey and the Middle East", Ronald H. Linden et al (Eds), *Turkey and its Neighbors: Foreign Relations in* Transition (Boulder, CO: Lynne Rienner, 2012).

Alexis de Tocqueville, *Democracy in America*, various editions.

Bennaz Toprak, *Islam and Political Development in Turkey* (Leiden: E.J. Brill, 1981).

————, "Islam and Democracy in Turkey", *Turkish Studies*, Vol. 6, No. 2, 2005.

Selva Tor, "Büyük resmin küçük adamı: Sarraf ", *Al Jazeera Turk*, 25 March 2016.

Pinar Tremblay, "How Erdogan used the power of the mosques against coup attempt", *Al-Monitor*, 25 July 2016.

Ozlem Tur, "Economic Relations with the Middle East Under the AKP— Trade, Business Community and Reintegration with Neighboring Zones", *Turkish Studies*, Vol. 12, No. 4, December 2011.

Berna Turam, *Secular State ad Religious Society: Two Forces in Play in Turkey* (New York: Palgrave Macmillan, 2012).

Ilter Turan, "The Military in Turkish Politics", *Mediterranean Quarterly*, Vol. 2, No. 1997.

Pinar Turker-Devecigil, "Urban Transformation Projects as a Model to Transform Gecekondu Areas in Turkey: The Example of Dikmen Valley— Ankara", *International Journal of Housing Policy*, Vol. 5, No. 2, 2005.

Asuman Turkun, "Urban Regeneration and Hegemonic Power Relationships", *International Planning Studies*, Vol. 16, No. 1, 2011.

Hasan Turunc, "Islamist or Democrat? The AKP's Search for Identity in Turkish Politics", *Journal of Contemporary European Studies*, Vol. 15, No. 1, 2007.

Ozgur Mutlu Ulus, *The Army and the Radical Left in Turkey: Military Coups, Socialist Revolution and Kemalism*, (London: I. B. Tauris, 2011).

Emrullah Uslu, "From local Hizbollah to Global Terror: Militant Islam in Turkey", *Middle East Policy*, Vol. 14, No. 1, 2007.

Kadir Ustun, "Turkey's Iran Policy: Between Diplomacy and Sanctions", *Insight Turkey*, Vol. 12, No. 3, 2010.

Martin van Bruinessen, "Between Guerrilla War and Political Murder: The Workers' Party of Kurdistan", *Middle East Report*, No. 153, July–August 1988.

Simon A. Waldman, "The military's last stand: what went wrong for Turkey's coup plotters?", *The Globe and Mail*, 16 July 2016.

BIBLIOGRAPHY

Joshua Walker, "Turkey and Israel's Relationship in the Middle East", *Mediterranean Quarterly*, Vol. 17, No. 4, 2006.

————, "Learning Strategic Depth: Implications of Turkey's New Foreign Policy Doctrine", *Insight Turkey*, Vol. 9, No. 3, 2007.

————, "Introduction: The Sources of Turkish Grand Strategy-Strategic Depth and Zero-Problems in Context", *Turkey's Global Strategy*, LSE Publications, London, 2011.

Washington Institute for Near East Policy, "In His Own Words: Erdogan on Israel, Hamas, and the Gaza Conflict", PolicyWatch #1475, 11 February 2009.

Nicholas Watt, "Europe Embraces Turkey as Diplomatic Deadlock is Broken", *The Guardian*, 4 October 2005.

Zia Weisse, "Allegations of torture in Turkey as rule of law erodes", *Politico EU*, 25 July 2016.

Lois Whitman and Thomas Froncek, *Paying the Price: Freedom of Expression in Turkey* (New York: Human Rights Watch, 1989).

Robin Wright (Ed.), *The Islamists Are Coming: Who They Really Are*, (Washington, DC: United States Institute of Peace, April 2012).

L. Todd Wood, "Russia supporting Kurdish groups in Syria to Turkey's detriment", *Washington Times*, 8 February 2016.

Lerna Yanik, "The Metamorphosis of Metaphors of Vision: 'Bridging' Turkey's Location, Role and Identity After the End of the Cold War", *Geopolitics*, Vol. 14, No. 3, 2009.

M. Hakan Yavuz, "Turkish Identity and Foreign Policy in Flux: The Rise of Neo-Ottomanism", *Middle East Critique*, Vol. 7, No. 12, 1998.

————, "Towards an Islamic Liberalism?: The Nurcu Movement and Fethullah Gülen", *Middle East Journal*, Vol. 53, No. 4, Autumn 1999.

————, *Islamic Political Identity in Turkey* (Oxford: Oxford University Press, 2003).

————, *Secularism and Muslim Democracy in Turkey*. (Cambridge: Cambridge University Press, 2009).

———— (ed.), *The Emergence of a New Turkey: Democracy and the AK Parti* (Salt Lake City, UT: University of Utah Press, 2006).

M. Hakan Yavuz and John L. Espisito (Eds), *Turkish Islam and the Secular State: The Gulen Movement* (Syracuse, NY: Syracuse University Press, 2003).

M. Hakan Yavuz and Nihat Ali Ozcan, "The Kurdish Question and Turkey's Justice and Development Party", *Middle East Policy* Vol. XIII, No. 1, 2006.

Serap Yazici, "UPDATE: A Guide to Turkish Public Law and Legal Research", *Global Lex*, May/June 2012, http://www.nyulawglobal.org/globalex/turkey1.htm#laws (last visited 28/09/2016).

Birol Yesilada and Barry Rubin (Eds), *Islamisation of Turkey under the AKP* (London: Routledge, 2011).

BIBLIOGRAPHY

Nuri Yesilyurt and Atay Akdevilioglu, "Türkiye'nin Ortadoğu Politikası (Turkey's Middle East Policy)", in Bulent Duru and Ilhan Uzgel et al. (eds), *AKP Kitabı (AKP Book)* (Istanbul: Phoenix, 2010).

Ahmet Yildiz, "Politico-Religious Discourse of Political Islam in Turkey: The Parties of National Outlook ", *The Muslim World*, Vol. 93, No. 2, April 2003.

Guney Yildiz, "Turkey-PKK Peace Process at 'Turning Point'", *BBC News*, 12 November 2014.

Kerim Yildiz, *The Kurds in Turkey: EU Accession and Human Rights* (London: Pluto Press, 2005).

Kamil Yılmaz, "The Emergence and Rise of Conservative Elite in Turkey", *Insight Turkey*, Vol. 11, No. 2, 2009.

Hale Yılmaz, *Becoming Turkish: Nationalist Reforms and Cultural Negotiations in Early Republican Turkey, 1923–1945* (Syracuse, NY: Syracuse University Press, 2013).

Piotr Zalewski, "The Self-Appointed Superpower: Turkey Goes it Alone", *World Policy Journal*, Vol. 27, No. 4, Winter 2010/2011.

Amberin Zaman, "Turkey spy chief's resignation: power play or family feud?", *Al Monitor*, 13 February 2015.

Unal E. Zenginobuz, "On Regulatory Agencies in Turkey and their Independence", *Turkish Studies*, Vol. 9, No. 3, 2008.

Fatma Disli Zibak, "İstanbul becoming uninhabitable with mega construction projects", *Today's Zaman*, 30 May 2013.

INDEX

INDEX

INDEX

INDEX

demns Egyptian coup, 15, 222; recommends families have four children, 73; announces democratic package for Kurds, 183; condemns co-ed dormitories, 73; declares closure of *dashane* schools, 76; seeks to affirm relations with TSK, 38–9; AKP corruption investigation, 76–7, 99, 128, 129, 139

2014 announces Twitter ban, 139; scandal over Baykal sex tape, 112; condemns Israeli operations in Gaza, 223; outburst against Zaman, 133; elected president, 38, 49, 78, 92, 94, 112, 116, 129–30, 157, 229; Davutoglu appointed prime minister, 78; Gul blocked from AKP leadership, 116; construction of Ak Saray, 38, 78; establishes Conquest Unit, 38

2015 Suleyman Shah incident, 39; declares end to peace process with PKK, 40, 194; resignation of Fidan, 115; supports AKP in general election, 78–80, 94; arrest of Baransu, 113; arrest of Bulent Kenes, 63, 113; re-run of general election, 80, 94

2016 Davutoglu resigns; Yildirim appointed prime minister, 92, 117, 200, 203, 228; condemns birth control, 74; apologises for shoot-down of Russian jet, 225; attempted Gulenist coup, 4, 11, 41–7, 117; expresses regret over cooperation with Gulenists, 11; meeting with opposition leaders, 195; refuses to rule out reinstatement of death penalty, 226; anger at EU response to coup, 227; drops court cases against critics, 233; meets with Putin, 228

Erdoglu, Aykut, 158
Erez industrial park, Gaza Strip, 210
Ergenekon, 10, 11, 31–8, 46, 48, 129, 131, 133, 186
Eruygur, Sener, 35, 96
Eskisehir, 32
esnaf, 51
Euphrates river, 167, 217
Eurobarometer, 198
European Commission, 23–4, 130
European Convention on Human Rights, 101, 120–1
European Court of Human Rights, 132, 138, 140, 176, 187
European Economic Community (EEC), 198
European Union (EU)
    accession process, 16, 21–7, 32, 35, 48, 60, 67–8, 71, 74–5, 87, 91, 97, 104, 130–1, 160, 176, 198, 200, 204–5, 209, 216, 225
    and AKP, 21–2, 59–60, 67–8, 71, 74–5, 87, 97, 104, 125, 130–1, 160, 198–200, 204–5, 209, 216, 226–7
    Copenhagen criteria, 22, 176
    and Cyprus, 25, 26, 199, 209
    and Gulen movement, 64
    and human rights, 99, 101, 104, 132, 138, 140, 176
    and Iran, 214–15
    and Kurds, 24–6, 176–8
    and Milli Gorus, 64
    and Palestine, 210
    refugee crisis, 92, 225–7
    Schengen zone, 225–7
    support for, 198, 200
    trade with Turkey, 207–8
    and Welfare Party, 202
Evren, Kenan, 51–2
executive, 4, 79, 89, 91–2, 97–9
extra-judicial killings, 7–9, 34, 124, 125, 168, 170–1, 174, 186, 188

INDEX

INDEX

human rights, 22, 99, 101, 120–1, 124, 169, 170, 176, 181, 186–7, 194, 215, 220
Human Rights Watch (HRW), 99, 124, 169, 170, 186–7
hunger strikes, 177, 183
Hurriyet, 122, 125, 127, 135
Hussein ibn Ali, 220

identity politics, *see* cultural identity
Ihsanoglu, Ekmeleddin, 94, 130
illiberal democracies, 84–5
illiteracy, 144
Imam Hatip high schools, 19, 28, 47, 58
Imam's Army, The (Sik), 132
Imrali Island, 163, 176, 180, 182
Independent Industrialists' and Businessmen's Association (MUSIAD), 67, 76–7
inflation, 56, 68, 76, 148
Inonu, Ismet, 4, 92
Inspection of Cinema, Video and Musical Works, 23
interest rate lobby, 70
Internal Service Law No. 211 (1961), 18
International Criminal Court (ICC), 213
International Crisis Group, 193
International Monetary Fund (IMF), 68–9, 199
Internet, 5, 38, 77, 84, 104, 107–14, 117–18, 136–41, 231
Internet Law (2007), 137–8
Internet legislation (2014), 138–9
Ipek, Akın, 126
Ipsos KMG, 107
Iran, 20, 26, 57, 75, 202, 204, 205, 206
 golden loophole, 70
 Green Movement, 215, 218
 Iraq, relations with, 217

Israel, relations with, 212, 213
 nuclear programme, 197, 207, 214–15, 232
 and Kurds, 167, 169, 206, 214–15, 217
 Syria, relations, 215–16, 221–2
Iran-Turkey High Security Council, 214
Iraq, 205–6
 Gulf War (1990–1), 173, 201–2
 Iraq War (2003–11), 26, 171, 177, 199, 201–2, 205–6, 215, 216
 Islamic State in Iraq and Syria (ISIS), 39, 40, 135, 189–92, 223–6, 232
 Kurds, 164, 167, 171–4, 179–80, 182–3, 189–93, 197–8, 206, 210, 214, 216–17, 228
 Syrian War (2011–), 221
 trade with Turkey, 186, 201–2, 220
 Turcomans, 216
IRIS, 100
Islam
 and alcohol, 57, 73, 94
 Alevis, 10, 54, 98, 104–5, 180, 234
 call to prayer, 55, 114
 education, 19, 28, 47, 53–4, 58
 Hajj, 54
 hocas, 52
 Koran, 54, 55, 93
 Milli Gorus, 50–1, 55, 57, 58, 59, 64, 65, 66–7, 71
 mosques, 36, 53, 54, 55, 57, 78, 113, 154
 Muhammad, Prophet of Islam, 136
 Naksibendi, 50, 55
 Nurcu, 55, 63
 Ramadan, 62, 100, 150, 172
 Sala prayer, 114
 Sharia, 13, 62
 Shi'ism, 54, 104, 217, 220, 221
 Sufism, 54, 65
 Sunnism, 75, 105, 220

INDEX

331

INDEX

INDEX

2016 Ankara bombing, 194

Kurds

AKP, relations with, 3, 38, 40,
75–6, 80, 86, 115–16, 133,
163–4, 176–96, 214, 216–17,
221, 225, 228, 232, 234

Democratic Society Party (DTP),
178–9, 180, 181, 182, 184

destruction of villages, 2, 149, 169,
170, 187

and elections, 30, 79, 90, 94,
178–9, 183–4, 191–2, 234

and Ergenekon, 33

and European Union (EU), 24–6,
176–8

extra-judicial killings of, 7–9, 34,
124, 168, 170–1, 174, 186, 188

and *gecekondu*s, 149, 152

and Gezi Park protests (2013), 105,
188

Hezbollah, 169–70

insurgency, 1–3, 7–8, 25, 38, 40,
116, 124, 134, 149, 163–4,
166–96, 202, 214, 216–17, 221,
232, 234

in Iran, 206, 214

in Iraq, 164, 167, 171–4, 177,
179–80, 182–3, 186, 190, 192,
197–8, 206, 210, 216–17, 228

Israel, relations with, 210

and judiciary, 98

Kurdistan Communities Union
(KCK), 75, 134, 173, 182, 183,
185

language, 22, 86, 165, 167, 175,
176, 177, 180, 181, 184, 185

media, 3, 124, 130, 131, 132–3,
134, 135, 176

migration, 2, 149, 167

and military, emergency rule, 3,
6–9, 22, 40, 163, 168–76, 179,
181, 191–5

Newroz, 175, 191

Peace and Democracy Party (BDP),
30, 172, 178, 180, 182, 183,
184, 188

peace process, 1, 3, 40, 75–6, 80,
163–4, 171, 172–96, 217

Peoples' Democratic Party (HDP),
44, 79, 80, 94, 105, 111, 130,
185, 188, 191–5, 224, 234

Seyh Said uprising (1925), 166

society, 168

Solution Process, 173, 183, 189–95

in Syria, 39, 163, 167, 171, 174,
182, 184, 189–92, 202, 206,
221, 222, 224, 225

torture of, 124, 167, 169

Uludere massacre (2011), 133, 173

Video Documentation Collection,
109

Village Guard, 31, 168, 169, 186

Kurkcu, Ertugrul, 111, 185

Kusadasi, 171

Lake Terkos, 159

Lavrov, Sergey, 209

Law of Printing Presses, 121

Law of Treason, 121

Law on Compensation for Damage
Arising from Terror, 187

Law on Crimes Against Ataturk, 121

Law on Public Financial Management
and Control, 24

Law on Public Procurement, 89

Law on the Establishment of Radio and
Television Enterprises, 137

Law on the Introduction and
Application of the Turkish Alphabet,
121

Lebanon, 167, 169, 189, 206–7, 212,
207, 215

leftists, 6, 10, 18, 33, 52–4, 103, 134,
148, 167, 175, 192

INDEX

INDEX

INDEX